ENCOUNTERS WITH UFO OCCUPANTS

CORAL AND JIM LORENZEN

A BERKLEY MEDALLION BOOK
published by
BERKLEY PUBLISHING CORPORATION

FOR

Our Dear Friend

MADELEINE H. COOPER

Published by arrangement with the authors.

Berkley Publishing Corporation
200 Madison Avenue
New York, N.Y. 10016

SBN 425-03093-8

BERKLEY MEDALLION BOOKS are published by Berkley Publishing Corporation 200 Madison Avenue New York, N.Y. 10016

BERKLEY MEDALLION BOOKS ® TM 757,375

Printed in the United States of America

Berkley Medallion Edition, APRIL, 1976

ACKNOWLEDGMENTS

When two people have been associated so closely with so many others for so many years, it is difficult to decide whose names to include here. It goes without saying that we are deeply indebted to APRO's Scientific Consulting Staff, whose names are listed at the back of this book, for their support and willingness to apply their talent and expertise to the absorbing UFO problem.

Also of invaluable assistance have been APRO's foreign representatives who have helped make APRO the central depository of thousands of UFO cases from around the world.

In addition to our permanent staff, Mrs. Sheila Kudrle, Randy Rice and Betty Darr, we thank the local volunteers, Mrs. Madeleine H. Cooper. Mr. Lou Daugherty, Jean Oberg, Al Kudrle, Dan Harris, Richard Guy and Lynn and Sue Hutchinson for their dedication in keeping the files in good condition and the flow of paperwork at a reasonably steady pace.

We also thank APRO's corps of Field Investigators who are a special group: they are often called upon to undertake interviews many miles from their homes in trying circumstances and sometimes difficult weather conditions.

We extend a special thanks to the following whose efforts greatly contributed to the subject matter of this book or have supported APRO in other ways: Lance Johnson and James Stavem of Arizona; Neil Davis, Ross Graham, Jan Herr, Paul Smith of California, Robert Achzehner, Donald Johnson, Mr. and Mrs. Donald Richmond and Lee Trenholm of Colorado; Harvey Courtney and Paul Holmes of Connecticut; Judy Allison, Helen Hartmann, Irving Lillien, Sandra Thomas and Everett Walter of Florida; Di Etta Cunnigham and Paul McCarthy of Hawaii; Paul Kiepe of Idaho; Delight Bonvouloir, Laird Carter, Dale Dufelmeier, Fred Merritt, Herman Muenchen and Douglas Williams of Illinois; Donald Worley of Indiana; Celia Block and Kevin Randle of Iowa; Joyce Davis, Roger Epley and William Thornton of Kansas; Joe and Doris Graziano of Maryland; Raymond Fowler,

Joseph Nyman and David Webb of Massachusetts; Clinton C. Williams of Michigan; Joyce Shapiro and Gerald Waltry of Minnesota; Joseph Breuning, and Glenn Bryant of Mississippi; Ted Phillips of Missouri; Josephine Myers of Nebraska; Kenneth Hing of Nevada; Betty Hill of New Hampshire; Harold Redner of New Jersey; Terry Clark and Gary Kinemond of New Mexico; Robert Barrow, Douglas Daines and Richard Ruhl of New York; Carl Funk, Iris Maack, J. Robert Reiss and Virgil Tarlton of Ohio; Dwight Dauben and Lewis Sikes of Oklahoma; Carroll D. Watson of Oregon; Michael McClellan of Pennsylvania; Donald Todd of Rhode Island; Dr. Luckett V. Davis and Thomas Deuley of South Carolina; Robert Davis, Leonard Janetzke and David Wuliger of Texas; Lowell Maw of Utah; Hobart W. Whitaker and Beatrice Zimmer of Virginia; David Akers and David Mischke of Washington; Theodore R. Spickler of Virginia; Andrew Andropolis, Leonard Bongle, Gail Busse, Margaret Davis, Ed Cushman, William F. Johnson and David Weier of Wisconsin.

From Canada: William K. Allan, Donald Stromberg of Alberta; Gregory Kanon of Nova Scotia; Arthur Bray, Gary Jopko and Louis Normandin and Carol White of Ontario; Wido Hoville and Dean Clausen of Quebec.

From other countries: Keith Basterfield and William Chaulker of Australia; Irene Granchi of Brazil; Jorge Enrique Parr O. of Colombia; Flemming Ahrenkiel and Ole Henningsen of Denmark; Fernando Tellez Pareja of Mexico; Frank Cordero of Puerto Rico; August Moraru of Romania; Ignacio Darnaude Rojas-Marcos of Spain; Ake Eldberg and Sven-Olaf Fredrikson of Sweden; Tova Bratt of Switzerland.

We sincerely wish that we could list the names of all of APRO's members and Field Investigators but unfortunately space does not permit. However, we do take this opportunity to thank them.

Last, but certainly not least, are APRO's staff artists, Richard Beal, Brian James, Norman Duke, Robert Gonzales and Lance Johnson whose works through the years have served to illustrate various reports in our periodical, the *APRO Bulletin*.

Like the rest of us, these gentlemen volunteer their services. Some of Mr. Duke's, Mr. James' and Mr. Gonzales' artistic renditions grace the pages of this book. Inasmuch as the old saying "a picture is worth a thousand words" certainly holds true where UFO reports are concerned, their contributions are appreciated, and we feel will help to illustrate the quandary that researchers the world over find themselves in when attempting to evaluate the UFO occupant phenomenon.

FOREWORD

One cannot spend the better part of one's life researching a subject without forming some kind of opinion or at least favoring one theory over another. Such is the case with UFOs and with the writers. After considering all the suggested explanations for the elusive objects, including plasmas, balloons, aircraft seen under unusual conditions, misinterpretation of astronomical objects, man-made secret weapons and, yes, messengers from God or the devil, we have accepted the extraterrestrial hypothesis as the one theory which best fits the available facts. The continuous recurrence of occupant reports seems to us at this time to rule out all other explanations which are not at odds with contemporary physical science.

As the reader makes progress through this book he may at first think that the cases discussed comprise a jungle of puzzle pieces none of which fit. It is a feeling that was often shared by us until 1965 when so much more new data came to hand as a result of (1) concentrated UFO activity on a world scale and (2) APRO's increasing size, and therefore increasing ability to investigate.

As more data became available, a few correlations became obvious, and as time went by, more cases involving alleged occupants came to light. Our first book dealing with UFO occupants (*Flying Saucer Occupants*, New York, New American Library, 1968) was published under the Signet imprint. Although the idea of occupants or entities was only beginning to be accepted by a few people actively engaged in UFO research at the time, the general public's fancy was caught immediately. The book enjoyed a brisk sale and was partially responsible for an increase in APRO's membership and the recruiting of scientific personnel to aid in the evaluation of data.

Therefore, at this time when UFOs are no longer only occasionally reported but are a matter of daily routine, we deemed it our obligation to the members of APRO as well as the general public to update our findings.

We feel that it is desirable to provide everyone with the opportunity to become aware of the bizarre occurrences being reported in increasing numbers by individuals and groups of people who in other circumstances would be considered quite reliable. The veracity of all of these reports cannot be vouched for. They are very likely not all true and they are very likely not all false—but if only a few are true the connotations are sobering.

In the interest of better understanding of the complete UFO problem we have, in addition, undertaken to discuss "contacteecultism" sympathetically from the standpoint of religious need, and "Government secrecy" in the light of national defense considerations as well as for the emotional security of the individual.

Traditionally our culture has relied heavily on the authority of the orthodox clergy for the tenets which shape our society. In recent times we have seen this reliance shift substantially to the authority of orthodox science. The appearance of the unidentified flying object, however, is fraught with connotations which challenge their validity.

In this situation, when people's usual tower of strength seems rather shaky, when they are obliged to rely largely on their own judgement, it becomes of prime importance that they be as well informed as is possible at this time.

We hope that our observations—the result of twenty-four years of study—are of some help toward this end.

Coral and Jim Lorenzen
August 28th, 1975

Contents

INTRODUCTION

Historians like to speak of the Stone Age or the Iron Age. What will be the designation of our age? It was suggested that the first atomic bomb ushered in the Atomic Age. Or how about the Age of Technology, encompassing modern communications, transportation, and the numerous other facets of contemporary civilization? Having just read the manuscript for *Encounters With UFO Occupants* I would like to suggest (if someone hasn't already) that our time should be called the Age of Paradox. On the one hand, we have knowledge and understanding; on the other, mystery and confusion.

Technology is only the outward, everyday manifestation of the Age of Science; the real revolution lies in man's exploding knowledge and understanding of his universe. There are many individuals today who can outline in intricate and logical detail the inner workings of the atom, the molecular manifestations of genetic material, the machinery of an ecosystem, or the structure and function of a galaxy. The paradox is that with all this understanding modern men and women are, nevertheless, faced with mysteries that seem as unsolvable as those ever before faced by mankind. The questions of purpose remain as challenging as ever, and in spite of our scientific knowledge, many observed phenomena remain to be understood and explained. This is so true for the problems and challenges faced by each of us in our lives that many people have retreated from rationality to astrology and other mystic pseudosciences, which allow effects to happen without acceptable causes, or at best assume that unknown forces in the universe—the gods or the demons—are responsible for everyday events. The paradoxes of understanding may have contributed to the equally important paradoxes of behavior: it seems that the best and the worst individuals, the most moral and the most corrupt, are living in our time.

One of the most perplexing mysteries is the UFO. Here we really seem to be faced with something beyond our understanding. The phenomenon is vast, almost beyond our comprehension. Millions of people from all parts of the world have seen unidentified flying objects. Furthermore, the variety of the UFO experience is almost as great as its statistics. There are patterns all right, and the Lorenzens document them in this book, but the range of experiences is, nevertheless, fantastic. There are those who see a distant brilliant light they are unable to understand in terms of their knowledge of the universe. This may be true even if the light is hanging suspended in the sky, but if it is moving in some way that seems atypical of airplanes, helicopters, satellites, or balloons, it may be much more perplexing. If the unknown vision comes close enough to exhibit an unexpected form—a disc, ball, egg, or cigar shape, for example—then it becomes still more perplexing, especially when it appears in the daytime. If it is seen to have windows, landing gear, antennae, flashing lights, tubes or cables, flames, or other strange accoutrements, or if it lands, stops cars, hums, departs at unbelievable speeds, or otherwise behaves in an uncivilized fashion, it may be not only perplexing but downright frightening—especially if its overt actions seem directed toward the witness! When it is possible to see occupants inside the object, or when the object lands and the occupants disembark and move toward the witness, sometimes by walking in a fairly normal fashion, but other times by floating, moving with "sliding motions," or with a tottering gait, then we really seem to be in the world of the unknown. And what if the occupants take the witness on board their craft, examine him or her (sometimes in rather debasing ways), and then perhaps leave the witness with mental blocks that destroy clear memory but may give rise to horrendous dreams and sometimes even physical illness? Or what if the occupants contact the witness in a benign fashion, perhaps telling him or her that he has been chosen as a messenger between the space people and mankind, instructing him in the ways of the Big Brothers, and finally releasing him to evangelize his fellow earthlings?

Your reaction to this scale of UFO experiences may be a sort of Rorschach inkblot test providing insight into how you relate to the universe. If you recognize that the distant, brilliant, unblinking light in the west after sundown or in the east before sunrise was probably the planet Venus, then you may be rational, skeptical, educated, and quick to see how some apparently mysterious phenomenon can be placed in its proper position in the scheme of things. Of all the unidentified objects or apparitions seen around the world the vast majority, probably well over 90 per cent, could be understood and explained if the true facts were presented to a suitably knowledgeable investigator. If you are willing to consider other reports, such as the close encounters or the observations of occupants, although you are unable to fit these ideas into your concept of the universe, this may indicate you are curious in the best sense of the word and you can be objective when confronted with unfamiliar information. On the other hand, if you believe all the details of all the contactees or all the details presented in this book, you are probably overly gullible and perhaps not very well educated about the realities of the universe.

In the spectrum of UFO experiences this book concentrates upon the occupants but stops short of those who claim benign contact: the contactees. The authors point out that numerous books have been written documenting moving lights, odd shapes and behaviors, and close encounters. Fewer writers have attempted to bring together current knowledge about occupant sightings. This book (and the earlier version by the same authors) attempts to fill this gap in UFO research. The contactees are discussed in one brief chapter, but the authors felt that it would be impossible to do full justice to that sociological phenomenon without going into much more detail than limited space would permit.

It is probably safe to say that UFO research has finally achieved a certain level of scientific respectability. The Aerial Phenomena Research Organization (APRO), the organization headed by Coral and Jim Lorenzen, now lists forty-eight scientific consultants. The Center for UFO Studies, headed by J. Allen Hynek, has a Board consisting only of scientists who are recognized (e.g., by research and publication) in their own fields. All these individuals are devoted to the goal of solving the UFO enigma. This does not indicate, by any means, that they are committed to the hypothesis of extraterrestrial spaceships; but it does mean that they are willing to put their reputations on the line in an attempt to solve problems in a very difficult field. The Lorenzens, though with limited formal training in the sciences, take this same objective approach.

What do investigators have to work with? So far, there is precious little in the way of artifacts, photographs, or other tangible materials that can be studied in the customary scientific manner. There are a few tangibles, and they are being studied, but the question usually revolves around whether they are fraudulent or misunderstood earthly objects, rather than what they might tell us about the UFO phenomenon. For that information we have only the reports. This book summarizes a great many reports that relate to UFO occupants. Of the tens of thousands of available reports it is, of course, essential to specialize somewhat, and that is what the Lorenzens have done in this publication. Personally, I found this vast body of data almost overwhelming, especially in the early chapters. Thus I would suggest that you skip around a bit in the book if you find yourself being numbed by the succession of one case following on the heels of another. But if you are really interested in the UFO phenomenon you should certainly read every word, either in the order presented or at your own choice. The more UFO occupant cases you get into your mind, the better the chance that you might be able to contribute something to an understanding of what is going on.

There are rewards beyond the detailed summaries of occupant cases: the book is extremely exciting reading. Some stories compare in terms of sheer fascination with the best of science fiction. But there is an added twist; the stories might be true! And for still another twist; they might not be true! So you are confronted with the baffling mystery that keeps you reading a whodunit until far past bedtime. This mystery is not solved by the authors, however; the reader is left with it to haunt him. And if the stories are true, what do they imply?

The Lorenzens offer some thought-provoking guideposts along the way although they do their best to leave the decisions to you. In their more than two decades of directing APRO, they have accumulated an amazing mass of information. They have personally investigated hundreds (perhaps thousands) of reports, with many more being submitted by APRO representatives. Surely it would be amazing if the Lorenzens had no convictions. They believe we are being visited by extraterrestrial intelligent beings. But they don't proselytize, and if you reject this idea, you can still enjoy the book. The Lorenzens leave it up to you to decide which accounts you accept as the truth and to what extent.

And what accounts they are! You will meet many "little men" (even a couple of little *green* men) but you will also make the acquaintance of seven-foot giants as well as bug-eyed, monkey-like creatures that run on all fours and "float" from tree limbs to the earth. There are hairy little bipeds with pumpkin-shaped heads and even humanoids dressed in outfits apparently designed to protect them against infestation by earthly microorganisms. And there is a naked blond space goddess with slanting eyes and fiery red hair in her armpits! Perhaps most perplexing of all, at least one UFO harbored a bald gentleman who seemed to be an ordinary human in every respect, including his "bedside manner." These various entities move in a variety of ways; some even seemed to float, as though they controlled gravity, once or twice levitating the witness or his automobile! Some seemed clumsy while others were superbly agile; some exhibited great strength while others seemed frail with delicate features. Skin was sometimes swarthy, dark, or unimaginably pale, emitting *light* in some stories.

The really amazing thing is that all these details, as well as many, many more, were reported by people who appeared to be, at least before their experiences, normal in every way. Typically, they were terror-stricken by the events they chronicled, but often their accounts were substantiated by several other frightened witnesses. There were a few marks on the ground, burning bushes, and other physical items to bolster their stories. Sometimes their lives were profoundly influenced, often adversely, for months or even years after their experience. In more than one case, it was the desperate attempt of a witness to find help against a developing mental strain that led to the story becoming known or at least better known.

The Lorenzens make it clear that the reader need not, probably *should* not, accept it all. But what if only *one* of the stories is true? The real impact of this book concerns the implications that arise in your mind if you are willing to entertain the possibility that one or more of the accounts may be true. As a scientist, I must return again and again to the question of the veracity of the accounts, but also as a scientist (as well as a normally curious individual), I am deeply intrigued but also troubled by the implications.

The psychological implications are obvious. How much can a witness observe and recount vividly? How much is imagination or even hallucination, motivated by the technology of the Space Age? How much do the visiting entities, if they exist, use such powerful psychological tools as hypnotism in their interactions with the witness? In a special chapter, Leo Sprinkle, a topnotch psychologist at the University of Wyoming, provides some useful suggestions as to how to approach some of the problems, and the Lorenzens continually allude to the principles of psychology. Indeed, because of their UFO interest, they have become rather expert in the field.

If the entities are both real and extraterrestrial, what can the reports about them teach us about our universe, especially the stars and planets in the vicinity of our sun? The very fact that they are able to visit us implies much about the possibilities of space travel. Our technology is presently totally impotent when it comes to traveling beyond our own solar system; we can't imagine how it might be done in reasonable time intervals. The visitors imply that there must be a way. In the famous Betty and Barney Hill case, they also inform us about their home base and other stars that they have visited. You will read about Marjorie Fish's study of Betty Hill's star map, especially in the chapter by astronomer Walter M. Webb.

I am particularly intrigued by the biological implications of the UFO occupants. Biologists have had a lot to say about the kinds of intelligent beings that one may encounter in other worlds. The poet-anthropologist Lorin Eiseley, for example, in his book (*The Immense Journey,* New York, Random House, 1957) has a chapter entitled "Little Men and Flying Saucers." After reviewing much of the scientific as well as the theological speculations about our place in the universe, he summarizes the concepts of evolution developed by Charles Darwin and his intellectual descendants. Considering the many chance steps involved in the evolutionary development of a being as complex as man, he concludes that it could, under no circumstances, happen the same way more than once: "Life, even cellular life, may exist out yonder in the dark. But high or low in nature, it will not wear the shape of a man.... nowhere in all space on a thousand worlds will there be men to share our loneliness." George Gaylord Simpson, the "dean of American evolutionists," has elaborated on this idea in his article entitled "The nonprevalence of humanoids," *Science* 143:769, 1964. Eiseley or Simpson would be shocked to see a humanoid from another world.

But there is another line of reasoning. It is now recognized to be extremely likely that life on other worlds will be at least chemically similar to our own. When the postulated primordial conditions of our planet, which are thought to be closely similar to those of countless other planets in the universe, are duplicated in the laboratory, and some energy source such as an electrical spark or ultraviolet light is then introduced, the common chemicals of life appear in the resultant "soup." Amino acids, sugars, fatty acids, nucleotides, and other molecules are observed, the majority of them being identical with the basic building blocks of our own bodies. Thus it is suggested that life nearly anywhere in the universe would be based upon the same molecules. The cell seems so fundamental to life that (even as Eiseley suggests) it, too, might be a common feature of life everywhere. But beyond that, the argument becomes more tenuous. After all, the fantastic diversity of life forms on earth is also based on cells and a few fundamental molecules.

Would it be possible to imagine that in spite of the arguments of Eiseley and Simpson (and many others) the only form of an organism that might develop enough intelligence to fly between the stars would be a form similar to that of man? Robert Bieri took this approach in his article entitled "Humanoids On Other Planets?" (*American Scientist* 52:452, 1964). He points out that man is extremely well-constructed to meet the requirements of an intelligent organism capable of using tools and developing high intellectual capacity. Wouldn't it be essential to have two hands that are not necessary for walking? Or sense organs including eyes for stereo vision located at the front and close to the brain, elevated some distance above the ground? There is more to the argument, and the Lorenzens consider it. Prof. Bieri and others who agree with him would be convinced that an extraterrestrial humanoid would differ in extremely fundamental ways from mankind. Certainly the details of structure would probably be very different, so that any possibility of interbreeding between humans and humanoids from another world would be totally and completely eliminated. This is, indeed, the message of Darwin and modern biology. But Bieri would not be surprised to see a humanoid disembark from an extraterrestrial spaceship.

There is a third possibility that should be considered. It is conceivable that intelligent beings on different worlds might not be as totally unrelated as the modern biological theory of evolution would suggest. On the one hand, their creation may have been directed by God, so that the similarity of structures would not be left to chance. On the other hand, ancient and extremely advanced civilizations may have been traveling among the stars for countless ages, seeding the planets with similar life forms, including related humanoids.

One thing seems clear from the accounts presented in this book: except for a small minority involving robots, monsters, and the like, the great majority of UFO occupants are indeed humanoid. If, and always there is the if, we can accept any of the data in this book as evidence of extraterrestrial UFO occupants, then the question seems to be answered: extraterrestrials are humanoid.

Some other implications are especially perplexing. It was the Villas-Boas incident that most disturbed my sleep when I first encountered it. It is a wild tale, as the Lorenzens indicate, but there are reasons to consider that it might be true. For example, some details are impressive—things remembered by the witness that he did not understand but that make rather good sense in light of later speculations. I was also impressed by the sores on his body after his sexual encounter with the space goddess. Was this a form of interplanetary V.D.?

What about the problem of contamination between worlds? Could organisms from another planet infect us, or could our parasitic organisms be parasitic to the creatures of another planet? Some say yes. Bacteria are capable of metabolizing many substances, and only a specific resistance against specific organisms seems to protect us. Some say no. The relationship is too specific; an organism may only be able to parasitize those organisms to which it is specifically adapted. Villas-Boas says yes. His visitors perhaps wore suits and took other precautions to protect themselves against the possibility of infestation and infection by earthly organisms—and Villas-Boas may himself have been infected by extraterrestrial organisms.

But most disturbing of all is the apparent breeding experiment between Villas-Boas and the space lady. If this is the implication, then the visitors are not only humanoid but human, and we are certainly not alone in the universe. Our modern understanding of genetics leaves no alternative. Unless, of course, the visitors were not interested in breeding but only in playing a lewd and purposeless game!

Just what are the visitors up to? If, even tentatively, you accept their existence, then this question becomes all-important. Indeed, these accounts could be the most important data of our time, dwarfing to insignificance such matters as detente and even the destruction of the earth's environment. What could they mean? The Lorenzens piece together a great deal of information to arrive at a fairly reasonable story of planetary exploration. Are we being observed and explored by the visitors? Perhaps. This will be a primary concern as you read through the accounts. I find myself no longer content with this idea in its most simplistic forms. And the Lorenzens also express their discontent. What if the extraterrestrials are interested in more than simple exploration and a search for knowledge about our world? What if they have some purpose in wanting to manipulate us? What if it's all a show, a display, a circus—a charade in which we are led to guess answers they want us to guess? Are the silver-suited little men who are pulling up plants out in the meadow really on a botanical expedition? Or is that just what they want us to think? If so, why? These thoughts are troubling, because I can't understand what's going on or what motives might direct the visitors. Yet, as I read the stories, I can't dismiss these thoughts. Nor can I divorce my musings completely from my religious convictions. Indeed, the stories are so profoundly moving that I find myself devoting at least as much thought to their religious implications as to their scientific evaluations. But that's what this book is all about: to stimulate you to apply every thought you have ever had in an attempt to understand what is going on.

Frank B. Salisbury
Professor of Plant Physiology
Plant Science Dept. UMC 48
Utah State University
Logan, Utah

CHAPTER I

The Metamorphosis of UFO Research

When the so-called "flying saucers" came into national prominence in the summer of 1947, after Kenneth Arnold's historical sighting of nine disc-shaped objects over Mount Rainier, there was no known organization or governmental department to accommodate the rash of sightings which ensued around the country. The fledgling U.S. Air Force had just been created, becoming a full-fledged military organization, as opposed to its prior status as a division of the U.S. Army when it was the Army Air Corps.

In September 1947 "Project Sign" was created and housed at Wright-Patterson Air Force Base near Dayton, Ohio. Little was known about the project or its functions except that Dr. J. Allen Hynek, a relatively unknown astronomer, was scientific consultant Hynek was chosen mainly because he was near Dayton, being Director of Ohio State's McMillin observatory. Like the majority of the population of the United States he was a skeptic and his main function was to peruse the files of the current case reports at Project Sign and weed out the obvious reports of meteors, planets, stars, balloons, etc. It was years later that we learned the limited scope of the project, which indicated that it would have been nearly impossible for the project to do an efficient job.

By 1952 enough had happened, and there continued to be a dribble of reports each month, so that Mrs. Lorenzen broached the subject of starting an information and news clipping service to at least collect and store the data. We talked it over and decided that even with caring for two young children she would be able to handle the necessary paperwork.

Mr. Lorenzen had been a professional musician until 1950 when he entered the electronics field. We had traveled extensively and had made many friends and acquaintances, some of whom were interested in astronomy as was Mrs. Lorenzen. She contacted them, and the embryonic organization came into being. To avoid the use of the term "flying saucer" she chose Aerial Phenomena as the words describing the subject of research, adding Research Organization which described the function. It was January, and with the cold weather and the children confined to the house most of the time, she was able to achieve her goal of making contacts and planning for a publication. We realized that in order to make it work there would have to be financial support, so annual dues of three dollars were instituted. For that amount the membership received a mimeographed periodical, the *APRO Bulletin*, which contained the most recent reports, mostly taken from newspaper accounts.

In 1953, *American Magazine* (now defunct) carried a one-page feature on Mrs. Lorenzen, which brought worldwide publicity for APRO, and membership began to climb. At that time we were living in Sturgeon Bay, Wisconsin, and during a trip to Milwaukee when she visited with an official of the Milwaukee Astronomical Society who was also interested in UFOs, Mrs. Lorenzen had the opportunity to meet Dr. Hynek. She learned that he seemed interested in the UFO, but was not deeply engrossed and certainly skeptical of the reality of the UFOs as well as the extraterrestrial hypothesis of the UFOs.

In 1954 the family was in Alamogordo, New Mexico. Mr. Lorenzen was with the electronic maintenance division of the data reduction facility at Holloman Air Force Base, and Mrs. Lorenzen decided to seek a position with the Air Force there. Since the UFOs had been popularized by the press in 1947, it had been the contention of most UFO enthusiasts that the Air Force had much more information than they admitted to and was instituting a censorship of the press as well as the news media. Her main reason for taking the position was to find out if such a scheme could be implemented. After eighteen months she was forced to resign due to ill health, but during the time she was employed she came to the conclusion that there was no censorship as claimed and that various circumstances led the Air Force to choose this public stance.

During our six-year stay in Alamogordo several things happened that led us to change our philosophy about the UFOs as well as to make changes in the organization. Our affiliation with the various branches of the armed services (the Navy and Army were represented there as well as the Air Force), as well as civilian, scientific, and technical personnel, allowed us the opportunity to talk about the seriousness of the UFO problem with responsible people who in turn joined us in our efforts. Also, our experience indicated that the U.S. Air Force Project (by then renamed Blue Book) was more of a public relations effort than a study or research project.

In 1957 when the big UFO wave occurred, several sightings were made in the Tularosa basin, where Alamogordo and Holloman are located. At the height of the "flap" the UFO Officer from Holloman came to visit us in our home one evening to talk about the subject and learn what we were doing. We found that the UFO Officer position was an extra-duty assignment which was given to an officer who already had a full-time job. With such a loosely knit organization where untrained men were sent out to investigate a phenomenon about which, in most cases, they knew absolutely nothing, we felt that the Air Force could not have been doing an adequate job. At the end of the conversation the UFO officer asked us about our methods of interrogation and asked for advice in investigating cases.

Our first foreign representative had been a young drama and music critic in Venezuela who joined APRO in 1954. He recruited Horacio Bonzales G., who ultimately represented Venezuela. APRO began to acquire more and more foreign members capable of conducting and overseeing investigations in their countries, and as we approached the 1960's we had representatives in New Zealand, Australia, a few European countries, and several in South America.

We were in Tucson, Arizona, in 1960 where Mr. Lorenzen had accepted a position on an exotic new project for the Associated Universities for Research in Astronomy at Kitt Peak National Observatory. At first the goal was an orbiting telescope controlled from the ground, but that project was later scrapped. However, a communications system was set up whereby a telescope at Kitt Peak, located forty miles west of Tucson, could be programmed by computer from the laboratory in downtown Tucson.

The *APRO Bulletin* had changed from a mimeographed format to typesetting in 1956, and except for arranging for a new printer, things changed very little. It was necessary to acquire a home with adequate space for our family of four in addition to the burgeoning files, and in 1965 we bought a rambling, brick home on the north side with a large sunporch which became the new APRO headquarters.

Our consulting panels were instituted in 1962. Mrs. Lorenzen read an article about research done by a young biologist, Dr. Frank B. Salisbury, at the Utah State University at Logan, Utah. She wrote him a letter and also sent along a copy of her book, *The Great Flying Saucer Hoax*, (New York, William Frederick Press, 1962). Dr. Salisbury responded with a telephone call and they discussed the current status of the UFO phenomenon. Salisbury in turn recommended APRO to a colleague, Dr. James A. Harder, a professor of civil engineering at the University of California at Berkeley. A year later these gentlemen were joined by Dr.

R. Leo Sprinkle, a professor of psychology. APRO was well on its way to acquiring the necessary scientific talent to carry out in-depth investigations and supply the know-how for analyses of reports.

When UFO activity increased in 1965 the organization was in better position to actually put investigators into the field to interview witnesses, make measurements, and so on. The 1965 activity brought so much attention to the subject that the U.S. Air Force contracted with the University of Colorado to institute a study of the UFO phenomenon and make recommendations. The study began in 1966. APRO was asked to furnish the project with its best cases and two hundred and fifty case reports were copied and forwarded to the project, which was popularly called the Condon Committee, named after Dr. Edward U. Condon, the chief of the project. Before long there were disagreements among the committee members concerning various matters, resulting in resignations and outright firings.

Meanwhile, Mrs. Lorenzen had revised her 1962 book at the suggestion of the New American Library in New York, and it was published in the fall of 1966, resulting in further organizational growth. We then co-authored *Flying Saucer Occupants.* In 1967 we went to South America to contact representatives in six countries. It was in Lima, Peru, that we made the acquaintance of our Peruvian representative, Richard Greenwell. A young, intelligent, and energetic young man, he was deeply concerned with the UFO problem and in 1968 came to Tucson to join the headquarters staff as Assistant Director. At that time the staff consisted of the Lorenzens and three part-time workers.

Greenwell's dedication and energy enabled us to expand our foreign representation as well as fill out the scientific consulting panels. In January of 1969 the *Bulletin* announced the formation of our field investigators network. New application blanks were forwarded to all members which asked for specific details about education and experience, and on the basis of this information the field investigators were chosen. Field investigators and consultants were asked to furnish comments and suggestions for a manual and comprehensive report form which would help the investigators get the best possible complete report from witnesses. In addition to including spaces for the all-important date, time, and place, it helped the inexperienced investigator to measure angles, obtain samples when necessary, and evaluate the witness.

The Condon Committee formally closed its doors in 1968 and published its report (New York, Bantam Books, 1968). Their investigatory methods had been sadly lacking (we had visited the project in October 1967 at their invitation to brief them on our South American trip), and what we saw of their files indicated that they had no standardized report form, no set method of investigations, and generally the project was haphazardly conducted. We had learned from the experience, however, and tightened our own procedures.

After the public announcement that the project was closed, and that the committee did not feel that scientific inquiry into the UFO problem was justified, the APRO membership, which had swollen to about 4,000 in 1967, began to dwindle. In 1969 the U.S. Air Force announced the closing of Project Blue Book, and it appeared that with no official investigatory body the problem was left squarely with civilian researchers. APRO accepted the challenge and five years later, after having dwindled to a paltry 1,500 members, we have restructured the organization, built up the membership to approximately 3,500 with a crew of over 750 field investigators around the world. Although field investigators in the United States, Canada, and Mexico work directly with headquarters in Tucson, investigators in other countries channel their reports through their representatives.

One of the biggest problems with international research has, of course, been the language problem. Today APRO has the capability to translate nearly all major foreign languages into English. Because of the growth of interest in UFOs, journals have sprung up all over the world. A project now underway at APRO headquarters is the translation of all cases contained in the bulging periodical files. When translated, these reports are filed in the main case files.

In 1970 a major step was taken when the offices were permanently moved out of the Lorenzen household, and in 1973 the organization acquired its own building on the north side of Tucson. Mr. Lorenzen, who operates a thriving electronics service and marketing business, carries out his APRO obligations as director in the evenings and on weekends, while Mrs. Lorenzen spends full-time on her duties as secretary-treasurer as well as editor of the *Bulletin*, in her office at our home. The headquarters office is staffed with office manager Mrs. Sheila Kudrle, clerk-typist Douglas Price, and part-time clerk-typist Betty Darr. Volunteer helpers aid with the on-going work of report filing and preparing mailings.

The most recent project undertaken by APRO is a five-minute radio program dealing with the current "state of the art" as well as news about the most recent cases. At this writing it has been accepted for syndication by a California company.

Future projects include a course in UFOs to be taught in schools where interest is intense. It will not be an effort to teach the students that UFOs are real or attempt to identify them, but rather it will be taught to promote critical thinking. APRO has received hundreds of requests from elementary and high school teachers who feel this would be a subject of interest to their students.

UFO research is a unique field. It requires the expertise of many scientific disciplines. In the early 1960's when it became obvious that some witnesses, out of fright, tended to repress certain details of their UFO experiences, APRO began to recruit qualified psychologists and psychiatrists in order to have their advice and skills, if needed, to reassure witnesses, and in some instances use hypnosis to obtain information which might have been suppressed.

Engineers and physicists are a vital part of the staff of any research organization since it will ultimately be their answers to the problem of what type of propulsion is utilized by the UFOs.

Although great emphasis has been put on the astronomer's role in UFO research, actually it is a minor one; mainly sifting reports to weed out those which are misidentified planets, stars, comets, and the like. Astronomy is most important in the context of work such as Marjorie Fish's models of the Hill star map, but surprisingly, it was not an astronomer who did the work and produced the model (see Chapter VII).

The landing cases, which have become a repeating phenomenon, seem mostly likely to yield best information about UFOs to date. APRO is now utilizing the skills of a soils engineer who, provided with samples from a landing site, can compute the weight-bearing capacity of the ground and ultimately the weight of the object which had rested there.

Ultimately we hope to put the data concerning occupants in the hands of a team of anthropologists, but it is not likely that they will come up with many answers because if we are, in fact, dealing with aliens from other worlds, it will be next to impossible to learn much about them without having a specimen to examine.

Therefore, although we are making progress, feeling our way as new problems present themselves, we have yet to perfect a method or set of methods by which to make any hard and fast conclusions about the UFOs. There is much work ahead of us.

CHAPTER II

Landing Traces

UFOs have been reported flying around the skies of this planet for hundreds and possibly thousands of years and many books have been written about that aspect of the UFO puzzle.

But they have, in many instances, landed and left evidence of their presence behind. It is this phase of UFO activity which we will deal with in this chapter.

In our 1967 book *Flying Saucer Occupants* we documented several landing cases which involved landing traces and also demonstrated a correlation between certain types of UFOs and specific types of terrain.

Briefly, we will describe the more important incidents. A pilot driving through the desert in the summer of 1956 and bound for Nellis Air Force Base experienced a sudden and inexplicable engine failure. He tried to start the car with no success, then started walking. He saw a strange shape at the side of the highway and, being curious, approached it. To his surprise it took off. Before it left, however, he got a good look—it was circular and disc-shaped with a dome on top. When it took off he clearly saw three circular appendages underneath. The pilot went back to his car which started with no trouble. When he reached Nellis he reported the incident to Intelligence and he and one of their officers immediately drove back to the scene. On the ground at the location of the sighting they found three clearly defined concave impressions in the sand.

About ten years later, on the Emmanuel Rotenberger farm near Gwinner, North Dakota, landing impressions which closely resembled those seen by the pilot were found in a plowed field. At 7:30 A.M. on September 13, 1966, eleven-year-old Randy Rotenberger ran excitedly into the house and told his mother that a strange object had landed in the field. Mrs. Rotenberger told him to lock the door and stay inside, which he did, but he watched through the window and made these observations: the object appeared to be metallic and shaped like two bowls fastened together, lip to lip. Two red lights and a green one were arranged along the joining. It sat on three "legs" which ended in "feet" or gear which were circular and looked like bowls with the rounded part down.

The legs jutted downward and slightly outward, giving the boy the impression of the legs of a camera tripod. There was what appeared to be a transparent "bubble" on the top of the object. No forms or movement could be observed inside. Randy thought the object was perhaps 8 to 10 feet high at its thickest portion and "about one and a half times as wide as a Cadillac is long"—or about 30 feet in diameter.

After sitting on the ground for about one minute, the object took off. There was a blue glow on the bottom, and it made a roar followed by a "buzzing" sound. Randy called his mother again just before the object left, and she heard the noise which accompanied its departure.

This incident was investigated by General Homer Goebel, State Air National Guard Commander at Fargo and Assistant State Adjutant General for Air. Goebel inspected the site of the landing and found three impressions in the soft earth. Each was a foot in diameter, round in shape, tapering down to a rounded base. They formed a triangular pattern with sides 26, 23 and 22 feet apart, and they gave the impression of indentations made by pressing three bowls into the ground. Goebel told the St. Paul *Dispatch:* "They look pressed, not dug" and "I'd hate to call it a hoax because the boy sounded as if he was quite sincere."

When interviewed by telephone from APRO's office, Randy Rotenberger was cooperative but not overly talkative and positive of what he saw; he readily admitted he had been frightened.

Another type of landing impression was documented in 1957 when three different landings took place within days of each other. One was at La Madera, New Mexico, another at Canyon Ferry, Montana, and the most famous and well-investigated one occurred at Socorro, New Mexico.

On April 24, 1964, Patrolman Zamora of the Socorro police department, was chasing a speeder on the southern edge of town when he saw a blue flame in the sky and heard a loud roar in the direction of a dynamite shack in the desert. Fearful that youngsters had been "messing around" the dynamite shack, he gave up the chase and headed his patrol car toward the shack over a desert trail leading up over one mesa, down through a wash, and up onto a second mesa at the far end of which the dynamite shack stood. At first it seemed that his patrol car could not make it up the incline but on the third try he succeeded. At the point of entering the wash he looked "upstream" and spotted what appeared to be a light-colored car standing on end and two humanoid figures beside it (he said they looked about the size of young boys) about 600 feet away. One of the figures seemed to look toward Zamora as if startled by his presence. Zamora could not make out any details, because of the dust (apparently kicked up by the object's landing) as well as the distance. At this point he radioed police headquarters and asked State Patrolman Sam Chavez for assistance. Chavez immediately set out and might have viewed the object himself had he not taken the wrong street.

Meanwhile Zamora continued. As he topped the second mesa he heard two metallic bangs. Pulling his car up to where he thought the object was, he got out and took three steps toward the wash. The figures were gone but the object, white and egg-shaped, was still there. Then a roar filled the air and the object lifted off the ground. Zamora turned and ran in the other direction to the other side of the mesa and threw himself into the wash northwest of the patrol car. With a blue jet of flame about 3 feet long issuing from underneath, the object elevated toward the dynamite shack and when approximately 20 feet above it the roar was replaced by a high-pitched whining sound and the flame vanished. It headed into the southwest at low altitude and high speed and was out of sight in seconds.

Only seconds later, Chavez arrived upon the scene to find a thoroughly frightened, dirty, and disheveled Patrolman Zamora.

Afterwards Zamora reported that the strange vehicle had rested on four girder-like legs which retracted when it elevated from the ground. In the gully were found four depressions which appeared to have been made by four wedge-like members pressing outward at an angle from a central area. Imaginary lines connecting opposing depressions intersected at right angles. Those downhill from this imaginary intersection were at greater distances from it than were those uphill from it. Desert growth in the area of this intersection—a clump of range grass, a shrub, and a small barrel cactus—showed signs of short term high heating. The grass and the shrub were charred and smoldering in upper portions toward this imaginary intersection and the cactus had been scorched and burned in the same manner. The desert soil was of the general character of beach sand underscored with coarse gravel. It was not possible for a human being to walk in it without leaving obvious tracks. When Chavez and Zamora descended to the landing site the absence of tracks made it obvious that no one had preceded them. Deputy Luckie, who arrived as Chavez and Zamora began their examination, verified this point.

When we examined the scene less than forty hours later we were able to patrol the perimeters of the landing area and determine that no one had entered it except by the trail that Zamora took. Because it had rained heavily in the three days previous to the incident, Zamora, Chavez and Luckie were able to testify to the fact that no ground vehicle or pedestrian had preceded them to the area since the rain. Because of the residual moisture we found two days after the incident, the range grass in question could not sustain burning when we attempted to ignite it with matches and a cigarette lighter.

Chavez, following the methodical instincts of an experienced law officer, had "checked out" his friend despite the absence of tracks. Zamora had no implements with him with which to dig.

Besides ourselves, within the space of one week of the incident, Zamora was questioned by Army Intelligence officer Captain Holder, an F.B.I. agent named J. Arthur Byrnes, Dr. J. Allen Hynek of Northwestern University, Sgt. David Moody of Air Force Project Blue Book and Major Connors of Kirkland Air Force Base. None of these individuals expressed a need to call Zamora's integrity into question. One characteristic noted by all of the above was Zamora's intense wish for an explanation of his experience.

As with many others, the documented details of this case exceed the psychological threshold of acceptability in many who are confronted with it, and they refuse to accept its reality but none, to our knowledge, has come up with a tenable alternate theory which accommodates the facts.

Self-appointed UFO debunker, Phillip Klass, has worked the hardest at it (*UFO's Identified*, New York, Random House, 1968 and *UFO's Explained*, New York, Random House, 1974), but the best he can do is hypothesize a hoax in which Zamora took part designed to attract tourists to the community. His job was made easier by two basic facts. He arrived on the scene years after the fact and he avoided primary investigators of the case (ourselves, Captain Holder, Dr. Hynek) like the plague.

But even after applying his usual techniques he was unable to come up with an alternative explanation of the evidence. He implies that the landing leg marks were dug but does not explain how one could accomplish that without leaving tracks. His strongest objection is at best a negative proposition. He points out that a couple living near the site did not hear the roar that Zamora reported even though they were closer to the location. He does not mention the fact that their house is near a busy highway—that sounds of evaporative coolers, TV sets, etc., in the normal house serve to mask considerably louder sounds occurring at a distance.

Of course, the sound of the patrol car would have the same effect. However, Zamora told us that the sound and the blue flame occurred suddenly and simultaneously. We conclude that the visual stimulus supported the audible stimulus.

In Klass's account the UFO had already landed when Zamora first saw it: an impossibility obvious to anyone who has visited the site. What Zamora told us was that the flame appeared suddenly accompanied by a roaring sound and the object to which he was thus alerted dropped straight down into the area near the dynamite shack which could not be seen from the road. In pointing out that there was no sign of an "intense blast" at the site, Klass is merely knocking down a "straw man" of his own building. Zamora at no time describes an intense blast—quite the opposite. He stated that the flame only "kicked up a little dust," that it was an intense bluish-white color, and that it was accompanied by a loud roaring sound.

Without belaboring the issue further, the above serves to demonstrate the difficulty that Mr. Klass gets into when attempting to explain the better close encounter cases. He is forced to abandon so many elements of significant data (and distort others) that what he eventually ends up explaining is a pseudo-case of his own fabrication. He is accepted by a fairly wide audience, however, because of a complicity in the minds of those readers who so very much wish not to believe in the reality of UFOs that they will accept arguments they would find unacceptable in connection with a less emotionally tinged subject.

We personally think that Phil Klass is "putting us on" and having a good laugh (all the way to the bank) at the expense of us "buffs" whom he scorns and that portion of the reading public that is taken in by his pseudo-science.

Steve Michalak is a Polish-born industrial mechanic living in Winnipeg, Canada. A chance meeting with a UFO on the ground while prospecting in a wild area in the vicinity of Falcon Lake, Manitoba, which is about 75 miles east of Winnipeg, resulted in strange second- and third-degree burns on his chest and a minor burn on his face. After several years the burn scars are still evident, and he claims that they occasionally become reddened as though the burns are recurring.

The incident took place at 12:13 P.M. on May 20, 1967, when Michalak's attention was arrested by the noise of a number of geese which had been aroused when he first arrived in the area, but they quieted down shortly after becoming used to his presence. Michalak looked up to see what was disturbing the birds and saw two red objects approaching at about 14 to 15 degrees from the horizontal and on a heading of 240 degrees. The first was about 15 feet above the ground and the second slightly higher and they approached at very high speed. The first object came to rest on the ground, blowing leaves and rock lichen from the landing spot. Michalak was crouching in the brush, examining a rock sample and out of sight of the object. The second object hovered for a few seconds, then took off at high speed.

The machine just sat on the ground for the next half hour and radiated heat in "rainbow-like" colors. While airborne it had been a dull red color, but when on the ground it had the appearance of stainless steel. During the period that it sat on the ground Michalak took out pencil and paper and sketched the object. After about 25 minutes a square door with rounded edges opened and a "fantastic" purple light emanated from the opening. He pulled his welding glasses down over his eyes and was then able to see flashing red, green, and blue lights inside the object but could not discern whether or not they were on a control panel. At this time, Michalak said, he heard a high-pitched whining sound like that of a motor running at high speed and smelled an odor resembling that of a burned-out electrical motor and heard a "whooshing" sound as if air was being taken in and expelled. Michalak then approached the machine, noting the heat that radiated from it. He claims he heard the sound of voices, so he spoke to it but got no answer. He tried English, Russian, German, Italian, and Polish. While he was talking the sound of the motor stopped, he heard voices again, and then the door closed and moved out to become flush with the outside of the object. Although he saw the door and knew it was there, he said, when it was closed there was no evidence of an opening or seam nor were there any seams or rivets of any kind visible over the rest of the vehicle.

Michalak then reached out and touched the side of the object with his canvas-base, rubber-coated glove, which melted and slipped off the surface. As he looked down at the glove, the machine began to move in a counter-clockwise direction and he was blown to the left by a blast of hot air or exhaust which set his clothes on fire. The machine then took off in the direction from which it came.

After putting out the fire on his clothes, Michalak packed his gear into his briefcase and headed back for the highway. He felt dizzy occasionally but went into town, called the Royal Mounted Police at Falcon, but they told him they could do nothing about it. When he went to the Misericordia Hospital for treatment, he told the doctors who treated him that he had been burned by airplane exhaust.

Mrs. Michalak was one of the first to note her husband's odd condition. He could not keep food on his stomach, was nauseated and vomiting and had a strange odor about him, which she said, "Seemed to come from the inside." When he did begin to eat and accommodate food on the fourth day after his experience, he seemed to derive no nourishment from it for he lost a total of 22 pounds. Blood counts were taken and the lymphocyte count was down considerably below normal.

That, in essence, is Michalak's story. Because it is a one-witness case it would ordinarily not be considered to be the best, but Michalak's reputation, the burned glove and shirt, added substance to his claim. Additionally, when Field Investigators James B. Thompson, Edward Barker, and Brian Cannon investigated, they found the circular area where leaves and lichen had been blown away, indicating that something might have hovered above the ground even if it had not landed. Examination of the glove and shirt yielded nothing—there was no residue of any kind which could contribute anything to the case. Examination of the landing site gave us no further clues either.

However, 11 days later, another landing took place near a farm outside Beausejour, Manitoba, about 45 miles from Winnipeg. A farm woman, who requests anonymity, was sitting on her front porch at 11:30 P.M. waiting for her husband to come home. She said she saw a brilliant red light with a smaller blue light beside it come toward her from the south. It illuminated the ground and appeared to land, whereupon she became frightened and went into the house. The next morning she and her husband investigated the area where the object had apparently landed and found a semi-circular area 30 yards by 50 yards in flames. The strange aspect of this case is that on the 15th of June the area was still smoldering despite the fact that there had been considerable rain in the interim. Soil samples taken at the site yielded nothing.

As we proceed in this examination of the ground markings associated with the landing of unidentified flying objects, it will become extremely clear that there are many ways in which the UFOs manifest themselves on the ground, such as in the following case:

At 4:20 A.M. on the 5th of July 1967 on Route 31 near the Depot Road area in Coventry, Connecticut, a motorist sighted an orange ball of light which appeared to be hanging from a tree. The driver immediately drove into Coventry and notified the police, but by the time officers arrived on the scene the area was deserted. After receiving the full report from the police, APRO Field Investigator Larry Fawcett examined the area and found a grassy spot which had been swirled flat as if compressed by some rotating force just a few yards off the road from the point where the ball of light had been seen.

This particular type of ground marking, which had been found quite frequently in Australia several months before the Coventry case, had been dubbed "saucer nests" by the press, alluding to the original designation for a UFO which had been popularly used in the 1940's and 1950's.

Another such "nest" was found by Ronald E. Januzzi, a mineralogist of Danbury, Connecticut, near his museum on the Danbury-Brewster highway. It was found on the morning of the 9th of January 1967 and was considered to be too large to have been caused by an animal; however, no UFO was seen in the vicinity which could be linked to the spot.

Another case with a different marking involved young (18-year-old) Barbara Fawcett of Pompano Beach, Florida, who was driving to Islamorada where her mother was staying, at 11:30 P.M. on July 20, 1967. Her small Ford was the only vehicle on the highway at the time, so when a large yellow light showed up in her rear-view mirror she became frightened. It made a constant high-pitched roaring sound, and when she tried to speed up to get away from it, it overtook her car, swayed up a few feet as if to land on top of it. But at that moment a car approached from the opposite direction and the bright yellow glow coming from the object covered the road for a second, and then completely disappeared.

Arriving at her mother's home at Islamorada, Barbara told her mother of her experience, rested for a couple of hours and, convinced that it had been an illusion, decided to return to Pompano in order to elude early morning rush hour traffic. She and her sister and a toy poodle began the journey back on U.S. Highway 1 and reached the Jewish Creek area at 2:30 A.M. on July 21st. The only other car on the road had turned off at Ocean Reef, and the girls were alone when the dog suddenly began to shake violently, not making a sound. Then the girls saw the yellow light again as it rose out of the swamp west of the highway. This time it did not look perfectly round as before, but somewhat jagged. "It wobbled and floated up, down, and from side to side," Miss Fawcett reported.

When the object appeared in front of the car about 15 feet off the ground, Barbara thought she was going to collide with it. But as the car nearly reached the object, it veered to the right under the power lines and landed on one of the large sand dunes to the right of the road. At this juncture the light became smaller and smaller until it reached the size of a pinpoint and finally disappeared. Less than a minute later the large light again appeared in the rear-view mirror of the car, and Barbara kept going as fast as her car would go and reached Pompano Beach. She later reported the incident to officers at Substation Four in Homestead, the Air Force and Homestead police. Investigation showed an immense scorched area on top of a particular sand dune near the edge of the road where Miss Fawcett estimated the object had landed.

Our next ground marking report came from a 14-year-old Tucson, Arizona, boy who observed a "maverick" as far as UFO prototypes are concerned, at 5:40 P.M. on the 9th of October in 1967. Richard (he and his parents ask that he remain anonymous) had ridden his bicycle part-way home with a friend and was returning alone, following the track of a minibike. He decided to ride along the floor of a wash (a wash is a deep ditch-like affair in the desert floor which carries run-off water in the rainy season) and was nearly home when he had to ride up the side of the wash to avoid a tree which was growing across the wash in his path. There had been some rain and the floor of the wash was hard packed. As Richard detoured, he spotted a cylindrical object sitting on two legs about 44 feet away from him. He rode a little further until he was about 35 feet from the object whereupon it left the ground, ascended straight up with a discernible side-to-side motion, and disappeared from sight within 12 seconds.

Later questioning indicated that the object was approximately 8 feet tall, 2½ feet wide, and it was shaped much like a water heater except that the top was rounded. It appeared to be metallic, reflecting sunlight, but not reflecting the images of trees, brush, etc., in the vicinity. The object was supported by two legs which angled out from the bottom, ending in two "feet" in the shape of round "pads." A curved bar ran between the "legs" just above the "feet," indicating that it was a strengthening or bracing member.

Richard proceeded immediately to his home and told his mother what he had seen, and the two of them went back to the wash where she took several color photos of the impressions left by the object and of the general area. The imprints indicated that the "legs and pads" made a twisting motion as they left the ground. The tracks measured 13 inches across and the area of the impressions from edge to edge measured about 42 inches.

In checking Richard's claims, the area was observed and the terrain clearly showed Richard's bicycle tracks and his footprints indicating, as he stated, that after the object left he approached to within about 2 feet of the place where the object had rested. It would not have been possible for the boy to have made the impressions without aid and there were no other tracks indicating the presence of others.

Probably one of the most interesting aspects of this case is the fact that the magnetometer at the Tucson Magnetic and Seismological Observatory, which is located within a few miles of the sighting location, registered a perturbation, and inasmuch as UFO movements in other cases have produced the same reaction, we can at least speculate that the UFO and the magnetometer action were linked.

As the reader will note, the year 1967 was a year of very heavy UFO activity and in particular involved a considerable number of landings and close encounters. Subsequent chapters will document the occupant cases which were most outstanding but before getting into that phase, we go to Fordingbridge, England, for the adventure of one Karl Barlow of Dawley, Shropshire, at 2:30 A.M. on the 6th of November.

Barlow was driving his truck on Highway A 338 near Fordingbridge and as he rounded a bend in the road he became aware of a strange object above some trees on the right hand side of the road. It was approaching and when about a quarter of a mile away, the lights and radio of the truck went dead although the truck's diesel engine continued to function. Without lights, Barlow decided it would be best to stop and brought the truck to a halt as he observed the object descend toward the surface of the road about 15 yards ahead of him. He sat transfixed and watched as an opening or porthole in the bottom of the thing began to put out a tube-like attachment which resembled the flexible hose of a vacuum cleaner. At the end of this tube was a box-like affair from which four short tubes protruded. During this maneuver the main object seemed to emit a high-pitched whine. The box was then directed to the side of the road and the four short lengths of hose sucked up grass, gravel, and dead leaves from the roadside. The box was then transferred to the other side of the road where it did the same thing; then the box and the hose were withdrawn into the porthole and the porthole closed.

The craft hovered for another half a minute, still making the whining sound, then ascended into the air, taking off in the same direction from which it had come—to the right of the truck. Barlow described the main object as about 15 feet in width, egg-shaped, with an "out of this world green color." A small, white, saucer-shaped form was visible on its underside during its departure.

During the time that the object hovered over the road and sucked up material from each side, another vehicle, a white Jaguar with one passenger, which was coming from the opposite direction from that of the truck, pulled up when its engine and lights failed. When it stopped, the UFO was between the truck and the Jaguar and both drivers got a good look at the object.

Upon the departure of the UFO, Barlow went to a phone and called the police who came upon the scene shortly thereafter. The Jaguar driver was still there as he could not start his car since the battery was dead, as was the truck's battery. Barlow, described by police as being in a terrified condition when he reported the incident, duly made his report which was carried in the English press. The Jaguar driver, however, had had a couple of drinks and did not want to submit to a "breathalizer" test and therefore did not make a report. Both vehicles were tested by the Royal Automobile Club official testers and were found to be in good mechanical condition. The truck's battery had been charged shortly before the incident took place and there was no reason found for the condition of either of the batteries. Other interesting points of information about this case include the fact that the truck's lights and radio came back on (he had not turned them off) when the UFO was about a quarter of a mile away on its exit flight.

Constable Roy Nineham who was in the patrol car and who had investigated this report said, "the most startling part of his report is that his lights failed and came on again when the object he saw disappeared." Another police spokesman made this statement: "There is no explanation for this. We have no reason to suspect the informant's story." The ground clearly showed that two areas, one on each side of the road, were absent of leaves, gravel, and grass.

Eighteen days after Mr. Barlow's experience in England, two technicians in Rio de Janeiro, Brazil, witnessed an astonishing sight from the window of an apartment building where they were repairing a record player. In the Barlow case it seemed obvious that the object in question was taking samples for some unknown reason, but the motivations of the Rio UFO leave much about which to speculate.

It was 2:30 P.M. on the 24th of November on the eighth floor of a building on the Rua Gomes Carneiro, the front of which faces the hills which run parallel to the coastline. From this apartment a large area between Praca G. Osorio and the spot where the tunnel comes out onto Rua R. Pomepia is visible.

Carlos Alberto do Nascimento, 14, the helper to Ugo Battaglia, 39, a radio technician, was standing by the window when he heard a high-pitched sound which made the glass vibrate, and looking out the window he saw a brilliant metallic disc-shaped object which appeared to be landing just below the skyline among the trees opposite the building. One tree stood well above the others, and as the object passed over it struck the tree and the leaves scattered about and the tree itself appeared to "blow up." Settling close to the ground, the craft hovered and out of the bottom of the object came three white-clad men who proceeded to walk around it. Carlos excitedly called Mr. Battaglia to the window and the two watched the spectacle. Both were struck with two strange characteristics of the three forms: they walked around the object side by side, in a row. Their arms hung down from their sides as though made of lead—they did not swing as do the arms of a normal man.

The only disagreement between the two about the scene was that Carlos thought the clothing worn by the three figures was white like the type worn by service station attendants (coveralls), but Battaglia said he thought they were yellow.

Mrs. Irene Granchi, our field investigator for Rio de Janeiro who conducted the investigation, suggested that Battaglia, who had been further inside the room, had been focusing his attention on his work and that the sudden bright sunshine when he went to the window may have affected his color perception. Carlos had been at the window for some time before calling Battaglia.

After about five minutes of the "walking," the three figures went under the disc, which continued to hover. Carlos noticed a spinning cupola with "slat windows" on top and a red light at both ends of the saucer-shaped object underneath. The day was clear with perfect visibility. Their business at the apartment concluded, Battaglia and Carlos left the building at 2:55 P.M. and on their way to their shop at the corner of the street they both looked up to the hill and saw that the UFO was still there. When they reached the last corner near a square, they looked again and the object was gone. Upon arriving at their shop, Carlos and Mr. Battaglia told about their observation to another man in the shop and they all decided to visit the spot the next day. Their friend took a new camera along with him. At the scene of the landing the three found the wild grass trampled or pushed down and the tree which Carlos had seen appeared to have been wrenched apart, had no leaves on it, and the bare trunk looked burned and charred. The other trees in the area were perfectly normal. Samples of the bark and tree trunk were obtained and turned over to APRO, but as usual, beyond the fact that they were burned, nothing was learned.

The men noted that the grass, which was very high, would have covered them completely had they tried to walk through it. However, Carlos and Ugo testified that the three figures they had seen were walking only knee-deep in the grass, indicating that they were not, in fact, walking on the ground, but that by some means of locomotion, were moving about *above the ground.* Carlos, who had never put much stock in UFOs, was badly shaken by what he had seen and suffered from a severe headache, no doubt due to shock, for the rest of that day. Battaglia, on the other hand, had convinced himself that he had seen a helicopter until he talked with his colleague at the shop.

Another apparent witness had called the police station after having fainted at the sight of the object and its crew. This information was picked up from a local radio station and attempts were made to locate the witness, but to no avail.

This case is included here because of the ground traces, but from what was described it seems possible that it could have been discussed in the chapter dealing with the infallibility of UFOs, or in the chapter dealing with the "floating, flying UFOnauts."

If Battaglia's and Carlos' observations were accurate, it can be theorized that the object came in too close to the ground, struck the tree, and then stopped while the occupants got out and searched for exterior damage to the craft. Whether or not the close approach was intentional for some unknown reason or there was some malfunction of the controls cannot even be guessed.

Our next ground trace case has received wide attention, probably because of the photographs taken from an airplane showing the marks allegedly left by an unidentified flying object. The only testimony that an object was there at all comes from two young girls who, on the night of July 13, 1969, were preparing to retire in the upstairs bedroom of the Warren Barr home 7½ miles south of Garrison, Iowa. Pat Barr's attention was caught by what sounded like a low-flying jet and she went to the north window and looked out in the direction of a neighboring farm. She called to her cousin Kathy Mahr, 17, and the two girls watched what they described as a strange object which appeared to be hovering over a large bean field on the Barr farm. Kathy described the object as follows. It had a dull metallic finish which was easily discerned because of the two rows of lights which were arranged across the face of it at its midline. It had the appearance of "two coffee saucers" placed rim to rim, and it rotated as it hovered. The sighting lasted only a few seconds, after which the object left at such high speed that the girls did not know precisely which direction it went, except that it went past their window. But they claimed that the area where it had hovered was glowing red after the object disappeared from sight. Neither of the girls was frightened but they were curious about the strange craft.

At breakfast the next day the girls told the Barrs about what they had seen, and Mr. Barr tended to be skeptical and attributed the whole thing to "a figment of their imagination." However, later that morning he discovered, at the spot indicated by the girls, a nearly circular patch of ground in his bean field which was almost bare. The bean vines appeared to have been burned although there was no evidence of flame.

The area in the field which was "burned" was approximately 40 feet in diameter and was easily seen from the air. The local news media showed interest in the incident and a taped interview with the Barr girl was made which was played on a local radio station. Most of the area's residents were inclined to think that the scarred field resulted from a "fireball" or lightning, and Mr. Barr did not rule out lightning entirely. When interviewed, he said that he hadn't informed authorities at first because he was skeptical. Pat Barr, on the other hand, was convinced that the object she had seen had caused the damage to the bean crop and that it was an "air-flying object from outer space." Mr. Barr told interviewers that he "would hesitate to guess" at the object's identity and the cause of the scar on the field but did say that he felt it was "something unusual—I'll put it that way."

APRO Field Investigator Glenn McWane and member Leroy Latham conducted APRO's investigation and Mr. McWane furnished the photo of the field. Samples of the beans were submitted to APRO Headquarters but nothing could be learned from them other than the fact that they had been burned in some manner.

As the reader will no doubt notice, the concentration of landings was in 1967, gradually becoming more and more infrequent in the ensuing years. This may be due to the fact that there were simply more landings in 1967 or it may be that landings took place in later years and were not reported. There are, of course, other cases of claimed landings, cases in which strange marks were found on the ground but they are not included here because no UFO was observed before or after the marks were discovered.

Stewart, Minnesota, is the location of our next ground trace report. Field Investigator Michael Stone did not learn of the case until five weeks after it allegedly occurred so when he examined the field he could find only one stalk of damaged corn.

At 12:30 A.M. (C.D.T.) on the morning of June 25, 1971, members of the Arnold Windschitl family were awakened by the sound of a sudden, strong gust of wind. Mrs. Windschitl noticed that a small electric night light in the house went out at the same time but came back on a couple of seconds later. Mr. Windschitl, thinking a heavy storm was beginning, rushed outside to check the weather but found that the sky was cloudless and there was no wind or lightning. Their ducks, however, were "wild," and the electric yard light had gone out.

The yard light is actuated by a photo-sensor; it extinguishes when the ambient light exceeds a certain value and turns on, after a few minutes' delay, when it becomes dark. Mr. Windschitl theorized that a bright flash had accompanied the wind and extinguished the light. After a couple of minutes the yard light came back on and the ducks quieted down. They could find nothing else wrong so the family retired again for the night. An older son was returning home from Stewart on his motorcycle at the time of the incident and saw what appeared to be the flash of a meteor in the direction of the farm.

The next morning Mr. Windschitl was cultivating corn in a field a few hundred yards east of their farmhouse when he noticed that a portion of his field was flattened and scorched. The area affected was circular and about 25 feet in diameter. The corn was bent over about one inch from the ground with the stalks all pointing radially out from the center. In the center of the circle was a circular dish-shaped depression approximately 2 feet in diameter and 6 to 8 inches deep in the center. Inside the depression, near the edge, were five or six small holes, approximately three-fourths of an inch in diameter and 2½ inches deep.

A day or two later, according to the family, they were weeding a bean field about a quarter of a mile south of the corn field when they discovered a similar burned and flattened area. They estimated the diameter of the circle to be 25 feet, as in the corn field, but there was no evidence of the dish shaped depression in the center. Mr. Windschitl offered his opinion that the two areas could have been damaged at the same time.

During his investigation Mr. Stone examined the fields. Heavy rains had occurred in the meantime and the corn was over 6 feet tall by then so it was difficult to find the damaged area in the corn field. The dish-shaped depression had been almost completely obliterated but was still noticeable and over half of the corn in the damaged area had recovered and appeared to be as big and healthy as the corn in the rest of the field. Two of the Windschitl boys, Tony and Paul, and Mr. and Mrs. Stone examined the bean field but found nothing to indicate damage; apparently the beans had managed to recover completely.

After the interview Mr. Stone showed Mr. Windschitl an article in the July-August 1969 *APRO Bulletin* describing a similar occurrence in the Barr case. Mr. Windschitl said that if an aerial photograph of his bean field had been taken at the time the damage was discovered, it would have appeared the same as in the photograph accompanying the article. He estimated the diameter of the circle in the photograph to be about 25 feet, assuming a 44-inch spacing between rows, making it about the same size as the burned areas in his field.

The explanation which comes most readily to mind in the Windschitl case is, of course, lightning, but the atmospheric conditions do not support this, and fulgurites, a fused soil condition which almost always accompanies lightning strikes, were not found. A meteor strike seems to be ruled out, too, in view of the circular shape of the damaged areas in both the corn and bean fields. What the holes in the corn field were leads only to speculation—along the lines that core sampling was taking place, for instance. As we examine occupant cases later in this volume, perhaps some light can be cast on this particular case.

In 1972, the *National Enquirer,* a weekly magazine published at Lantana, Florida, sponsored an ongoing contest to award various sums of money for the best UFO cases, the ultimate prize being $50,000 for a report that would prove that UFOs are from outer space. A $5,000 prize was awarded to Ronald Johnson, a 16-year-old farm boy who lives near Delphos, Kansas, for his report of a landed object on the family farm on November 2, 1971. A whitish ring of soil which glowed and would not absorb water was the physical evidence that something quite strange had happened in the small clearing on the Johnson farm.

On that date, at 7 P.M., Mr. Johnson and Ronald were in the farm yard. Mrs. Johnson called them to dinner and Mr. Johnson went in while Ronald stayed in the yard. The Johnsons ate a leisurely meal which took about 30 minutes, then Mrs. Johnson called to Ronald again. The Johnsons do not remember whether or not Ronald answered. However, he shortly came to call them out to see a bright light disappearing from view in the southeast sky.

Then Ronald related what had happened during the time that his parents were eating. Unfortunately, Ronald is not completely clear concerning the time involved and cannot account for all of the 30 minutes between the time his mother first called him and when he called his parents out at 7:30. However, Ronald claimed that he heard a rumbling sound, took a couple of steps to the north and around the corner of the barn about 90 to 95 feet from him was a strange craft hovering above the ground. It stayed there for about five minutes, then it ascended over a low shed and headed south.

At this point he called his parents who came out and saw the object leaving. They walked over to the spot where the object was first seen and saw a glowing, phosphorescent, ring-shaped area on the ground and also noted that portions of trees adjacent to the area were also glowing. Mrs. Johnson took a photo of the ground immediately. Mr. and Mrs. Johnson claimed that upon touching the soil in the ring their fingers became numb. This condition persisted with Mrs. Johnson, she said, for about a week. She was employed at a local rest home and said that she could not feel the pulses of her patients during that period of time.

After receiving the preliminary report on this case, APRO asked Mr. Clancy Tull, a lawyer and field investigator from Kansas City, Missouri, to visit the Johnsons and attempt to get answers which had not been covered in the original report.

According to Tull, Ronald saw an object but could not describe the surface. The bottom of the craft was about one foot above ground level, but Ronald could not recall seeing the actual ground level. The base seemed stationary but the upper portion was moving or vibrating from side to side or perhaps wavering up and down. The illumination of the object apparently began some minutes after Ronald first saw it. The sequence of events was: he heard the "rumbling" sound, then he took a step or two to the north, then he observed the object approximately 1 foot above the ground level although he could not see the ground, and the base of the thing was stationary, then the illumination began. He described the illumination as appearing like an arc, such as the electric light between an electric welding rod and metal being welded. This arc flash began at the base of the object and almost instantaneously involved the entire object. The arc flash allegedly caused an apparent flash burn in both of Ronald's eyes. He described blue, red, and orange. There was a partial loss of vision but not "total black" or absense of light. Mr. Tull assumed that something akin to a flash burn caused total constriction of the pupils and perhaps even temporary dam age to the rods and cones in the eyes.

The evidence gathered by Mr. Tull indicated that the sheep were not disturbed until after the observation began and that Ronald was perhaps 90 feet, 235 degrees S.S.E. from the assumed center of the ring when he first observed the object after taking one or two steps to the north. Ronald's eyes watered, burned, and were bloodshot for at least two days. The object in question was estimated to be about 9 feet in diameter, the ring was a foot wide, and the outer diameter of the entire ring was about 8 feet.

The preliminary investigation by Ted Phillips of Sedalia, Missouri, had been carried out 32 days after Ronald Johnson allegedly had the experience and there had been considerable precipitation. The inside of the ring was very muddy as was the terrain outside of it. However, the ring itself was dry down to 1 foot, whereas the soil outside the ring was wet down to 8 inches. A truly interesting set of circumstances and evidence.

When Phillips first saw the ring it was distinguished by the fact that it was still covered with snow, while in all the surrounding area the snow had melted. His report states: "Although the surrounding area was extremely moist, we found that if the snow was removed from any part of the ring the soil directly beneath the snow was dry and light brown in color—this was in contrast with the black moist soil in the ring center and around the ring."

Ted Phillips returned to the site on August 8, 1972, in the company of APRO Research Director Dr. James Harder. They found that the ring seemed to be "widening" and that differences between ring soil and the surrounding soil were becoming less pronounced compared with samples taken by Phillips during his earlier visit.

Writing of the August 8, 1972, visit, Harder says, "In trying to clarify some of the earlier witness testimony, I asked many questions of Mrs. Johnson and Ronny. The following points I thought to be pertinent. During the initial period of the sighting, when Ronny felt himself to be paralyzed, the sheep seemed not to move. I questioned Ronny about his paralysis, asking if he could move his eyeballs (this being inferred if the larger muscles are paralyzed). He seemed not too sure, but said that he could not. Mrs. Johnson still suffers a numbness in her leg just above the knee in front of the right leg, where she rubbed her fingers after first reacting to the numbness induced when she put her right hand into the glowing soil. She was wearing slacks which may have caught the dirt; she did not change clothes for some time. This may have given a longer or more intense exposure to that spot. Mr. Johnson experienced the numbness in his fingers, too, from handling the dirt.

"I talked to some other non-family witnesses and got some additional provocative information, but nothing that adds to the probative evidence. Besides the family (two sons and the parents) there were at least three others who saw the ring at night within four days—Judy Stout (friend of the older son, I think) and the reporter Thaddia Smith and her husband (both the night of the 3rd, second night from the event). All the witnesses agreed it was very bright. 'About as bright as the floor of a lighted room if you came in from the dark. You could almost read a newspaper by it.' The older son saw it four or five days later (he was out of town, apparently, at the time of the sighting) and described it to me as 'about like a fluorescent light bulb.' He said that a week or two later you could still see it at night, that it had a greenish tint like a tinted fluorescent bulb. Judy Stout told me that it was almost like walking into a room with the light on. She saw it within an hour and said that three days later it was about the same. On another occasion, however, she said that it was about half as bright on the third night. The first night she said, 'You could have read by it.' It could be photographed by its own light with a camera using color daylight film. The Polaroid camera aperture was 'set in the middle.' The camera was a Polaroid model 104, with 108 film. This model does not take time exposures. All of this indicates that the light source was pretty intense—far greater than anything that could be produced by luminiscent organisms—especially at very cool evening temperatures. So those that want to invoke luminescent fungus, etc., just don't know what they are talking about. The light output must have been on the order of 50 foot lamberts (50 foot candles at 100 per cent reflectance) in order to have exposed the film the way it did.

"The whitish filaments collected on Dec. 4th were fungal in origin, and there is no evidence that this whitish substance was the same as the material that covered the ground earlier and gave rise to the light. However, the fungal mycelium can also give a hydrophobic water-rejecting reaction, so there has been some confusion. However, even the parts of the soil that were not obviously connected with the fungal growth were hydrophobic. Thus it would appear that the hydrophobicity and the fungus were not necessarily connected. A series of soil cultures that I made in Berkeley showed a great deal of scatter in the amounts of bacteria and fungus, but generally there were, by my colleagues' estimates, about ten times the usual ratio of fungus to bacteria in the samples taken in August 1972. One inference is that the UFO produced some differential sterilization that favored fungus over bacteria, or that there was some substrate laid down that favored fungus.

"Stanton T. Friedman has claimed that the glow could have resulted from elemental (white) phosphorus that was produced by micro-wave heating of manure and organic matter deep in the soil and which then condensed at the soil surface. This is nonsense, particularly because one cannot sublime or vaporize phosphorus in the presence of air without its burning. It burns spontaneously in air at temperatures over 37°F. Besides, there was no evidence of steam or other production of heat at the time immediately after the landing when Mrs. Johnson went out and touched the surface. She said it was cool. However, she said that several days later there was something that looked like steam in the photographs she took, but that one could not see this with the eye. This may be significant, but I'm not sure what to make of it. Maybe there was a strong UV emanation? She said it looked like a volcano (on film); I did not see the film, as she did not tell me this until later by telephone.

"There had been quite a bit of rain the previous day (Nov. 1), 1.82 inches at Concordia, nearby. The dryness of the ring was apparent on Nov. 3, the next day, and continued in spite of rains between then and Dec. 4. We can conclude that not only was there an initial drying-out but an induced hydrophobicity. These two data have been confused. Furthermore, there seemed to be no way for the water to have been driven out by heat at the time—and what happened to it? Did it get incorporated into the whitish substance which subsequently decomposed in the process of giving off light? There is not enough chemical energy available to have accounted for the total quantity of light emitted over several weeks from any normally occurring reactions. This suggests that there is a form of matter involved that does not have the chemical nature of normal matter and takes part in different reactions which are much more energetic."

An incident which took place at Rosmead, South Africa, on the evening of November 11, 1972, was indeed baffling to all who investigated it thoroughly. At about 9:30 P.M. policemen at Middleburg watched a strange glowing object through binoculars. It appeared to change color, and its shape went from circular to elliptical. They said the light hovered over a hill at Rosmead, then disappeared and reappeared. A while later the principal of Rosmead School, Mr. Harold Truter, was just arriving home when he saw "a beam like a searchlight" in the sky and he and his wife and children watched it for some time. He then discovered that chunks of tar had been gouged from the school tennis court near his home. The next morning he made a closer inspection and found that there was no damage to the fencing around the court and that the gate was still firmly secured with wire as it had been before the object was seen. He thought it significant that lumps of tar were found caught high up in the tennis court fence. On the 13th, police who were searching the area found lumps of tar on a hill some distance away.

Lt. Col. B. J. van Heerden, district commandant of police at Middleburg, stated that the reports on the object from his men tallied with those of the UFO seen at Fort Beaufort earlier in the year.

As the investigation continued, it was found that a tree next to the tennis court at Rosmead High School had started to die. It was a large blue gum tree which showed signs of scorching, according to van Heerden. Theories were advanced that the 10 to 12 foot chunks of tar which had been ripped up from the court's surface were caused by a gas explosion or a whirlwind, but were discounted because not a piece of tar had been overturned and the other trees in the vicinity had not sustained any damage. After the news about the mysterious damage was reported, four men who had been guarding the petrol dumps 400 meters away on Sunday night made independent statements to the police that they had observed red lights on the court.

"It looked as if someone in a car without headlights but with tail lights burning were riding around in circles on the tennis court," they told police. The lights disappeared, they said, and then the whole petrol dump was illuminated with a "strange incandescent light." Riflemen P. K. Nel and S. J. Rosseau said that the lights were on the court and not next door.

Mr. E. van Zyl, who held a B.Sc. in astronomy and lectured at the University of Witwatersrand, investigated the case and concluded that the damage was caused by a whirlwind.

In a letter to Mr. T. Geary, director of the planetarium, he argued that upon examining the surface of the tennis court: "I saw no signs whatever of melting and no signs that could have been made by a rocket or jet blasting off" (here van Zyl makes the error of assuming that whatever was over the court was using a mundane type of propulsion). He also made the flat statement that two holes pressed into the asphalt surface at each end of the court "definitely could not have been made by a leg or stay pressing down into the tar," without listing his reasons. Van Zyl further said, "The whirlwind does not explain the light which was seen on Sunday night—some folks say they saw a red light, others yellow and some blue! So it must have been a piece of hardware left over from a satellite burning out."

Mr. van Zyl's explanation of the cause of the damage to the tennis court conveniently ignores some of the evidence or distorts it, whichever is most effective in bolstering his theory.

Although we do not have *exact* times for the sightings involved, we can reconstruct to some extent. The petrol dump guards saw two red lights going around in circles—*not next to*, but *on* the tennis court. Then the lights disappeared and the petrol dump was lit up. Meanwhile, Principal Truter, arriving home (which is located next to the school), saw a "beam like a searchlight" in the sky. Shortly afterward he discovered the damage to the court. Now, the question is: Did the guards first see a UFO with rotating lights over the court? When they disappeared and the dump was lit up, was Mr. Truter *at the same time* looking at the "searchlight" which was spotlighting the petrol dump?

Where Mr. van Zyl's hypothesis is concerned, we must again ask some questions. Can a whirlwind pick up material as heavy as the material which was torn out of the tennis court? Why was asphalt found on a hill some distance away, but there was no evidence of the ravages of a whirlwind between the tennis court and the hill? Why were the green shoots at the *base* of the gum tree dying the next day? The tree was partially denuded and the remainder of the foliage withered—it is doubtful that a whirlwind could do that.

Being desert dwellers, the writers are most familiar with whirlwinds, which in the desert are called "dust devils" and are very frequently seen. Some information about the physics of a whirlwind is very beneficial at this point. A whirlwind and a tornado are of the same family of physical phenomena, but the latter is tremendously more powerful. Tornadoes can uproot trees, carry houses off their foundations, etc. But it is doubtful that there is any case of a tornado tearing up an asphalt or cement pavement. Why? Because the tornado depends on its vacuum to give it lifting power. It is the air in and around an object rushing up to fill the vacuum of the tornado that gives the "twister" its power. Similarly, but on a much smaller scale, the much weaker "whirlwind" depends on the vacuum principle for its power. There is little *if any air* in asphalt so the odds against a whirlwind tearing up an asphalt pavement are astronomical. It is also difficult to conceive of a whirlwind "sucking" up *two-inch thick* chunks of asphalt, dumping them next to the holes they were torn free from, and also carrying other chunks a half mile away before dropping them—and with no disturbance to trees or other vegetation *between the two points*!

One last point concerning the whirlwind theory: whirlwinds depend upon the sharp temperature gradients offered by sunlight in order to form and thus (unless South Africa operates on a different set of physical laws than elsewhere) could not form at night.

A case which was carefully investigated and later documented in Aime Michel's excellent book *Flying Saucers and the Straight Line Mystery* (New York, Criterion Books, 1958) bears considerable resemblance, at least where the physical traces are concerned, to the Rosmead incident.

On October 4, 1954, Madame Yvette Fourneret of Poncey, France, walked toward a window to close it. The time was approximately 8 P.M. and, she saw, about 20 yards from the house in the Cazet's meadow, a luminous body which appeared to be balancing lightly in the air to the right of a plum tree, as if preparing to land. She estimated that the object was about 3 yards in diameter, elongated, horizontal, and orange-colored. The glow from the object threw a pale light on the branches and leaves of the plum tree. Frightened, she seized her son and ran next door to a friend's house where they tightly closed the door. At that point two neighbors arrived, and seeing how frightened the women were, asked and were told what had happened. Armed with shotguns, the men ran toward the meadow, but when they arrived there they found no object, but rather a very strange hole.

Mr. Fourneret had been at a meeting at the Mayor of Poncey's house and was sent for. The men then went about examining the hole in Mayor Cazet's meadow. What they found was strange indeed. An area measuring 27 inches wide at one end and 20 inches at the other appeared to have been "sucked up." White worms wriggled on the fresh soil of the hole, and the earth that had been torn up was scattered all around the hole in clumps 10 to 12 inches across over a radius of approximately 4 yards. On the *inner* edge of the hole similar clods hung down, and the soil had been pulled out in such a manner that about halfway down the aperture was wider than at ground level. There was no trace of any instrument which could account for the extraction of the earth and also the tiny roots and rootlets in the soil were intact everywhere on the surface of the hole. None had been cut, as would have been the case had an excavation taken place.

Another detail was outstanding: in the center of the hole lay a plant with a long root which was still attached by the end of the root to the soil at the bottom of the hole with all its rootlets exposed to the air and completely undamaged. It appeared that the mass of earth spread over the surrounding grass had been sucked out by a gigantic vacuum. The same was true of the earth which was strewn about on the grass. There were no cut roots, no trace of an implement, no evidence of burning, and no impressions in the ground. Many attempts were made to duplicate the hole but were met with no success.

During the next few days it was learned that many of the citizens in the area had seen a luminous object rise on one side of Poncey and shoot off into the southeast at 8 P.M., indicating that they had likely seen the same object that Mrs. Fourneret had seen hovering above the ground in Mayor Cazet's meadow.

Many have theorized that the phenomenon at Poncey and the incident at Rosmead, South Africa were the result of a craft utilizing an anti-gravity method of propulsion, i.e., when the craft comes in contact or close to the ground some of the earth is attracted to the object, and when it elevates and ascends into the air the suspended earth material drops off. Of course, no exacting theory can be proposed until the mystery of the actual propulsion is solved. Until then speculation is about the best that we can do.

During the excitement of the 1967 UFO activity, we received a letter from Mr. Buzz Montague of Twin Falls, Idaho, who claimed that he and a companion had observed a strange set of circumstances involving what he called "mining UFOs." It was some time before we could investigate that particular case because at that time APRO was not well represented in Idaho. However, in 1971 Field Investigator (now Staff Librarian) Allen Benz moved to Twin Falls and was able to contact and interview Mr. Montague concerning his experience, and he obtained the details of one of the most interesting cases in the annals of UFO research.

Mr. Montague often hunted in the area of the Spring Creek Mines which is near Spring Creek Ridge in the Sellway wilderness. He claimed he had often sighted unidentified flying objects, but the two outstanding experiences occurred during the 1960's. The first was during the early sixties and he could not pinpoint a date. The last sighting was in the middle 1960's (no date for this one either) in the company of his friend, William Andrews. Both sightings were approximately the same, so we will describe the latter, during which he had a corroborating witness.

The two men were camped on a bluff overlooking a valley. When they awoke in the early morning at about 6 A.M., they noticed a shiny spot on the ore dump of a Spring Creek Mine across the valley. Neither took particular notice of the exact time as they were engrossed in looking at the objects. Using the 10-power scopes affixed to their rifles, they observed the "shiny object" which actually was one of our which were hovering over the ore dump. Protruding from the top of each of the objects were four hose-like devices which were inserted into the slag piles and moving around. After a period of time, one by one, the objects elevated and ascended into the air. At this time the large object, hovering at about 1,000 feet above the terrain, was spotted. An elongated, cigar-shaped object, it had four depressions on its underside. When the small objects reached the larger one, they fitted themselves into the depressions, after which there was no indication that there had been a depression there to begin with. After another short period of time the objects detached themselves from the cigar-shaped craft and returned to the slag heap.

The two men were so engrossed in what they were watching that they made no attempt to note the time but later estimated that they had watched the objects for approximately forty-five minutes to an hour and a half while they made four trips from the slag heap to the craft hovering overhead. After the last trip they remained watching a part of the large object as it moved slowly into the northwest and out of sight, ascending all the while. All of the craft were silvery in color, windows or ports were visible in the large one. The smaller craft, which Mr. Montague referred to as "miners," had transparent domes on the top but nothing visible inside.

Two theories are offered to explain the purpose of the crafts in this incident. One is that mining operations were being carried out. On the other hand, the earth which was being probed had already been mined by men so that if the occupants of the craft were engaged in research they might have been obtaining samples to analyze later to determine the nature of man's mining in that area. One theory appears to be as valid as the other.

Our next trace case took place on the 16th of November, 1973, at about 7:00 P.M. when Richard T. and David F. (both they and their parents requested anonymity), eleven years of age, were playing outside near their homes in Lemon Grove, California. They went down into a vacant area next to the group of four houses where they live. The area measures approximately 80 by 100 feet and contains a couple of small trees. The ground consists of hard clay covered by dead field grass and the entire area is surrounded by a chain link fence. Several neighboring houses surround the field, about 150 feet distant.

The boys passed through a neighbor's yard on the way to the field, passed a clump of bamboo, and then came out into the open where they saw a dark object apparently sitting in the darkened field. They slowly approached the object and after about five minutes, Richard, who had a plastic-cased flashlight in his hand, walked up to the object and rapped on it three or four times with the flashlight. The rapping made a metallic sound. Immediately a dome on top of the object, which was about as high as its diameter, became illuminated with intense red light, a very brilliant spectral or Chinese red which illuminated the entire area. At the same time the object, which had been about 18 inches off the ground, rose up to about 3 or 4 feet from the ground, whereupon a row of green lights around the peripheral rim of the craft started to blink in sequence and the object began to rotate, making a sound which resembled "woooo-shooooo-woooo-shooooo." The rate of rotation became very high with the red light blinking on and off, then the red light went out momentarily, came back on, and the object rose into the air, still making the sound.

The boys, by then frightened, started to run, feeling chills and a tingly feeling, weak "like we were going to black out or die," and "like we were running in slow motion." They said the object took off toward the southwest, and after they had left the field and got to the street they saw it disappear into the clouds.

Both of the boys' mothers told Field Investigator Donald R. Carr that the boys were not in the habit of telling tall tales and stated that the boys were very excited when they came to the house after their experience.

During the questioning it was learned that the object was approximately the size of the living room, kitchen, and bathroom area of the houses in which the boys live, or 20 feet in diameter. The interview was conducted in the field where the object was seen, and the height of the craft was set at 10 or 11 feet, based on the size of an adjacent tree. Further investigation revealed two holes in the ground which measured 6 inches by 6 inches square by 6 inches deep, about 6 feet 8 inches on centers. A third partial depression, forming an equilateral triangle with the two holes, was apparent on a slight rise of the ground level. The holes were located 400 feet from the back fence and the hole nearest the side fence was about 23 feet 3 inches from it. Dead grass in the field seemed to be lying in a counter-clockwise circular pattern. The ground was extremely hard dry clay and the holes appeared to have been sheared by something extremely heavy.

Residual magnetism was checked but nothing out of the ordinary was detected. Mr. Carr also found that several residents in the area had experienced television interference at about 7:20, the time that he estimated the object took off. Another strange coincidence, if it is that, is that the X-Axis and the Z-Axis of the magnetometer at La Posta registered a perturbation at exactly 7:20 P.M. that evening.

The latter information compares favorably with the Tucson sighting by the boy mentioned earlier in which a perturbation on a magnetometer was also registered.

A report of an incident involving young girls at a boarding school at Valenii de Munte, Rumania, was forwarded to APRO by Field Investigator Moraru Augustin in March 1974 and detailed a strange case. The girls were roommates, and at dawn on February 8, 1974, they observed two bright orange spheres side by side which were separated by a gap much less than the width of either one. They were fairly sharply outlined and both were surrounded by a whitish halo which was much more intense in the area between them. Their apparent size was that of a circle 2 inches in diameter held at arm's length.

After about 15 seconds the two spheres slowly approached one another (this operation took about 15 to 17 seconds) and fused, forming a long object which was oval in shape and exhibited the same color and halo as the single objects. This object then moved very slowly into the southwest (approximately 6 to 7 seconds), then accelerated and disappeared into the distance within a time span of about 3 to 4 seconds. After the object had left, a whitish mist remained in the area where they had hovered.

Later that day an examination of the fields in the direction where the object(s) was (were) seen revealed two concave ditches similar to those made by a skidding automobile tire. The earth was not pressed but the soil was gouged out. There was no indication that these marks were made by ordinary means.

So we have another case of soil missing from the ground after a UFO sighting. Unlike the Poncey and Rosmead cases, however, the missing material was not found in the field, and so it can be hypothesized that this was a sample-collecting operation rather than tracks left by UFOs which had landed on the ground. Had the two spheres been merely appendages of a larger, darker object overhead, the object would have been difficult to observe because of the brilliance of the light from the sphere. Similarly, had the "gouging" been done by appendages from the spheres themselves, the brilliance of the spheres would have cloaked the operation.

Three incidents widely separated (in distance and in time) yielded a similar "residue," the last of which came to our attention in a report forwarded by our South American members in 1962. The first incident took place in Meral, in the department of Mayenne, France, on October 14, 1954. It was first reported by Aimé Michel in his excellent book *Flying Saucers and the Straight Line Mystery* (New York, Criterion Books, 1958).

On October 14, 1954, a farmer was getting ready to leave his home when he saw an orange-colored ball arrive and land on the ground not far from him. He approached the object and saw that it was a dome-shaped disc with a flat bottom, and it emitted a blinding light which illuminated the field for about 200 yards around. The craft appeared to be translucent, and a dark shape could be seen silhouetted inside it. For approximately ten minutes the witness watched the thing. Suddenly the color of the object changed from white to red and it took off and disappeared into the north at great speed

After the thing had left, the witness went to the spot where the craft had been and found a sort of "luminescent stream" that was falling to the ground. He watched for a while and then went home. When he arrived there and took off his jacket he found that his clothes were covered with a layer of white, somewhat sticky residue, not unlike paraffin, which soon disappeared without leaving any trace.

This particular phenomenon is very similar to the substance called "angel's hair" which has been seen streaming from the objects in flight. It usually melts when it comes into contact with heat, and this may be the reason for the fact that the witness in the

Meral sighting did not discover any of the stuff on his face or hands. His body heat would have dissipated it as it came into contact with his skin.

The next incident in which a residue was observed took place on December 21, 1957, on the road leading from Ponta Poran to the farm of Mrs. Ivonne Torres de Mendonca. (See our book *Flying Saucers: The Startling Evidence of the Invasion from Outer Space,* # T3058, New York, Signet, for the complete details.)

Before this sighting was over, the object, which ultimately chased a jeep-load of people for approximately a half hour, had made a couple of landings. On the last of these landings, before leaving the area, the object left an odd, luminous haze floating in the air where the object had hovered. The observers stayed and watched the material slowly dissolve in the faint, warm wind blowing from the north.

On October 21, 1963, a family was held under siege by two discs giving off light beams which heated up their house near Tranca, Argentina. Activity was taking place at the railroad tracks about a half mile away, where a lighted object could be seen. At the conclusion of the incident, in the area where the two closest discs had hovered, there remained a misty, smoke-like deposit for several minutes.

So here we have three separate incidents in which peculiar residue was left after the departure of an unconventional disc-shaped object. In all three cases the residue disappeared shortly after appearing. It is another correlation which may be very important to our overall study of the UFOs.

Our next two ground marking cases come from Canada and the two incidents happened within two weeks of one another in two different provinces. On August 16th at approximately 7:30 P.M., David Bates, seven, Steven Stillie, nine, and Henry Stillie, seven, were playing along the banks of the Coquitlam River at Port Coquitlam, British Columbia, when they saw a craft shaped like an inverted dish which landed in a graveled area some 200 feet north of the Canadian Pacific Rail Bridge over the river. They reported the incident to their parents and to a neighbor, Mrs. Lola Rogers, who investigated the area the following morning and found two strange black circles on the gravel.

The boys said that the object first flew over the river at 7:30, then stopped, reversed course and began descending into the clearing beside the river. The boys watched from a vantage point approximately 150 feet from the site. They said the craft had no markings, made a buzzing sound as it descended, and gave off a blast of hot air as it touched down. All three described the object as dish-shaped with a squarish protuberance on top with what looked like a door in it, and lights which seemed to change from red to green to white. Mrs. Rogers stated that she had walked through the area several times prior to the sighting and the black spots were not present then.

The boys did not observe the object's departure as they were frightened and ran into the house. They guessed that the viewing time, from the time that they first sighted the object coming across the river until they left the scene, was about ten minutes.

After questioning the boys, Field Investigator R.J. Halishoff noted that the only areas of disagreement between the boys was in reference to a flashing light on top of the object. The Stillic boys thought that the light was a red flashing light, whereas the Bates boy thought the light changed colors. David Bates also stated that there was a row of lights around the aperture which they took to be an exhaust hole on the bottom, whereas the Stillie boys said it looked like a "bright chain."

Mr. and Mrs. Stillie said that when the boys came running home they were very frightened, exhibiting glazed eyes and pale skin as they related their experience.

Mrs Rogers, who accompanied the boys to the site the next morning, said that there was a nauseating odor of burned material much like the smell of ashes from a fireplace. She said she picked up a rock in this black spot and it stained her hand and took a week of daily scrubbing before it came off. She admitted that she had not believed the boys' story until she visited the site, but was willing to admit that the boys had never pulled any pranks before.

Mr. Halishoff did not learn about this incident until a month after it had allegedly occurred and, upon digging down into the large 5-foot 6-inch spot, found that the black residue lay about 4 inches below the surface, and felt that the surface residue had been washed below the surface by rain. This was unfortunate, for it is felt that earlier examination of the material might have revealed something. However, examination of the material merely indicated that the rock and gravel had been subjected to great heat.

About two weeks later, on September 1 at 11:30 A.M., Edwin Fuhr, who operates a farm about six and a half miles out of Langenburg, Saskatchewan, Canada, was harvesting his rape (a seed oil plant) crop. As he approached a slough on his land, he saw what he thought was a "spun aluminum duck blind." (He said later that he had seen such a blind advertised in *Field and Stream* magazine and assumed it had been placed there by a neighbor.) He also described it as looking like stainless steel. He dismounted from his swather (a mowing machine) and approached the object on foot. As he drew near, he noted that the object was a symmetrical bun shape and that it was hovering about a foot off the ground. He noted also that the grass underneath was being imparted a clockwise swirling motion.

While watching for about two minutes from a distance of 15 feet, he noticed that "the whole thing was turning." Returning to the swather, he noted four additional identical objects to his left. He sat motionless for about 15 minutes and watched. He said he wanted to leave but couldn't (the inference here is that he was too terrified to operate the controls of his swather properly). After about 15 minutes, the objects all left simultaneously moving straight up into the air, exhibiting a gray mist underneath and a "strong downwind."

The Royal Canadian Mounted Police heard about the case by word of mouth, and after launching an investigation offered the opinion that Mr. Fuhr's account was reliable. In his investigation, the R.C.M.P. constable found a circular swirl of grass for each UFO position reported by Mr. Fuhr. In the center of each swirl the grass remained erect. This case was investigated by Mr. Don Coulthard who also forwarded a photo of Mr. Fuhr standing in the field pointing to one of the swirled areas.

This, then, concludes our examination of UFO incidents involving landed objects and the residue or impressions left behind. Other selected cases are discussed in Chapter XVI, "Are They Infallible?"

CHAPTER III

The Contactee Conundrum

Jacques Vallee, author of several books on UFOs, observes that an outstanding characteristic of the UFO as a subject of discussion is the passion that it evokes. Most of us experience difficulty in attempting to deal with UFOs in a detached, objective manner. Why is this so?

The social scientists tell us that our judgments, actions, and reactions in dealing with any given situation are habitual, based more or less on the sum total of our individual experience, plus the thought-habits of our cultural heritage. Herein may lie our difficulty.

Inherent in the idea of the UFO as a space probe is the prospect of an imminent confrontation *unprecedented in human experience.* History records many examples of confrontation between relatively advanced and primitive cultural/racial groups of men but these provide little in the way of useful example (and less in the way of solace).

Expeditions to alien areas were usually launched for purposes of conquest or exploitation, say our history books, and even in those rare exceptions where this was not clearly the case, the more primitive party to the confrontation was nonetheless the loser for the contact. In the resultant conflict of ideas, the concepts and value systems that had previously given his life meaning and direction lost their validity.

The example of conflict (whether physical or ideological) between man and man projects a dark enough picture, but at least it's a picture which displays certain elements common to both parties in the area of motivation. At least it's man dealing with man. And all men, if for no other reason than common nativity (this earth), have *some* common bonds of understanding.

But what about men (or near-men) with a nativity other than this earth? We don't know. We have nothing in history or personal experience on which to base our judgments. Thus arises the passionate reaction to which Vallee calls attention—our external manifestation of the repressed fear resulting from our realization that we are treading on uncharted ground.

The only precedent for the idea of extraterrestrial visitation which exists in all our sociocultural history is the angel of religious mythology.

The idea of UFOs as vehicles of reassurance carrying Big Brothers here for the express purpose of straightening out the difficulties we already have has many comforting aspects—an obvious one being that, in one fell swoop, it converts an ominous menace into a source of reassurance.

Carl Jung says (*Flying Saucers: A Modern Myth of Things Seen in the Sky*, New York, Harcourt, Brace & Co., 1959), "No Christian will contest the importance of a belief like that of the Mediator, nor will he deny the consequences which the loss of it entails. So powerful an idea reflects a profound psychic need which does not simply disappear when the expression of it ceases to exist."

Due to our attitude toward modern technology the ready acceptance of such ideas does not come easily, but our vociferous objections to the contrary notwithstanding, most of us simply do not believe the traditional religious myths any longer. Otherwise we would find, for instance, NASA investigating all facets of The Ascension for helpful techniques in our effort to get men into space.

There can be no doubt that we live in tense times. The problems of coping with a complicated world on a personal as well as a national level produce an emotional tension which faces no visible prospect of release, since the future promises only further complications. For the most part, the traditional avenues of release through religious expression are blocked, because in the face of modern technology the traditional mediators have lost their validity.

We are faced with a growing spiritual hunger. If a spiritual hunger exists, a need for reassurance and solace, it should not surprise us to find certain self-appointed prophets profiting from it. Several have emerged from obscure backgrounds, assuming titles such as doctor or professor, and proceeded to spread the new doctrine. For one of these, at least, this simply meant a change of props. In a previous self-appointed position as Grand Lama of the Royal Order of Tibet (operated, by his own admission, as a front for prohibition bootlegging activities) he had attributed certain gems of wisdom and salvation to the ancient masters of the Orient. In his new role he simply attributed the same gems of our "space brothers," gave lectures, sold books and pictures—a much more suitable line of pursuit for an aging gentleman than the rigorous and insecure avocation of bootlegging.

There seem to be, however, a considerable number of "contactees" who are not charlatans—who, conversely, give accounts of experiences which are, to them, very real.

They, as a rule, profess to revelatory experiences which become the basis for their preachments. Their revelations, as might be expected, do not arise from contact with traditional gods, saints, or angels, but from gentle individuals who have traveled here in flying saucers from another world.

It should be pointed out (an idea also endorsed by Jung) that whether or not UFOs are physically real has little to do with the real nature of the "contactee" myth. Rather, the *idea* of the flying saucer as an extraterrestrial machine provides a form which is acceptable from both a traditional and a modern standpoint, one through which the tension-motivated psychic projection can be expressed.

In a traditional sense the "saucer" is the mandala, a symbol of wholeness; it represents a wish for unity by confining disassociated parts within a circle, the smallest possible circumference for a given area. Its role as a potential holder of the "cup of knowledge" should not be overlooked either. The appearance of archetypal components and mediators in a space vehicle provides a technical touch which makes the pageant more easily swallowed by twentieth-century man.

In the epilogue to his *Flying Saucers: A Modern Myth of Things Seen in the Sky*, Jung repeats the story of an early "contactee," one Orfeo Angelucci, as related biographically in *The Secret of the Saucers* (privately printed), which serves as a classic example of psychic projection. Jung says, "Without having the faintest inkling of psychology, Angelucci has described in greatest detail the mystic experience associated with a UFO vision.... The story is so naive and clear that a reader interested in psychology can see at once how far it confirms my previous conclusions. It could even be regarded as a unique document that sheds a great deal of light on the genesis and assimilation of UFO mythology." We will not indulge in the presumption necessary to synopsize Jung's masterful treatment of this case, but will satisfy ourselves with recommending it to the reader in its original form.

We begin our own illustration with a case in a California beach area in the late 1960's.

The principal is a man who suffered from insomnia and therefore worked his "ham rig" late at night, or took solitary nocturnal walks in the beach area. He had, according to the opinion of a psychiatric social worker who had the opportunity to observe his home environment, a wife with a paranoid fear of Communists.

During one of his nocturnal walks he observed a UFO which moved in close to him and assured him through a voice that seemed to be all around him in the air that no harm was to befall him. The saucer did not land but came so low that he could walk right into it without going up steps or a ramp or anything of that sort. He was greeted by a Mr. Zno who was one of the party of eight men and one woman aboard the craft. Zno and party whisked our contactee away to the hills where he spent the greater part of two hours walking and talking with Mr. Zno through two levels or floors of the ship. Each level had seven rooms. Mr. Zno had a curious habit of always keeping his right side toward his guest. He answered questions freely except for two which he simply did not respond to. They were: (1) a request to compare their time base with earth's and (2) a request to describe the ship's power source.

Information on other matters was as follows: The purpose or reason for the visit was observation. Our contactee took this to mean that he was to observe them, because Mr. Zno asked no questions and appeared to know all about the contactee (and the earth) already. Their origin was a planet which we do not see because it is hidden by a planet which we do see. Zno was careful to phrase this as "*do* not see" rather than "*can* not see." Among other important bits of information was: "There is only one Supreme Deity." Also, they assured our contactee that they were not hostile and never would be.

After alighting from the craft which he described as egg-shaped, 70 feet long and 30 feet high, our contactee suddenly realized that there must have been a higher level to which he was not taken. The occupants of the craft were described as "just about like us—human, I'd say."

Here we have a troubled man (the insomnia and nocturnal walks are common symptoms of emotional tension and conflict) undergoing an experience whose consuming theme is reassurance of an extremely one-sided kind.

The chief performer, Mr. Zno (whose name more or less equates phonetically with *snow*), conducts our subject through two levels of an egg-shaped ship over a period of two hours, after appearing to him at 2 A.M. Most of this time is spent in the hills. In the concomitant conversation, Mr. Zno lives up to the phonetic equivalent of his name (snow) by covering all ominous, pessimistic, mundane possibilities with a blanket of bright prospects and reassurances. In addition to this, he restates his role in his physical attitude by keeping his *right* side toward his interviewer at all times. This also may have a compensatory value, for the contactee's wife in real life concentrates on exposing the dangers of the hidden left (Communist conspiracy) which no doubt contributes to his general tensions, while Mr. Zno never exposes his left side.

The trip to the hills is completely pointless unless we consider the traditional tendency expressed in the Bible to look to high places for help in times of trouble. Judaic altars were built on hilltops. Moses walked with God and obtained the Ten Commandments on a mountaintop. The Psalmist says (Psalms 121:1): "I will lift up mine eyes unto the hills, from whence cometh my help." "His foundation is in the holy mountains." (Psalms 87:1).

Our subject's sudden realization upon leaving the craft that there must have been another level merely emphasizes once more the general one-sidedness of his reassuring experience. In other words, the complete interior nature of the egg-shaped object (the egg in mythology is said to contain the secret of life within its shell) was not revealed to him. The two unanswered questions concerning time and propulsion simply served no purpose to the general experience.

The contactee was assured that the whole pageant was staged for his sole benefit. Their reason for the visit was observation—that is, for our subject to observe them, since they apparently knew all about him already.

Where were they from? Mr. Zno stated about as clearly as can be said in allegorical language, "We are from a planet which you don't see (he didn't say *can't* see) because it is hidden by a planet which you do see."

The existence of such a planet is, from an astronomical viewpoint, pure nonsense. However, the field of psychology has much to say about a hidden world, the unconscious, which is normally, though not necessarily, obscured by the familiar world of the conscious.

Another older case which bears some similarity to this one is that of Truman Betherum. He began with a report that ran roughly as follows: He had been driving by himself at night on a lonely road, became tired, and pulled over to sleep. He awoke sometime later to find his car surrounded by space people who were called Clarionites because they came from the planet Clarion. The captain of the saucer-shaped craft was a beautiful woman named Aura Rhane.

Without going into detail concerning the conversation that

followed, it seems germane to point out that, though a clarion is a small trumpet, it is so named because it makes a clear sound. It is suggested here that the symbolic meaning relates more closely to the Latin root word *clarus*, meaning clear; that the intended function of the Clarionites was to clear up the clouded, confused aspects of Betherum's life. Supporting this is the fact that their woman captain's name translates almost directly as "characteristic of rain." We all know that a dominant characteristic of rain is that it "clears the air."

The planet Clarion is quite close, Betherum tells us, but is hidden from us by the moon. We should not be too surprised to find in the case of a gentleman whose ship is captained by a woman that the source of that vehicle is hidden from sight by the lady of the night, La Luna. We might further conjecture that such a gentleman might be in trouble in the area of masculine prowess. When we consider, in addition, the fact that Mrs. Betherum subsequently sued for divorce, naming Aura Rhane as correspondent and complaining that Truman had neglected marital duties because of the space woman, our conjecture seems justified.

Even though he misunderstands the message of the unconscious, the contactee sometimes finds that his life takes on a meaning and direction which it previously lacked, aided by the fact that others in whom the symbolic content of his experience seems to strike a chord become his staunch advocates.

The contactee, whose experience springs from internal need rather than external fact, contributes nothing useful to the question of whether or not physical UFOs exist. If anything, his contribution is of a negative order for it seems to lead many otherwise objective students to discount out of hand all reports of landed UFOs with occupants.

In our twenty-five years' experience we have not come up with any hard and fast set of rules for distinguishing between the mythical and the real, but we have formulated a few "rules of the thumb," or general guidelines.

The contactee, if he reports ostensibly physical beings, describes them in terms of their similarity to man—"just like us" or "beautiful, by human standards." He occasionally describes ethereal beings and/or disembodied voices. He is always the recipient of messages and/or warnings, sometimes including a rationalization as to why he was "chosen" for contact. He usually does not offer any physical evidence or corroborating witnesses to support his theory.

If a contact claimant presents bogus proof, he is a charlatan attempting to enter the field for reasons of his own by means of forged credentials.

By contrast, the non-contactee describes occupants in terms of their dissimilarities to man, has no messages to repeat, and is generally puzzled and frightened by his experience. Whether or not he has corroborating witnesses is generally consistent with other circumstances of the sighting.

Quite apart from the contactee myth there is evident another manifestation of the tendency to cast the visitors in the role of angels. It is a rationalistic process which concludes that they *must* mean us no harm and is generally stated like this: "If they are so much more technically advanced than we are, they *must* be more spiritually advanced as well." A comforting thought but one not easy to support empirically. Man's technical advances in the past fifty years are phenomenal. Can we say the same for his spirituality?

It is not the purpose of this treatise to prove that UFOs contain conquerors from space. There doesn't seem to be proof one way or the other. What we (the authors) are trying to do is point out the emotional pitfalls which prevent objective evaluation of the situation. It may be that our visitors are neither inimical nor friendly, and probably this is the hardest possibility of all to accept. It's pretty deflating to think that we may not even be important enough to qualify as an enemy.

CHAPTER IV

UFO-Car Encounters

Through the years, beginning with the early 1950's, reports of strange lights diving on or chasing cars have increased in number, and in 1967 there was a proliferation of such sightings. Whether the UFOs are interested in the vehicles or merely the reaction of the passengers to their antics we cannot know at this time but the weight of evidence indicates that it is a growing problem. In the words of one witness: "You won't catch me driving a lonely road at night anymore," and that is the general reaction of most people who have had such an experience.

In 1967, which was a year of very heavy UFO activity, there was a record number of UFO-car encounters, some of the most outstanding of which we will examine. In early January of that year (no exact date because the event was not immediately reported), Robert Blaine of Villard, Minnesota, was on his way to Kensington to attend the Villard-Kensington basketball game. Riding with him were Mrs. James Galvin, wife of the Villard basketball coach, Billy Smith, and three of Blaine's children, all youngsters ranging from seven to thirteen years. At about 7:30 P.M. at about two miles east of Farwell, Minnesota, on Highway 55, the engine of Blaine's 1964 car died and the lights went out. To his left Blaine spotted an orange flash at about the level of the hood, then tiny beads of lights crossed in front of the windshield. Mrs. Galvin also said she saw an orange and red flash go by the driver's side of the car at about the level of the window.

The car coasted for some distance, then the engine and lights came on again without warning or aid. Blaine first thought a short had started the trouble, was startled when the engine started again by itself, and inspected the car under a streetlight when he arrived at Farwell. There had been no trouble with the car that night and there was none thereafter. Blaine admitted he was startled and that because of his fear he did not attempt to investigate the light.

On the 12th of March, Larry Burke, Dick Makens, Junior Edinger, and Charles Warren of McIntosh, South Dakota, encountered four unusual lights over the road near McIntosh. Burke initially saw a strange object with red, white, and green flashing lights southwest of McIntosh at 7:15 P.M., then picked up his friends to go with him to investigate. On a country road a mile west of the town they saw four lights low over the road ahead of them. As they proceeded up a hill their car engine stopped and, frightened, they coasted backward down the hill. The car started again, and they drove into McIntosh and brought back the sheriff.

Nothing was found, however. The boys disagreed on the altitude, size, and shapes of the lights but all were in agreement on the color, which they described as fluorescent green. One of them said he got the feeling that the lights were attached to something huge which was towering over them. Sheriff Kittleson said that Makens was definitely shaken up when he came into the office to report the incident. The report was printed in a local paper, and Reverend Terry Nelson came forward and reported that he and others had seen an object with red, white, and green flashing lights flying parallel to the highway between Morristown and McIntosh while on the way to conduct a class in Morristown on the same night.

Reports of this nature were almost commonplace in the early months of 1967. One out of Ohiopyle, Pennsylvania, was the claim that Wilbur Daniels, thirty-seven, and his wife Janet had watched a light which appeared to be following their car for the distance of a mile at an altitude of 100 feet on the 17th of March. Several neighbors claimed they also saw the object as it perched over the Daniels' home for about five minutes shortly before 8 P.M. It was round and orange as if it was on fire, they said.

On the evening of the 21st of March at about one mile west of Hillsboro, Kansas, near U.S. 56, Miss Mary Beth Neufeld of Lehigh and several friends were attracted by a brilliant light. They were interested as it was a very cloudy night and there were no stars visible. For a lark they started toward it, whereupon it flashed and began moving toward them. They described it as flat like a pancake with an upside-down cup on the top of it. The object caught up with the car which "started rocking real bad," causing considerable consternation among the girls. The engine stalled and after several seconds of the rocking motion, the object left as suddenly as it had arrived on the scene. The car started up again by itself and the girls went into Hillsboro to report the incident.

An incident involving an actual chase took place on March 24th when Air Force Staff Sergeant Johnny Ferguson, who was stationed at Vandenberg Air Force Base, California, was on route to Memphis, Tennessee, to visit his parents. He and his wife and three children were traveling by car on an FM Highway in the vicinity of Loco, Texas, at 5:30 A.M. when he pulled his car to the side of the road in order to consult a road map and noticed a red light which he first thought was on another vehicle.

As it approached, however, he noted that it made no noise. It first appeared to be "about 8 inches in diameter" but as the distance closed between itself and the car it grew in size until it was as wide as the road. At that point Ferguson decided to depart, and as he drove the object followed him, so he increased his speed until he was attaining speeds as high as 100 miles per hour in his attempt to escape the thing. He noted that the object followed the terrain of the country, going down with the dips and up over the knolls. It was gaining on his car when he approached a farm house, then it split into two separate lights and disappeared into the sky at a high rate of speed. Ferguson then drove into Wellington, Texas, where they notified officers of their experience. On the following Monday Air Force investigators Colonel Hallmark and Lt. Nicholson of Altus Air Force Base arrived in Wellington, and with Sergeant and Mrs. Ferguson proceeded to the area of the chase. Sheriff's Deputy Hooten told the press that no report was disclosed by the Air Force concerning the investigation but that the Altus team seemed to be "open-minded" about it.

A press report out of Mangum, Oklahoma, carried the story related by E. A. Griffith, who claimed that on the 28th of April his auto had been chased by a silent object with flashing lights. He said that he first thought the object was a helicopter but decided that couldn't be the explanation as it made absolutely no noise. The craft either beamed a light down on his car or its lights illuminated it, he said. One state trooper reported that he interviewed a farm family who said they saw the object above the car but could not make out the shape because of the darkness. The chase lasted only a few minutes and the object disappeared into the night sky at about 8:30 P.M.

Young Dennis Whitley of Monroe, North Carolina, made the mistake of trying to signal a large, white light which he spotted above the road ahead of him as he was returning home from a church meeting on April 28th. When he reported it he said it was shaped like an umbrella on top "with crystals on top of it" and that he tried to get it's attention by blinking his lights. The thing then "seemed to lock in on the road or my car" for it began to follow his car at 45 to 50 miles per hour, making the same curves that the car did. Shortly after the chase began the thing turned from white to orange, coming closer to the road as if it were going to land. He said he stopped his car once but was too frightened to get out. When he reached home his mother also saw the object which she said was orange and that it hovered near the house for about thirty minutes. After the Whitley sighting was published, a neighbor, Mr. George W. Hilton, claimed he and his wife saw the object as they left the Celanese plant in Rock Hill. Hilton said that he didn't report it to the police until he learned of Whitley's experience because he was afraid of ridicule.

The same pattern was found in an incident at Arnett, Oklahoma, on May 7th when Jerry Luck, a junior at the High School, was driving home at night. Passing in front of a school located in open farming country about a mile from his home, he glanced to the west and spotted a large white light which was later determined to be the size of a dime at arm's length. As he continued on his way the object moved toward his car. It had been at approximately 40° elevation when he first saw it, but as it approached it became parallel with his car. When Jerry arrived at home he rushed inside and his parents came out and observed the object as it hovered for a few minutes, then moved into the west at high speed and disappeared from sight. The light was white, they said, and they got the distinct impression that it was solid.

One of the few instances of a firearm being used against a UFO allegedly took place on May 13th about seventeen miles west of St. George, Utah. Michael Cameadore, twenty-four, a resident of National City, California, was en route to Salt Lake City to attend the funeral of his grandmother and told officials at St. George that he heard a strange, loud humming sound. At first he thought it was a truck trying to pass so he moved over but could not see any lights in his rear-view mirror. He then put on his brakes and jumped off the truck. An object was hovering over his truck at an estimated altitude of 25 to 35 feet. It was an amber-colored circular object which he estimated to be 40-50 feet in diameter. Thoroughly frightened, Cameadore reached into the truck, got his .25 caliber handgun, inserted a clip of ammunition, and began firing. He said he heard the bullets strike and ricochet and the sound convinced him that they were striking metal. At this point the object simply put on a burst of speed and was out of sight in just a few seconds.

Another trio of young men experienced a typical car-buzzing incident on May 26th at 10:15 P.M. The three boys were driving on Atrisco Avenue north of Central Avenue in Albuquerque, New Mexico, when they spotted a white light approaching from behind. The light darted back and forth across the road and at first they thought it was the lights from a car being driven by a drunk. When the object got above the car it kept their speed and moved along with them and then the engine and lights died. They said they jumped out of the car and as they looked up the object flew away into the southwest at high speed. They all said there was no sound connected with the incident.

There is a thread of continuity running through all of these cases. They all took place at night; in all cases the object was seen at a distance; and then it zeroed in on the car and either hovered over it if it stopped, or followed it if it continued on its way. In some instances when the car and its occupants reached a home or destination the object stayed around just a short time, then demonstrated its amazing speed by darting off into the night. In others, engines and lights were apparently neutralized, so that the driver couldn't proceed. Yet if the driver got out of the car the object would leave immediately. We might speculate here that the object and its occupants were experimenting—to learn the speed of ground vehicles and/or to determine how human beings react under stress.

Different people react differently to UFO encounters as we shall see in the next two cases. On the night of June 29, 1970, at approximately 9:32, Mr. and Mrs. R. and their two sons of Apopka, Florida, were returning home from Orlando when Mrs. R. spotted a glowing green oval object with a smaller blue ring about 1,000 feet to the right of their car and approximately 100 feet off the ground. She called it to the attention of her husband who was driving, and when Mr. R. spotted it, it was descending at about a 45° angle toward their car. They estimated the blue ring to be about 20 feet in diameter and Mrs. R. got the impression the ring was depressed into the object. Both witnesses noted that the object had a hazy edge and that the bottom was convex.

The R. car was traveling at about 45 miles per hour when the object was first sighted but after it moved in and over the car Mr. R. accelerated to about 90 miles per hour. He felt the object was higher than the nearby service power lines but his wife felt it was lower. It paced the car for about a mile but as the car passed under a street light it was temporarily lost from sight.

Mr. R. slowed the car to turn into the driveway of his home which is located in the orange groves surrounding Apopka, and the UFO moved slightly ahead. As the Rs ran from their car to their house the object made a level close (100 feet in diameter) sweep of the area and moved off, leaving a trail of mist about 20 feet wide which gave off an apple-green light. It hung in the air a few minutes before dissipating. Mrs. R.'s father, who lived next door, also observed the mist which spread out evenly and lost its glow but did not fall to the ground. The path of the mist left by the UFO was thick on the outside of the turn and thin on the inside. At first the R.'s could see the stars through the thick part of the mist.

The R.'s dog, which was in the car during the incident, did not react to the object's presence whereas a second dog, belonging to Mrs. R.'s mother, ran off howling just before the Rs and the UFO arrived at the house.

Oklahoma is the site of our next car UFO encounter, only in this instance one of the witnesses not only felt fear but also a sort of strange desire to stay and watch. On the 16th of October, 1973, Mr. and Mrs. Bill Hatchett and their daughter Valerie, nine, and their four-year-old son were driving to their rural residence near Cushing, Oklahoma, after having visited with relatives who live between Sand Springs and Tulsa. It was about 12:20 A.M. when Mr. Hatchett noticed a very bright light south and east of his pickup truck as it traveled west on the county road between State Highways 97 and 33. He at first thought it must have been an REA pole light at a nearby farmhouse, but the light seemed to be moving with the truck and getting closer. By this time Mrs. Hatchett was also watching intently and said it appeared to be getting closer to the ground and turning to an intercept course with the pickup. She began begging her husband to stop the truck and he finally complied with her wishes.

The object, which was emitting the light, moved closer and hovered at a point about even with the front of the pickup and just south of the fence row on the south side of the road at an apparent altitude of 150 to 200 feet above the ground.

The Hatchetts heard or felt, or both, an intense and penetrating low-pitched humming sound and a stillness fell roundabout just as one might experience before a storm. The very air seemed charged and oppressive as the gigantic thing hovered there. Mr. Hatchett estimated the size of the object to be equal to the dimension of a Boeing 707 jetliner and he had to shield his eyes with his hand from the blinding white lights which were emitted by the forward part of it. His wife, during this time, had gotten out of the pickup and had walked to the side nearest to where the object was hovering. She walked there by walking around the back of the pickup rather than around the front, because of her fear of the craft. Mr. Hatchett, very frightened, ordered her back into the pickup. She complied but got out of the pickup two more times and repeated her short journey each time and each time was ordered back into the truck by her husband.

The Hatchetts observed that the object appeared to change shape as it hovered, and neither could determine what, in fact, it really was. The whole object emitted a white light, and the forward section had an intense emission of white light that seemed to revolve from the top to the bottom of the front end. Behind this front area were three belts of lights that appeared to encircle the craft and blinked all the time.

The first belt of these lights from the front were white in color. The other belts probably were also white, but neither could be certain of this because of the intense white light being emitted from the forward section. Behind the object were two red lights toward the top, one white light near the center and two red lights near the bottom.

Although Mr. Hatchett was constantly expressing his desire to drive on and put some distance between them and the object, his wife kept imploring him to remain there. The last time that he ordered his wife back into the pickup he did, however, drive away. As the pickup moved west down the country road, the object crossed the road and proceeded off in a northeasterly direction toward the distant lights of Tulsa, increasing altitude as it did so never getting up very much speed. As it was going away from them they observed that there were three red lights visible on the back end of the object which were in the form of a triangle and in the center of this triangle was one white light. The way in which the lights on the craft had blinked while it hovered reminded Mrs. Hatchett of the lights on a computer.

During the time that the object was near the pickup, both of the Hatchetts had an intense feeling that the object or its occupants "knew everything," and that the power that they or the object possessed was limitless. Mrs. Hatchett stated that she felt chilled when she was out of the pickup, even though the night was not sufficiently cold to chill her. She further stated that the feeling of being chilled may have been caused by her excitement and other emotions stimulated by beholding such an awesome sight.

Valerie, their nine-year-old daughter, was extremely frightened during the encounter. The humming sound the object made and its tremendous size completely overwhelmed her. She expressed the feeling that her four-year-old brother had been fortunate in that he had remained asleep during the entire episode.

When the Hatchetts arrived at the next town, Drumright, Oklahoma, they stopped and reported the incident to a police officer but he did not take the report seriously, which was still fairly typical of the attitude of law enforcement agencies at that time.

UFO reports, which involved objects pacing, chasing, or hovering over motor vehicles, continued to come into APRO Headquarters but a large number of such incidents during a relatively short space of time did not occur again until 1974. On May 3, 1974, Mr. Lorenzen had appeared on a half hour special on UFOs on KPHO-TV in Phoenix, Arizona, under the aegis of the Junior

Achievement Program of the Phoenix, Arizona school system. Shortly thereafter APRO received a letter detailing the experience of four adults and a low-flying UFO near Kingman, Arizona, in early 1974.

It contained the following information. "We and two friends from Lansing, Michigan, were returning to Phoenix from a trip to Las Vegas, Nevada, on the night of March 27, 1974. Bob (our friend) stated that he had read that UFOs had been seen in the area of Kingman and asked me if I believed in UFOs, to which I responded that I didn't, and the subject was dropped."

(Mrs. A. interjected at this point that none of them had been drinking because of the long drive back to Phoenix.)

"I asked Bob to pull over at a look-out point outside of Kingman as I wanted to drive. I was in the back seat and when Bob got out he looked back and said, 'God, what is that?' We all got out and were scared speechless. There was no sound whatsoever and a huge form, platter-shaped, silver, and as big as a football field with three huge spotlights beaming down approached, stopped, and hovered over our car. My husband and I started praying. It hovered over us for five minutes and then took off (thank God) and left behind a steel-blue haze all around where it had hovered."

Our second 1974 case does not precisely represent a car chase, but the object seen by Mr. and Mrs. Y. of Brock, Nebraska, has yet to be identified.

Again, the lady in the case narrates the experience: "We had just returned from a Thanksgiving trip to Roswell, New Mexico, and had our first unexplainable UFO experience coming home. We started at 2 A.M. for home since we wanted to make the trip in one day. It was a bright, moonlit, early morning (Saturday, November 30, 1974) and we had just left the city lights behind us when my husband spotted what he thought was a large plane just on the horizon to our right. Then we thought it might be a huge oil rig but before we could make up our minds it had moved, in darkness, parallel to us, and again lit up with a white brightness that one could hardly focus on for long. You may know this countryside. It is rough, wild, and almost uninhabited but for the few and far between ranches—hardly a road anywhere with canyons, arroyos, and rough range everywhere.

"We watched this thing for sixty miles or more and I am curious as to whether anyone else has described anything similar. It *seemed* to be a mile or so to our right, but moving for the most part parallel to the highway, now and then going away from us, up canyons or down arroyos as though exploring. In this position it seemed to be a solid column of *very* white, bright lights, with only twice a flicker of red at the base. The odd part was the *way* it moved. You remember the "sing-along" bouncing ball we used to follow on movie screens? That is the way it moved.

"The column would light up with what *seemed* to be revolving lights—then for two to three seconds all was dark—but in the meantime it had moved farther on and again lit up! It simply hopped—or bounced—seeming to be hovering on the ground. Once it started coming closer and since we were the only car on that lonely road, we were really relieved when our road veered left at Elida and we lost it behind hills.

"We did notice several well-lit big installations farther on and wondered if there could have been some connection. We know this part of New Mexico well, and there just isn't *anything* that could move over that terrain in the way that this object did. I have always been interested in the UFO thing, since many of our friends had had such experiences—but this, though our first, really has us wondering."

Our next case involved a husband, wife, and father-in-law from Lordsburg, New Mexico, who, on January 6, 1975, observed a strange phenomenon in an area outside that town.

Mrs. M. tells her story. "I am not really a UFO buff and have never seen any such craft. However, about three months ago a *very odd* experience occurred some few miles south of Lordsburg, New Mexico. Whether you believe me or not is not important. What happened, happened, and that's it—whatever it was. I've just been reluctant to say anything to anyone. The reason I am writing now is probably because the experience still haunts me and I'd finally like to mention it and mainly inquire from you if you have received any similar reports, at anytime in the past, from this area. Nothing like this has ever happened to any of us before.

"It was January 6, 1975, on a Monday night. My dad, husband, and I were out for a short drive to get some fresh air after a tiring day. We drove about three or four miles south on Animas Road south of Lordsburg, found an area just perfect for viewing the night sky and stars, and to talk and relax. It was about 10:30 P.M. or perhaps a few minutes later. The sky was perfectly clear with no clouds, a slight wind, and a little chilly. After driving a few miles we came to the old Lady Mary Mine Road (the mine is abandoned now). We drove off onto the road and shone our headlights around the area to make sure we were safe from anyone out ready to hijack cars. There was no one around on the dirt road, we were out in the open, there were no fences, high lines, etc. We turned the car around so that we faced Animas Road, turned out the headlights, rolled a window down and turned on the Citizen's Band radio. The channels were fairly clear that night and we enjoyed listening to other CBers.

"We had not been there for more than fifteen minutes or possibly less when Dad noticed lights coming up from behind the small hill behind us directly on the Lady Mary Mine Road. It looked like another vehicle coming. Dad had his keys in the ignition just in case something like this should happen. He assumed it was a car and was preparing to move aside. My husband was up in front with Dad and I was in the back seat on the driver's side. Neither my husband nor I looked back.

"Then Dad panicked—the car would not start. It was still quite warm, in good condition (brand new battery and tune-up, etc., only a month before). No matter what he did it still wouldn't start. He looked back again and said, 'Hey, what's going on here?'

"Before my husband or I could react a very strange blue-white (more bluish) light shone near the car on the driver's side. It lit up only a section near my door and the driver's side. My husband's side was pitch dark. The light was strong enough to light up and show in detail the foliage on the side of the road and part of our car. It lasted for only a brief few seconds—prolonged, yet brief—and kind of maneuvering like a person directing a light back and forth. It moved—it was not merely a quick flash. At the same time we had problems with the CB radio—lots of static. The car wouldn't start but the radio worked until the flash of light.

"After the flash of light the car started. We were stunned when we turned around, expecting to see someone in a car or something, but nothing was there. All during this time there was no sound except one similar to electricity humming through the wires. Yet there were no high lines at all nearby.

"We pulled our car onto Animas Road and looked back toward the old mine road. There just over the hill was a fabulous, blue, glowing light similar to a halo effect and yet not arched, solid from its highest point to the ground. It was just beneath the hill. The glow, as I said, was blue with a more turquoise hue and beautiful. We checked the directions and it was definitely not the lights of Lordsburg or any town or mining operation. Besides, the color of the horizon of city lights definitely do not match that beautiful color.

"The incident unnerved us as it was late, sudden, and the area deserted. What we thought had been a car never appeared, yet something was there. We checked on possible aircraft in the area that night, but there were none. Also, the light was very bright, a most definite, concentrated beam, and directed specifically at us. I don't think the whole thing lasted any more than five or six minutes from the time we tried to move the car, then saw the flash, to the time we moved to Animas Road.

"My face felt hot, maybe because it shook me up when we checked and nothing was there except the eerie glow back over the hill several hundred yards. Dad wanted to investigate it but I had a very strong feeling that we shouldn't and insisted upon leaving the area and getting closer to town.

"Several days after the incident my brother let slip about our experience to a fellow at work. This young man said that he and five other workers were near that same area some two weeks before at about 11:00 P.M. on a Saturday night. They were trying out a new Bronco (car). Well, they were going down an arroyo and nearing a hill when a brilliant blue-white light came around the hill, shone its light on them, and then zoomed southwest at terrific and incredible speed. They said it lit up their jeep and was out of sight afterwards in a matter of seconds. They were all petrified.

"We drove out to the area the morning after our experience but could find no traces or proof that anything had been there, but Dad had to get a new battery as one cell was dead."

Thus ends Mrs. M's account. She did add that the area is rich in copper.

In the first 1974 case we have offered, the UFO seemed to have been examining the car and the people, in the second case the UFO appeared to have been pacing the car, but in the third case it seems obvious that the people had intruded upon *something* and the spotlight was calculated to get rid of them, which it did.

Another, more recent report comes from Mr. Willie Campbell of Spartanburg, South Carolina, and took place between 9:30 to 9:40 P.M. on February 25, 1975. Until his experience Mr. Campbell had always linked UFOs with pink elephants and the like and he had always thought that people who saw them were drunks or crazy.

Mr. and Mrs. Campbell and their four children had just left a movie theater in Spartanburg and were heading up Byrnes Boulevard to go home (in Inman) when they spotted the object in the west. They said it was much too large for a star and the light was "too massive" to be an airplane. It appeared to be nearing town and getting larger. Mr. Campbell described the mysterious thing as a glowing ball of fluorescent blue, red, and silver light.

The Campbells were not too concerned with the object until it swung right and followed them up the Asheville Highway, hovering over the trees along the way and keeping pace with the car.

Campbell stopped the car at a shop just before the entrance to the Riverdale subdivision where they lived, bought some ice cream for the children, and was surprised to see the object stop over a field across the road. When he came out of the store with the ice cream it was still there.

"It was just hovering less than fifty feet off the ground and just sort of rocking back and forth gently," he said.

At this point Mrs. Campbell was frightened, and when Willie decided to go up the highway past 1-26, she protested but he was curious, and they drove on. When they stopped to turn around the object stopped, and when he headed for home it followed. When he pulled the car into the driveway the object stopped about 200 to 300 yards away, hovering between two houses, just below the rooftops. Meanwhile, Mrs. Campbell ran into the house. Mr. Campbell stayed outside watching it. Then his four children, wife, and mother-in-law came out and watched for another fifteen minutes. The object did nothing; just hung in place while they watched it. Next, Mr. Campbell and his son, Scottie, age twelve, got into the car and played tag with the globe. It followed them almost to Campton Heights where Willie stopped and turned off the headlights. At that point the sphere swung in front of their car and went up much higher and further away. The two watched it for about fifteen minutes more, then returned to Inman. The object followed them part of the way back home but by the time they arrived at home it was gone. They stood in the yard ten or fifteen minutes more to see if it would come back, and all of a sudden it showed up. It came over the house at about 500 feet altitude, let off a blue and silver streamer (like a jet) which was 15 or 20 feet long, in their estimation. "After that," Campbell said, "it just disappeared and we never did see anything."

When interviewed by Field Investigator William Steiner, Mr. Campbell said, "I really don't believe that I could sketch what I saw that night. It was spherical in shape and had a glow to it. Toward the inside I could make out the colors red, blue, and silverish but they blended into each other, so it would be hard for me to say one area was one color and another area another color. The lights appeared to me to be sort of pulsating. From where I was, it appeared to be maybe 20 to 25 inches in diameter. I guess that the distance was probably about 150 to 200 yards at the closest point from me. The last time my son and I saw it was after we got back home the second time. There was no noise from it at all. As low as it was, I know I would have heard something if it had been an airplane."

Mr. Campbell's experience is typical in two ways: it demonstrates how quickly an individual can change his attitude about UFOs once he's had a personal experience, and it is one of those incidents where curiosity on the part of the UFO is apparently the motivating factor. But it is also one of the few times that a UFO has been viewed below rooftop level.

The only UFO-car collision incident to come to our attention begins with a telegram received at APRO Headquarters on July 15, 1967. The telegram was from Robert Richardson of Toledo, Ohio. He informed us that he had struck a UFO with his auto, and that police would verify the incident. He had supplied his telephone number and so a call was immediately put through. During our conversation with him he told us that he had retrieved two bits of physical evidence—a small lump of metal from the road and a fiberlike substance from the front of his car. At the close of the conversation we gave him the name and address of our investigator in Toledo. We then called member Nils Paquette who immediately went to work.

Richardson's story follows. He and a friend, Jerry Quay, twenty-one, were on their way to Whitehouse, Ohio, to see if the Whitehouse Quarry, a well-known picnicking and swimming spot, would be open for the coming weekend. It was Thursday night, the 13th, and the time was 11:30. At a point about midway between Maumee and Whitehouse, Richardson, who was driving at about forty miles per hour, turned around a bend in the road and saw before him a very brilliant blue-white source of light which completely blocked the road. Instinctively, he slammed on the brakes and closed his eyes, knowing that he would probably smash into the object. Quay also closed his eyes. A distinct bump was felt and heard by both at the moment of impact, but when they opened their eyes the road ahead was clear—the object was gone. Quay was shaken up, but neither of the young men was injured.

Following the incident, the two drove to Waterville to phone the police, but they were not taken seriously. They then went to Maumee, Ohio, where they contacted the state police. They were instructed to proceed to the Maumee police station and await the arrival of highway patrol officers, which they did. Present at the station during the questioning were Richardson, Quay, two Maumee policemen, and two state highway patrolmen. After their testimony was taken, Quay and Richardson revisited the scene of the accident along with the two state patrolmen. Nothing was found except the skid marks where Richardson had applied his brakes.

On the next day, however, Richardson went back to the spot and found a small lump of metal. Examination of his car revealed that there were dents and scratches on the hood of the automobile and that some of the chrome plating on the bumper seemed to have been stripped off in some unknown manner. The area surrounding the dent on the bumper was not scratched, cracked, or lifted away from the plating base metal of the steel bumper. Mr. Paquette, who investigated the scene of the alleged collision and also examined Richardson's car, later observed that the sound and sensation of the impact indicated that the object was probably lifting off just as the car struck it. This was also indicated by the small amount of damage done to the automobile.

To us, one of the most interesting aspects of this case was the series of visitors received by Mr. Richardson in the days following the incident. On the 16th of July at 11:00 P.M., two men in their twenties presented themselves at Richardson's home and asked to talk to him about the incident. They stayed about ten minutes, mainly asking questions about the incident and its location. They seemed somewhat friendly. They did not identify themselves, however, and Richardson neglected to ask them for their names. When they left he noted that they were driving a 1953 black Cadillac sedan with the license number 8577-D. He later checked with the Toledo police department to see if he could get a lead on their identities and found that that license plate *had not yet been issued.*

One week after the first two visitors' arrival, two other men came to Richardson's home when he was alone. They were dressed in black suits and were of dark complexion. They impressed Richardson as being "foreigners"; one had an accent but the other spoke fluent English. From the conversation of the two men, Richardson gathered that they were trying to make him think he had not hit anything on the road that night; they then contradicted themselves by demanding the two pieces of physical evidence that he had retrieved. Mr. Richardson told them that the material had been turned over to APRO for analysis. They asked if there was any way he could get it back. Richardson said no.

Just before the two men left, one of them said, "If you want your wife to stay as pretty as she is, then you'd better get the metal back."

Richardson was very upset about this, particularly since his wife was pregnant; he had been very concerned for her safety. He confided in us that he hated to leave her alone to go to work because of what the man said. When those two men left he noticed that they were driving a 1967 tan two-door Dodge sedan. He couldn't make out the license number because of the way the car was parked.

In view of the fact that the piece of metal was discussed only on the phone between Mrs. Lorenzen and Mr. Richardson, and later in private between Richardson and Paquette, those concerned are wondering how the information got out. Richardson swears he did not discuss it with anyone but Paquette, his wife, and Mrs. Lorenzen. So it would seem that the telephone call from Mrs. Lorenzen to Richardson was somehow monitored. Considering the evidence reviewed in Chapter XIV, it seems logical to assume that the Lorenzen telephone has been monitored for some time. This aspect of the UFO mystery will be discussed further in that chapter.

Dr. Allen Utke of the Wisconsin State University at Oshkosh, then consultant to APRO in chemistry, examined the lump which was found on the road. He found it to be iron and chromium with traces of nickel and manganese.

On March 13, 1968, a test conducted at the request of Dr. Roy Craig of the University of Colorado UFO Project, showed the following distribution:

iron—75 per cent	nickel—1 per cent
chromium—20 per cent	silicon—1 per cent
manganese—3 per cent	

In conjunction with the above, a test was run on the fibrous metal taken from the front bumper of Richardson's car. The distribution was reported as follows:

magnesium—92 per cent	
zinc—2 per cent	aluminum—5 per cent
manganese—1 per cent	

The test results furnished to APRO by the University of Colorado do not specify the types of testing utilized or the accuracies of the tests.

While there is nothing unique or mysterious about the alloys involved, an alloy containing 92 per cent magnesium is not what one would expect to find on one's front bumper.

The Richardson-UFO collision obviously was an accident and not by design. But the following two cases had to have been engineered by the UFOs and, to our knowledge, represent the only two of their kind in the annals of UFO history.

Referred to as "car levitations," these cases involve the physical lifting of automobiles off the road by an unknown source. It has come to our attention that in order to make the specific phenomenon more "scientific sounding" in upcoming tomes relating to the UFO mystery, these events will be referred to as "mass displacements." However, not wanting to attach any more mystery to the subject than is already present, we will simply state what happened and let the reader make up his own mind concerning which is the better designation.

On May 14, 1971, Mr. and Mrs. Wilton Raw Eater, Blackfoot Indians of the Blackfoot Indian Reservation near Gleichen, Alberta, Canada, were on their way home at the end of the work week. They had stopped at a bar for a "few beers," as was their custom.

At a certain point in the road, after having passed some houses on a hill, they became aware of a very bright light. Both Mr. and Mrs. Raw Eater had difficulty in describing what happened, but said the light persisted for a few seconds, whereupon Mrs. Raw Eater informed her husband that the car was off the ground. He said he kept steering the car, but it kept to the center of the road and apparently his efforts to steer it had no effect.

According to Raw Eater, the car seemed to float from the crest of the hill to the bottom at a speed of about forty to forty-five miles per hour, with no feeling of the characteristic bumps in the road. Mrs. Raw Eater looked outside and saw that the wheels were about two feet above the level of the road. She said that the car felt like a new car, which theirs wasn't, and that she was very frightened. When finally the light went out, the car descended to the surface of the gravel road with a decided bump. Then the couple drove to Mr. Raw Eater's house where they discussed it with his brother and his wife.

Most might consider the foregoing to be the result of hallucinations of inebriated Indians. However, considering that it was Mr. Raw Eater's custom to have a "few beers" (he was the reservation's school bus driver) on the last work day of the week, there is no reason that he should have had this particular type of hallucination on that particular night. Also, there is the problem of simultaneous hallucination in both husband and wife. And in view of what had happened two years before, which had not been published and which only came to our attention in 1973, it seems that both couples might have had an experience with a similar craft.

Mrs. L. B. (anonymity requested) was bringing her husband home from the hospital after treatment for an injury suffered in an industrial accident. At 12:30 A.M. on Saturday, January 25, 1969, they were within a quarter mile of their home at Yorkville, Illinois, when a bright light to the right of the car at 30° elevation became evident. It resembled a brightly illuminated ice cream cone (*sans* ice cream; no rounded portion) flying broad end first, with the pointed end slightly elevated above the front portion. It came out of the northeast and when at an estimated quarter mile from the car at treetop level, it righted itself, giving the appearance of a triangle with the point up and flat portion pointed toward the ground. It appeared to Mrs. B. to be two or three stories in height as it hovered, showing horizontal strips on the body which resembled siding on a house. On the bottom there appeared to be a lattice-like affair which impressed Mrs. B. as looking like "diamonds and rubies," indicating the presence of red and white lights.

The object lit up the ground below, spun on its axis two or three times, flashing an exceptionally bright light. Then a strip peeled back (down toward the witness) and the object tilted back, revealing the bottom portion. In this position Mrs. B. could see a dim, luminous light like an I-beam and was afforded a view of the inside of the object which she compared to the "spongy" appearance of iron ore.

At this point the car engine and lights died. The car, a Chrysler Imperial, stopped completely. The front end of the car rose up until it was off the ground. Mrs. B. screamed, waking her husband who had been dozing in the seat beside her. He said, "I'll start this car" and reached over and turned the key, but with no results. It apparently hadn't dawned on him what had happened. The car wouldn't start and both were aware that the car was definitely elevated in front.

Then the lighted object moved off in a smooth motion to the northwest. As it left the area, the car came down slowly, but with a noticeable bump when it again rested on the roadway. Mrs. B. was then able to start the car and all was normal.

Arriving at home, they found no marks on the car, but the next day when visiting their landlord who lived a short distance up the lane from them, they found that his wife had been up at approximately 12:30 A.M. to use the bathroom and had become aware of a very bright light which shone through the picture window of the living room. She thought at the time that it was most unusual to have lightning that morning as the sky was clear and cloudless. The testimony of the landlord's wife, given to Field Investigator Fred Merritt, is corroboration of a kind, in that an unusual and unidentified light was in the area at the time of the Bs experience.

Admittedly, the cases offered in this chapter are not a listing of *all* of the UFO-car encounter cases on file at APRO. However, it has been our intent to include the most interesting cases, which demonstrate the different types of UFO shapes and lighting patterns as well as those cases involving multiple witnesses, so that the reactions of more than one human observer can be noted. The presentation only proves one thing: that intelligent, thoughtful people are seeing incredible things which have impressed them sufficiently to risk ridicule and report them.

Report on the Villas-Boas Incident*

By Olavo Fontes, M.D., and Joao Martins
Translated by Irene Granchi

The Antonio Villas-Boas report is probably the most controversial ever to come into our hands. We present it here because the qualifications of the co-author, the late Dr. Olavo Fontes, APRO's Brazilian representative, are indisputable. Dr. Fontes was Professor of Medicine at the National School of Medicine of Brazil and is recognized as one of the top authorities on UFOs in South America.

Coral and Jim Lorenzen

Testimony, furnished by Mr. Antonio Villas-Boas, given in my consulting room on the afternoon of February 22, 1958, in the presence of a witness, journalist Joao Martins:

"My name is Antonio Villas-Boas. I am twenty-three years old, and a farmer by profession. I live with my family on a farm which we own near the town of Sao Francisco de Salles, State of Minas Gerais, near the border with Sao Paulo State in Brazil. I have two brothers and three sisters who all live near me, and I had two more that died. I am the last son but one. All of us men work at the farm where we have many fields and plantations; we also own an International petrol tractor for plowing. When the time comes around for plowing we take turns with the tractor. During the day time the work is done by two laborers who are paid for the job. At night it is usually I who work alone (so I sleep during the daytime), or sometimes it is one of my brothers who goes with me. I am single and a healthy man. I work hard, though I also find time to follow a correspondence course, studying whenever I have the time for it. It was a sacrifice for me to come to Rio, for I should not have left the farm, where my presence is needed. But I feel it is my duty to come here and relate the strange happenings in which I became involved. I am ready to comply with anything you gentle-

* Reprinted by permission of the authors.

men may deem necessary for clearing up this case, such as giving evidence before civil or military authorities, though I would very much appreciate returning home as soon as possible, for I am very worried about how the farm is faring.

"It all began on the night of October 5, 1957. There had been a party at my house and we had gone to bed a little later than usual, at eleven o'clock. I was in my room with my brother Joao Villas-Boas. Because of the heat, I decided to open the window which looks out upon the corral. Right in the middle of it I then saw a silvery fluorescent reflection, brighter than moonlight, casting light all around it. It was very white and I don't know where it came from. It was as if it came from on high, like the headlight of a car shining downward, spreading its light around. But nothing was to be seen in the sky from where the light seemed to be coming. I decided to call my brother, and showed it to him, but he is a very incredulous sort of person, so he did not look and advised me to go to sleep. I closed the (window) shutters and we both lay down to sleep. A little while later, spurred on by curiosity, I opened the shutters once more: the light was still there, where it had been before. I kept on watching until, all of a sudden, it slowly began to move toward my window. I closed the shutters very quickly then, so quickly that the noise woke my brother, who had already gone to sleep. Together we watched the light appear through the crevices of our shutters and shine through the tiles of the roof, lighting up the darkness of our room. It finally disappeared for good that night.

"The second episode occurred on the night of October 14. It must have been between 9:30 and 10 P.M., but I cannot guarantee the hour, for I had no watch with me. I was in a field, plowing it with a tractor when it happened, and my other brother was with me, too. We suddenly saw a very bright light, so bright that it hurt our eyes, at the northern end of the field. When we saw it, it had been there already, and it was big too, about the size of a cart-wheel. It seemed to be standing at about 100 meters up from the ground (1 meter = 3.28 feet), its light-red light shining over a large surface. There must have been some kind of object hidden by the light, but it could not be seen so I cannot declare its existence, for the light itself was much too bright for me to be able to make out anything. I called to my brother to come with me to find out what it was, but he did not want to, so I had to go alone. When I began to approach it, it moved suddenly and with enormous speed it went to the southern end of the field, where it stopped again. I went after it, and the same maneuver was repeated, this time back to where it had been before. The same maneuver was then repeated no less than twenty times. By that time I felt tired and gave up going after it, so I went back to my brother. The light kept still for a few minutes longer in the distance. Now and again it seemed to throw forth rays in all directions, the same as the setting sun, sparkling. Then it suddenly disappeared, as if it had been turned off. I am not quite sure if this is what actually happened, for I cannot remember if I kept looking in the same direction all the time. Maybe for a few seconds I glanced elsewhere so it may have lifted up and disappeared before I had the time to look back again.

"The next night, which was October 15, I was alone, plowing the ground with my tractor at the same spot. It was a cold night and the sky was very clear and starry. At exactly 1 A.M. I suddenly noticed a red star in the sky. It really looked like one of those big, brightly shining stars. But I soon discovered that it was not, for it slowly grew larger and looked as if it were coming in my direction. In a few moments it had grown into a very bright, egg-like object, flying toward me at a terrific rate of speed. It was moving so quickly that it was on top of me before I could make up my mind what to do about it. The object then stopped suddenly and hovered at about 160 feet above my head, shining all the while as brightly as daylight, lighting up the ground and my tractor so strongly that the light from my headlights could not be seen anymore, because of the strong, light-red glare. I was terrified. I thought of running away with my tractor, but owing to the low speed I could develop, my chances of escape were few, as the object had patently proved that it could travel at an enormous speed, even though at the moment it was standing still above me in the air. I also thought of jumping to the ground and running away. But the earth was soft and had been turned up by the tractor, so that it would have been a difficult obstacle to overcome in the dark. It would have been nearly impossible for me to run with my legs sinking knee-deep into that treacherous ground. In putting my foot into a hole I could even break a leg. For about two minutes I was kept in a terrible state of mind without knowing what to do next. Then the bright object dived forward and stopped again at about 35 or 45 feet in front of my tractor, when it began to really land, though always moving slowly. As it came closer I noticed for the first time that it was a very strange type of machine. It was rather rounded and was full of little purplish lights all around it and it had a large red headlight in front from which the light had been coming which I had noticed when it was higher up, and which had hampered my vision. But now the shape of the machine could clearly be seen and it looked like a large elongated egg with three metal spurs in front of it (in the center and the sides)—they were three metal bars, thick at one end and spiked at the tip. Their color was indistinguishable, for it was hidden by a bright phosphorescence (or fluorescent light, such as that of a brightly lit poster), and this was reddish, of the same shade as that of the front headlight. Over the machine there was 'something' which rotated at a great speed, also having a sharp, fluorescent, reddish light, which gradually became greenish the moment the machine started to slow up its speed for landing, so that it seems to me that it corresponded to a decrease in the speed of rotation of that part, the revolving part, that began to look like a round plate, or like a squashed cupola, something I hadn't been able to distinguish before. I cannot declare whether that was the real shape of the revolving part at the top of the machine or only the impression given by the movement it made, for it never stopped moving, not even later on after the machine had landed.

"Of course, the majority of the details I am describing now were only observed by me later. At that first moment, I felt very nervous and upset at seeing so many things happen all at the same time. So much so that when I saw three metal props (forming a tripod, as it were) coming out from under the machine when it was only a few meters up from the ground, I completely lost control, the little of it that I had left. Those metal legs were obviously meant to hold the weight of the apparatus when it touched the ground upon landing. I cannot tell when this happened, for I began to work the tractor (the engine of which was on all the time) and I managed to move it sideways, trying to make my escape. But I had only gone forward a few more meters when the engine died suddenly while at the same time the light went out by itself. I can't even try to explain how this happened, for the key was in and the lights were also connected. I tried to get the engine to start again but the starter gave no sign of life. I opened the door on the opposite side of the tractor and jumped out of it, trying to make my escape by running away. I may have lost a few precious moments when I tried to get the tractor to move as I had only gone a few steps when my arm was caught.[1]

"My pursuer was a small figure (it only reached to my shoulder) dressed in strange clothes. (I later deduced that this was the woman I met inside.) In my despair, I turned round and gave the creature a violent push which sent it reeling off-balance, and in so doing it let me go, and fell on its back to the ground about six feet away. I took advantage of this to try to continue my escape, but at the same time I was attacked by three others, men, both from the sides and at the back. They took me by my arms and lifted me off the ground, so there was no possibility to defend myself. I could only twist and turn, as their hold upon me was firm and they didn't let me go. I began to call for help and yell and curse, demanding to be freed. I noticed that as they were dragging me to the machine my talking had aroused their curiosity and surprised them, for they stopped to watch me closely every time I opened my mouth to talk—though they never loosened their grip on me. This relieved me a little as to their intentions, but even so I did not stop struggling for one moment. In this manner they carried me to their machine, which had landed about 2 meters above the ground, squatting, as it were, upon its three metal spikes which I mentioned before. A door was open behind it in the middle, and it opened out from top to bottom forming a kind of bridge the end of which was held to a metal ladder, seemingly of the same silvery metal the walls of the apparatus were made of. This ladder had been lowered and unrolled to the ground. I was lifted up to it, which wasn't an easy job for the men to handle, for the ladder was narrow, not being really large enough to hold two people at a time, one beside the other. It was also movable and flexible, and kept swinging from one side to the other with the efforts I made to free myself. There was also a round railing on both sides of the ladder to help climb it, and it was about the thickness of a broomstick. I caught at it several times in my efforts to avoid being hauled away, and by doing so succeeded in making them stop to unclasp my hands. The rail was also flexible, and as I got off it later, I had the feeling that it was not made of one piece, but of small pieces of metal, each single clasp linked to the other.

"Once inside the machine, I noticed that we were standing in a small square room. Its polished metal walls were bright with the reflection of fluorescent light coming from the metal ceiling and shining from the many little square lamps fitted into the border where the walls met and circling it entirely. I could not count how many of them there were, for as soon as we got in they made me stand on the floor while the entrance door was being closed and the ladder rolled up and fastened to it. The lighting was excellent, the same as broad daylight. But even so, it was impossible to make out where the entrance door had been only a second before, for when it closed by lifting up, it became part of the wall. I could only tell where it had been because of the metal ladder attached to it. There was no time for me to notice anything else because one of the men—there were five of them altogether—made a gesture to me with his hand for me to go to another room, which could only be half-seen from an open door at the opposite end of the room, the other side of the entrance. I cannot tell whether this second door had already been open when I first arrived, for it was only then that I looked that way. I decided to obey him, for I was still being tightly secured, and anyhow I was now closed in there with them and had no other alternative.

"We left the little room, in which I hadn't seen any furniture or machines, and went into another larger and more spacious one. This room was oval in shape, lit in the same manner as the preceding one, and had the same silvery polished metal walls. I believe this room must have been in the center of the machine, for there was a metal bar running from floor to ceiling right in the middle of it, and it was thick at both ends, much narrower in the middle. It was well-rounded and looked solid. I do not believe its only purpose was decorative; perhaps it was holding up the weight of the roof. The only furniture visible was an oddly shaped table that stood at one side of the room surrounded by several backless swivel chairs (something like barstools). They were all made of the same white metal. The table as well as the stools were one-legged, narrowing toward the floor where they were either fixed (such as the table) to it or linked to a movable ring held fast by three hinges jutting out on each side and riveted to the floor (such as the stools, so that those sitting on them could turn in every direction).

"For endless moments I stood in that room, both my arms held fast by two of the men while those strange people watched me and apparently talked about me. I say 'talk' as a manner of speech, for what they said had no resemblance whatever to human speech. They talked in growls, like dogs do, in a way. This comparison is not quite fitting, but it's the only one I can think of to attempt to describe those sounds, so different were they from anything I ever heard before. The grunts were emitted slowly; they were neither high-pitched nor too low; some were longer, others shorter, sometimes containing several different sounds at the same time, at other times ending in a tremor. But they sounded to me only like animal growls and there was nothing that could be taken for the sound of a syllable or for a word in a foreign language. Nothing whatsoever! To me it all sounded the same, so now I cannot remember a word of it. It baffles me how those people could understand each other. Those sounds still make me shiver when I think of them! It isn't even possible for me to reproduce them for you gentlemen; my vocal organs are not made for it.

"After the grunts had ceased, it seemed as if they had all come to a decision, so the five of them caught hold of me again and began forcibly to undress me. We fought, and I tried by my opposition to make it as difficult as possible for them to accomplish their goal. I protested all the while and cursed at them in loud yells. They obviously couldn't understand me, but they stopped and stared at me as if trying to make me understand that they were being polite.

Besides, though they had to employ force, they never at any time hurt me badly and they did not even tear my clothes, with the exception of my shirt perhaps (which I believe had already been torn before; this I cannot be sure of).

"They stripped me naked, and I was again in anguish, not knowing what would happen next. One of the men got near me. He was holding something in his hand that looked like a wet sponge and with it he began to spread a liquid all over my skin. It wasn't a rubber sponge, for it was much softer. The liquid was clear as water but much thicker and odorless. At first I thought it was some kind of oil, but I was mistaken, for my skin did not get oily. They spread the liquid all over my body, and I was feeling cold by now, for (outside) it was nighttime and cold, of course, but it was much colder inside the machine in those two rooms. As they began undressing me I had begun to shiver and now this liquid made me shiver all the more. But it dried quickly and after that I didn't feel much difference anymore.

"The three men who were growling and making signs at me took me to a door at the opposite end of the one we had come in by, keeping me in the middle. The man in front pushed something in the middle of the door, which was closed, that may have been a button or a hook which made it open in half, inward. It was like a barroom swinging door. It was also made of metal and stood from floor to ceiling, and at the top there were some inscriptions (or something like that) in bright red lettering and the light effect was such that it seemed to stick out about two inches from the door. The inscriptions were the only ones of their kind that I noticed on board. They looked like scribbles of a kind entirely unknown to us. I did my best to remember what they looked like and drew some in a letter I sent to Mr. Martins. Now I don't exactly remember any more what they looked like.

"But to get back to the subject, the door led into another, smaller room. It was small, squarish, and it was lit up in the same way as the others. After we had gone in (I and the two other men) the door closed again behind us. I looked back and saw something that can't be explained; there was no door anymore, only a wall like the other, behind me. I do not know how that was done, unless when the door closed some kind of blind came down with it to hide it from view. I can't make this out. All I can declare is that a moment later the wall opened again and it was a door once more, though really I could not see any blind. This time two more men came in carrying in their hands two very thick rubber pipes which were each over a yard long. I can't say if there was anything inside them, but I do know that they were hollow. One of the pipes was fixed into a chalice-shaped glass vessel at one end. The other end had a spout like a supping glass which was put to the skin of my chin, right here where you gentlemen can still see this dark mark that is now a scar. Before applying it the man who did it squeezed the tube with his hands as if he were pushing out the air. I did not feel any pain or prick at the time this was being done, only the feeling that my skin was being sucked in or absorbed. But later on the spot began to burn and scratch and I discovered that the skin had been torn. The rubber pipe being fitted into place, I noticed that my blood was little by little filling the chalice, until it reached halfway up. Here the thing stopped working and the pipe was taken off; another was put there to replace it, and I was bled once more, this time from the other side of my chin, which you gentlemen can verify because of the other dark spot here, the same as the first. This time the chalice was filled to the brim and the cupping glass was taken away. The skin was torn here too, burning and scratching the same as the other side had done. I was finally left alone; the men left too, and the door was closed behind them.

"I was left alone for quite a long time, perhaps for over half an hour. The room was empty, except for a large couch in the middle of it. It looked like a kind of bed, though it had no legs to it nor any headboard and it looked a little uncomfortable to lie on, for it was very high in the middle, like a hump. It really was soft though, as if made from foam-rubber, and was covered with some soft kind of thick gray material; all this I discovered when I sat on it, as I was feeling tired after so many emotions and so much struggle. It was then that I began to notice an odd smell which was also making me feel sick. It was as if a thick smoke was stifling me, and it smelled like painted cloth burning. Perhaps that is what it really was, for on examining the walls I noticed for the first time that there were many little metal tubes jutting out at the height of my head, which were closed but pricked full of holes like those of a shower; from them there spread tufts of gray smoke which were dissolved by the air. It was the smoke that was causing the smell. I cannot tell if they had been working when the men were taking the blood from me, but I hadn't noticed them before. Perhaps, as the door opened and closed better ventilation was afforded, and I hadn't noticed anything. But now, as I wasn't feeling well anyway, my feeling of sickness increased, and I ended up by vomiting. As I was about to do so I hurried to a corner of the room where I was very sick indeed. Then the difficulty I found in breathing ceased, though I still did not feel well because of the smoke. So I felt very much discouraged, and began to hope that something else would happen.

"I must declare that up to that moment I hadn't the slightest idea as to how those weird men looked nor what their features were like. All five of them wore a very tight-fitting siren-suit, made of soft, thick, unevenly striped gray material. This garment reached right up to their necks where it was joined to a kind of helmet made of a gray material (I don't know what it was) that looked stiffer and was strengthened back and front by thin metal plates, one of which was three-cornered, at nose level. Their helmets hid everything except their eyes, which were protected by two round glasses, like the lenses in ordinary glasses. Through them, the men looked at me, and their eyes seemed to be much smaller than ours, though I believe that may have been the effect of the lenses. All of them had light-colored eyes that looked blue to me, but this I cannot vouch for. Above their eyes those helmets looked so tall that they corresponded to the double of what the size of a normal head should be. Probably there was something else hidden under those helmets, placed on top of their heads, but nothing could be seen from the outside. Right on top, from the middle of their heads, there spouted three round, silvery, metal tubes (I can't tell whether they were made of metal or of rubber) which were a little narrower than a common garden hose. The tubes, which were placed one in the middle and one on each side of their heads, were smooth and bent backward and downward, toward the back. There they fitted into their clothes; how, I cannot say, but one went down the center, where the backbone is, and the other two, one on each side, fitted under the shoulders at about 4 inches from the armpits—nearly at the sides where the back begins. I didn't notice anything at all, no hump or lump to show where the tubes were attached, nor any box or contrivance hidden under their clothes.[2]

"Their sleeves were narrow and tight-fitting to the wrists where they were followed by thick five-fingered gloves of the same color that must have somewhat hindered their movements. As to this, I noticed that the men weren't able to double their fingers altogether, so as to touch the palms of their hands with the tips of their fingers. The difficulty did not prevent them from catching me and holding me firmly, nor from deftly manipulating the rubber tubes for extracting my blood. Those overalls must have been a kind of uniform, for all the members of the crew wore a red badge the size of a pineapple slice on their chests, and sometimes it reflected a shiny light. Not a light of its own, but reflections such as those given by the rear lights of a car, when another car lights it up from behind. From this center badge there came a strip of silvery material (or it might have been flattened metal) which joined onto a broad tight-fitting claspless belt, the color of which I can't remember. No pocket could be seen anywhere, and I don't remember seeing any buttons either. The trousers were also tight-fitting over the buttocks, thighs, and legs, as there was not a wrinkle nor a crease to be seen. There was no visible hem between the trousers and shoes, which were actually a continuation of the former, being part of the selfsame garment. The soles of their shoes were different from ours: they were thick, about 2 or 3 inches thick, and a little turned up (or arched up) in front, so that the tips looked like those described in the fairy tales of old, though the general appearance was that of common tennis shoes. From what I saw later, they must have fitted loosely, for they were larger than the feet they covered.[3] In spite of this the men's gait was free and easy, and their movements were swift indeed. Perhaps the closed siren-suit they wore did interfere slightly with their movements because they kept walking very stiffly. They were all about my height, perhaps a little shorter because of those helmets, except for one of them, the one who had caught hold of me out there—this one did not even reach my chin. All seemed strong, but not so strong that had I fought with them one at a time I should have been afraid of losing. I believe that in a free-for-all fight I could face any single one of them on an equal basis.

"But this has nothing to do with what was happening to me at the time.

"After what seemed to me an enormously long time a noise at the door made me stand up with a start. I turned to look and received a terrible shock. The door was open and *a woman* was coming in, walking toward me. She came in slowly, unhurriedly, perhaps a little amused at the amazement she saw on my face. I stared openmouthed, which is not surprising, for the woman was entirely naked, as naked as I was, and barefoot too. Besides, she was beautiful, though of a different type of beauty compared to the women I have known. Her hair was blond, nearly white (like hair dyed in peroxide). It was smooth, not very thick, with a part in the center, and she had big blue eyes, rather longer than round, for they slanted outward like those pencil-drawn lines girls make to look like Arabian princesses and look as if they were slit. That was what they were like, except that they were natural; there was no makeup. Her nose was straight, not pointed, nor turned-up, nor too big. The contour of her face was different, though, because she had very high, prominent cheekbones that made her face look very wide, wider than that of an Indian native. Underneath her cheekbones her face narrowed to a peak, so that all of a sudden it ended in a pointed chin, which gave the lower part of her face a very pointed look. Her lips were very thin, nearly invisible in fact. Her ears, which I only saw later, were small and did not seem any different from ordinary ears. Her high cheekbones gave one the impression that there was a broken bone somewhere underneath, but as I discovered later, they were soft and fleshy to the touch, so that did not seem to be made of bone. Her body was much more beautiful than any I have ever seen before. It was slim, and her breasts stood up high and well-separated. Her waistline was thin, her belly flat, her hips well developed, and her thighs were large. Her feet were small, her hands long and narrow. Her fingers and nails were normal. She was much shorter than I am, her head only reaching my shoulder.[4]

"The woman came toward me in silence, looking at me all the while as if she wanted something from me, and suddenly she hugged me, and began to rub her head against my face from side to side. At the same time I also felt her body glued to mine and it also was moving. Her skin was white (as that of our fair women here) and she was full of freckles on her arms. I didn't notice any perfume on her skin nor on her hair, except for a natural female odor.

"The door had closed again. Alone with that woman embracing me and clearly giving me to understand what her purpose was, I began to get excited. This sounds quite incredible, considering the circumstances. I suppose the liquid they had spread on me may have caused it; they must have done so on purpose. I only know that I became uncontrollably sexually excited, something that had never before happened to me. I ended up by forgetting everything and held the woman close to me, responding to her favors with greater ones of my own. We ended up on the couch, where we lay together for the first time. It was a normal act and she reacted as any other woman would. Then we had some petting, followed by another act, but by now she had begun to deny herself to me, trying to avoid me and to escape, to end the matter. When I noticed that, I too became frigid, seeing that that was all they wanted, a good stallion to improve their own stock. After all, that was all they were concerned with. I was angry, but decided not to attach any importance to the fact, for anyhow I had spent a few agreeable moments with the woman. Of course, I would never exchange her for one of ours! I like a woman one can talk to, understand, and get along with, and with this woman that was impossible. Some of the growls that came from her at certain times nearly spoiled everything, as they gave me the disagreeable impression of lying with an animal.

"One thing that I noticed was that she never kissed me. I remember that at one time she opened her mouth as if to do so, but instead of that she bit me softly on the chin, which of course wasn't a kiss.

"Another thing that I noticed was that the hair in her armpits and her pubic hair was bright red, nearly the color of blood.

"A little while after we separated the door opened. One of the men appeared at the doorstep and called out to the woman, who left the room. But before leaving she turned to me, pointed to her belly, and smilingly (as well as she could smile) pointed to the sky —southward, I should say. Then she went away. I interpreted the signs as meaning to say that she intended to return and take me with her to wherever it was that she lived.[5]

"That is why I still feel afraid: if they came back to fetch me, I'd be lost. I don't wish to part from my folks nor from my country, by no means!

"The man came back again bringing my clothes with him. He beckoned to me to get dressed, and I obeyed in silence. My things were all in place in my pockets except for my lighter, which was missing. It must have been lost during the struggle when I was captured, so I didn't even attempt to protest.

"We then left the room and went to the other one where three of the crew were sitting on swivel chairs talking, or rather, growling, among themselves. The one who was with me joined them, leaving me to stand in the middle of the room by the table I have mentioned before.

"I was by now feeling altogether calm for I knew no harm would come to me. I tried to pass the time, while they were deciding what to do, and began to observe closely and fix in my memory all the details of what surrounded me (wall, furniture, clothes, and so on). I noticed on the table, near the men, a square box with a glass lid that covered a clocklike face, like that of an alarm clock. There was a hand on it and a black mark that corresponded to our six o'clock. Other markings of the same kind were to be seen where our nine o'clock and three o'clock stand. But where twelve o'clock usually stands, it was different: there were little black marks, one beside the other. I can't understand what they stood for, but that's how they were. At first I thought the thing was a kind of clock, for now and again one of the men looked at it. It couldn't have been, though, for I kept looking at it for some time and at no time did I notice the hand moving, which it would have done had it been a clock, for time was passing.

"The idea of possessing it came to me when I remembered that I had to take something with me to prove my adventure later on. By having that case with me, I would have proof. Who knows, if seeing my interest in it, those men would realize how much I wanted it and would end up by giving it to me. At the moment they were looking elsewhere so I unobtrusively got nearer to it and made a grab at it. There wasn't even time for me to have a good look at it, for one of the men immediately darted toward me and as quick as lightning took it from me, shoving me angrily to the side, and placed it back on the table. I backed to the wall till my shoulders touched it and stayed there quietly, though I wasn't really feeling afraid. I am not afraid of any man. Obviously, though, it was better for me to keep still, as it had been proven that only when I behaved properly did they respect me. It was to no purpose to try to do anything, so all I did was to try to scratch the wall with my nails, so as to get some of it under them. But they slipped over the polished surface where there was no hold. The metal was so hard, there was nothing to do about it. So I kept on waiting.

"I never saw the woman again, either dressed or naked, after she had left the other room, though I believe I discovered where she was. In front of the larger room there was another door through which I hadn't passed. It was now ajar, and now and again I could hear some noise coming from beyond it, as if somebody was there moving about. It could only have been the woman, for the rest of the crew were all in the same room as I was, wearing their odd garments and helmets. I suppose the front room was where the pilot sat directing operations. But that I couldn't check myself.

"At last one of the men got up and motioned to me to follow him. The others went on sitting without even looking at me. We walked to the little entrance hall, straight to the front door that was open once more and the ladder was down. We didn't go down it, though, for the man had given me to understand that I should follow him toward a platform that jutted out on both sides of the door. The platform went all around the machine. In spite of its narrowness one could walk right around it in both directions. First we walked it one way and I soon noticed a square piece of metal jutting outward and sideways (there was something similar on the opposite side too), firmly fixed into the metal machine. If these metal supports had not been so small I should have thought they were wings for flying purposes. By the looks of them, I suppose their purpose was to move up and down for taking off or landing. I must admit that I never noticed any movement to prove this, so I really cannot explain what they were there for.

"Farther on, the man pointed at the three metal poles I mentioned before, which were solidly fixed into the sides and into the front part (the middle) of the machine like three metal spurs. They were all alike in shape and length, thick at the base and narrow and sharp at the top. They were laid horizontally. I cannot tell if they were made of the same metal as the machine because they spread a slight reddish phosphorescence, as if they were on fire. In spite of this, I couldn't feel any warmth coming from them. A little higher up, where they fitted into the metal, I could see some reddish lamps fitted into each one of them. Those at the sides were rounder and smaller; the one in front, which was also round, was enormous and corresponded to the front headlight which I described before. Uncountable little square lamps, like those used inside the apparatus, surrounded the body of the machine slightly above the platform over which they spread a purplish light. In front the platform did not close around to form a circle, but was stopped short by a thick broad sheet of glass, which was securely fitted into the metal. It was rather prominent and elongated at both ends. Perhaps it was for looking outside, *as there were no windows to be seen anywhere at all.* But whether this was the purpose I cannot say, because as seen from the outside, it looked too dull to see through. Of course, I don't know what it looked like from the inside, but I don't suppose it was any clearer.

"I suppose those front spurs I was talking about were the ones that loosened the power that worked the machine, for when it took off, their lights brightened considerably, and blended entirely with the light coming from the headlights.

"After visiting the front of the machine we turned back to the back of it that jutted out more than the front. But before doing this we stood still for a few seconds while the man pointed up to where the enormous saucer-shaped cupola rotated. It turned slowly round and round and was lit up by a greenish, fluorescent light which came from I know not where. Despite the fact that it rotated slowly, a noise could be heard as that of a vacuum cleaner sucking in air, a kind of whistle (just like air passing through a lot of little holes, though I did not see any, and am only making a comparison). Later on, when the machine began to take off from the ground, the rotating saucer turned round and round so quickly that it became quite invisible, so much so that only the light could be seen and the brightness increased so that the color changed too, turning from the original shade to a bright red. At the same time there was more noise, showing there was some relationship between the saucer's speed of rotation and the noise itself, that soon grew into a strong buzz or squeak. I could not make out the reason for such changes, nor can I even now understand what the bright rotating saucer was for, but it never stopped turning. Obviously, though, there was some reason for it to be where it was.

"There seemed to be a small reddish light at the center of the cupola or rotating saucer. But of this I cannot be quite sure because it moved so fast.

"Walking to the back of the machine, we went past the door once more and, going ahead, followed the curve to the back. Right behind, where the tail of an airplane would naturally emerge, there was an oblong piece of metal standing up back to front, crossing the platform. But it was low, no higher than my knee. It was quite easy for me to step over it to get to the other side, and then come back again. As I was doing this, I noticed that there were two reddish lights embedded one on each side of it, at ground level, looking like two thick, slanting-out jutting lines. They looked like the head spotlights of a plane, though they didn't twinkle. I believe that the metal slab must have been a kind of rudder to change the ship's direction. At least that was what I noticed, seeing the thing moving to one side at the very moment the ship, which had already stopped still in midair at some height after taking off, suddenly changed direction just before heading up at a fantastic speed.

"The visit to the back of the machine being over, we walked back to the door. My guide pointed to the metal stair and signaled to me to go down it. I obeyed and when I got down I looked up to see if he was coming too, but he was still there. He then pointed to himself, then to the ground, and then in a southerly direction to the sky; he again signaled me to step back, and forthwith disappeared inside the machine. The metal ladder began to shrink, each step fitting into the other like a pile of boards. When it reached the top, the door (which, when open, was part of the floor) began to lift until it fit right into the wall and so became invisible. The lights from the metal spurs, the headlights, and those of the rotating saucer got brighter, and this last kept turning round faster and faster. The machine began to lift slowly straight up. At the same time the three legs of the tripod began to lift sideways so that the lower part of each (which tapered, was round, and ended in a broader foot) began to fit, or telescope, into the upper part (which was thicker and square). When this was over, the top contrivance entered the bottom of the machine. Finally nothing was to be seen of the legs, and the bottom looked as smooth and polished as if that tripod had never been there at all in the first place. I couldn't see any sign of where the legs had disappeared. These people really knew their business.

"The machine kept rising slowly into space till it was a little over 114 feet above the ground. It stopped for a few moments then, while it grew increasingly brighter. The buzz formed by the dislocation of air grew louder and the revolving saucer began to rotate at a terrific speed while the light turned to many different shades of color, finally settling on a bright red. As this happened the machine abruptly changed noise, a kind of 'shock,' and it was then that I noticed what I have called the 'rudder' turn to one side. When this was over, the strange airship darted off suddenly like a bullet, southward, holding itself slightly askew, at such a heady speed that it disappeared from sight in a few seconds.

"I got back to my tractor. It was about 5:30 A.M. when I left the airship. By all accounts I must have entered it at 1:15 A.M. So I had spent *four hours and fifteen minutes on it.* Quite a long time, in fact!

"As I tried to start the engine, I noticed that it still wasn't working so I tried to find out if there was something wrong with it and discovered that the wire ends of the battery had been unscrewed and were out of place. Somebody had obviously been at them, for a well-screwed-on battery wire doesn't come loose by itself, and I had checked them all on leaving home. That must have been done by one of the men when the tractor was standing still with the engine dead, probably to prevent me from running away in case I had been able to free myself from their grasp. Those were really sharp-witted people; there was nothing that had escaped their notice.

"Except for my mother, I haven't told anyone of my experience up to the present moment. She asked me never to get mixed up again with those people. I didn't feel bold enough to tell my father about it because I had already told him about the light that had appeared in the 'corral' and he hadn't believed me, adding that I was 'seeing things.' Some time later I decided to write to Mr. Joao Martins of *Cruzeiro* magazine, after having read one of his articles in it in November, in which he appealed to his readers to send in their experience with 'flying saucers.' If I had had more money I would have come here long ago. But since I didn't have enough money I had to wait until he told me that he would pay my expenses for the journey here.

"Here I am at your disposal, gentlemen, and if you think I had better go home, I shall leave tomorrow. But if you find my presence here useful, I agree to stay on. That is why I came."

COMMENTS

The sworn evidence transcribed above was given spontaneously by Mr. Antonio Villas-Boas in my consulting room. For about four hours we listened to his story and submitted him to close questioning—all the while trying to clear up certain details, trying to make him fall into contradictions, to call his attention to certain inexplicable facts in his deposition, to see whether he would get mixed up or fall back upon his imagination. Right from the beginning it was obvious that he was not a psychopath. He was poised, spoke fluently, didn't reveal any signs of emotional instability or other movements, all reactions being perfectly normal to the queries made to him. He never once hesitated or lost control of his narrative. All his uncertainties were those natural to a person faced by a strange situation which offered no natural explanation. When he reached such points, even though he knew that the doubt expressed by certain questions might produce incredulity, he answered quite simply, "This I do not know!" or "This I cannot explain!" There are several examples of this attitude of his when relating facts that are entirely unexplainable to him: (1) the reflected brightness which lit up the corral, the origin of which he did not know; (2) what made the tractor engine stop and what turned off its headlights; (3) the reason for the rotating saucer at the top of the machine that kept on turning round ceaselessly; (4) the reason for which his blood had been taken; (5) the door that by closing itself became part of the wall; (6) the strange sounds that came from the throats of the characters in his story; (7) the symptoms he showed during the days that followed his adventure (these are related further on), and so on, and so on.

On the other hand, in one of his letters to Joao Martins he declared that certain details could not be put into writing, for he was ashamed to do so. That was, of course, the references to the "woman" and the "sexual contacts." These details were not given spontaneously, nor were any descriptions of them given freely. Upon questioning, he revealed embarrassment and shamefulness, and it was only after much insistence that we obtained the foregoing details from him. He also seemed embarrassed when he confessed that the shirt he had been wearing had been torn before, when I asked him if his clothes had been torn at the same time. Such feelings are quite plausible in a person coming from his environment and upbringing and are to be considered psychologically normal. No noticeable tendency toward mysticism or superstition was observed either. The man did not think that the crew were angels, supermen, or demons. He believed them to be human beings such as we are, only coming from other countries on some other planet. He declared that because one of the crew, the one who had taken him on a visit outside the machine, pointed to himself, then to the earth, then to some place in the heavens, that this gesture could only mean above, according to him. Besides, the fact that the crew kept their helmets on and their uniforms closed all the time can only mean, according to him, that the air they breathe is different from ours. Taking this declaration as an indication that he considered the woman, the only one who appeared without a helmet or a uniform, to be of a different race than the others, possibly of human origin (perhaps brought up and adapted to the condition of another planet), I asked him what he thought of it. He peremptorily denied the possibility, saying that she was the same as the others, physically speaking, when dressed in her uniform and helmet, except for a small difference in height. Besides, she spoke the same as the others did with gutteral sounds coming from the throat. She, too, had taken part in his capture, and it never occurred to him that she was ever at any time under any constraint from the others, being quite as much at ease as any of them. I then asked him if the helmets were not by any chance some kind of disguise, as the woman had proved to be able to breathe our kind of air. He said he did not believe it was so, for she had only been able to breathe the same air when she was in the small room with smoke coming from the little tubes fixed into the walls. That was where the "meeting" had taken place that had caused him so much trouble. This, besides the fact that the smoke had not appeared in any of the other rooms (where he had not seen any of the crew take off the helmets), led him to conclude that it must have been some kind of gas used to help her breathing—put in there purposely for her to be able to appear without the protection of the helmet.

As can be judged from the preceding account, Mr. Villas-Boas is an extremely intelligent man. His power of reasoning is surprisingly logical for a man brought up in the country and nearly illiterate, for he only had primary schooling. The same can be said as to the possible aphrodisiacal effects of the liquid that was spread over his body, in spite of the fact that in this case the explanation may have been more to satisfy his own "ego" than for any other reason (if what he says is true), for his sexual excitement may have been perfectly spontaneous. His unconscious repulsion may be due to the fact that it was hard for him to have been overcome by purely animal instincts. On the other hand, the liquid may have been only an antiseptic, a disinfectant, or a deodorizer, for the purpose of cleansing him or getting rid of any germs harmful to his mate.

He was asked if he thought that his actions could have been carried out by his captors' willpower or from telepathic suggestion. The answer was negative. He declared to having been the master of his own actions and thoughts throughout his adventure. At no time did he feel he was being mastered by outside power or suggestion. "All they got from me was by the fist" was his only comment. He denied having received the slightest mental influence or telepathic message from any one of them. "If they thought themselves capable of such things," he said, "I must have let them down flatly."

When the questioning was over, Joao Martins told him that unfortunately his story would not be published in the *Cruzeiro* weekly, for it would hardly be taken seriously with no further proof unless another similar story were to appear somewhere else. Villas-Boas showed his disappointment (either because he had wanted his name to appear in print in *O Cruzeiro* or because he had noticed from Joao Martins' expression that his story was not believed). He showed embarrassment but did not protest or try to argue the point.

He only added: "Therefore, if you do not need me anymore, I shall go home tomorrow. If you want to visit me there someday, I shall be very pleased to receive you. If you need anything else from me, you may write."

To comfort him somewhat in his disappointment, I told him that if he wanted to see his story in print he need only go to the newspapers—that they would most certainly publish it at a time when the subject was back in the headlines with pictures taken of a "flying saucer" off the island of Trindade. But I also warned him that as in the case of the photographer Barauna, many people would consider him crazy or a quack.

He answered: "Those who accuse me of being a liar or crazy I would challenge to come to my home and find out who I am. They would soon find out that I am known as a normal and honorable man. If they still continued doubting, the worse luck for them."

All the foregoing comments serve to confirm the impression of frankness given by Villas-Boas in telling his story. It also clearly establishes that we are not dealing with a psychopathic case, a mystic, or a visionary subject. In spite of this, the very substance of his story becomes the heaviest argument against it. Some details are too fantastically imaginary to be believed—unfortunately for him! Therefore the possibility of his being an extremely clever liar must also be considered. He could be a mystifier admirably gifted with imagination and uncommon intelligence, capable of making up an entirely original story, something altogether different from anything that has ever before been told. In that case, his memory must also be extraordinary. For instance, the detailed description of the strange machine corresponds exactly to the model carved in wood, which he sent to Joao Martins last November. Notice should be taken that this apparatus is entirely different from the "flying saucers" described heretofore, as if the man made a point of being original in this too. The coincidence of the model made months ago and the oral description, with one more sketch made now, shows that the man must have an excellent *visual* memory.

Another experience we put him through was to show him several pictures of Brazilian blondes to see if he thought any of them looked like the fair woman of the crew, either in her features or type of hair. The result was negative. At last we presented him with a picture published by *O Cruzeiro* magazine (1954) in which Adamski's picture of a Venusian appeared, drawn after his own specifications. Villas-Boas did not find any resemblance at all and pointed out that the face he had seen was much thinner and had a pointed chin, the eyes being larger and more deeply outlined, the cheekbones higher too. The woman's hair was shorter, coming only halfway down the neck, and was made up in a very different style. Neither did he recognize any resemblance in their clothes.

•

NOTES

[1]The description made of the first moments after the engine appeared standing over the tractor differs from the one Villas-Boas gave in one of his letters to Joao Martins in November 1958. In it he describes having seen the "object" hovering over the tractor, and finding it impossible to escape from it because of the slow speed of his tractor, as well as his own speed if he had been on foot, and the danger and trouble involved by the lumpy ground with its freshly plowed soil, he decided to *stop* the engine and wait and see what happened. He then saw the object land a little farther away, resting on the metal tripod, saw a door open in it, a ladder being pushed out from it, and two strangely dressed men step down. One of them started walking down, while the other waved at him as if to ask him to get nearer and get into the apparatus. It was only then that panic seized him and he tried to start the engine of his tractor. As it would not go, for the starter failed (there was no reference made to the headlights), and seeing one of the men already on the ground and the other one coming down the steps, he rushed away from his tractor, going out from the opposite side and was caught only a few yards away by his first pursuer. From here on both reports agree.

This was the only contradiction that we were able to ascertain during the questioning. We do not offer any explanation for it and only take note of it for future reference. It is because of this contradiction that Joao Martins' distrust was aroused regarding the case.

[2]This remark gave rise to a question on my part. I told Villas-Boas I could not understand how the crew could breathe, being fas-

tened into those clothes and wearing those helmets all the time, with no portable reserves in sight like those worn by divers and deep-sea swimmers to obtain the oxygen needed in such cases. He replied, repeating in part what had been said earlier: "I didn't notice anything at all, no bulge or lump to show the tubes were fastened somewhere to a box or contrivance hidden under their clothes."

[3]The description of their clothes was made by comparing them to those of Adamski's "Venusian." The main difference noticed by Villas-Boas was that his men wore them tighter, very tight-fitting in fact, especially their trousers, which in Adamski's sketch are drawn baggy with a lot of surplus cloth. The described shape and thickness of their shoe soles, and the lack of a clear-cut division between trousers and shoes, making them only a continuation of the former, are also a departure from the classic "contactee" spaceman clothing.

[4]If the woman had been wearing a helmet, according to Villas-Boas, she would have looked a little taller and would have just about reached his chin. With this premise and taking into account the fact that four of the crew, *with* their helmets *on*, were about his own size, he declared not to have any doubt that the woman and the first person who had caught hold of him were one and the same. Villas-Boas is 1.64 meters (5 feet, 5 inches) tall with his shoes on (this measurement was taken in my consulting room). Considering his remarks as to the thickness of the men's shoe soles and the further increase in height given by their helmets, and with due reserve as to the statement, each male member of the crew must have measured about 1.55 meters (5 feet, 2 inches) or a little less. The woman being considered much shorter, it was figured that she must have been about 1.35 meters high (4 feet, 5 inches).

His declaration that the woman reached only to his shoulders (referring to her height) would make it impossible for her to rub her head against his face, according to Joao Martins. In fact, this seems to be the second contradiction in his story. I am not of the same opinion. I believe that if the woman stood on the tips of her toes she could easily have acted as she did.

[5]This sign, according to Villas-Boas, was perhaps the main cause of the fear he still lived in since the preceding October, expecting the strange creatures to return at any moment to catch him and take him away definitely. Evidently this is not the most reasonable explanation for that sign. This is what we pointed out to Villas-Boas, suggesting instead that her pantomime must have meant the following: "Someday I shall bear a child that will be

yours and mine, over there in my planet." He agreed that this could be a much more reasonable explanation than the one he had thought of.

CLINICAL REMARKS AND MEDICAL EXAMINATION

Identification:

Antonio Villas-Boas, twenty-three, white, single, a farmer, resident in Sao Francisco de Salles, Minas Gerais State.

Medical History:

As was registered in the annexed deposition, he left the apparatus at 5:30 A.M., October 16, 1957. He was feeling very weak, for he had not eaten anything since the foregoing night and had vomited several times while still inside the machine. When he got home he was feeling worn out and slept the whole day. He woke up at 4:30 P.M., feeling refreshed, and had a good dinner. On the next night, however, he was able to get a little sleep, but soon after he began to dream of the events of the night before as if all were happening over again. He woke up with a start, crying out, as if his captors were at him again. On repeatedly going through the same experience, he decided to get up and try studying. But this he was unable to do, for he could in no way whatsoever concentrate on what he was reading, his thoughts straying back to the events of the night before. The day dawned with his feeling restless, walking to and fro, and chain-smoking. He was feeling tired and had pains all over his body. He took a cup of coffee and nothing else, which was not his custom. But soon after he felt sick again, just as if he had been eating, and this kept on for the rest of the day. A very bad headache also settled in, beating at his temples, and this also went on for the rest of the day. He had also lost his appetite altogether and was not able to touch food for two days.

The second night he was still sleepless, the same as the first, and during it he began to feel troublesome burning in his eyes, but the headache had disappeared completely and did not appear again.

On the second day his feeling of sickness still persisted, as well as his lack of appetite. He did not vomit again, though, perhaps due to the fact that he had not forced himself to eat. The burning in his eyes got worse and his eyes kept shedding tears. In spite of this he did not notice any congestion of the conjunctival tissue nor any other sign of visual irritation. He did not notice any decrease in vision either.

On the the third night sleep returned, and he slept normally. But from then on, for about a month, he was overcome by excessive sleepiness. Even during the day he often dozed off, and it even happened when he was chatting with someone wherever he was at that moment. It was enough for him to sit or stand still for a short time for him unwittingly to drop off to sleep. During all this period of sleepiness, the burning in his eyes persisted, as well as the weeping. His feeling of sickness had disappeared from the third day—and that was when his appetite returned too, so he started to take food normally. He noticed that his visual symptoms got worse in the sunlight, so he was obliged to avoid too much daylight.

On the eighth day, he hurt his forearm slightly while at work, and there was a little bleeding from the wound. On the next day, he noticed the appearance of a slight amount of infection and there was a spot of matter and it felt scratchy. After the wound had healed, however, a purple spot still appeared around it. Four to ten days later more wounds of a similar kind appeared on his forearms and legs: these were spontaneous and had not been provoked by any external cause. All appeared "with a little lump and a spot in the middle of them, which felt very scratchy and lasted for ten to twenty days each." He referred to them all as "staying purple all around after drying up," and the scars are still visible.

On no occasion did he notice any kind of skin eruption or burning sensation, and he denied having seen any part of his skin bleeding (crusts) or bruises formed by any smaller hurts (spots formed by bleeding). If any were present he had not noticed them. However, he refers to the fact that on the fifteenth day two yellowish spots appeared on his face, one on each side of his nose, more or less at symmetrical points. They were kind of "palish patches" as if there was little blood there and they disappeared spontaneously after ten to twenty days' time.

At present he still has two little wounds on his arms which have not healed up, besides the scars of all the others, that keep appearing on and off during all those months. None of the symptoms described above have appeared again up to the present. He feels well and supposes he is in good health.

He denies having suffered from fever, diarrhea, bleeding phenomena, or jaundice, not only during the acute phase of his illness, but also later on. No loss of hair occurred either on his body or on his face, nor did he suffer from unusual loss of hair at any time since October.

All through the time he suffered from sleepiness his willingness to work did not subside. Neither did he notice any decrease in libido or of his power or any change in the sharpness of his sight. He did not suffer from anemia nor from open wounds in his mouth.

Past Diseases:

He only refers to eruptive illnesses pertaining to childhood, such as measles and chicken pox, with no subsequent complications, no chronic venereal disease either. For some years he has been suffering from "chronic colitis," but he is not bothered by it at present.

Physical Examination:

Subject is of male sex, white, smooth black hair, brown eyes, no visible acute or chronic illness. Bio type: long-limbed asthenic. Untypical fancies. Medium height: 1.64 meters with shoes on. Slender and sturdy, his muscle structure well-developed. Presents good state of nutrition; no sign of lack of vitamins observed. Absence of any kind of deformity or anomaly in growth of body. Hair of normal appearance, evenly distributed over the body as is fitting to the sex. Conjunctival mucous membrane slightly discolored. Well-kept teeth. Superficial glands unnoticeable to the touch.

Dermatological Examination:

The following changes are to be noted:

1. Two small hyperchromic spots, one on each side of the chin, small in size, rather roundish shape; one of them is the size of a small coin, the other slightly larger and of more regular shape. The skin in this region is firmer and smoother, as if it had been renewed recently, or as if there had been some kind of atrophy. There is no sign to enable an estimate to be made as to their nature or size. It can only be said that they are scars resulting from some superficial lesion with associated bleeding under the skin—of at least a month or at the most a year since they came into existence. Apparently these marks are not permanent and will probably disappear by the end of a few months. No other spot or similar mark to be detected.

2. Several scars resulting from recent skin lesions (a few months at the most) on the back of the hands, on the forearms, and on the legs. All of them present the same appearance, like little pimples or scarred tissue, with some scaling around them showing they are comparatively recent. Two of them are still fresh, one on each arm, and their appearance is that of two lumps or nodules, reddish, harder than the skin around them, painful upon pressure, having a small central opening from which a yellow serous substance is emitted. The skin around them is modified and in a state of irritation, showing that the lesions are irritated, for marks made by the patient's nails appear on them. The most interesting aspect of these lesions and scars is that of the existence of a purplish hyperchromic area around all of them, with which we are not familiar at all. We cannot say if these areas signify something special or not. Our

experience in the field of dermatology is not great enough to be able to interpret them correctly, as this is not our specialty. We limit ourselves to signaling these alterations, that have also been photographed.

Examination of the Nervous System—Psychism:

Good orientation as to time and space. Feelings and affections within normal limits. Spontaneous and provoked attention, normal. Tests for perception, thought association, and reasoning powers show apparently normal mental mechanism. Forward and backward memory working well. Excellent visual memory, with great ease in reproducing drawings or sketches of what was first explained verbally. Lack of any outward or inward sign of mentally unbalanced state. Note: These conclusions, although precise, must be completed, if possible, by a psychiatric examination made by a specialist. Examination of movement, reflexes, and superficial sensibility presents nothing abnormal.

Olavo Fontes, M.D.
Rio de Janeiro, February 22, 1958.

AUTHORS' SUMMARY

The seeming inconsistencies in this case may not be so at all if approached calmly and logically.

Mr. Martins felt that if the woman were only four feet five inches, and Villas-Boas was five feet five inches tall (in his shoes), she would not have been able to rub her head against his cheek. Dr. Fontes points out this might have been accomplished if she were standing on tiptoe, and this is quite possible as she was, after all, the aggressor.

Another point to consider is just precisely how tall Villas-Boas is. Most people, and especially men, stretch a little or "stand their tallest" when being measured and/or exaggerate a little when telling their height especially if they are average or less. It is understood that Villas-Bòas is average or just under average height for a Brazilian.

Now, considering that Villas-Boas was the captive of strangely dressed entities in a strange ship, had been gassed, and sexually accosted by an unusual-appearing woman, it is unlikely that he was "standing tall." His testimony also indicates that he cooperated with the woman from the beginning. So perhaps he bent down?

The problem of the strange headgear on the "men" may be a simple one also. If the generous space in the helmet above the heads of the creatures was occupied by a filtration system, we have the answer. They could have been breathing the same air as Villas-Boas and the woman, only filtered so they would not be exposed to Villas-Boas' germs. The woman had to be in close contact for the purpose of sexual intercourse, but it would not be necessary to expose the entire crew. The liquid which was spread on Villas-Boas' body and the ill-smelling gas which was forced into the room he occupied may both have been antiseptic in nature—the latter for the purpose of neutralizing any respiratory germs.

It is important here to recall that the helmets of the crew were "high," and although tubes leading from the helmet to the body of the suit were present, there was no indication of a package or capsule containing air supply. We must examine, of course, the possibility that the "gas" used on Villas-Boas was an atmospheric component which was necessary for the woman and her companions. This conjecture arises from the fact that the men as well as the woman wore those suits when Villas-Boas was first accosted in the field, and the only one who appeared without one was the woman, and that was only during the time she was in the room with Villas-Boas, as far as we can determine. It is just as likely that the "gas" was an antiseptic agent, as we have suggested, as it is that it was a needed atmospheric component for the woman. Also, the "gas" was inserted into the room only once as far as we know and was not reinforced at any time, despite the fact that it was being breathed by two individuals for quite a long time. Also, it seems that if a certain gaseous ingredient was needed, it could have been distributed throughout the air in the whole ship and not just in the one room.

When the Villas-Boas report was first given to APRO in 1958, we tried hard to explain it as a sexual fantasy, but the reported facts did not fit. If Villas-Boas (who Dr. Fontes said was a normal man in every way) were to indulge in a sexual fantasy either during sleep or while awake, he would logically make a glamorous, beautiful woman the center of his thoughts. He would not hallucinate a strange woman who lacked one of the physical attributes generally ascribed to a sexy woman—lips. Kissing is one of the very normal overtures leading up to the act, yet the woman in the Villas-Boas case would not kiss but rather used a biting technique. This, in itself, is not out of bounds in lovemaking procedures, but it hardly replaces good old-fashioned osculation—for humans, anyway.

In this case, as in many UFO incidents in which strange clothing, equipment, or creatures are involved, criticism of the possible authenticity of the report arose out of the very differences between the purported facts and "normal" people, ships, clothing, etc.

If, indeed, these UFOs are ships from another planet and are occupied by alien beings, we should expect that the beings, their ships, their technology, culture, and habits would be considerably different from ours. And if they are technologically hundreds or thousands of years in advance of humans, we should expect the differences to be even more pronounced.

CHAPTER VI

The Interrupted Journey Continued

What started out to be a lark for the Barney Hills in September 1961, turned out to be a series of nightmares. On the 19th, on their way back from a relaxing trip to Canada, Betty and Barney Hill saw an unusually bright star in the sky, kept their eyes on it, and at Betty's insistence, eventually stopped to observe it for some time. And therein lies the tale.

John Fuller, professional writer and columnist for the *Saturday Review*, heard about the Hills' adventure, contacted them, and eventually came up with the most fascinating adventure story of modern times. But certain details of that adventure take it out of the story category and make it seem, in actuality, the record of a harrowing experience.

A little about the Hills: although of secondary importance, the Hill marriage is one of mixed races. Mrs. Hill is Caucasian and Mr. Hill was a Black. Barney worked for the United States Post Office and Betty is a state of New Hampshire social worker. Both were highly regarded in the community of Portsmouth, New Hampshire; both were active in social work as well as in the civil rights movements.

Prior to the experience we will relate, Mrs. Hill had been curious about the subject of UFOs, having friends who had seen the things, and Mr. Hill was gently scoffing and generally tended to dismiss the subject.

On the night in question, the couple were making their way down U.S. Highway 3 through the White Mountains. At Colebrook, where they stopped for coffee, they noted that the clock read 10:05 when they left to get back into their car. They expected to be home in Portsmouth by 2:30 or 3:00 at the latest.

In order to paint a picture of that night it is necessary to note that the sky was clear with bright stars and the moon was out. Shortly after the couple drove through Lancaster, Mrs. Hill noticed a particularly bright star near the moon. It had not been there before. It appeared to be getting brighter. She brought it to Barney's attention and he dismissed it as a satellite.

The Hills drove on, occasionally noting the "star." Delsey, their pet dachshund who had been asleep on the back seat, began to stir restlessly. They stopped the car so that Delsey could have a little walk and they took the opportunity to watch the star a little more closely. Mrs. Hill snapped the leash onto Delsey's collar and walked her along the side of the road. At this point she noted that the "star" was moving. Barney joined her in the road, and she turned over the custody of Delsey to him and went back to the car and got the binoculars. Barney noted that the light in the sky was moving and concluded that it was an off-course satellite.

Mrs. Hill looked at the object through the binoculars and later began to occasionally call Mr. Hill's attention to it as it moved about the sky. They got back into the car and continued their drive, stopping at intervals to look at the object again. At about 11 P.M. they approached Cannon Mountain and Barney slowed the car near a picnic turnout and turned his attention to the light again. The light then terminated its northern flight, turned into the west, then east, and then completed the turn until it was coming directly toward the Hills. Barney braked sharply and pulled into the picnic area.

Betty, by now very curious and a little excited, argued with her husband, who insisted at this time that the object was an airliner. He looked through the binoculars and made out the shape of a plane's fuselage without wings and a series of blinking lights. Betty took her turn at the binoculars, and saw the object getting closer, for it moved in front of the moon in silhouette and appeared to be flashing different colored lights which were rotating around the object. The lights were red, green, amber, and blue.

The dispute about the identity of the light was beginning to cause friction between the two and they argued about it. Betty got back into the car where she found the dog whimpering and cowering.

Mr. Hill put the binoculars to his eyes again and looked at the object. It made absolutely no sound and he strained to hear an engine. When he got back into the car he realized that he was afraid, but tried not to let it show. He told Mrs. Hill he got the impression that the object, whatever it was, was observing them. So they drove on toward Cannon Mountain at low speed, occasionally glimpsing the object as it moved erratically about the sky.

Before too long the object had approached and seemed only about 100 feet off the ground to the west and keeping pace with the Hills' car. With the car barely crawling at a low rate of speed,

Betty looked through the glasses again and was startled to see a double row of windows. She commanded Barney to stop and take a look at it. He demurred, saying it would probably be gone by the time he stopped anyway, but after some coaxing he brought the car to a halt in the middle of the road. Betty handed him the binoculars and Mr. Hill got out, left the engine running, and leaning his arm on the door of the car, brought the glasses up to his eyes. By now the object had swung toward them and seemed to hover no more than a city block away and a few degrees above the treetops. The object was tilted toward them and its configuration was clear for the first time. It was obviously a large, glowing disc-shaped thing. The vibration of the car jiggled his arm so he stepped away from the car to look. Betty, by now very excited, asked if he could see it. For the first time he noted the emotion in her voice and snapped, "It must be a plane or something." Mr. Hill looked again. The huge thing at that moment swung in a silent arc across the road and was now not more than 100 feet away. The double row of windows was clearly seen.

By this time Hill was gripped by fear but could not stop himself from moving across the road on the driver's side of the car, and then across the field toward the object. Two finlike projections on either side, with a red light on each tip, were sliding out from the central object. There was still no sound. Barney approached to within 50 feet of the thing which was now at about treetop level. Back at the car, Betty had begun to call Barney, but he did not respond.

Out in the field, Barney used the binoculars again and clearly saw the structured windows and about six beings behind them. They seemed to be braced against the windows and looking down at him. One, who seemed to be the "leader," wore a black leather jacket and reminded him of the German officers of World War II. Suddenly, all but one of the creatures turned their backs toward Barney and seemed to be doing something like pulling levers. The craft began to descend even lower, just a few feet at a time. As the fins bearing the red lights spread out further on the sides of the craft, something extended toward the ground under the object.

Barney sharpened the focus on the binoculars and looked at the one remaining face at the window on the huge disc. Blind fear gripped him and he suddenly had the conviction that he was going to be captured. The eyes of the creature at the window seemed to affect him. He pulled the binoculars away from his face and ran screaming back across the field toward Betty and the car. He arrived at the car, tossed the glasses in the seat, put the car into first gear, and drove off down the road at breakneck speed, shouting that they were going to be captured. He told his wife to look for the thing. She rolled the window down and looked but the object was apparently gone. So were the stars, which had been so brilliantly obvious only seconds before.

Shortly, a strange electronic "beeping" was heard by both. The whole car seemed to be filled with it. The sound seemed to come from behind the car, in an irregular rhythm. Then the pair both began to feel a strange tingling drowsiness come over them.

Some time later the sound was heard again. Mr. and Mrs. Hill soon saw a road sign which said: Concord—17 miles. They drove on home. They arrived at about 5 A.M.

The big adventure was over—but it had just begun.

When the Hills arrived home, Barney was concerned with a spot on his groin. Betty unpacked, took a bath and, for no reason whatsoever, bundled up the dress and shoes she had been wearing and shoved them back into the deep recess of her closet.

During the next few days the Hills discovered some unaccountable shiny spots on the trunk of their car. They looked highly polished and were about the size of a half dollar. Barney discovered that his almost-new shoes were scuffed on the tops of the toes and could not account for it.

As time wore on, these unaccountable circumstances bothered the Hills. They eventually realized that there were approximately two hours missing from the night—and a distance of approximately 35 miles. Barney began to have stomach trouble which led him to consult a physician. On March 25, 1962, both of the Hills saw Dr. Patrick J. Quirke of the Baldpate private sanitarium, who ruled out simultaneous hallucination, a possibility which had been worrying both of the Hills.

By the summer of 1962, Barney Hill was in a bad state. His anxiety had increased, and ulcers and high blood pressure were giving him a lot of trouble. Eventually he began therapy with Dr. Duncan Stephens of Exeter, New Hampshire.

At first Mr. Hill did not associate his problems with the experience with the UFO, blaming everything on various other personal problems. From the summer of 1962 through the summer of 1963, Barney only discussed the UFO incident with Dr. Stephens in passing. His only concern with it had been his panic when confronted with the object in the field. He was not generally susceptible to panic, so it bothered him. Otherwise it did not seem to be a contributing factor to his ill health. Betty did not seem to have been bothered much, if at all, by the experience although she occasionally had some strange dreams about UFOs.

In order to pare down the space ordinarily allotted to an incident of this sort, we will jump at this point directly to December 1963 when Barney was referred to Dr. Benjamin Simons in Boston, a well-known and qualified neurosurgeon, who eventually performed hypnotherapy on both of the Hills.

During the course of this treatment, both of the Hills would go to Dr. Simon's office at the same time, but only one would be put into a trance. The entire transcript of these hypnotic sessions were presented in an excellent book, *The Interrupted Journey* by John Fuller. He is also the author of *Incident at Exeter.* We will deal here only with the main details which resulted from the trance questioning.

Barney Hill, who was suffering from physical illness, was put into trance first. Each session seemed to lessen his feelings of anxiety, and eventually the following information was elicited from his subconscious: After the first series of "beeping" sounds were heard, the Hills found themselves on a dirt road and there appeared to be a roadblock ahead of them. Betty became afraid, the engine quit, and the car stopped. Mr. and Mrs. Hill were confronted by several men who guided them through a wooded area to a huge disc-shaped object which was resting on the ground. Mrs. Hill did not look at the man to whom she referred as the "leader" to any extent, but did note that the crew had a mongoloid appearance with broad, flat faces, large slanting eyes, and small, flattened noses. Their bodies seemed out of proportion with large chest areas.

Barney Hill kept his eyes closed most of the time, and this was noted by his wife during the episode. They were taken aboard the huge object and put into separate rooms. Mrs. Hill noted the details of a rather strange physical examination. Unusual instruments were touched to her body in various places, a sample of skin obtained by scraping was taken from her arm, a piece of fingernail was cut off, and a hair was pulled from her head. Then a long needle was inserted into her navel, causing her considerable pain, and she protested to the "examiner" who was doing it. The "leader" (these are two separate entities) passed a hand over her eyes and the pain stopped. She was told that this was a test for pregnancy.

Mr. Hill noted that the "leader" had very large, almond-shaped eyes, which seemed to extend around the side of his head to some degree, giving the impression of a greater peripheral vision than men. The mouth of this entity, he said, was only a slit, completely without lips, and with a vertical line on each side. There was no nose as such, he said—only two slitlike holes. Mr. Hill also recollected that the table on which he was put during his "examination" was quite short; his legs hung over it from the knees down. He was about 5 feet 8½ inches tall. The table was hard and cold and by its side there was a stool, probably used by the "examiner."

The room in which the Hills were "examined" was pie shaped with the "point cut off," suggesting that it was a section of the round-shaped craft. When they were taken aboard the craft they went up a ramp and into a corridor which seemed to encircle the ship on the outside circumference. From this they were taken into the rooms mentioned before.

Mrs. Hill got the distinct impression that the "leader" was trying to keep the crew away from her. The "leader" and "examiner" seemed to be taller than the others, but Mrs. Hill thinks this might have been because she was closer to them than she was to the crew. She became visibly disturbed when questioned about the "leader" under hypnosis, could not describe the "leader" or "examiner" except for the personality of the "leader," with whom she conversed while waiting for the completion of Barney's "examination."

This conversation is one of the really strange things about the whole experience, for although there seemed to be conversation between the crew members and the "leader," the exchange of thoughts between Barney and Betty and the "leader" seemed to be just that—an exchange of thoughts. The sounds made by the entities in communicating with each other sounded like "mmmmm" sounds.

The "examiner" became quite excited about Barney Hill's denture and some discussion took place concerning this. Betty explained to the "leader" that Barney had been injured and had to have artificial teeth, and that sometimes old people lose their teeth and must be fitted with dentures. This seemed to be a novel thing to him, as well as the term "old age" which Mrs. Hill did not succeed in explaining to him.

Because of the light in the object described by Antonio Villas-Boas (see preceding chapter), specific questions were put to the Hills by Mrs. Lorenzen concerning the lighting in the craft they were in. Mr. Hill said that it was like a mercury vapor light he had seen while visiting the Hayden Planetarium at one time. This may be quite revealing where the physical characteristics of the crew of the ship are concerned.

Mr. Hill kept his eyes shut during the experience and did not see his wife inside the ship. On the other hand, Mrs. Hill saw Barney until they took him to the examining room and noted that he was "sleepwalking" and had his eyes shut, missing a lot, as she put it.

The important point here is the skin pigmentation of the Hills. Mrs. Hill has quite light skin. Mr. Hill might have noticed a faint bluish or grayish cast to her skin if he had been able to see her. Barney's color, on the other hand, might not have been affected by the light because of his darker skin. Although not a very dark Black, his skin was several shades darker than that of his wife.

This is all in an attempt to analyze the most puzzling aspect of the physical descriptions of the creatures: Mrs. Hill described them as having a bluish-gray cast to their skin; Mr. Hill said he got the impression of a metallic appearance. If the entities had a particularly light skin they might have looked grayish, depending on the exact nature of that light. It is possible that if Mr. Hill had seen his wife on board the ship he might have noted the same type of bluish-gray or metallic appearance in her skin color.

In a telephone conversation with Mrs. Lorenzen the two agreed to answer specific questions, to fill in what information they had which had not appeared in Mr. Fuller's book. It developed that after hypnotherapy the Hills were able to find the spot on the road where they were captured, and found that it was a dead-end road. Also, from their reconstruction, they decided that their car had been turned around after their capture so that they were headed in the right direction to get home after the experience was over and they were released. They also theorized that the creatures unlocked the trunk of the car, for it had been locked before, and was unlocked when they arrived home that morning. Nothing was missing, however.

After hypnotherapy began and the details of the experience began to emerge, Mrs. Hill began to have dreams about the capture, but in her dreams the crew members had quite large noses instead of flat, mongoloid-appearing noses, and had dark skin and hair. Hair had not been specifically recalled under hypnosis. One of the specific questions submitted to Mrs. Hill by APRO concerned the difference between the dreamed characteristics and those revealed under hypnosis. Mrs. Hill offered the opinion that her dreams were rationalizations and that in them she tried to make the crew appear to be more humanlike than they really were, which was precisely the thought we entertained concerning the meaning of her dreams. It should be recalled at this juncture that questioning under hypnosis concerning the "leader's" physical description brought about considerable upset to her, and Dr. Simon did not pursue the point because of the disturbing effect.

Mr. Hill, while under hypnosis and later during recall of the experience after hearing the tapes, again and again mentioned the fact that the "eyes" of the "leader" seemed to have some strange effect on him.

In answer to questions put to him by APRO he wrote: "The tapes of us under hypnosis seem to indicate that I was being controlled while walking toward (the) craft and Betty does not become affected until (the) first sound of (the) beeps, when I returned to (the) car. Beep sound seemed to refortify what was happening to me in (the) field, thus my amnesia became complete."

Everything considered, a reconstruction can be made in this way. The entities aboard the craft were initially attracted to the Hills by the fact that they were on a lonely road at night, stopped occasionally, and seemed to be watching their ship. As they approached, with or without the aid of optics, they may have noted the racial difference between the two and became curious.

Waiting for a likely spot along the road when the Hills stopped to watch, the ship approached. At that time some type of influence was brought to bear on Mr. Hill. After he "broke" the contact with great effort and returned to the car, a mechanical means of influencing both of the Hills was possibly employed—the "beeping sounds" which both described. At this time the object was not visible, and it may be that the car was literally taken up off the road in some manner and moved to an isolated spot, although this does not seem too likely, for it would have been set down in a correct position for them to continue their journey later. Recall that the Hills said that the car was in a different position when they returned to it. Under hypnosis they also said that they approached a road block.

So it is more possible that the "beeping sounds" set up some type of control by which the Hills were guided to the spot where they were taken aboard the ship. The same type of beeping sounds which were heard hours later when they came out of their somnambulistic state in the car could have been a release from "control." The shiny spots on the trunk of the car may have had some connection with the "beeping" phenomenon.

Although Dr. Simons and Mr. Fuller leave the question open as to whether the Hills had a real or a psychic experience, one gets the definite impression that Dr. Simons feels they did see some strange object in the sky, but that it triggered an emotional experience which was shared by "thought transference." This position is untenable, however, when the information revealed by both of the Hills' subconscious minds correlates with known facts about other cases, such as the experience of Villas-Boas about which the Hills could have had no knowledge. The Villas-Boas case was published in English for the first time in March 1965, by the British UFO magazine *Flying Saucer Review*, and did not receive wide distribution in this country, for it went only to subscribers. By that time, however, the Hill case was a matter of history and the information gathered through hynotherapy concerning their amnesiac period had been made a part of the record.

Certain details about the whole episode, however, should be taken with a grain of salt, as it were, for if it was a true experience as we suspect, then the "leader" gave a clue to the various, however, slight, discrepancies. When he told Betty Hill that she would not be able to remember the incident, she insisted that she would, whereupon he said that it wouldn't matter because Barney would remember it differently. And Mr. Hill was the one subjected to influence first—the "leader" seemed to have the ability to influence him much more than he could Mrs. Hill.

One might wonder why Villas-Boas was not "conditioned" or "influenced" to forget his experience, but the explanation is really quite simple. It has been the consistent characteristic of the UFOs that they operate surreptitiously and do not seem to have the desire to make a lasting contact of any kind. Villas-Boas was alone and his captors no doubt knew that he would not be believed if he did relate his experience. In the case of the Hills, however, they were dealing with two people, and if the two had the occasion to undergo hypnotherapy as a result of their experience, certain details, if recalled by both, could lend credibility to the tale. Therefore, the logical thing to do would be somehow to plant different impressions and memories in the minds of each. Quite likely the strongest influence brought to bear on Barney Hill was accomplished by the "leader," whose eyes seemed to be the key to Barney's hypnotic state. Mr. Hill told Dr. Simons that while he was on the ship he was aware of the "leader" and those strange eyes, their reassurances or suggestions, whether he was with the entity or not. Betty, on the other hand, seemed to respond only and directly to the "beeps." She kept her eyes open on board ship and observed more than her husband did.

A clue to the different approaches used by the entities on each of the Hills may be found in the personality of each. Mr. Hill seems to have been a repressed individual, not prone to panic nor emotionally inclined—at least outwardly. Mrs. Hill (we believe that being a woman may have some bearing here) readily expresses her emotions although she is the type, who in times of stress, "rises to the occasion," and it is only after the stress is over that she realizes or admits that the strain was present. (Maybe, we believe.)

Revolting as it may be, we must come to grips with the problem involving Mrs. Hill's inability to describe the "leader." It just may be possible that his appearance was so repugnant to her that she completely suppressed any memory of it, preferring to remember only that despite the situation, he was kind to her. The forcible kidnaping by strange "people" and submission to an altogether strange kind of "physical examination" would be a considerable strain on anyone, let alone being observed and examined by an alien-appearing creature. The "leader" may have realized this also, and planted a suggestion which would cause her automatically to resist any attempts to elicit the information about his appearance.

The famed astronomer, I. M. Levitt, was interviewed concerning his opinion about "flying saucers" on the Mike Douglas television talk show one afternoon in November 1966, and his observations and opinions are characteristic of most scientists who do not seem able to face the situation squarely. When asked about the story told by the Barney Hills he tended to discount it. One of his reasons was that he felt the "physical examination" was not exotic or advanced enough to have been carried out by superior beings. He noted that in the future man would be able to place a human on a table, and with the use of electronic instruments and computers give him a physical examination, diagnosing any problems without laying a hand on him.

This is interesting, for Dr. Levitt was discrediting observational evidence and testimony with a theory concerning diagnostic equipment which does not exist. At any rate, the physical examination to which the Hills were subjected did not appear to be concerned with diagnosis of illness but with a scientific evaluation of physical makeup, according to the description given by the Hills. A machine such as that predicted by Dr. Levitt would have to be designed with knowledge of the creature being examined. Lacking this knowledge, the examiners would have to use such equipment as was available.

The whole Hill affair seems to indicate that the UFO and its occupants were attracted by the car and its occupants which occasionally stopped and viewed them, and possibly, eventually, by the fact that the couple were of different races.

There can be no doubt that the details of the Hills' experience is disturbing to most people and that scientists especially do not care to face its implications. There has been a strong resistance to the idea of the UFOs being occupied by men ever since the mystery of the UFOs became newsworthy in 1947, and even a very large segment of UFO researchers resist the idea of humanoid occupants to the extent of attempting to suppress information about reports involving these observations.

At a seminar given by atmospheric physicist, Dr. James MacDonald, at the University of Arizona in the fall of 1966, he lamented the publication of the Hill story in *Look* magazine, stating that he felt it would "set UFO research back ten years." This was a surprising statement to come from a scientist, for it would seem that *any* information about the objects would tend to further the study. It appears to be another demonstration that people do not care to carry their examination of UFOs beyond a certain point. It may be due to the possibility that if the humanoid occupants are accepted as fact, then we must logically progress to consider the reason for their presence. And man knows what his own motivations for exploration are—exploitation or conquest.

Although one of the two motives may account for the presence of the space travelers, we cannot be certain, for it is certain that we are not only dealing with alien beings, but that their psychology, and therefore their motivations, are alien also.

During the course of several hours of discussion of the UFO subject at our house in the summer of 1966, Dr. MacDonald's main theme was the alleged "censorship" and his conviction that the subject had been scientifically mishandled. He seemed totally oblivious of the various psychological aspects involved. He mentioned Dr. Hynek's responsibility (J. Allen Hynek was consulting astrophysicist to the Air Force UFO project) and stated his opinion that Hynek should have spoken out long before he did. MacDonald did not explain his own actions in collecting data for years, but waited until others had paved the way before publicly stating his own opinions.

There have been few rational and honest approaches to this subject, which is fraught with emotion, and therefore it is not ethical to attempt to blame any one person or group of persons for the scientists' lack of attention. The whole situation, since the end of the summer of 1966, resembles the period of buck-passing and name-calling which followed Russia's launching of Sputnik 1 in 1957.

In our opinion, the public airing of the Hill case, rather than being a setback for the field of UFO research, is a definite step forward. If the human population can face the implications of humanoid occupants, then we are on our way to a solution of some of the knotty problems involved.

The general resemblance between the entities in the Hill and in the Villas-Boas cases is inescapable. If we have any problem in this area, it concerns how much description is retained in the subconscious of Betty Hill and how well it would match up with Villas-Boas' description of the woman in his experience. Even the physical characteristics of the crew as recalled by Betty Hill closely resemble the woman in the Villas-Boas case. Barney Hill's recollection was sadly lacking, however. His main impression of the appearance of the "leader" seems to have been that of his first glimpse through the ship's window while in the field. He was already under the "influence" of something—so what did he really see?

Could the two "slits" or "holes" (nostrils) have been an impression because they were not observed directly? Recall that his attention was drawn to the strange eyes; he did not even note the presence or lack of hair. A very straight nose, viewed from the front, might give the impression of slits only.

Were those eyes wrap-around eyes—extending around the side of the head—or were they some kind of advanced corrective lenses? The latter was brought to our attention by a young colleague in his late twenties who was getting his first pair of glasses. We have both worn glasses most of our lives and they are nearly a part of us. Our friend, however, is much more aware of the drawbacks of eyeglasses and pointed out the advantage of correctly-ground peripheral lenses, if the technique of grinding them could be perfected.

Going back to that strange nose—or lack of it—there is considerably more purpose for a protruding proboscis than one usually thinks there is. It is a protection for the face and especially the eyes in case of impact, for one thing. It keeps the rain out, for another. And it also provides an adequate filter system to keep dirt out of the delicate membranes in the head. So what kind of creature would have evolved into a noseless one? What sort of environment would promote such evolution?

Such questions can give rise to endless and seemingly useless speculation. But it is the purpose of this book to present information, arouse curiosity, and stimulate legitimate scientific speculation concerning the nature of the reported occupants of the UFOs.

Unfortunately Mr. Hill passed away suddenly in 1969, the victim of a massive stroke. In January 1971 Mrs. Lorenzen was one of the scheduled speakers at the APRO Eastern Symposium at Baltimore, Maryland, which Mrs. Hill and her mother attended, and they had a chance to meet and discuss the Hill's experience among other things. Mrs. Hill stopped in Tucson for a visit with us when she was returning from a television appearance in California in the fall of 1971, and both of us had the opportunity to further discuss the "interrupted journey."

In 1973 when the National Enquirer's Blue Ribbon UFO Panel met in Tucson, Betty was invited to attend and brought along the tapes of her and Barney's hypnotic sessions. We were privileged to listen to the most interesting portions as well as to discuss the contents. During that visit Betty remarked that she felt she had total recall of all the experience, but in a later discussion of the "leader" and "examiner" tears came to her eyes and she said that she suddenly recalled that they only had three fingers. She expanded on that by saying that they reminded her of the hands drawn on Walt Disney cartoon characters (i.e., a thumb and three fingers).

Even though we have been examining reports of UFOs and interviewing witnesses for over twenty-three years, and many relate to UFO occupants, we were very impressed with the Hill tapes and with Mrs. Hill as a person as well as a witness. She is a thoroughly warm, friendly woman. She is stable, possessed of a lively sense of humor, and fame has not changed her in the least.

Therefore, when APRO Field Investigator Marjorie Fish undertook to identify the stars represented in the map which Betty Hill had seen while on board the craft, and later drew while hypnotized, we were very pleased. But the story of Marjorie's success is best told by the man who was with the Hill story from the beginning.

CHAPTER VII

An Analysis of the Fish Model

By Walter N. Webb, B.S.
APRO Consultant in Astronomy

INTRODUCTION

The Betty and Barney Hill experience has become one of the classic cases of its type in UFO annals. The Portsmouth, New Hampshire, couple claimed they suffered a puzzling memory loss immediately following a close-range UFO observation on the night of September 19 to 20, 1961. About a week and a half to two weeks later Mrs. Hill said she had a series of vivid dreams in which she and her husband were abducted by humanoid beings and subjected to a physical examination aboard the UFO. These dreams so impressed Betty Hill that in November 1961, she wrote a five-page account of her dream episodes describing, among other things, a star map that allegedly showed her abductors' home star and routes of trade and exploration between the star and others nearby. But it was not until 1964 that Mrs. Hill, under post-hypnotic suggestion, reproduced the map in a drawing. (Both Mr. and Mrs. Hill were hypnotized by a Boston psychiatrist and, while in a trance state, independently told similar stories of being captured and examined aboard a UFO.)

Since the star pattern represented, in a sense, something tangible from the Hill experience, the existence or nonexistence of this pattern might be tested. If the map were a genuine portrayal, several assumptions would be obvious at the outset: (1) the home star must be one of two large circles connected by many lines; (2) the map was made from a vantage point near the origin star; (3) our sun was present somewhere on the map with a line drawn to it; and therefore (4) the map depicted our local stellar neighborhood.

Nevertheless, the task of isolating and identifying a unique pattern of a dozen stars from thousands in the sun's vicinity presented a formidable challenge. Only a few interested amateurs made any serious attempt to uncover the pattern. In 1968 one gentleman with some knowledge of the heavens wrote to me, discussing his approach to the problem, and then closed his lengthy letter with the following: "I would like to add that this is one amateur's attempt to solve a riddle that, I believe, deserves professional help." Of course he was right, but unfortunately few professional astronomers would have dared tackle such a project because, in the first place, the UFO subject in general is frowned upon by the scientific community and, secondly, the Hill case simply is too sensational a report to warrant the expenditure of even a modicum of energy when there are "more important" problems awaiting solution. That, I sadly report, still is the prevailing attitude toward UFOs among the vast majority of scientists.

THE FISH MODELS

In 1966 Marjorie E. Fish, a thirty-four year old elementary school teacher in the little town of Oak Harbor, Ohio, decided to search for the star pattern by constructing a three-dimensional model of the volume of space surrounding the sun. Ms. Fish, though self-taught in astronomy, is an extraordinarily gifted and dedicated person. She has a B.S. degree in sociology (with a minor in science), is a MENSA member, and includes among her many interests anthropology, biology, photography, art, and sculpture. Her persistent quest for the precise pattern shown on the Hill map makes a fascinating story which can only be summarized here.

After completing her first small model of all known stars out to five parsecs (16 light years), Marjorie realized she would have to cover a larger volume at increasing radius from the sun if she expected any hope of success. Subsequent models consisted of up to 259 beads suspended on string, each bead representing a star, colored and sized according to spectral class, and positioned at its correctly scaled distance and direction from the sun.

Ms. Fish anticipated discovering many patterns that would resemble the Hill map. But this was not to be the case, and eventually only one remarkable set of stars emerged. It was a search that required six years, more than twenty models of the solar neighborhood out to 20 parsecs (65 light years), the checking of thousands of stars in a dozen catalogs, and thousands of hours of photography and visual inspection of the models from diffferent angles. Because she experienced difficulty in obtaining the star catalogs she needed, it took Marjorie two years to locate what she believed were the first five stars in the pattern. Another seven or eight months revealed the next four stars. Finally, more than three additional years of intensive work were necessary to find the last three stars in the pattern.

A visit to Betty Hill's home proved especially helpful in 1969. For the first time, apparently, Mrs. Hill disclosed that the star map she allegedly viewed seemed three-dimensional (like a reflective hologram), appeared about 3 feet wide and 2 feet high, and contained tinted stars that glowed.

The star Zeta Tucanae, though not a visible part of the Hill drawing, led directly to the discovery of the final stars in the pattern in the early autumn of 1972. For some time Zeta Tucanae had been a prime candidate as the tenth pattern star but stubbornly refused to fit into the network. Finally, Marjorie realized the star might be occluded by Zeta^1 or Zeta^2 Reticuli from Betty's viewing position (the latter two stars were described as being larger than the others—the size of nickels—and could have hidden another star). For Zeta Tucanae to be obscured, Marjorie found she had to view it from below the model at a 45° angle. When this was tried, the full pattern appeared at once. The difficult angle plus blockage by the base and frame in various models had prevented earlier discovery of the complete pattern.

CONDITIONS FOR LIFE

Before we can understand the significance of Marjorie Fish's results, we must know something about the evolution and types of stars in our galaxy. Stars form when the heat of a contracting dust and gas cloud causes hydrogen fusion to occur in the core. After an unstable period of some millions of years, the star attains a state of equilibrium and begins to shine evenly, arriving on the so-called main sequence where it spends most of its life. When the core has exhausted a large fraction of its supply of hydrogen, the star leaves the main sequence, swelling into a red giant (or exploding), and then shrinking into a white dwarf or a tiny neutron star.

Depending upon its original mass (the total quantity of matter in the star), the star normally falls into one of seven primary spectral classes—O, B, A, F, G, K, and M—arranged in order of decreasing surface temperature. O stars are large, blue, and hot; G types (our sun) are yellow and of medium size and temperature; M stars are small, red, and cool. Each class is further divided into ten subgroups from 0 to 9, again with decreasing temperature.

If planetary life is to arise and evolve into complex intelligent organisms, a star must satisfy several criteria: (1) It must reside on the main sequence for at least three to four billion years to allow complex life forms time to evolve. This implies a fairly constant, nonvariable heat and light output over this long interval. The more massive a star, the more fusion reactions are going on, and the shorter its lifetime. Hot O, B, and A stars have stable lifetimes of less than three billion years. Stars F through M meet the age requirements for life with residence times ranging from about four to one hundred billion years.

(2) The planet must orbit in a habitable thermal zone around the star called the ecosphere. Although O to F stars have wide ecospheres, their short lifetimes most likely rule out the possibility of life. Late K and M types have long lifetimes but also small ecospheres and sometimes life-destroying stellar flares. The most suitable main-sequence stars for the evolution of life, according to exobiologists, range from about F2 (Sagan, Dole) or F5 (Oliver, Huang) to Kl (Dole) or K5 (Oliver, Sagan). G types probably offer optimum life zone conditions.

(3) Single stars are more likely than multiple stars to have habitable planets. Binary stars, for example, could perturb planets into unstable orbits although such effects would depend upon how closely separated the stars were in the system. The problem is a complicated one, but at present it seems best to favor single stars over multiple systems as better prospects for life.

(4) Massive O to early F stars tend to have high rotational speeds (100 to 230 km per sec) with an abrupt slowdown occurring between F2 and F5, decreasing to only a few km per sec in G stars like our own. Such slow rotations may indicate planets are absorbing the angular momentum of the star from early F through M. If this is true, it is interesting that the emergence of planetary systems coincides with the estimated cutoff for spectral types suitable for life.

Ms. Fish restricted her selection of stars even further, confining her search ultimately to only single, nonfluctuating, main-sequence stars between F8 and K1—her "Group 1" stars—those with the best chance for producing terrestrial planets with intelligent life. (According to Carl Sagan, F8 is the point where intelligence may emerge.) She reasoned that if the Hill story were true and extra-terrestrials visited our solar system and the earth, other stars similar to our sun should be of interest to them. In fact, by reversing the argument, it also was likely their origin star was similar to our sun. Marjorie discovered that about two hundred stars within 22 parsecs (72 light years) of the sun lie in the F8-K1 spectral range.

RESULTS OF THE FISH STUDY

Marjorie Fish's six-year search yielded only one unique three-dimensional duplicate of Betty Hill's star map, and a continuing inspection since then has not uncovered any pattern remotely resembling the original discovery. The matchup includes not only the twelve-star network connected by lines but also three background (actually foreground) stars that formed a prominent triangle in Mrs. Hill's drawing.

The stars that make up the pattern in the Fish model fulfill the above exobiological criteria. For example, *the lines in the map connect stars that are exclusively the type defined as suited for life.* All twelve stars are single, nonfluctuating, slowly rotating dwarfs residing on the main sequence for lifetimes of from about seven to thirty or forty billion years, ample time for the evolution of life to take place. Tau Ceti seems to be a special borderline case. It has been listed either as lying between the main-sequence dwarfs and subdwarfs or as a subdwarf. Sagan believes full-fledged subdwarfs would not likely possess terrestrial planets although they might have Jovian-type gas giants orbiting them.

The pattern stars range from F6 to K1. All twelve are "Group 1" stars (having terrestrial planets with intelligent life) except Tau^1 Eridani, which is F6. This latter star is a member of Ms. Fish's "Group 0" stars possibly possessing terrestrial planets with *nonintelligent* life. Marjorie feels such bodies would be suitable for colonization or the establishment of bases. One of the most striking features is that *eight of the twelve stars are G types, probably the optimum range for intelligent life.* The so-called "base stars," Zeta^1 and Zeta^2 Reticuli, are included in this category; they are G2 and G1, respectively. It should be emphasized the two stars are not components of a binary system (they share a common motion through space) and therefore fulfill the single-star requirement for life. Both bodies are quite similar to our sun (G2) in mass, temperature, luminosity, and residence time on the main sequence. Marjorie, it will be recalled, assumed from the beginning that the home star of the Hills' abductors probably would resemble our sun and that they would seek out stars similar to theirs.

Especially noteworthy is the fact that *the pattern happens to contain a phenomenally high percentage of all the known stars suitable for life in the solar neighborhood.* Employing her own critical standards, Ms. Fish found only twelve (5 per cent) of two hundred fifty-nine known stars within her 10-parsec model that were suitable for life; *five of the twelve (42 per cent) occupy positions in the Hill pattern* (six, if we include the occluded Zeta Tucanae): Interestingly enough, when multiple stars, probable variable stars, and stars later than K1 are removed from Sagan's list of twenty nearest stars (and Dole's list of fourteen stars), those most likely to have habitable planets within 6.7 parsecs (twenty-two light years), only two stars meet Marjorie's stringent requirements —Tau Ceti and 82 Eridani—and both are in the Hill pattern: (The former object has been the target of at least four radio-telescope searches for artificial signals.)

The star pattern fills a volume of space determined by Marjorie to be 48 light years (14.7 parsecs) wide by 48 light years deep by 32 light years (9.8 parsecs) high (plus or minus 1½ light years per side)—a two-thirds cube. *This volume actually contains over a hundred stars and yet all the stars within the volume compatible with life are included in Betty Hill's drawing.* This would hardly seem coincidental.

The solid and broken lines allegedly representing trade routes and expeditions do indeed *depict a logical travel sequence from star to star.* The routes link Zeta[1] Reticuli with only the nearest stars having spectral classes that favor the emergence and evolution of life—especially intelligence. For the reasons cited previously, all other stellar types appear to be avoided: fast-growing stars earlier than F2, stars later than K1, multiples, and variables.

Concerning discrepancies between the drawing and the model, Ms. Fish feels, and I tend to agree, that these differences are relatively inconsequential and can be justified in a reasonable manner. The drawing, as mentioned earlier, was created under post-hypnotic suggestion, and a comparison with the model demonstrates what would appear to be astonishing accuracy in recalling forgotten details. During a moment of conscious control, Betty erased the Zeta[1] Reticuli- Gliese 86 line twice before settling on the *wrong* position. *The longest erasure appears to be the correct angle for the Zeta[1] Reticuli—Gliese 86 line while the short erasure is the correct length.* Improving the angle would also correct the angle of the line to Alpha Mensae on the opposite side of Zeta[1].

Both Zeta[1] and Zeta[2] Reticuli are probably large and widely separated in the drawing according to Ms. Fish, because (1) the two stars were located very near the map's front surface and (2) they may have been deliberately dramatized by using a larger scale (on the original map).

Mrs. Hill's representation of the background triangle (stars Gliese 86.1, 95, and Kappa Fornacis) is larger than the one in the

PROBABLE STARS IDENTIFIED BY FISH IN THE HILL MAP

NAME	SAO CATALOG NUMBER	GLIESE CATALOG NUMBER	CONSTELLATION	SPECTRAL CLASS	DISTANCE FROM EARTH (LY.)
Zeta Tucanae	248163	17	Tucana	G2 V	23.3
54 Piscium	074175	27	Pisces	K0 V	34.3
—	167134	59	Cetus	G8 V	52.6
—	037434	67	Andromeda	G2 V	37.5
107 Piscium	074883	68	Pisces	K1 V	24.3
Tau Ceti	147986	71	Cetus	G8 Vp (or V1)	11.8
—	232658	86	Eridanus	K0 V	36.6
—	167613	86.1	Fornax	K2 V	42.3
—	167697	95	Fornax	G5 V	44.7
Kappa Fornacis	167736	97	Fornax	G1 V	42.3
Tau_1 Eridani	148584	111	Eridanus	F6 V	46.6
$Zeta_1$ Reticuli	248770	136	Reticulum	G2 V	36.6
$Zeta_2$ Reticuli	248774	138	Reticulum	G1 V	36.6
82 (e) Eridani	216263	139	Eridanus	G5 V	20.2
Alpha Mensae	256274	231	Mensa	G5 V	28.3
Sux	—	—	—	G2 V	—

model. Marjorie believes it was drawn larger because it is near the front surface of the map and would have been relatively easy to recall in contrast to most of the other background stars. Indeed, the other objects were included by Betty simply to show there was a backdrop of other stars.

Marjorie is satisfied any residual differences between the drawing and model can be explained plausibly as being due to (1) Betty Hill's recall and sketching ability and (2) the possibility of somewhat incorrect star positions in the model owing to still inexactly known parallaxes (by which the distance to each star is calculated).

An important piece of evidence uncovered by Ms. Fish, strongly suggesting the map is not a hoax, is the fact that *the background triangle could not have been drawn prior to the publication of the 1969 edition of Gliese's* Catalog of Nearby Stars. Not only was the star Gliese 86.1 not listed, so far as is known, in any (earthly) star catalog in 1964 when Betty drew her map, but also Gliese 95 and Kappa Fornacis, their parallaxes imperfectly known in 1964, would not have created the triangle Betty drew on the map. I checked this out myself in several of the catalogs Marjorie used and confirmed the accuracy of her discovery.

In addition, it is improbable Mrs. Hill could have devised a pattern of twelve stars, all of which would turn out to be candidates for life; it is improbable she could have had access to the proper star catalogs; and even if she had located the catalogs, it is improbable she knew how to interpret them. As the initial investigator of the Hill affair, I happen to know Betty's knowledge of astronomy is severely limited.

The twelve stars connected by lines have the following ranges as a group: spectral classes F6 V to K1 V (sun G2 V), surface temperatures about 4800 to 6500° Kelvin (sun 5800°), masses about 0.7 to 1.2 solar masses (sun 1.0), luminosity about 0.3 to 2.1 plus (sun 1.0), radii about 0.7 to 1.2 solar radii (sun 1.0), absolute visual magnitudes plus 3.7 to plus 5.9 (sun plus 4.8), apparent visual magnitudes plus 3.5 to plus 7.0 (sun minus 26.7), distances from earth 11.8 to 52.6 light years, and main-sequence residence times about 7 to 30 or 40 billion years (sun about 13 billion).

All but one (Alpha Mensae) of the twelve pattern stars can be seen from parts of the United States in the winter evening sky or late summer morning sky. Zeta^1 Reticuli, the probable origin star, is a faint fifth-magnitude star located in the tiny, undistinguished, southern hemisphere constellation known as Reticulum the Net and is visible in the United States only from the southern tip of Florida and Brownsville, Texas. Under favorable conditions, nine, and possibly eleven, of the twelve stars are detectable with the naked eye. The remainder require binoculars.

A Scenario of Exploration From Zeta^1 Reticuli

Based upon data from the Fish model, the star map, and Betty and Barney's testimony of their UFO encounter, I believe it is feasible to construct a speculative but rational scenario of interstellar exploration from the alleged origin star, Zeta^1 Reticuli. It was felt Ms. Fish's careful research supplied enough usuable scientific data to justify such an exercise in subjective probability.

We have already seen how similar Zeta^1 Reticuli is to our own sun in its spectral characteristics although we have no way of knowing at present exactly how long the former body has been on the main sequence. From both the star's spectrum and the Hills' description of their captors, it may be assumed the home planet of the hypothetical "Zeta Reticulans" possesses a mass, gravity, and environment at least somewhat like our own. Bieri (1964) argued that extraterrestrial intelligence probably will resemble *homo sapiens* because evolutionary pathways are strictly limited and air-breathing, land-roaming humanoids offer the optimum adaptive solution to terrestrial environments. He postulated that life-supporting planets will evolve bilaterally with symmetrical animals with an anterior brain and closely associated sense organs, paired appendages, and hands for tool-making. Variations in atmospheric density and composition, stellar distance, and radiation output and intensity from the star would account for the reported appearance of the Hill entities: large slanted eyes, wide nostrils, mouth-slit, gray skin, and thick chests.

Although it is impossible to tell how long this race may have been conducting interstellar spaceflight, it is obvious from the Hill map that it has been a spacefaring society for a very long time. Participants at the 1971 Byurakan Conference on Communication with Extraterrestrial Intelligence (CETI) estimated the lifetimes of such civilizations which do not destroy themselves as ranging from perhaps ten thousand to one billion years (Sagan's value was ten million years).

Since interstellar exploration would doubtless be an expensive venture, it is entirely conceivable the Reticulans are members of a linked community of intelligent species, possibly composed not only of various cultures contacted in planetary systems represented on the Hill map, but also embracing other societies as well. Participation in such a "galactic federation" would bestow definite advantages: a galactic heritage of knowledge about innumerable planets, their histories, and the life forms that evolved on them; a detailed astronomical record of the origin, history, and probable fate of the universe, some of the data perhaps originally acquired by long dead civilizations; the development of sciences not easily contrived by one civilization alone but achievable through combined efforts; and the transfer of information that would help extend the life expectancy of participating societies.

When the Reticulans mastered the principles of relativistic spaceflight, their first expedition must have been a rather easy hop to neighboring Zeta², a yellow dwarf star much like their own. Ms. Fish assigned limits of about 1/20th to 1½ light-years separation between the two stars—about 470 billion to 14 trillion kilometers. (This distance may be compared to that of the sun's nearest stellar neighbor, the Alpha Centauri triple system, 4.3 light-years or about 41 trillion kilometers from earth.) From the many lines running between the two stars on the Hill map, it seems likely contact was established with another intelligent race on a planet (or planets) orbiting Zeta^2 and the consequence was what appears to be a heavy commerce between the two solar systems. We might further speculate that the unusually close proximity of another star to the origin star could have provided the impetus for additional deep-space explorations. (The average distance between stars in the solar neighborhood is about 8 light-years.)

Undoubtedly, other nearby stellar candidates were monitored for the likelihood of intelligent life and were eventually visited, ultimately leading to voyages along five or six branches of stars—those in the Hill map. The next logical planetary system to receive a visit from the Reticulans probably was Zeta Tucanae, another G2 dwarf like Zeta^1. (While this star was occluded from Betty Hill's vantage point, it would be surprising if it were not part of the Reticulan network.) Although the distance from the origin star to Gliese 86 is estimated by Marjorie to be only 9.8 (plus or minus 2) light-years, the latter is a K0 type star. Zeta Tucanae was several light-years farther but a more promising candidate for the emergency of intelligence.

Alpha Mensae, a G5 dwarf 14 (plus or minus 2) light years distant, probably became the next target followed by 82 Eridani, another G5 sun 19 (plus or minus 2) light-years from the home star. The sequence of travel after the latter star grows more problematical and depends upon many unknown factors including whether single or simultaneous expeditions to various stars were launched from Zeta^1 Reticuli. In any case, we might conjecture that solid lines to Alpha Mensae, 82 Eridani, our sun, Gliese 86, and quite possibly Zeta Tucanae, indicate repeat trips to planets of extraordinary interest orbiting those stars. (Communication with, or observation of, intelligent cultures on the worlds visited could be an important reason for return trips but certainly not the only aim.)

Ms. Fish has proposed a very logical explanation for the existence of *two* dashed lines between 82 Eridani and Tau Ceti (G8 type): the first expedition to arrive at the latter star used it as a jump-off point to our own sun, the next G2 dwarf beyond Zeta Tucanae and of the same spectral type as the home star itself. From Tau Ceti the choice was either the sun or 107 Piscium, a lesser K1 prospect 5 light-years more distant than our star. After the sun and earth were visited, the dashed line from Tau Ceti to the sun was eliminated in favor of a direct link between the home star and the sun, the longest single traverse to another star from Zeta^1 Reticuli (36.6 light-years, one way).

Employing the time-dilation paradox, a one-way trip from Zeta to the sun might take about eleven years at a constant one-gravity (normal earth weight) acceleration and deceleration near the velocity of light. However, this interval could be cut in half at two- or three-g accelerations and reduced even further if higher forces could be tolerated. Obviously, whatever the propulsion mode, the earth and its inhabitants appear to be a priority objective, not only of the Reticulans but also apparently of other humanoid races, in spite of the sun's relative isolation on the edge of a 30-light-year-diameter gulf nearly devoid of stars, one of the many facts disclosed by the Fish model.

Eventually, another expedition, according to Ms. Fish's supposition, proceeded from 82 Eridani to Tau Ceti, accounting for the second dashed line between the two stars, and then probably continued to 107 Piscium.

If we continue our hypothetical exercise, it is apparent other branches of interstellar exploration were established. Gliese 86 (AK0 star) became the jump-off point to Gliese 59 (G8) and to Tau[1] Eridani (F6). It is not clear to Marjorie why Gliese 86.1, 95, and Kappa Fornacis—all G or early K dwarfs—were bypassed, but she points out 86.1 is a K2 star and therefore not a "Group 1" candidate for intelligent life, while the other two might have peculiarities not yet detected by earth astronomers, such as variability; or they might be recent arrivals on the main sequence; or perhaps both deficiencies are present.

The Gliese 67 branch, connecting a total of six stars, represents what appears to be the deepest penetration of space by the Reticulans from their home star. The route spans 78 (plus or minus 2) light years or 24 parsecs! Of course, it is possible, as Ms. Fish suspects, that the volume depicted in the star map is only *one of several volumes* of space explored by the Reticulans!

SUMMARY AND CONCLUSIONS

Much credit for escalating my interest in Marjorie Fish's work goes to Robert J. Durant, Assistant Editor of *Pursuit,* quarterly journal of Society for the Investigation of the Unexplained (SITU). Durant ghosted an excellent article for SITU regarding Marjorie's research. In November 1973 he paid me a visit and later forwarded copies of his *Pursuit* story (Jan. 1974 issue) and a provocative *SAGA* article by Friedman and Slate (July 1973 issue). Finally, on July 18, 1974, I spent six hours with Ms. Fish discussing her work and viewing her models. Returning with copies of some of her voluminous notes and photographs, I checked her data in six star catalogs and found no errors. I am satisfied her investigations have been carried out in a completely thorough, scientific manner.

Although initially, Marjorie believed the models would reveal many star patterns similar to the one in Betty's map, only one select group turned up after years of painstaking study. She feels the pattern in her model and in the map are one and the same, and moreover she is satisfied her work has ruled out a hoax and coincidence. I must agree the reasons she cites are compelling. From my own personal inspection of the model, I can attest the star pattern in the model does indeed match amazingly well the one in the map. The presence of the prominent background triangle lends strong additional support.

The few discrepancies between the map and the model are rather minor and, in my view, are logically accounted for by Ms. Fish. Even Betty's two erasures, which match the correct angle and length for the Gliese 86 line, help to build a case for the pattern's reality.

Most impressive is the fact the twelve network stars fulfill all required exobiological criteria—that is, all are single, nonvariable, slowly rotating, late F to early K main-sequence dwarfs with stable lifetimes of at least three to four billion years. The lines in the map connect stars that are *solely* candidates for life. Furthermore, all but one of the stars are possible for *intelligent* life (eight of the twelve are optimum G stars including the suspected origin star itself which is the same spectral type as our sun); the pattern is composed of an abnormally high number of all the known life-supporting candidates in the solar neighborhood; all the life-supporting stars found within the Hill volume are included in Betty's map; and the lines in the map represent a logical travel sequence from star to star.

It is extremely significant that the background triangle was not known to exist when Betty Hill drew her map in 1964. One of the stars was not even listed in catalogs at that time. In addition, based upon Mrs. Hill's nonscientific experience and limited knowledge of the heavens, it appears highly improbable she had the capability to devise a unique pattern of a dozen life-supporting stars.

For all of these reasons Marjorie believes, and I tend to agree, that the evidence appears to eliminate both fabrication and coincidence. It is just possible that Ms. Fish has achieved a stunning breakthrough with enormous implications for UFO research, exobiology, and astronomy—not to mention the cultural impact. If the Hill map was evidence, as a result of contact with extraterrestrial beings, a whole series of exceedingly important facts are immediately evident: (1) the reported abduction of Betty and Barney Hill represents reality, not fantasy; (2) the map is evidence of interstellar visitation and indicates the origin of at least some UFOs; (3) the map, together with the Hills' testimony, provides valuable clues about the abductors, their probable home star, their planetary environment, their sequence of space travel between stars, and something about the actual abundance of life-bearing stars in the sun's vicinity.

If this is correct, we may conjecture that we are "dealing" with a very old and incredibly experienced galactic culture which has crisscrossed the vast spatial seas for probably thousands, perhaps millions, of years in starships that, to us, are "indistinguishable from magic" (A.C. Clarke). Such an advanced race—apparently capable of manipulating mental, electrical, and other forces in a manner we are powerless to comprehend—would so far surpass our own technology it might very well have little interest in communicating with us and nothing to gain by it.

Even ignoring the stupendous UFO implications of Ms. Fish's accomplishments, her models stand on their own merit as detailed representations of the solar neighborhood. Conceivably, the models may reveal new data regarding local stellar distribution. For example, Marjorie has observed that hot, bright A stars in the sun's vicinity form a plane. Other types cluster in separate groups: G and early K's in one group; late K and early M's in another; late M's, white dwarfs, and some subdwarfs in still another cluster; and double stars in a curved band. The sun's somewhat isolated position in space has already been mentioned.

Astronomers and exobiologists everywhere owe a debt to Ms. Fish, a former elementary school teacher, who accepted a challenge to science that was not met by professionals—in my judgment, a tragic indictment of the science community. Although she received some help on non-UFO aspects of her research from several astronomers—most notably, Walter Mitchell of Ohio State University—most scientists are either totally unaware of her considerable achievement or choose to disregard it altogether. So far the only professional recognition of Marjorie's work has come from Ohio State's Department of Astronomy, where her 10-parsec model has been used for student study for five years. Northwestern astronomer and director of the Center for UFO Studies, J. Allen Hynek, also has a few of the Fish models but has not yet offered a formal evaluation statement. Finally, David R. Saunders, former member of the Colorado UFO Project, reproduced the Hill star map on a computer, using the Fish data.

Though thus far unappreciated by the scientific community, Marjorie's prodigious research will continue. She now is preparing to construct an even more precise, larger scale model of the nearby stars.

Someday confirmation of Ms. Fish's discoveries could be forthcoming. CETI itself has gained a new respectability. A just completed radio-telescope search by Zuckerman and Palmer examined some five hundred stars for artificially generated signals at twenty-one centimeters (the results have not yet been published). Even though it is possible most space communications occur via direct spaceflight, and not by radio transmission, an effort should be made to scan Zeta[1] Reticuli and other stars in the Hill pattern for intelligent signals. While the fixed 1,000-foot antenna at Arecibo, Puerto Rico, can acquire only a few of the Hill stars, the Australian radio telescopes are at the right latitude to examine them all.

In conclusion, I wish to point out the bulk of this report is a presentation and interpretation of Marjorie Fish's own results. My contributions were limited to supplementing her findings with additional astronomical data, to writing what I hope was a credible "interstellar scenario" based upon her results, and to offering my evaluation of those results.

CHAPTER VIII

The Entities in Europe

The earliest report in Europe of an unconventional aircraft on the ground accompanied by extraordinary beings took place on August 14, 1947, nearly two months after a sighting by one Kenneth Arnold of nine UFOs over Mount Rainier. (We will discuss the latter in further detail later in the book.)

On that August day at 9 A.M., Signor R.L. Johannis, an artist, was out painting near Chiarso Creek at Villa Santina, close to Carnia, Italy. He was startled to see a disc-shaped object, later estimated to be about 30 feet in diameter, land some distance from him. Next, he was confronted with the presence of two child-sized beings (about 3 feet tall) standing by the object. They were wearing dark blue coveralls with bright red collars and belts, and a spherical, transparent helmet on their oversized heads. Their faces appeared to have a greenish color, their eyes were large and plum-colored with a vertical line in the center and no lashes or brows. Their hands were clawlike with eight fingers, four opposed to four, on each hand.

Johannis hailed the creatures. The gesture may have been interpreted as hostile, for one of the beings touched its belt and projected a thin vapor, which dazed the artist and he fell onto his back. The little beings then approached to within 6 feet of the artist and stood looking at his easel. Though weak, Johannis managed to roll over and saw the creatures pick up the easel which had been knocked down. He noted that it was taller than both of them, and that they were panting hard. Shortly they returned to the disc and entered it, whereupon it rose from the ground, hovered, and—disappeared.

No other entity accounts are recorded in Europe until 1954, the same year that South America was overrun with little folk. On October 21 of that year, Mrs. Jennie Roestenberg reported that at 4:45 P.M. on that day she and her two children watched an aluminum-colored disc as it hovered over their home at Rampton, near Shrewsbury, England. Through transparent panels Mrs. Roestenberg claimed she saw two "men" with white skin, long hair, and very high foreheads, giving the impression that all features were located in the lower half of their faces. They were wearing transparent helmets and turquoise-blue suits like ski outfits. The object hovered at a tilted angle as the occupants apparently observed the area below.

No exact day is recorded, but in November 1958 two "part-time" soldiers reportedly observed two huge figures who made "gurgling noises," from their slit trench at Deeside, England, not far from Balmoral, Scotland. The men were on maneuvers in the area and had been left to guard a small hilltop. The incident took place in the early hours of the morning just as daylight began to break. The light was insufficient to see clearly, but the soldiers estimated the intruders to be at least 7 feet tall and dressed in strange clothing which seemed to impede their movements.

Needless to say, the witnesses fled the scene and shortly after saw a huge, brightly glowing, disc-shaped object coming down the road behind them, only a foot or so above the ground. It swooped up over their heads and flew away, pulsating and giving off a shower of sparks. The men were in a state of shock when they were given shelter shortly after their experience by post office engineers in a hut near the scene.

A human-sized, headless, bat-winged creature approached a couple of teenagers on November 16, 1963, after the boys saw a bright object land in a field near Sandling Parke, Hythe, Kent, in England. Later investigation by teenagers curious about the report turned up an expanse of bracken that had been flattened, and three giant footprints, an inch deep, 2 feet long and 9 inches wide.

Crossing the Channel to France, we find a proliferation of reports of "little men" or "occupants" in the year 1954, where we will start our study of the situation on the Continent.

On August 23 in Lugrin, near Thonon, France, a man approached a landed object which looked like an aluminum trailer. Standing nearby were two small beings in silvery clothing who grunted like pigs. The object glowed red and flew away after the little fellows entered it.

Another type of ship was seen at Mourieras, France, on September 10. A farmer returning to the town at nightfall saw a man of average height, wearing a helmet, who made friendly gestures and entered the brush, after which a cigar-shaped object, estimated to be 16 feet in length, took off.

One of the best-known sightings of UFO occupants took place near Valenciennes, France, on the night of September 10. It was such a strange incident that it received some international press notice.

Maruis Dewilde was thirty-four years old in 1954, married, a father, and a serious, reliable metalworker in the Blanc-Misseron steel mills on the Belgian frontier. He lived with his family in a small home in the midst of fields and woods about a mile from Quarouble. His garden was adjacent to the National Coal Mines railway track running from Blanc-Misseron to St.-Amand-les Eaux, and grade crossing 79 was next to his house.

On the night in question, Dewilde was reading after his wife and children had retired. It was 10:30 P.M. when he heard his dog Kiki barking, and thinking there was a prowler in the vicinity of his property, he took a flashlight and went outside.

Dewilde walked to his garden, found nothing en route, then spotted a dark mass on the railroad tracks less than 6 yards from his door. He thought at first that someone had left a farm cart there. At that point his dog approached, crawling on her belly and whining, and simultaneously he heard hurried footsteps to the right of him. The dog began barking again and Dewilde directed his flashlight toward the sound of the footsteps.

What Dewilde saw startled him greatly. Less than 3 or 4 yards away, beyond the fence, were two creatures, walking in single file toward the dark mass at the tracks. Both creatures were dressed in suits similar to those of divers, and light was reflected off glass or metal in the area of their heads. Both entities were small, less than 3½ feet tall, but had very wide shoulders and the helmets covering their heads looked enormous. The legs looked very short in proportion to the height of the little "men," and Dewilde could not make out any arms.

After the first fright passed, Dewilde rushed to the gate, intending to cut them off from the path or to grapple with one of them. When he was about 6 feet from them, he was blinded by a very powerful light somewhat like a magnesium flare which came from a square opening in the dark mass on the tracks. He closed his eyes and tried to scream but couldn't, and he felt paralyzed. He tried to move but his legs would not function.

Shortly, Dewilde heard the sound of steps at his garden gate, and the two creatures seemed to be going toward the railroad. The beam of light finally went out and he recovered the use of his legs and headed for the track. But the dark object had begun to rise, hovering lightly, and Dewilde saw a kind of door closing. A low whistling sound accompanied a thick dark steam which issued from the bottom of the object. The object ascended vertically to about 100 feet altitude, turned east, and when it was some distance away it took on a reddish glow. A minute later it was completely out of sight.

After he regained his senses, Dewilde woke his wife and a neighbor, told them of his experience, then ran to the police station in the village of Onnaing, a mile distant. He was so upset and his speech so confused that the police thought he was a lunatic and dismissed him. From there he went to the office of the police commissioner where he told his story to Commissioner Gouchet.

Dewilde's fear was so evident that Gouchet realized something extraordinary must have taken place, and the next morning his report brought investigators from the Air Police, and the Department of Territorial Security. These teams, along with police investigators, questioned Dewilde and then examined the area where the dark object had rested. They found no footprints in the area, but the ground was very hard. However, they did find five places on three of the wooden ties which had identical impressions, each about 1½ inches square. The marks were fresh and sharply cut, indicating that the wooden ties had been subjected to very great pressure at those five points.

The impressions were never satisfactorily explained, but railroad engineers who were consulted by the investigators, calculated that the amount of pressure required to make the marks was approximately thirty tons.

An examination of the gravel of the roadbed showed that at the site of the alleged landing the stones were brittle as if calcined at very high temperature.

And lastly, several residents in the area reported that they had seen a reddish object or glow moving in the sky at about the time Dewilde indicated that the object had left.

The next landing incident took place on September 17, 1954, between Vouneuiel-sur-Vienne and Cenon on Route D-1. Monsieur Yves David was bicycling along the road at about 10:30 P.M. The night was dark and the moon had not risen. The region is wooded with many bushes and hedges. David's headlight gave only a dim light and he could not see very well.

As David drew near Le Pontereau, near Cenon, he felt a sensation of prickling and/or itching all over his body, somewhat like an electric shock. Unable to continue, he stopped and got off the bicycle. Since his light worked from a generator fed by pedal power, it went out, and he was in total darkness. The prickling sensation had not left, and he felt paralyzed. However, his eyes were getting used to the darkness and he noticed, not far ahead on the road, a strange machine which appeared to be about 9 feet long and 3 feet high.

By this time, David was terror-stricken. He was unable to move, and he saw a silhouette move away from the dark mass and approach him. It was a small "creature," much smaller than a man, and it came to him and touched him on the shoulder, uttering an incomprehensible and completely inhuman sound at the same time. It then moved back to the machine where it disappeared and seconds later the dark object gave off a greenish light and flew off at great speed and vanished in the sky.

As soon as the object left, David recovered the use of his limbs, got onto his bike, and headed for home at Pontgame where he told of his experience. He was trembling with fear.

With just these few sightings we begin to see a general correlation—little men at night in lonely places. In some instances they seem afraid of the people who happen upon them unexpectedly; in others they seem bold enough to attempt some sort of contact.

There is a considerably larger number of landings of UFOs which involve the observation of strange beings than we cannot possibly present within the pages of this book, and so we have chosen those which are a fair representation and, specifically, of different types. The actual number of reported landings, recorded throughout the world and especially in Europe, number several hundred.

Quite a famous landing took place on September 26, 1954, and it is quite familiar to UFO students the world over. On that date Madame Leboeuf, of Valence, France, had gone to gather mushrooms in the woods not far from the cemetery at Chabeuil about 4:00 o'clock. There were a few people visiting the cemetery at the time. The dog began to bark and then began howling as if in misery. Madame Leboeuf looked around and saw that the animal was standing at the edge of a wheat field in front of something which she thought at first was a scarecrow.

Upon approaching the dog, she saw that the "scarecrow" was some kind of a small diving suit which appeared to be made of translucent material. The whole affair was about 3 feet or a little larger, and the helmet was translucent also. But suddenly she realized that something was inside of that suit and that "it" was looking at her. She later said she got the impression of eyes, but that they seemed to be larger than human eyes. At this moment the thing began to move toward her with a sort of quick, waddling walk.

Until the creature, or whatever it was, began to approach her, Madame Leboeuf had only experienced slight surprise and mild curiosity, but when it started toward her she became frightened, screamed, and fled into a nearby thicket to hide. When she turned to look again she saw nothing unusual, but the dog had begun to howl again, accompanied by the howls of the other dogs in the village.

Next, to her surprise, a large, circular, and somewhat flattened metallic-appearing object rose from behind nearby trees and moved away at low altitude, making a whistling sound as it flew. It gained elevation as it crossed about the wheat field, then veered and took off toward the northeast at high speed, gaining altitude all the time.

Meanwhile, Monsieur Leboeuf heard his wife's scream, as well as the whistling sound, and ran to her as did some of the people at the cemetery. Soon practically the whole village was on the spot.

At the place from which the "aircraft" had risen a circular area was found about 10 or 11 feet in diameter, in which the shrubs and bushes were crushed. A 3-inch branch on an acacia tree at the edge of the circular area was broken as if from pressure from above. The branch on another acacia tree, which hung over the circular area at about 8½ feet from the ground, was stripped of leaves. For a few yards at the beginning of the wheatfield across which the object had flown, the wheat was flattened out in radiating lines.

Police and reporters were struck by the nervous shock suffered by Madame, the physical traces left by the object, the number of people who had heard the whistling sound. Madame Leboeuf suffered a state of nervous collapse and spent two days in bed with high fever. The dog was still visibly frightened and tremulous after three days had passed.

A half an hour after Madame Leboeuf's ordeal, witnesses at Col du Chat, which is 65 miles northeast of Chabeuil, saw an object arrive at that location.

On September 30, eight construction workers near Marcilly-sur-Vienne, France, saw a disc-shaped object on the ground, and a small man-shaped being wearing a helmet standing nearby.

On the same day, Bernard Devoisin and Rene Coudette, both eighteen years old, of Vron (Somme), France, were riding their bicycles on route D-27 at about 6:45 P.M. At a point about two and a half miles from Ligescourt they both suddenly spotted a luminous object in the middle of the road. It emitted an orange light, was circular, estimated to be 6 feet high and reminded the boys of a haystack. It seemed to be about 150 yards ahead of them.

Near the object something moved, which they first thought was an animal, but as they approached it they saw that it was a creature "the height of a child" and dressed like a diver. It got into the glowing object which took off when they were about 70 yeards from it.

Investigators of this incident found the boys to be sincere and of good reputation in their home community. Subsequent events in the area (investigated and studied after days, weeks, and months later in some cases) indicated that an object or objects of the same description were reported by hundreds of other witnesses in the hours that followed the sighting on D-27. Two and a half hours later, a car was pursued by a UFO near Rue and Quend. The driver, butcher M. Galant, said an orange-colored glowing object flew low along the road and followed his car for about 800 feet. He had no knowledge of the incident on D-27.

The hairy ones come onto the scene on October 5 at Loctudy (Finistere). A baker, drawing water from a well at night, was surprised to see an object about 10 feet in diameter on the ground nearby. From the object emerged a small being with a face covered with hair and large eyes "as large as the eggs of a raven." The strange little creature approached the man, touched him on the shoulder, and made unintelligible noises. The baker called his boss, whereupon the dwarfish creature got back into the craft, and it flew away.

On that same day, near Mertrud (Haute-Marne) a road mender named Narcy saw a strange object on the road. A small, hairy creature approached it, got in, and it took off. Investigation showed traces on the road where the object had sat.

The little men put in an appearance at Rinkerode, near Munster, Germany, on October 9. Herr Hoge, a projectionist, reported to authorities that he had seen four occupants of a cigar-shaped craft which landed about 250 feet or more off the road. According to his story, he was returning home that evening when he saw a blue light on the side of the road which at first appeared to be an aircraft making an emergency landing. Hoge watched four small men, about 4 feet tall, who appeared to be wearing rubber overalls at work near the underside of the craft. Further description in the poor light yielded only the fact that they seemed to have large chests and heads and very small, thin legs.

On the same date as the Hoge incident, Jean Bertrand was driving on a road near Carcassonne (Aude), France, when he came upon a metallic sphere sitting on the road ahead of him. The top half, he reported, seemed to be transparent material of some kind, and he saw two human-shaped figures standing inside. As he approached, the object took off at high speed.

A round machine was seen at about 6:30 P.M. in Pournoy-la Chetive (Moselle), France, according to four children. They told authorities that they had been roller-skating when they saw something bright near the cemetery. They approached and found that it was a round machine, about 8 feet in diameter, standing on three legs. A little man, about 4 feet tall came out of it. In his hand he held a light of some kind which blinded the children. They said they managed to see that the creature had large eyes, a hairy face, and was dressed in a "sort of black sack." The creature, the children reported, spoke to them but they could not understand what it said. Then it turned off the light it held. The children became frightened and ran away. When they overcame their fright sufficiently to look behind them, they saw something which was very bright flying through the sky at great speed.

A "little man" wearing boots "without heels" and a diving suit was seen that same night by a farmer in Lavoux (Vienne). He was riding his bicycle when he saw the creature which shone a "double-beamed" light at him. The witness reported that he was paralyzed throughout the incident. The creature, which had "very bright eyes," a very hairy chest, and two "headlights" walked along the road for a minute, then entered the forest and did not reappear. No object or craft was seen in conjunction with this appearance of a strange entity, but it is included in this listing because of the similarity of the "little man" to the descriptions of others in incidents involving UFOs.

A considerable distance away, at Teheran, Iran, three days later on October 12, Chasim Faili observed a disc-shaped object which hovered close to the ground. Inside the disc a small entity, dressed in black, was clearly seen. Faili, thinking he was about to be kidnaped, screamed, whereupon a crowd gathered. The object departed as the people began to arrive on the scene.

This particular incident is unique in that it took place in a densely populated area as opposed to little-traveled highways, dark byways, and other isolated spots.

Another object which left some familiar evidence was seen taking off from a field at La Croix Durade, France, at 4 A.M. on the same day. It was luminous, and it left the grass flattened in a 50-foot area.

Morocco was visited by a small being on October 12th also, when a French engineer was driving to Port Lyautey through the Mamora forest and saw a small being in silver clothing about 4 feet in height entering an object which soon took off. This incident took place in the afternoon, one of the few sightings of entities during the daylight hours.

M. Olivier, an ex-pilot, and two others saw a reddish disc about 12 feet in diameter with a small being close by. This incident took place on October 13, 1954, in Bourasole, near Toulouse, France. The three men were not together but all saw the same thing. They reported that a small being, about 4 feet in height, wearing a bright suit "like glass," with a large head and two enormous eyes, was near the craft, which was surrounded by a glow. One of the men approached the object, but was paralyzed. The object then took off, throwing the man to the ground.

These incidents, some of which are described in *The Humanoids,* a special issue of *The Flying Saucer Review,*took place during the UFO flap in France in 1954, and such a concentration has not occurred since. Aimé Michel analyzed the reports in *Flying Saucers and the Straight Line Mystery,* cited in Chapter I, including many landing incidents, both with and without occupants.

The rather indistinct figure of a human-shaped entity was observed by Dr. Henri Robert on October 16, 1954, in the village of Baillolet. Robert saw four objects flying at about 1,000 feet altitude, one above the other. Suddenly one of the craft dropped to the ground much like a dead leaf floating to earth, about 350 feet in front of Robert's car. Then Robert felt a kind of "electric shock," his engine stalled, and the headlights went out. The car stopped just as the object touched the ground.

The doctor, incapable of movement as though paralyzed, watched a figure which appeared to be about 4 feet tall moving in the light of the object, then everything went dark. Some time later the lights of the car went back on, and the witness saw the object taking off toward the north, above the road. The doctor called the authorities when he arrived in Londinieres and reported the incident.

The "dead leaf" movement of a landing or slow-moving disc has been described in many reliable and well-documented UFO reports throughout the world and was first noted as one of the outstanding characteristics of saucer-shaped craft over the United States in the early years of the mystery.

Two helmeted beings emerged from a gray, disc-shaped object approximately 40 inches high and 15 feet in diameter on October 17 at Cabasson near Corbieres, France. A sixty-five-year-old man, out hunting with his dog near the junction of a canal and a river, suddenly came on the object sitting on the ground less than 150 feet in front of him. The witness, frightened then by the helmeted occupants, turned and ran, but the dog approached the object. It soon retreated, however, and its master noted that it walked in a peculiar way for some time, as if partially paralyzed.

A mass sighting of an object took place at about 8:40 P.M. on the night of October 18 in Fontenay-Forcy, France. A man and his wife saw a glowing cigar-shaped object of a reddish color in flight. It suddenly dived toward them and landed not far from the road but hidden from sight by the surrounding brush. The couple walked to the top of a hill where they found themselves face-to-face with a human-shaped being about 3 feet tall who wore a helmet. The "eyes" appeared to glow an orange color. One of the witnesses lost consciousness. Four other witnesses reported observing the machine in flight at the same time as the couple from another location. A third group of independent witnesses in Sanson-la-Poterie observed the craft as it flew away at high speed and low altitude, illuminating the countryside.

An incident involving two of the "little folk" and one of normal size took place at Route N-437, on the shore of Lake St. Point in Doube, France, also on the 18th. Mademoiselle Marie-Louise Bourriot was returning to her home in Montperreux by motorcycle at 10:45 P.M. She had reached a spot near an orphanage when she spotted a bright red light ahead of her which illuminated the whole road. She thought little of it, taking it for granted that it was a car, and shortly the light went out. She continued along her way. Not much further along the road, near a mill, she saw to her left a creature of human form who appeared a little under average human height and dressed in some kind of light-colored one-piece garment. As Miss Bourriot came abreast of the "man," two small creatures, like dwarfs, walking on two legs but with shapes difficult to describe, crossed the road from the right and joined the creature.

Until this time, Miss Bourriot had not been too concerned, but she now became frightened and speeded up. A little further on, she turned around and looked behind and saw a luminous object rising vertically above the lake at great speed. She reported her experience and a search of the area the next day disclosed small footprints in the field from which the little creatures had come, as well as lightly marked "furrows."

One of the most puzzling incidents involving occupants took place at about 9 P.M. on the evening of the 18th. Mr. and Mrs. Labassiere of Royan, France, were driving on Route N-50 when they saw an object "shaped like a balance" at low altitude in the sky. One of the "pans" of the balance was orange, the other was red, and they appeared to be linked by a trail of luminous green. The whole apparition was swaying or "bouncing." Shortly the two "pans" stopped and hovered above a field not far from the witnesses. The two sat spellbound as the luminous beam uniting the two objects faded and disappeared, and the objects landed separately, but just a short distance apart. In the dim light emanating from the objects, the Labassieres saw two very small creatures which approached each other, passed without stopping, and changed vehicles. Then the two ball-like objects vaulted into the sky at a dizzying speed and disappeared over the horizon within seconds.

What is outstanding about this incident is the obvious fact that the pilots or occupants of the two vehicles changed crafts. The puzzling aspects are the luminous green beam, or whatever it was, which connected the two vehicles, the possible reason for the exchange, and whether or not the "beam" had something to do with the exchange. Inasmuch as this is the only incident of its kind, and the two objects with their connecting beam were seen by many others on the night in question (although without the added detail of the creatures and the exchange of crafts), this would seem to indicate that the sighting was a real one of a real object or objects, and leads one to conjecture on the meaning of the "beam." Was it a means of communication or a possible power exchange? Was one "pilot" relieving another who had been "on duty" for a considerable period of time? This might seem to be the answer, but it does not account for the exchange of craft, for they seemed to be identical. Could one have been having mechanical trouble, so that a replacement was delivered?

The questions about an involved, detailed incident such as this one are myriad and it seems that only through study of a considerable number of reports will we find any answers.

Another landing in a farm area took place on the night of October 27, during the 1954 flap. A farmer saw an elongated object with a light on each end which landed in a pasture. He was too frightened to investigate. Two hours later a motorcycle stalled and its rider fell from the machine. The farmer had notified residents of the village who went to investigate and found the object had moved somewhat according to the farmer's estimate of where it had first landed. Upon approaching the thing, the witnesses saw two beings about 40 inches tall who walked stiffly about in silvery clothing. The craft eventually took off without noise. This was at Les-Jonquerets-de-Livet (Eure) in France.

Three figures in light-colored clothing and transparent helmets were seen at Monza, Italy, on November 8, 1954, by a crowd of about a hundred fifty people who went to investigate a light in a stadium. The three were near a disc-shaped ship sitting on three legs. The beings made "guttural" sounds among themselves. One of them had a dark face and a "trunk" or hose coming up to his face. As with the others, this craft left upward without any sound.

Rabbit-stealing dwarfs figure in the last occupant case for 1954. At Isola, in northern Italy on November 14, a farmer watched a cigar-shaped craft land near him and hid to watch. Out of the machine came three small dwarfish beings dressed in metallic "diving suits," who centered their attention on the rabbits in their cages. The beings made strange noises among themselves.

Convinced the things were going to steal the animals, the farmer slipped away, got his rifle, and returned and aimed it at the dwarfs. The rifle would not fire and it became so heavy in the man's hands that he had to drop it. He also found that he could not move or speak. The dwarfs took the rabbits, got into their craft, which like most of its type, left soundlessly with a bright trail behind it. After the dwarfs had left, the farmer found he could move again and he picked up his gun and fired it, but the object was too far away to hit. He told the story to his family; it soon spread and was investigated. The witness is considered to be reliable.

Another incident, which may be a forerunner of the 1965 reports in the United States of UFOs around electrical installations and high tension lines, took place in France on May 10, 1957, a considerable length of time after the 1954 "flap." This one is most outstanding because of the number of witnesses and the duration of the sighting.

Michel Fekete, a twenty-nine-year-old Hungarian World War II refugee, was a railroad worker in 1957 and was riding his bicycle home on the Miraumont-Beaucourt road at 10:45 P.M. As he rounded a bend in the road he was blinded by a big, powerful light on the road, around which he saw four silhouettes of human-shaped beings less than 5 feet tall, who seemed to be barring the road. Fekete, thinking he was being ambushed, dismounted from his bicycle and ran off the road where he hid behind an electrical transformer installation. From there he found the footpath to the home of friends, Mr. and Mrs. Rene Lepot. The Lepots and some friends, Mr. and Mrs. Rene Iklef, were in the kitchen when Fekete arrived at the Lepot home. When they let him in he was almost incoherent with fright but managed to gasp out the word "attacked!" He pointed out the window to the road, a scant 50 yards away.

The Lepots turned out the lights and the five of them went to the window and looked out. They all saw quite clearly a luminous object, pulsating in color between red and white. Also viewed in the light of the object were three silhouettes of men between 4 and 5 feet in height who were visible from the thighs up. The lower extremities were hidden by the road bank. The color of their clothing appeared to be a grayish-beige except for their huge heads which were darker in color, nearly black. No features could be distinguished, however. The three were moving about the road and the adjacent field with a "tottering" gait.

The five witnesses watched the scene for about twenty minutes, when another railroad worker, Mr. Demanchaux, joined them. After a while a car approached and the object's light went out. In the light of the car's headlights, however, the figures were still visible. The six witnesses thought the driver must have seen them also. When the car had gone the white light reappeared, less brilliant than before, just above the road. It rose rapidly and silently into the sky at a 45° angle toward the northeast and by 11:15 it was completely out of sight.

Investigation of the spot where the object had sat revealed a 15 foot circle of apparently freshly deposited matter which was identified as asphalt. It was also found that the iron fence posts along the road were strongly magnetic, but all were equally so and no specific significance was attributed to it. No one was able to furnish an explanation as to why the object had dropped the asphalt, if indeed it had.

In a widely publicized explanation, the local mayor said that his wife had taken a lantern out to look at the cattle shortly before 10:45, and that the observers may have mistaken her and the lantern for the scene at the road. The incident was thoroughly investigated by Aimé Michel, however, who completely discounted the story. Also, the witnesses checked out as reliable, honest, and good observers.

Our next case took place on the first of July 1965 and has been exhaustively investigated by independent UFO researchers and organizations as well. It was the first sighting outside the United States that year which gained sufficient press attention to be carried on press wires in this country. The press coverage here, however, was totally inadequate and in some instances quite inaccurate.

The following is the account which came to French APRO members through a magistrate who wishes to remain anonymous at the moment: At 5:30 A.M., Monsieur Maurice Masse went to work at his lavender field a little north of Valensole. He was lighting a cigarette before starting his tractor when he heard a high-pitched whistling sound. He couldn't tell where the sound came from, so he stepped out from behind the stone pile, and saw before him an oddly shaped object which he assumed to be a helicopter. He immediately realized it was not, for the thing looked like a huge rugby football, about the size of a Dauphine car and was topped by a cupola. It rested on six "legs." Despite the odd nature of the object, Masse was curious and walked toward it along among the lavender plants. As he approached he saw two small beings of human shape bending over a lavender plant. Masse still was not frightened and walked toward them. When he was about 25 or 30 feet from them, one of the beings noticed him and pointed a kind of tube at him which paralyzed him on the spot. Although rooted to the ground, Masse was still able to observe what was going on.

He described the two "little men" as about the size of an eight-year-old child but their heads were huge, about three times the size of an adult's head. They were bald and completely hairless, and their skin as smooth as a child's and very white. Their bodies were covered by a coverall-like garment.

The size of the features of the beings was comparable to that of a human being except for the mouth, which was a lipless hole. Sounds made by the pair were unintelligible and did not seem to emanate from their mouths. Their general attitude as they looked at Masse was as if they were making fun of him.

After a few moments the little men jumped into their machine by way of a sliding door and it took off, flying into the west at an angle of 45°. Its speed was great as it moved away and a whistling sound like the sound which first attracted Masse was heard again.

The object left holes in the ground which were examined by many people including police personnel after they learned of the report. This incident is generally considered to be authentic, especially in view of Mr. Masse's good reputation.

In 1967 another possible electrical power-connected occupant case was reported to APRO's Swedish representative, K. Gosta Rehn. Mr. Gideon Johannson, sixty-seven, of Tranas, wrote to Mr. Rehn in September 1967, confiding that he and others had had a strange experience eight years before. After exchanging correspondence (Johannson wanted a guarantee that he would not be ridiculed), Mr. Rehn went to visit him on the 7th of October and got the full story.

It was 6:55 P.M. on September 29, 1959, in the little hamlet of Mariannelund where Johannson lived at the time. He was the electrician in charge of the central switch plant which served the plant where he was employed. He was on his way out of the house when his son, twenty-five, was coming in and they exchanged words about the blackout which had just plunged the area into darkness.

The son told Johannson: "It's jet black everywhere, but not up there in the air," and pointed at the sky. Looking up, Johannson saw a bright white light and thought it was an airplane with engine trouble and told his son to get the people out of the house because the thing was coming down toward the house and he was afraid it would set the house on fire. It took only seconds for the two men to realize that it was no airplane of any kind—it was completely soundless and hovering dead still in the air. Then it began to move, lowering itself slowly, passing over a nearby building, and buzzing the top of a maple tree, which when examined later, was found to be damaged. Johannson's son yelled at him to get out of the way as the thing was lowering itself toward the street. Not much could be made out of the craft itself because of the brilliant illumination inside the glass-enclosed top. Inside this transparent enclosure could be seen two figures. Johannson compared their size to that of twelve-year-old boys; they had chalk-white faces, long heads, very high foreheads, large dark eyes, long narrow noses, pointed chins, and were completely bald. He thought there were some kind of apparatuses sticking out of their ears and they wore black belts across their chests. One seemed to be very busy with something and the other just sat glancing from his companion to Johannson.

The object was now only 2 meters (6½ feet) above the street and Johannson later commented that it must have been quite small to have been able to navigate that street, which was 6 meters wide (20 feet). It came within 5 meters (16½ feet) of Johannson, enabling him to see the occupants quite clearly. Johannson followed it about 30 meters (100 feet) along the fence line of his lot and then it stopped and the light went out. They did not see where it went—there was just darkness everywhere. Johannson estimated that the whole incident took only two minutes, after which he hurried to the switch plant. He found nothing wrong there and in a few minutes the power came back on with no help from anyone. The power company never did find any cause for the blackout, but Johannson was of the opinion that the UFO was linked to it somehow.

In the following few days others approached Johannson and mentioned the blackout and what they had seen, verifying his own observations, but all indicated that they would just as soon forget about it, fearing that to talk of it publicly would only result in ridicule. Johannson noted that when the craft left, his pants flapped around his legs from the "draft" and he felt shaky. His wife told him that inside the house the radio rattled and went dead when the lights went out. Johannson noted that of the people in the town very few saw the craft because they were busy hunting for candles and lanterns.

In his report to APRO, Mr. Rehn said that he had interviewed the son who was living in Stockholm in 1967 and verified that although he did not see the occupants, he did see the object which frightened him badly. Rehn closed his report with these words: "The description (by Johannson) certainly gives the impression of rock-bottom honesty—that's all I can say."

We go to Scandinavia again for an interesting two-witness report of one occupant and a UFO which allegedly had a strange effect on the observers.

Aarno Heinonen, thirty-six, a forest worker, and Esko Viljo, thirty-eight, a farm worker, were avid and active skiers and on January 7, 1970, they were on their way to the ski area near Imjarvi, Finland, to redefine the ski track after a fresh snow. Upon arriving at the opening in the wood they stopped for a short rest. The time was 3:45 P.M., there were no clouds, no wind, and twilight was beginning.

Both of the men were startled to see a very bright light in the sky coming from the north. It was enveloped in a luminous fog, no sound was heard at first, and the "cloud" suddenly changed course, starting toward the two men while it gradually lost altitude. A humming sound was heard and it became louder as it neared the skiers. The "cloud" was red-gray in color, appearing to pulsate while brooms of smoke were emitted from the top of it, like smoke from chimneys. When it reached a distance of about 15 meters (50 feet) from the ground they could see that a round craft with flat bottom and of shining gray metal was inside the cloud. It was approximately 3 meters (10 feet) in diameter and around the lower rim there appeared three round balls. From the center of the bottom part a pipe-like affair protruded, estimated by the men to be about 2 meters (6¾ feet) in height and 5 meters (16¾ feet) in diameter. The humming sound increased and the object continued to approach them.

The cloud seemed to be thinning out more and more and the craft stopped at about 3 or 4 meters (10-13 feet) from the ground. At this short distance the men could see that the object was round and as it was inclined toward them they could see the dome on the upper part. Heinonen was watching the reddish-gray mist and said that suddenly he felt like something had seized him around the waist and pulled him backwards. He took a step back and at that instant noticed a creature was standing in the middle of the circle of light which issued from the "tube." The creature was about 90 centimeters (3 feet) in height, very thin with slender arms and legs, and a waxy, pale face. No eyes were noticeable and the nose gave the appearance of a "hook." The creature was clothed in some sort of overall material looking light green in color. The feet were encased in boots of a deeper shade of green and white gauntlets covered its hands and arms to its elbows. Claw-like fingers clutched a black box. Out of a round hole in the box a yellow light was pulsating.

Viljo said that he didn't get an impression of clothing on the little figure but noted that he glowed "like he was made of phosphorus." His head, Viljo said, was crowned with a conical helmet which appeared metallic.

According to the two men, the creature was in sight for only about 15 to 20 seconds. Then he turned, and the opening in the box was directed toward Heinonen and the light which it emitted was brilliant and almost blinding. The red-gray mist began pouring down from the craft and big sparks were jumping from the luminous circle on the ground. The sparks looked like luminous staffs, one centimeter (.40 inches) long and red, green and violet. They seemed to flow outward from the circle, quite slowly; some of them struck Heinonen and he was surprised that he did not feel them.

The red fog shortly encompassed the creature and he was no longer visible. The light cone on the ground then appeared to be "sucked up" into the opening at the bottom of the object. Then, when the red mist dissipated, the whole object was gone. The two men stood there for 2 or 3 minutes and Heinonen, who had been closest to the object and the lighted circle, experienced an insensitive feeling along his right side. When he attempted to step forward his right leg crumpled beneath him. Viljo had to half carry and drag his friend to his home which was located about 2 kilometers (a little over 1 mile) from the area where the object was seen.

Mr. Heinonen's mother, when questioned, revealed that when the men came home they pounded on the door and when she opened it they just stood there, Heinonen leaning on Viljo. Viljo's face was swollen and red. Heinonen was ill, complained of a backache, aching joints, and a painful headache. He later vomited, and in an interview with the writer of an article in a Finnish magazine, claimed that for a period of two months his urine appeared black in color.

Both men were examined by a doctor who stated that he had given them sleeping tablets because it was obvious to him that they were in shock. He attested to the complaints of Heinonen but said that both men were so excited in telling their story that they were nearly incoherent and felt that they had encountered some kind of electrical phenomenon.

More of the diminutive men type were reported to APRO by our representative for Yugoslavia in early 1973. The case was first reported to the Astronomical Geophysical Observatory which is the organization to which people report when UFOs are sighted. However, AGO doesn't take such reports seriously, so representative Milos Krmelj took it upon himself to investigate on behalf of APRO as well as his local UFO study group.

A Mrs. H. (anonymity requested), a sixty-year-old innkeeper at a village about 30 kilometers (17 miles) from Ljubljana where Kremlj lives, was on her way home from the hairdresser's at 9 A.M. on October 7, 1972. She was bicycling along a cartway when she spotted two figures a considerable distance away making their way along the edge of a hill.

The figures were dressed in "sort of white gowns" which reached the ground and there was a black belt around the area just below the chest and they wore black round-shaped caps on their heads. The faces appeared dark, she said, and she was not able to observe features (possibly because of the distance because at their nearest point they only came within 150 meters, approximately 475 feet).

The lady said that the spectacle was so strange that she descended from her bicycle and walked for awhile in order to watch them. Then she climbed back on her bicycle and proceeded to follow their tracks. However, because it was getting late she decided to go home, afraid that her family had not awakened and that the inn was not open. She looked around for someone else, but not seeing anyone, she left. By then the figures were out of sight. She told her husband of the experience, suggesting that they go back to see what it was all about, but he didn't want to go and the matter was forgotten.

Mrs. H. said that one of the figures was about 1 meter (40 inches) in height and she got the impression that one of the figures was a head higher than the other. They walked together, she said, with their shoulders touching.

When Mrs. H. told some local people of the occurrence they tended to ridicule the episode so she decided against talking about it further. During one discussion, however, one of the men at the inn asked where she had seen the figures and she told him and he then said that the night before his children had come running home very frightened, saying that they had seen two white figures near the field at the turnip plantation. The figures had "risen up" out of the turnip field and began to approach the children and they became frightened and ran home as fast as they could. The little girl was so frightened that her parents had to leave a light on in her room all night.

When questioned by Mr. Krmelj, the children gave the following information: At 7:30 P.M. the children saw two "strange creatures" with white hoods on their heads and the "rest of them" was black. They were moving slowly from the field toward the road. The children said that they were quite close when they rose out of the field, only about two meters (6½ feet) away. One of the youngsters said that their faces were "spotted" and that they wore a round, white cap and they seemed to be creeping on their hands and knees. They said they had seen them on two occasions, were not sure of exact dates, but that it was in the evenings, and that on the second evening the two figures walked upright and wore white "gowns" and one was larger than the other.

Although Mrs. H. did not see any sort of vehicle, whether on the land or in the air, the children said they saw what looked like a Fiat 750 which was behind the figures with its lights on. It could not be established that a Fiat 750 was, in fact, in the vicinity and inasmuch as small, compact-car-sized UFOs have been seen on the ground and flying through the air, it is possible that what the children assumed was a Fiat 750, was not. It was dark or fairly so, and the lights on the vehicle might have served to hide or camouflage the contours of the object.

It is interesting to note that the details of the second sighting of the figures by the children generally matches that of Mrs. H.'s description, i.e., that they were wearing "white gowns" and that one of them was taller than the other. Mr. Krmelj's report included information on other sightings of UFOs in that particular area of Yugoslavia indicating that at least some of them were operating in the vicinity around that time.

One of the most thoroughly investigated UFOnaut cases, and certainly one of the most interesting, took place in the middle of December 1973, and was published in *Inforespace* No. 18, the Journal of SOBEPS (Société Belge d'Etude des Phenomenes Spatiaux) which is a well-respected organization in Belgium dedicated to the study and research of the UFO phenomenon.

The weather was cold, although there was no snow, and a strong wind was blowing over the area of Vilvorde, some 12 kilometers (7 miles) to the northeast of Brussels, Belgium. The witness, Monsieur "V.M.," twenty-eight years old, and his wife, were in bed and asleep. At 2 A.M. he arose to go to the bathroom which is in a small outer yard adjoining the kitchen. In order to avoid waking his wife, he used a flashlight. Upon reaching the kitchen he heard a sound like shovel striking the ground which came from the outside. He also became aware of a greenish-colored light which filtered in through the gap at the left hand window curtain, and compared it with the diffused glow of an aquarium light. Knowing that the garden should be in total darkness at that hour, and puzzled by the noise as well, he went to the window and parted the curtain to behold an astonishing sight. At the other end of the garden was a small being about 1 meter, 10 centimeters (3½ feet) in height and wearing a shining green one-piece suit. The creature's back was to him in three-quarter profile, he was of medium build and his head, arms, and legs seemed normal in appearance. The green uniform was very bright and sparkling and Mr. M. compared it with the material of the upholstery of certain "buggy" types of cars (polyester tinged with metallic particles).

The entity's head was encased in a transparent globular helmet and a tube led from the rear of it down to join a sort of rectangular-shaped knapsack on his back. This knapsack covered his back from about the waist area upward to the level of the shoulder blade area on a man. The apparatus appeared to be the same material as the rest of the uniform.

The creature's clothing appeared to be smooth, without buttons or seams, and did not exhibit any evidence of fasteners of any kind, or pockets. The witness did notice a belt, and as the creature moved around he could make out a small bright red "box" on his abdomen at waist level, which was sparkling and luminous. The belt appeared to be about 3 to 4 centimeters wide (1¼-1½ inches) and the "box" about 8 centimeters (3¼ inches) long and 3-4 centimeters (1¼-1½ inches) wide. These estimates are very rough considering the distance involved. This box emitted a red light of constant intensity.

The creature's trousers, which were slightly baggy at the bottom, were thrust into close-fitting boots which had the same appearance as the rest of the clothing. At this time no detailed features of the entity could be made out. Although his hands were the same shape as those of humans, they were gloved and the sleeves of his suit were tight at the wrists, but like the trousers, the rest of them were slightly full. V. M. said that from the rear the head looked round and black and he thought the creature had short hair. A luminous halo surrounded him from head to foot and also partly illuminated the ground around him and the wall which was located at his left. The creature made no sound and the witness could not detect any respiratory movement.

The creature was holding a device in his hands which closely resembled a vacuum cleaner or metal detector which was slowly being passed to and fro over a heap of bricks that the witness had gathered together a few days previously. The device had a long shaft which was bent at one end to form a handle, with a small rectangular box just below the handle. The instrument itself consisted of a thick rectangular plate with the front edge bevelled and the rear consisted of a cylinder with about the same diameter as the thickness of the plate. The shaft was connected to the instrument between these two areas. The device was the same color of the humanoid's clothing and the witness could detect no sound or light coming from it.

V. M. noticed that the small man seemed to have difficulty moving about for he would move slowly, with a waddle, bending his knees slightly. His gait seemed very heavy. At this point, V. M. made use of his flashlight, flashing it towards the end of the garden twice. Thereupon the creature turned around; he did not turn his head around, but rather brought his whole body around, suggesting that his neck might not have been movable. Then V. M. caught sight of the dark face for the first time. Neither mouth nor nose was visible, but he could distinguish a pair of ears which appeared somewhat pointed. The eyes were oval and yellow in color, quite large, bright, and surrounded by a green rim. V. M. said that on the iris of the eyes he noticed small, black, and red veinlets, and the pupil was black and somewhat oval. At times the lids would come down over the eyes and at such time the face became completely dark for a few moments. But when the eyes were open these lids were not visible.

The creature stood there with the device in his left hand and seemed to answer V. M.'s flashlight signals by raising his right hand and giving the "V" signal, holding up the index and second fingers. Then he turned away and with waddling gait and arms gently swinging, walked off toward the back wall.

At the wall, the creature placed one foot flat against it and then without hesitation did likewise with the second foot and walked straight up the wall with no change of pace except that his knees did not bend. He continued to hold the instrument in his hand and to swing his arms as though walking normally on flat ground. When he reached the top of the wall, which is about 3 meters (10 feet) high, he walked over the top and down the other side, his body perpendicular to the side of the wall, and was out of V. M.'s sight.

About four minutes after this astonishing exhibition, a vivid halo of light appeared beyond the wall and the witness heard a faintly perceptible "chirring" sound which seemed to be muffled by the wind. Then a round object began to slowly rise above the top of the wall, probably only a few meters from it. After rising a short distance, the object halted and remained stationary for about another four minutes, still giving off the chirring noise which was compared to the sound of a cricket rubbing its wings together, and with the same amount of loudness. V. M. thought the diameter of the object might have been about 5 meters (16½ feet) based on the width of his garden. The upper half was an orange color, phosphorescent, and topped with a transparent cupola which emitted a greenish light. The lower half of the object was a dark red color and on this area, very much in evidence, were three lights arranged horizontally; the left one being blue, the middle one yellow, and the one at the right was red. These lights flashed on three times in sequence. The humanoid he had seen on the ground was clearly outlined in the greenish light of the cupola, but he could see no other detail in the "cabin." On the periphery of the object, the witness said, there issued what looked like showers of sparks like those from a cigarette lighter. They were located at the point where the dark lower part and the bright upper part came together. On the bright upper part was a round black circle traversed diagonally from right to left by a yellow lightning flash. This Mr. V. M. took to be an emblem of some kind.

The object then rose again vertically about 20 meters, still horizontal, and began to rock gently to and fro. The sparks were still coming out all around it. Then the "chirring" sound grew in volume and became a sort of hiss and the craft increased speed and shot straight up into the atmosphere, leaving behind it a luminous trail. Within a few seconds it was a tiny point of light among the stars, then lost to view.

V. M. said that at no point in the experience did he feel fear or hostility and that he found no marks on the ground or on the wall.

The investigation did not get under way until several weeks after the fact. The area where the object had allegedly been on the ground was on the property of the Ursuline Sisters' Convent but a search there revealed nothing. It was established that the Convent's vegetable garden, from which V. M. saw the object ascend, was sufficiently isolated so that a vertical rising aircraft such as a helicopter could have landed and taken off without being detected.

Another incident from the pages of *Lumières Dans La Nuit* was contained in their # 139 issue dated November 1974, but actually took place months earlier on February 28.

A single witness case, this report was made by a man who is described by his acquaintances and friends as a very simple man, fifty years of age, grown old prematurely by hard labor in an open forge. Until his observation he absolutely did not believe in the "humbug" concerning "flying saucers" and he knew nothing of UFO phenomena. Even his family, after being told of his experience, showed no interest, and his wife and two sons did not even bother to go see the place or the landing traces on the ground.

After his experience the witness proceeded on to work, where in response to questions, he revealed the details of his encounter with strange humanoids. As a result he was ridiculed and became the object of unsettling raillery and ultimately became quite depressed. Consequently, when the experience came to the attention of researchers the investigation was made quite difficult because the witness did not want to talk. Eventually he consented to an interview and the investigators learned the following.

At 5:30 A.M. on the day in question Mr. X left his home and took the road (State Route 38, then called RN 363) to Origney-en-Thierache (Aisne Province), France. He passed the last houses of the hamlet of Routieres and took the curve just before the bridge over the Thon (a river between Oise and Etreoupont), seeing nothing but that part of the roadway illuminated by his headlight. After crossing the bridge, he was suddenly stopped and was "nose to nose" with two "cosmonauts," as he called them. The man was stupefied and did not understand what had happened, so he asked them how they had stopped him since he had not slowed down or braked. He then noticed a large dark mass, circular, to the left in the grass below the level of the road (about 1 meter below or 3.3 feet) and at about 35 meters (110 feet) from him and immediately thought that this must be their "ship." He noticed nothing else—no signals, noise, absolutely nothing except the dark circular mass.

The witness had put his feet on the ground to keep his balance, the two figures were standing facing him on each side holding the handlebars, and it seemed that they were watching him. They appeared about 1.7 meters (5 feet, 6 inches) tall and wore dark uniforms like an astronaut's, including a helmet with an opening for the face, but nothing could be distinguished because it was dark inside and it seemed as though their faces were covered. No other details could be made out, except that the gloves had five fingers which were joined to the suit at the shoulders.

The witness later estimated the height of the object in the field as 1.8 to 2 meters (6 feet to 6 feet, 8 inches) and was "as large as two cars."

The "cosmonauts," after stopping the motorcycle, made very expressive gestures which the witness described as quasi-human, and seemed to be telling him that they needed food. He panicked. The two UFOnauts were looking at each other, turning their helmets. Then the one on the left made a sign to the one on the right and the witness saw the latter "search" with his hand behind his back for something which the witness could not see. Then this being showed a morsel of a substance of about 1.2 centimeters (.39 inch) on the palm of his right hand and made new signs with his left hand, seeming to indicate that the witness should eat what he was offered. Completely panicked, the witness grabbed the material (which seemed like a bit of chocolate), put it in his mouth, and ate it. The substance had no taste and was of a softer consistency than chocolate. The two entities watched as he ate; then when he was finished, they let go of his motorcycle and he left as quickly as he could.

Upon questioning later, the man could not tell whether the engine of his cycle had been stopped or not, and being glad to get out of the predicament, he did not come back nor did he even look back as he made his hasty departure.

The investigation of this case was carried out two months after the fact and inspection of the area where the dark mass had sat revealed nothing; however, neighbors and friends who went to the area after hearing the witness's story said that they had found an area which was circular in shape in which the grass had been flattened or compressed. This area measured 4 or 5 meters (13½-16½ feet) in diameter. The "beings" were about 1.7 meters (5 feet, 6 inches) tall and wore dark uniforms like astronauts, including a helmet with a transparent area for the face, although the witness could see no details because it was dark inside the helmet and their faces appeared to be covered. The only detail noted was the fact that the gloves had five fingers and the gloves were a part of the overall garment.

An editor's note at the conclusion of the article pointed out that the "forced" eating posed a problem to researchers, but that upon recalling the incident about the teeth in the Betty and Barney Hill case, there seemed to be a rational explanation. In the Hill case, during the examination the entities apparently found out that Barney's teeth were removable. One of the creatures brought them into the room where Betty was being examined and showed them to the entity who was examining Betty, whereupon he tried to take her teeth out. We can speculate that if there is any relationship between the entities in the Hill case and those who confronted the motorcyclist near Routieres, they might have wanted merely to see how human beings chew their food. In the Hill case, the entities had no teeth, and when they opened their mouth to communicate, a membrane inside vibrated and made a humming noise.

The range in size of the UFOnauts seems to be from diminutive to entities of almost gigantic proportions. The case we are about to examine involves entities, who by human standards, are much larger than the average man. It was first published in the June 1974 issue of the Spanish publication *Stendek*, and has since been disseminated in the UFO literature throughout the world.

Maximiliano Iglesias Sanches was twenty-one at the time of his experience, which took place on March 21, 1974, at 2:15 A.M. Maxi was a driver for one Aquilino Garrido Bernal in Lagunilla, Spain, and he lived in Salamanca. At 9:30 P.M. on the 20th Maxi drove to Pineda, completed his assignment, and went to visit his girl friend who lived there.

At about 2:15 the next morning he began his return trip and had just passed the town of Horcajo, enroute to Lagunilla, when he observed a powerful white light on the roadway some 700 or 800 meters (2,250 to 3,000 feet) ahead. He first thought it might have been the lights of a truck or car, but as the distance between him and the light decreased to some 200 meters (650 feet), he realized something was amiss for the lights of his truck went out and the engine stopped.

It then became apparent that the light was actually a craft of some kind, appearing to be metallic in composition with no rivets, joints, seams or openings, and it stood on three round legs. The object, Maxi estimated, was 10 or 12 meters (33 to 40 feet) in diameter and the legs were by comparison very short, about a ½ meter (1½ feet) in height. He was certain that the object extended beyond both sides of the highway which is some 7 or 8 meters (23 to 27 feet) wide at that point. The object gave off a faint light which was even all over its surface, and Maxi described it as a light "like nothing I have ever seen," making it difficult to describe. To the right of the object, at an altitude of some 15 or 17 meters (50 to 56 feet), was another object which was hovering motionless and gave off the same but a much weaker light.

Suddenly, to the right of the craft on the ground, two beings appeared and Maxi could not discern whether they were entering or leaving the object or, in fact, *where* they came from. They stood in front of the object in the center of the road and began to gesticulate with their arms. Maxi stood his ground and just looked at them and they continued to signal to him. Shortly, one of them made a half turn toward the object and disappeared to the right where he had initially made his appearance. The other remained where he was, watching Maxi, and then the other being reappeared from the right of the craft and rejoined his companion. They looked at each other and turned toward the craft, then went around the right side of the object and out of sight. A few seconds later the object ascended, making a noise which ceased when it hovered motionless.

When questioned about the "beings," Maxi said that they were between 1.90 and 2 meters tall (6 feet 4 inches and 6 feet 8 inches) and were dressed in tight-fitting outfits that covered their entire bodies. The material was brilliant and metallic looking like the ship, and rubbery-looking like the material of a diver's suit. They walked normally and were built like human beings although no detail of the face could be discerned because of the distance from Maxi and the fact that the only light was the light from the ship. This may have been the reason that the entities seemed to "disappear" when they went to the right of the ship and out of its glow.

The ship ascended very slowly until it was parallel to the other one and the distance between them was 1 or 2 meters (3½ to 6½ feet). At this time Maxi felt they would let him pass so he started the truck and continued his journey.

Some 150 to 200 meters (500 to 650 feet) down the road, Maxi stopped the truck to observe the two objects. He shut off the lights and got out, at which time the illuminated ship began to land in the same place. At this juncture Maxi decided he'd better leave and did so, rapidly.

The following morning Maxi told friends of his experience but no one believed him. However, when he described what had happened to him to his employer, Mr. Garrido, he believed Maxi and later told investigators that "he is a hard worker, very serious and incapable of lying."

Because he had another load of material to deliver to Pineda, Maxi returned to the town on the 21st and again visited his girl friend, telling her of his experience. She tried to convince him that he should stay in Pineda over night because she was worried about him; however he decided to return to Lagunilla anyway but left at an earlier hour—11:00 P.M.

Fifteen minutes later, and at the same spot where he'd had his experience earlier that day, he saw the same or similar objects again, only this time there were three of them and they followed his truck until they were about 200 meters (650 feet) away, then settled to the ground in a row in a field at the side of the road. Maxi decided to observe the objects so he turned off the engine and the lights and settled down to watch.

The light from each of the crafts was faint and Maxi could not detect any changes in the intensity, and the three were separated by a distance of some 8 or 9 meters (26.5 to 30 feet).

This time there were four "persons" instead of two, and like the first time the witness was not able to determine where they came from, only that they appeared and came to a position in the center of the highway in front of the crafts. They looked toward the witness while gesticulating among themselves. Then they signaled to Maxi and began to move in his direction, walking normally. At this point Maxi opened the door on the right side of his truck and began to run down the road, whereupon the entities quickened their pace. He turned around several times to determine their progress and realized that the gap between him and the beings was lessening.

Maxi then dove in the ditch along the side of the road and watched as the beings drew up to his location and passed him and then began searching for a distance of 14 or 15 meters (46 to 50 feet). Despite the fact that they at one point were so close that they almost touched him, they did not find him. When he saw them move off some distance he took that opportunity to flee and headed toward Horcajo, the nearest town. About 1500 meters (1 mile) from the town he saw its lights and when he got to town he talked to no one. After about ten minutes he worked up enough courage to return to where his truck was parked, hoping that the ships might have left, but they were still there. The beings were nowhere in sight.

Apparently feeling safe because the entities were not around, Maxi started toward his truck. The right hand door was closed and he distinctly remembered having left it open. Feeling apprehensive, he checked the inside of the truck before getting in. He tried to start it but with no success. At that juncture the four beings appeared again, walking along on the asphalt and moving toward the ship, and as before they disappeared from sight in the vicinity of the craft. Shortly, one of the ships began ascending, reached an altitude of 15 to 17 meters (50 to 56 feet) and then hovered motionless.

Then Maxi again tried to start his truck, was successful, and drove away. After driving about 200 meters (650 feet) he stopped his truck so that he could watch what was transpiring with the crafts behind him. Despite what had happened before he turned out the lights, got out of the truck, and walked toward the craft. Walking quietly Maxi approached to within some 8 or 9 meters (26.5 to 30 feet) and looked closely at the craft closest to him, attempting to learn how the beings entered and exited. But he could find no evidence of ports or doors—the entire surface was perfectly smooth. He then saw four beings doing something on the embankment of the roadway. Two of them were holding T-shaped instruments and a third held something which resembled a horsehoe. They did not speak or make any sounds and Iglesias could not make out what they were doing. Neither was he able to ascertain any details of the faces as they were covered with the same smooth material which encased the rest of their bodies.

Maxi estimated that he stood there for approximately three minutes and although he was extremely curious he decided to leave because his fear overcame any inclination to investigate further. The beings did not move toward him, indicating that they probably were unaware of his presence. He returned to the truck and without further difficulty proceeded on his way home.

On the following day he told his employer what had happened and was advised to report it to the Civil Guard. Investigators who returned to the scene with him found marks on the ground where the objects had landed in the field. On the highway where he said that one of the ships had landed they discovered a gouged spot which was in the form of a straight line, the depth indicating that it had been marked by a very heavy object. On the embankment were found two marks which the investigators assumed had been made by the "tools" or devices which Maxi had observed during his last observation. Nothing else was found.

This case, of course, raises more questions than it answers. It would seem that Maxi would have reported the objects when he went into Horcajo and bring witnesses back in order to verify what he had seen. But we must assume that these questions were thought of by the investigators and were answered to their satisfaction. Also, too often these reports lose something in the translation, no matter how careful and talented the translator. In a case such as this, the investigation can be on-going for months and sometimes years. Shortly after providing the interview which led to the report, Maxi Iglesias entered the military service, and investigators have had difficulty in contacting him for further interviews. Suffice it to say that Iglesias' report of the men with the covered faces is not unique, and unless he was a dyed-in-the-wool UFO researcher who has access to all of the literature, he would not have had knowledge of the "faceless" UFOnauts which have been reported in quite a few instances elsewhere.

His failure to report the happening when he went into Horcajo is perfectly understandable if one thinks about it in the context of a young man who does not want to face ridicule. American researchers have been living with the UFO enigma for twenty-eight years but there was relatively little UFO activity around the rest of the world until the wave of 1954. Even though France received the bulk of the "action" at that time, it was not until 1974 that the French people and the government came to grips with the problem. So it is not entirely unthinkable that a twenty-one-year-old Spaniard would hesitate to report having had such a bizarre experience as he claims he had near Horcajo.

CHAPTER IX

The Humanoids in South America

Early 1953 saw the emergence of a new kind of report out of South America. Prior to that time many incidents had been documented which concerned the presence of strange aircraft hovering or maneuvering in various areas. The new activity, however, concerned landed objects and humanoids of varying sizes apparently gathering plants and soil or rock specimens.

A strange case involving three entities apparently taking soil samples took place on January 3, 1953, near Santana dos Montes, Guanabara state, in Brazil. Mauricio Ramos Bessa, a hospital employee who lives some three hours from the town on a farm, had been shopping and was returning to his home via a shortcut when he saw a luminous object ahead of him. It appeared to be about the size of a Volkswagen bus, of metallic appearance, and hovered some 1.3 meters (4½ feet) from the ground. The lower half appeared flattened and the upper half was oval-shaped. Bessa stopped his car to observe. It approached to within 2 meters (6.5 feet) of Bessa's car, stopped, and two persons garbed in shiny gray clothing came out of the object from the bottom. One of them carried a cylinder of 12 to 14 centimeters (5 inches) in length which he used to scoop soil off the road.

When the figures first emerged from the object Bessa began to experience a severe headache and had difficulty seeing. When the two re-entered the object he did not see them climb upwards nor did he see the opening close because of the pain in his head. As soon as the two were gone the headache abruptly ceased.

Another entity was in the upper portion of the object behind a transparent panel. Bessa noted that this one wore an outfit which seemed to cover him completely, including his hands and head, and there was an open portion for the eyes but he did not note any detail of the eyes. The height of the beings he estimated to be from 1.30 to 1.40 meters (4 to 4½ feet). Their faces seemed to be flatter than a human's. They did not communicate with one another, except that one did make a motion with his head to the other. All in all Bessa had difficulty recalling details because of the headache and his terror which literally rooted him to the spot.

An extremely interesting case involving an object over a river took place on November 28, 1953, when Pedro Serrate was walking along the banks of the river Guapore in Bolivia. He saw the object some 50 meters (160 feet) from him and it approached to within 4 meters (13½ feet) of his position, making no sound. The thing was disc-shaped and Serrate estimated its dimensions as 4 meters (13½ feet) long, 2½ meters (8.5 feet) wide and 3 meters (6½ feet) in height. The hull seemed to be made of some kind of material resembling glass and was supported by metal beams in the material. It was of a dark blue color and in the rear and on each side there were curved tubes some 5 centimeters (5 inches) thick from which water was emerging. From the time he spotted the thing until it reached its nearest position to his location it had circled around over the river just above the surface. When close he noted six people, four of whom he assumed were men and two women, all of whom appeared no more than twenty years of age. They appeared to be of medium height and had blond hair and "rose-like" or pink complexions. All were dressed in outfits which were the same color as the ship, and when they became aware of Bessa's presence, the ship immediately ascended into the sky and was out of sight shortly.

There were no further cases involving occupants until the fall of 1954, when we received the following case forwarded by Joseph Rolas of Caracas, Venezuela: At about 2 A.M. on the morning of November 28, Gustavo Gonzales and his helper, Jose Ponce, set out from Caracas for Petare, a suburb, to pick up some produce to be put on sale in the markets of Caracas the next morning. Upon entering a street leading to the warehouse area, they saw a luminous spherical object hovering about 6 feet off the ground, and blocking their way. They stopped the truck and Gonzales got out to investigate. A dwarfish-looking, man-shaped thing about 3 feet tall, hairy, and with glowing eyes came toward Gonzales, who attempted to grab him. The little fellow struck Gonzales and sent him reeling about 15 feet. The little man then leaped at Gonzales, clawed hands extended. Gonzales drew his knife and made a stab at the creature, striking it in the shoulder, but the knife glanced off as though it had struck steel. Another of the little fellows emerged from a hatch in the side of the sphere, directed a light from what appeared to be a metallic tube at Gonzales, blinding him. At this point, the creature with whom Gonzales had scuffled leaped into the sphere, and it took off swiftly and was lost to sight in seconds..

During this scuffle, Ponce watched two other entities answering the same description as the first two, emerge from the side of the street carrying what appeared to be rocks or dirt in their arms. They leapt easily up into the sphere through the opening in the side. Alarmed, he ran to the police station about a block and a half away. He was telling his story when Gonzales arrived. Both men were questioned closely and it was determined that they had not been drinking and that both had obviously been badly frightened by something. They were given sedatives and Gonzales was put under observation for a deep, red scratch on his side.

On December 16, three young men were driving home from a dinner engagement in San Carlos, Venezuela. One of the men, Jesus Paz, asked the driver to stop by the road so that he could relieve himself. Shortly after he stepped off the side of the road, his friends heard him scream and, rushing to his aid, found Paz unconscious on the ground. A short distance away a hairy-looking little man was running toward a flat, shiny object which hovered a few feet off the ground. The object rose from the ground with a deafening buzzing sound and disappeared into the sky.

Paz was rushed to the hospital by his friends where he was treated for several long, deep scratches on his right side and along his spine. Authorities who interviewed the men said that all three were badly frightened and that Paz was in a state of shock.

On the same evening as the San Carlos incident, two young rabbit hunters, Lorenzo Flores and Jesus Gomez, were being interviewed about their reported encounter with strange little men on the night of December 10. The two had been hunting near the Trans-Andian Highway between Chico and Cerro de Las Tres Torres. They saw a bright object off the highway and approached it, thinking it was a car. They found it to be a shiny object which looked like two metallic soup bowls placed together lip to lip. They estimated its diameter to be about 9 feet and said it was hovering about 3 feet off the ground. Fire was issuing from its belly.

Then the boys saw four "little men" coming out of it. They said the creatures were about 3 feet tall and hairy. They spotted the boys and the four set upon Jesus and tried to drag him toward the "saucer." Lorenzo used his shotgun as a bludgeon and tried to beat them off, since he knew it was unloaded and he had no time to reload. "The gun seemed to have struck rock or something harder, as it broke in two," Flores reported later.

Jesus fainted during the melee, and Flores remembered only the apparent light weight of the "little men," their hairy bodies, and great strength. Investigation by authorities at the scene revealed signs of a struggle, and one of the doctors who examined the boys said both were almost hysterical when he questioned them. Both exhibited scratches and bruises and their shirts were torn to shreds.

In his evaluation of the incident, APRO's representative in Venezuela, Mr. Horacio Gonzales Ganteaume, pointed out that the gun is an expensive and coveted item for a young country boy and it wasn't likely that the gun had been deliberately broken in order to perpetrate a hoax.

December 19 was the next date for an "incident" involving small humanoids. Jockey Jose Parra dashed into the National Security office at Valencia, Venezuela, and told of his encounter with a half dozen "little men" near the local cement factory. Parra had been doing his running exercises in the cool of the night in an attempt to work off a little excess poundage. He had stopped when he spotted the little men pulling boulders from the side of the highway and loading them aboard a disc-shaped craft which was hovering just a few feet off the ground. Parra started to run away, but one of the creatures pointed something at him which gave off a violet-colored light and paralyzed him. He stood there helpless as the creatures got into the craft and it took off. Detectives who were sent to the area where Parra had his experience found strange tracks on the ground which could not be identified as either human or animal.

The publicity accompanying the aforementioned incidents moved a well-known Caracas doctor to come forward and tell of his experience with "little men," providing the press would protect his identity, which they did. On the same night as the Flores-Gomez incident the doctor was riding with his father between the La Carlota Airdrome and Francisco de Miranda Avenue at 6:30 P.M. His father suddenly pointed at the side of the road and the doctor stopped the car. Together, they watched two little men running into the brush. Shortly after they disappeared into the thickets a luminous disc-shaped object took off with a "sizzing" sound.

Two other incidents were then dug out of newspaper records and described in the large city dailies. One involved Jose Alves of Pontal, Brazil. Alves was fishing in the Pardo River on the evening of December 4 when a strange craft came down out of the sky in his general direction. He later estimated its size as 10 feet in diameter and said it looked like "two washbowls" stuck together, lip to lip. Too frightened to run, Alves sat transfixed as three little men, clad in white clothing and close-fitting skullcaps, emerged from a window-like opening in the side of the craft. Their skin appeared to be dark, but Alves could not get a good look at them because of the failing light. The little creatures took samples of grass, herbs, and leaves, and one of them filled a shiny tube with water from the river. They suddenly jumped back into the object, and it took off vertically and swiftly. Alves was sure the "men" were devils, never having heard of "flying saucers." His friends and acquaintances attested to his honesty and sobriety and believed his story.

The second story to come to light during the December interest in UFOs involved farmer Olmiro da Costa e Rosa, who on the evening of December 9 was working in his French bean and maize field in Linha Bela Vista, two and a half miles from Venancio Aires, Rio Grande do Sul, in Brazil.

Costa e Rosa heard a sound "like a sewing machine," whereupon the animals in the nearby pasture scattered and ran. He looked up and saw a strange object hovering "just above the ground," which looked like "an explorer's hat." It was cream-colored and surrounded by a smoky haze.

Three "men" were visible to Costa e Rosa. One was in the craft, his head and shoulders sticking outside an opening, and another was apparently examining a barbed-wire fence. Another approached Costa e Rosa, who dropped his hoe in surprise. The man then raised his hand, reached down and picked up the hoe, and gave it back to the farmer. He then stooped over, uprooted a few plants and started back toward the craft.

Somewhat reassured by these actions, the farmer advanced toward the craft. The man in the object and the one who had picked up the hoe made no motion toward him but the one near the fence made a gesture as if warning Costa e Rosa to stop, which he did. Some of the animals then approached, and Costa e Rosa, with gestures, told the strange creatures that he would give them one of the animals as a gift, but they didn't seem interested. Quite suddenly and unexpectedly the two men on the ground boarded the ship, which rose to about 30 feet, accelerated abruptly, and flew into the west at high speed.

The description of these men is most interesting: They appeared to be of "medium height," broad-shouldered, with long blond hair, extremely pale skin, and slanted eyes. Their clothing was light brown in color and seemed fastened to their shoes, which looked odd to Costa e Rosa as they had no heels. The farmer was questioned at length by authorities from Porto Alegre and it was determined that Costa e Rosa was a responsible, honest man.

Two days after the Venancio Aires affair, Pedro Morais, who lived less than a mile from Costa e Rosa, was preparing to go to a warehouse for supplies at 5:00 P.M. He heard a chicken squawking, and thinking hawks were raiding, he went outside to investigate. He could still hear the chicken but could not find it (and never did), for he saw an object which he described as looking like the "hood of a jeep," hovering just above the ground. The bottom resembled that of an enormous polished brass kettle. Morais then spied two human forms in a cultivated field nearby and he started toward the craft planning to register his displeasure at this trespass. As he did so, one of the "men" ran toward him while the other raised his arm in a gesture which appeared to be a warning to stop. Morais, angry, did not pay attention and continued toward the machine. The second man stooped quickly and pulled a tobacco plant out of the ground, then both of the creatures got into the craft which disappeared into the sky within a few seconds.

This particular incident involves a "new type" of occupant. Although human in shape, they both gave the appearance of being enveloped in a kind of yellow-colored sack—from head to toe.

Another renegade in the "occupant" reports involved seven-foot giants allegedly observed by Jose C. Higgins, a Brazilian survey worker on July 23, 1947, within days of a sighting by Kenneth Arnold over Mount Rainier in the state of Washington, U.S.A. This case surfaced in 1954. According to Higgins, a huge (150 feet wide) disc landed with a piercing whistling noise. Out of it came three giant creatures who were bald, had huge round eyes, no eyebrows, and were encased in transparent suits which covered their entire bodies.

Higgins reported that they seemed to shun bright sunlight, and when they attempted to lure him with gestures he eluded them, finally hiding in the brush where he watched them gamboling about, leaping, and tossing huge stones. They then re-entered the craft, which vanished toward the north.

A second sighting of the type just described was reported at Lago, southern Argentina in 1950. The observer, Wilfredo Arevalo, said that at 6:30 P.M. on March 18 he saw a huge disc land while another hovered above it. Through the transparent dome he saw "four tall, well-shaped" men, dressed in something like cellophane suits, who appeared to be working on some instruments. He was particularly struck by the pallor of their faces. When landing, the disc gave off a greenish-blue vapor. Arevalo had succeeded in getting within 500 feet of the object. The next day Arevalo and fellow cowhands found that the area where the object had rested exhibited burned grass, and they notified the Argentine Air Force and a Buenos Aires newspaper. It was later discovered that a similar object had been observed by others in the same area at the same time.

We have so far seen a couple of general types of UFO occupants, and it is obvious that unconnected sources are seeing the same thing. The bulk of the cases indicate a preponderance of small beings about 36 to 40 inches in height, but there is also another category made up of occupants ranging in size from about 4½ feet to 5 feet. Still another is "the giant" species, which is rare. The small hairy, animal-like beings with claws and hot tempers seem to be menial workers while the others are more docile and generally keep their distance, except on rare occasions.

We encountered another report claiming some sort of mental communication, related by Rubem Hellwig concerning his experience with average-sized beings near Santa Maria, State of Rio Grande do Sul, Brazil. Hellwig claimed that an object which looked like a melon or rugby football and about the size of a Volkswagen car landed at about 5:00 P.M. one day in March, 1954. He was driving, stopped his car, and walked to the craft. Two men were there with brownish faces and fair hair. One gathered specimens of grass; the other stayed in the machine. They spoke to Hellwig in a language he could not understand and yet he somehow knew what they wanted, which was where they could get some ammonia. He said he directed them to a nearby town, whereupon the craft glowed, gave off blue and yellow fumes, and vanished silently and instantly.

Hellwig further claimed that he met "the same" ship the next day, but with a different crew—a tall man with a fair complexion and two women with light-brown skin, long black hair, and large, dark, slanted eyes. They were clad in brown suede-like garments, and talked about the natural riches of Brazil, explaining that they were scientists. They also commented on the fact that Hellwig did not run away from them as had others in the past.

On November 14 at about 3:30 A.M. a Brazilian railroad employee allegedly saw three small human-shaped beings in tight-fitting, luminous clothing, who appeared to be examining the ground around the railroad tracks by the light of some kind of lantern. When the creatures spotted the man they entered an oval-shaped craft which rose into the sky and rapidly disappeared.

An unidentified motorist allegedly had a very eerie experience while driving on the highway some 15 kilometers (9½ miles) from the international airport of Pajas Blancas, Argentina, in April 1957. The engine of his car suddenly and inexplicably stopped and he said he got out to see what had happened and saw an enormous disc which he estimated to be about 18 meters (60 feet) in diameter and 4½ meters (14 feet) high, suspended some 15 meters (50 feet) above the ground in front of his car. Frightened, he ran and hid himself in a ditch beside the road.

With a sound like that of air escaping from a valve, the disc descended to an altitude of a little more than 2 meters (6½ feet) and from its base came a sort of elevator which came down almost to the ground. Out of this device came a man who approached the motorist and courteously asked him to come out of the ditch, all the time stroking him gently on the forehead as if to calm him. The being wore a tight-fitting outfit much like that worn by a diver and which seemed to be made of some kind of plastic.

This "man" took the motorist to the disc and they entered it by way of the elevator. Once inside he saw five or six men, dressed in a similar manner to that of the "man," who were seated in front of an instrument panel. A bright light illuminated the cabin and on the wall could be seen a series of large square windows which were not visible from the outside, which seemed very strange to the motorist.

The motorist was shortly taken back out and escorted to his car and the being put his hand on his shoulder as a gesture of departing and then got into the elevator which retracted rapidly into the disc. Then the disc, which appeared to be made of a blue-green, iridescent metal, ascended rapidly in a northwest direction. During the following hour the same or a similar object was allegedly seen in six or seven places in the same area.

Another instance of luminous suits, long hair, and diminutive size was reported by a Spanish naval officer, Miguel Espanol, and a companion, who claimed that on the night of October 10, 1957, they saw a huge oval or saucer-shaped object which stalled the truck in which they were riding. Then it hovered, during which time they could clearly see the seven occupants through an open hatch.

At 10 A.M. on November 18, 1957, one of the few daylight sightings of occupants took place near Maracaja, State of Santa Catarina, south Brazil. Farmers Joao Ernani and Pedro Zilli saw two aluminum-colored discs hovering about three or four feet above the ground from a distance of about 700 feet. Six medium-sized men of slim build with tight-fitting, dark-gray suits were returning to the craft. The discs appeared to be about 10 feet in diameter and rose with a sharp whistling sound, bending some palm trees almost double as they went over. At the same time three more discs rose from behind trees and all five craft headed out over the South Atlantic.

It was more than a year later before another occupant case was recorded when, on June 13, 1958, Remo Dall'Armellina left Cordoba, Argentina, by car, en route to Santa Fe. Because he wished to arrive by morning he left before midnight. At approximately

4:30 A.M. he was driving along route 19, at a speed of about 60 kilometers (37 miles) per hour, not far from Boca del Tigre (Mouth of the Tiger). He suddenly noticed a brilliance behind the hill ahead of him which he attributed to an oncoming car. But when he approached he saw that the lights did not belong to a car. Ahead, in the middle of the highway, he saw a strange individual. He was "taller than normal," was wearing strange clothing, but most surprising of all was the light which came from what resembled small metallic-like balls that covered him from head to foot. This "man" raised his arms above his head and appeared to signal. Dall'Armellina applied the brakes and stopped his car. He then picked up an iron crowbar which he made a habit of carrying with him for protection and got out of the car.

Dall'Armellina said he didn't take two steps toward the being. He brought the crowbar up, then the white light given off by the being turned rose-colored, and he felt dizzy as if he'd taken a narcotic, and fell to the road, quite senseless. When he regained consciousness he and his car were alone. He ran to the car, got in, and drove rapidly to the police station at Boca del Tigre. His back and shoulder hurt him and a doctor was called but the examination showed nothing but nervousness.

The last occupant case registered for the year 1958 occurred on the night of November 23 when Julio Marino Madeleto, an American technician of Spanish origin who was employed on a project for the construction of dikes in El Salvador, Central America, had a small auto accident followed by a strange adventure. He was driving on the highway between Cojutepeque and Zacatecoluca at about 11:35 P.M., and due to poor visibility and rain, he struck and ran over a can of gasoline which wedged itself beneath the car.

Madeleto got out of the car, took some tools and began to remove the can. As he worked he saw, illuminated by the car's headlights, a bell-shaped flying object appearing to be some 12 or 13 meters (40 to 43 feet) in diameter and coming to rest about 30 meters (100 feet) from him. He then noticed a human figure about 2 meters (6½ feet) tall and dressed in a kind of blue outfit engaged in examining the rim of the disc which he struck gently from time to time with a metallic instrument. Suddenly the pilot was no longer there, the transparent portion on the upper portion of the disc that was giving off a pulsating light greatly increased its brilliance, and Madeleto heard a buzzing sound and felt intense heat. The noise increased without stopping and the object began to rise slowly, giving off sparks from its lower part. When the disc began to oscillate, turning slowly on its axis, the witness was able to see two groups of portholes or windows on the circular exterior surface of what he assumed was the cockpit or command center. Through these openings he observed a greenish luminescense. When the disc rose upwards he saw that on the bottom portion there were three yellowish hemispheres which he estimated to be almost 2 meters (6½ feet) in diameter and separated from each other by 120°, placed equidistant from one another. Then the disc stopped oscillating and departed vertically at great velocity.

Exploring the area with his flashlight, Madeleto found three hemispherical depressions in the wet ground, arranged to form a perfect equilateral triangle. He also found the footprints of the "pilot," which were filled with water. The prints were much deeper than those produced by Madeleto himself, which indicated to him that the being was much heavier than he.

Two years passed with no occupant activity being reported in South America. But no condition ever remains static and researchers were rewarded for their vigil and patience. This time it was Brazil.

During the night of May 14, 1960, a six-state area of Brazil experienced an unusual number of UFO sightings and among them was the incident in which farmer Raimundo dos Santos saw two landed discs on the beach near Paracura, Ceara State, northeast Brazil, and several small, pale-looking human-like entities standing near them. They beckoned to dos Santos, who turned and fled in fright. Returning later with other men, he found marks in the sand where the discs had rested.

At this juncture it is necessary to mention the "robots" which have been reported less frequently than the humanoids, but nevertheless in sufficient number to be discussed.

One of the first of these came from the Province of La Pampa, Argentina, where, on May 24, 1962, a woman had to be taken to a hospital suffering from shock after seeing a disc-like object land and "two robot-like creatures" near it. The woman's husband was also a witness to the sighting. Argentine Air Force officials who investigated found a circle of scorched grass which was 18 feet in diameter.

On the same day that many people reported having seen a luminous object flying overhead, a seventeen-year-old student claimed that he was assaulted by a strange being. Ricardo Mieres, seventeen, a student at National College at Parana, Argentina, was riding his motorcycle on July 28, 1962. When in the vicinity of Bajada Granda, 5 kilometers (3 miles) from Parana, his engine stalled and he was accosted by a being with a round head, long hair that was almost white, and three eyes that looked at him fixedly without blinking. Terrified, he tried to run but the thing approached him and with a violent gesture grabbed him by the edge of his collar. He then did a "half turn, like a robot," released the boy and departed, leaving tracks.

On October 12, 1963, truck driver Eugenio Douglas was blinded by a bright light while driving from Monte Maiz, Brazil, to Isla Verde and ran his truck into a ditch. When he climbed out he found the road blocked by a huge, oval, metallic object which seemed at least thirty feet high, and from a door in its side emerged three huge "robots" which he estimated to be as much as 14 to 16 feet in height. He said their clothing seemed snug or "stuck to their bodies" and they had helmets bearing short antennae which resembled the "horns of a snail." Douglas fired several shots at them and fled. The "robots" re-entered their craft and pursued him, apparently beaming some kind of ray at him which caused a burning, prickling, heat sensation such as he had felt when his truck first stalled. Despite the heavy rainfall, investigators the next day found footprints some 18 or more inches in length near the disabled truck, the wiring of which was all burned out.

One incident, which we haven't been able to pin down as to the exact date, allegedly took place one afternoon in 1963, and is probably as weird as the weirdest cases we have collected to date. Three employees of the railroad were on a train going from Presidencia La Plaza to Resistencia in Chaco Province, Argentina, when they saw a towering person over 2 meters (6 feet 8 inches) tall and dressed in a red one-piece outfit, walking on the railroad tracks toward them. The being appeared human, had pale skin, long blond hair, and had his hands out in front of him as though offering something. They thought it looked like the body of a young boy. Suddenly, when the train was less than 5 meters (16½ feet) from the strange figure, he departed, "disappearing upward as if sucked up by a whirlwind."

Meanwhile, at Resistencia at about the same time, Justo Masin and his son were resting in the garden and eating when "a strange being descended towards them." Their description of the being was the same as that given by the railroad men. Unfortunately, these two cases were from a newspaper article which did not give dates nor did it mention what happened to the being in the Masin case.

An incident involving humanoid forms apparently interested in a railroad took place near Trancas, Province of Tucuman, Argentina, on the night of October 21, 1963.

The occupants of a farm house saw a strange lighted object on or near the ground near the railway some distance from the house, and human forms were moving about. The distance was too great to make out many details. After a flashlight was obtained and trained on the grounds outside the home, two of the discs came in toward the house, took up positions about 200 feet away, beamed a narrow nondiffusing beam of light at the house, after which it heated up "like an oven." When the discs finally left, a misty substance remained where the closest discs had hovered next to the ground, and was still there when reporters investigated later.

One of the strangest of the horde of occupant sightings concerns one in December 1963 at Sauce Viejo, Santa Fe Province, Argentina. Although no craft was seen, the "humanoid" was certainly "out of this world."

Cesar Tulio Gallardo, a railroad worker, was sitting and reading in a coach on a siding when suddenly the radio failed and his carbide lamp went out. He went outside, saw some strange lights, came in again, and closed the door. At that moment a "being," totally surrounded by "light," came in from the door at the other end of the coach. The dazzle from the light was so great that Gallardo shielded his eyes with the paper, whereupon the entity snatched the paper away from him and tore it up. The weird visitor then grabbed an oil can and emptied its contents into a sort of bottle he had with him, and left as abruptly as he had entered. The only thing Gallardo could see with clarity was the being's legs which were clad in some sort of dark, shiny material.

Shortly after Gallardo reported his experience to police, passengers on an incoming train told of seeing "a luminous man" walking along the railway track as their train approached the city.

At Pajas Blancas, Cordoba, Argentina, a doctor who preferred anonymity, and his wife, told of the failure of their car's engine on the night of June 5, 1964, and the subsequent sighting of a huge bright object in the road. The bright lights went out leaving only a violet light. A figure approached their car, spoke to them in Spanish telling them not to be afraid, that if they tried to start the car, it would start. They did, then the man walked away, joined two others dressed in gray clothing, entered the machine, and it left.

During the flap of July 1965, a daylight sighting took place at Quilmes, Province of Buenos Aires, Argentina. Senor Ramon Eduardo Pereyra was driving his van when he saw a parachute-like object drifting down from the sky into some trees. Upon investigation, Pereyra saw a chrome-colored, egg-shaped craft standing on metal legs. The top of it was transparent and beside it stood a blond young man dressed in a "plastic diver's suit" with small boots and a briefcase-like object attached to his leg. Pereyra approached the craft without being seen by the young man, looked into a porthole, and saw a second man seated at an instrument panel. The man outside noticed him, then came toward him with an angry expression on his face. Pereyra attempted to talk to the man, who immediately stepped into the craft which rose at once to a height of about 100 feet and moved away in swift, level flight.

An evening sighting on July 26, 1965, involved a fifteen-year-old boy named Adilon Batista Azevedo on his way to a movie. As he walked across a piece of open ground on the outskirts of the city, Carazinho, State of Rio Grande do Sul, Brazil, he heard a strange humming sound, then saw two cones of light, and two round craft landing not far from him. The boy hid and watched the following. Three human-like beings emerged from one machine and two from the other. The two parties combined and talked in a strange language. They were about 5 feet tall, wore helmets and one-piece suits of dark color, and boots. One held a brilliant object similar to a wand in one hand. The five conversed for about five minutes, walked around the machines three times, bending down and looking at the hull.

Sketches of the objects and the entities submitted to Dr. Buhler of the Brazilian UFO Investigation Group resemble the descriptions of the beings seen by Antonio Villas-Boas in 1957. After the inspection of the craft, the entities re-entered their machines which took off at great speed and were gone within seconds.

A reporter for the *El Territorio* in Apostoles, Argentina, claimed that Casimiro Zuk, twenty-seven, came to him with a tale about a landed UFO and an occupant who apparently landed just to "stretch" his legs. He said that on the night of August 23, 1965, at around 1 o'clock in the morning he was traveling on the outskirts of Apostoles when he saw a luminous object which was giving off, at intervals, very bright light. He stopped, got off his bicycle, and noted that little by little the object was getting closer to the ground and upon reaching an altitude of approximately 500 meters (1650 feet) it described a semi-circle from east to west. Later it touched down gently on the nearby beach area about 400 meters (1350 feet) from Mr. Zuk. He described it as "some kind of self-propelling vehicle of an elongated form some 5 meters (16½ feet) in diameter at the center." Around it, he said, was a kind of visor, similar to that in an automobile used to protect passengers from the sun's rays, and under this were several windows. The total height, Zuk said, he estimated to be 2½ meters (8½ feet).

Then a hatchway began to open slowly from which emerged a person of normal height, dressed in an outfit resembling that of an aviator, which covered him from head to foot and gave off luminous sparkles. The being walked several feet as if wanting to stretch his legs and then returned to the ship which, after the hatch was closed, began to ascend in a spiraling motion and made a howling noise. Asked if he had heard any other noise, Zuk said that when the individual came out of the device he could hear what seemed to be soft music.

A leaden-colored object landed on a road near Saito, northwest Uruguay, at about 11 P.M. on August 15, 1965, and stalled a car. The object sported a white light which changed to red, green, then yellow, and nearly dimmed out before repeating the sequence. Three of the astonished passengers of the car fainted and the other two sat transfixed with fear. Through a window in the object they could see three human-like beings moving about. As usual, it suddenly departed at high speed amid bursts of reddish-yellow flame and a deafening humming noise.

Several humanoid figures were seen moving about a UFO which landed within 700 feet of the home of Eduardo Lujan Yacobi at Mar Del Plata, Argentina, at 11 P.M. on August 20, 1965. The object was heard (a humming sound) and seen (a luminous oval in the sky overhead) before it landed. The sighting was corroborated later by witnesses who either saw the object go over or heard the humming sound.

"Little folk"—two of them—small enough to fit into a silvery disc about five feet in diameter were observed shortly before noon on August 20, 1965, by engineer Alberto Ugarte and his wife and Senor Elwin Voter. The three were sightseeing at the Inca ruins just outside Cuzco, Peru. The object landed on a terrace of the Inca stone fortress and the entities who emerged were "small beings of strange shape and dazzling brightness." The little creatures seemed surprised at the presence of the witnesses, got into their ship, and departed hastily into the west.

A tiny man (about 34 inches high) with a head about twice the size of a human's, was seen emerging from an oval-shaped object which landed on the private airstrip of a large estate near Huanaco, Peru, on September 1, 1965. The little man made gestures at the one witness (who requests anonymity), then entered the machine which vanished.

A strange hum accompanied the appearance of a disc 5 feet in diameter which reportedly landed at Sao Joao, State of Pernambuco, Brazil, on September 10, 1965, at 8:30 A.M. Farmer Antonio Pau Ferro was working his maize field when the object landed, then it ascended to about a foot from the ground, leaving two small man-like creatures (less than 3 feet tall) on the ground. They were well-proportioned, beardless, had smooth, reddish-brown complexions, and wore tight-fitting one-piece garments.

The witness clung to a tree in terror as the little men approached him, chattering to each other in an unintelligible language. They examined some tomato plants and picked a tomato, then got into their craft which took off vertically with a high-pitched hum. During the investigation carried out by Dr. W. Buhler, the doctor noted that Ferro literally shook while relating the experience, and had to sit down. Although no one else saw the landed discs or their occupants, several in the area heard the humming sound.

Lieutenant Sebastian Manche, military officer in charge of the Peruvian town of Santa Barbara, reported seeing two 32-inch beings walking about on the snow near Lake Ceulacocha in the Andes on September 12. On the same night many residents of Huancavelica watched two UFOs flying about above the town for about two hours.

The little 32-inch creatures made their next appearance at 4:30 P.M. on September 20, 1965, near the town of Pichaca, District of Puno, in southeast Peru. A shepherdess saw a half dozen of the little fellows emerge from a landed UFO, and talk together in a language which sounded "like the cackling of geese." They were dressed in white clothing which emitted intermittent flashes of light. She was so frightened that she fled the area and hid. Marks found on the ground later consisted of a liquid resembling oil.

When the concentrated UFO activity of 1967 began, researchers expected to obtain more cases of humanoids associated with the UFOs, and they did. It almost seemed a repetition of the phenomenal wave of 1954, as certain areas were revisited; Venezuela in particular.

Ricardo Hurtado and Antonio Piedra, two young residents of the Santa Monica section of Caracas, reported on the morning of the 23rd of August that the night before they had heard a strange noise "like horses galloping" in the kitchen of their apartment and when they entered the room to investigate they saw two small beings leaving hurriedly. There was no light in the kitchen so they said they were not able to discern any features, but they did not believe that the uninvited guests could have been children because of the late hour at which the incident took place.

Then, at 2 A.M. on the 26th, according to Marine Pfc. Estaban D. Cova, he was accosted by a small being about 3 feet tall and covered with a sort of hairy or wiry material who asked him to come along since he needed the company of an earthling. Cova had just gotten off duty at the hangar of the Venezuelan Airpostal Airlines at Maiquetia Airport, showered and changed clothes, and was leaving the building when he ran into the little creature. The little man had a very large head, he said, bulging eyes, and made a deep, whistling sound which Cova associated with a prickling feeling throughout his body. After the little man spoke to him, Cova fainted. When he woke, he went immediately to the office of the Commandant and made his report. The Commandant later told investigators that something had frightened Cova badly and that he believed the story.

The only Brazilian occupant case that came in during the fall flap was from a young sixteen-year-old boy named Fabio Jose Diniz, who claimed that on the night of September 26th he was going home after visiting a girl friend, when he encountered a landed half-sphere-shaped object of about 70 feet in diameter on a football field near the Hospital da Baleia. The object was brown in color, had a line of portholes along it, and a fixed triangular piece on top. It also had a black cylindrical support some 3 meters (10 feet) high by 2 meters (7 feet) wide. Two creatures, each over 6 feet tall, dressed in green clothing similar to that of a diver's underwater suit were near the object. They had wide-spaced and round eyes, their eyebrows appeared to be triangular in shape and very thick. Fabio said he did not see their noses which were covered by a long tube. He said they uttered two sentences: "Do not run—come back" and "Be here again tomorrow at this same hour or we shall take your family with us."

Because of this warning, Fabio decided to inform the police, who later stated that the boy was very frightened when he related his experience. Hulvio Brant, then president of C.I.C.O.A.N.I., a Brazilian UFO investigative organization, after interviewing the boy several times was convinced that the boy was not having hallucinations and was reporting what he had seen to the best of his ability.

Brazil again seemed to be the target of the humanoids in the latter part of 1968. A nightwatchman at the Central Electric Station of Sao Paulo claimed that at 1 A.M. on an October morning (as is often the case the press did not give the exact date) he was attacked by unusual creatures. He said he had just signed in to work when he noticed a light shining above the building so he went outside to see where it was coming from. He saw a man's face at a distance and ran toward it. The morning was very dark so he could only make out that the man's head had a covering of some kind. The watchman had an iron bar in his hand and he aimed a couple of blows toward the man's head, but the man dodged both of them quite agilely, then grabbed the watchman by the arm and threw him down. The two rolled about on the ground, whereupon the stranger was joined by another "man," then still another, and the watchman was overcome. He noticed that one of the "men" was dressed in yellow clothing and he tapped the watchman on the back, uttering unintelligible words. The watchman called to other workers, whereupon the three strangers got into a small vehicle which resembled a Volkswagen station wagon in size and it flew off into the air over the offices of the electrical complex.

The watchman described the "men" as being about his own height, one wearing dark trousers and polo shirt, with his face covered. The one who had been on top of the small building who first caught his attention had worn light-colored clothes which he thought were yellow and resembled overalls. The third wore dark clothing.

The vehicle, he said, was unlit and of a grayish color. The watchman's experience was reported to police who were impressed by the similarity between what he saw and the incident involving another encounter with UFO entities at Lins. A representative of the President of Brazil was sent to interview the watchman. Authorities at first thought that terrorists might have been involved in the incident but after the questioning was over they were forced to discard the idea.

We must call attention to the fact that so many of these occupant reports allude to a Volkswagen or Volkswagen station wagon-sized flying object being involved.

Another Brazilian occupant case which took place in August 1967, but did not become available to APRO for quite some time thereafter, ended up in tragedy for the primary witness. It is one of the few incidents in which a weapon was allegedly used against a human. The investigation was initiated by APRO's Brazilian representative, Dr. Olavo T. Fontes, who became ill in late 1967 and passed away in the spring of 1968. It was some time before Professor Felipe Carrion and Jader Pereira were able to carry the investigation to an end.

At 4 P.M. on the 13th of August 1967, Inacio de Souza and his wife, Maria, returned from an outing. De Souza was the tenant farmer and caretaker for a wealthy man who made his headquarters in Sao Paulo and commuted to the farm by private plane when necessary. Upon arriving at the farm they immediately saw a "strange, basin-shaped object" of approximately 35 meters (115 feet) in width resting on the landing field. Standing between the craft and the de Souzas were three strange looking creatures who appeared, to Inacio, to be naked. His wife, however, got the impression that the "men" were dressed in tight-fitting yellow jersey suits. They appeared to have no hair and were playing about like children. When they caught sight of the de Souzas they began running toward them. Inacio sent his wife into the house and he reached for his rifle and began to shoot. At the moment that Inacio began to fire, a jet of green-colored light erupted from the disc and struck him full in the chest, knocking him to the ground.

At this moment Mrs. de Souza ran out of the house to her husband's aid and took the gun and flung it away. But the three figures were already running toward the disc which thereafter lifted straight up off the ground making a sound like the swarming of bees and was shortly lost to sight.

De Souza was considered sober and reliable and his wife testified to the account he gave of the meeting of the humanoids and Inacio's ensuing illness.

Three days after the incident the owner of the farm arrived in his airplane. He found de Souza quite ill. Inacio complained of extreme nausea as well as a tingling feeling and general numbness throughout his body. He was taken to Goiana, the capital of Goias State, where a doctor examined him and found burns on his torso. The farm owner (who did not want to be identified and connected with the case) told the doctor the facts surrounding Inacio's condition and the physician decided to do some blood tests. The tests revealed that Inacio was suffering from leukemia and "malignant alterations of the blood." The doctor took the farm owner aside and told him that Inacio's probable life expectancy was about sixty days.

De Souza's weight dropped very fast, he suffered great pain, and yellowish-white spots appeared all over his body. Within two months Inacio de Souza was dead. Before his death he begged his wife to burn his bed and clothing as he was afraid that what had killed him might have been transmitted to his wife or their five children. De Souza had not been told that he had leukemia and not having much knowledge of medicine probably assumed that what he suffered from was communicable.

It is believed by Inacio's family, his employer, the doctor involved, as well as the investigators, that Inacio de Souza died of radiation poisoning. The incident took place on the farm which is located between Crixas and Pilar de Goias in Goias State.

Another occupants case involving little flying men and a "basin-shaped" object was reported at Pirassununga, Sao Paulo State, Brazil, in February of 1969. A parachute or basin-shaped object giving off a blue light was observed by many residents of that city at 7 A.M. on the 7th of February.

Among those who saw it was nineteen-year-old Tiago Machado, a fruit peddler who lived with his family. He had been in bed when he heard people shouting and upon looking out his window he saw the object. He dressed hurriedly, grabbed his binoculars, ran to the

Zootechnica Institute, and excitedly informed two guards, Francisco Hanse and Benedito Joana, of what he had seen and asked them to accompany him to the site where the object was located.

The three of them set out running, each by a different route, because of the obstacles presented by streams and trees and vegetation. Tiago reached the location first and stopped at about 10 meters (about 35 feet) from the object which now gave the appearance of an aluminum disc. A lid opened on the upper part of the disc and there merged two smallish men of about 1 meter, 10 centimeters (3 feet, 8 inches) in height. Two others could be seen inside the glass-enclosed "cabin." They appeared to "fly" down from the opening to the ground. Tiago later described them as wearing silvery-colored clothing, including gloves and boots, and through the helmets their faces appeared to have a yellowish tinge, their noses "squashed" at the ends. A tube projecting down from the area of the cabin seemed to be where their hoarse, guttural sounds were coming from. Tiago could not understand the noises they made.

The creatures seemed to be afraid of the binoculars which he had around his neck so he took them off and laid them on the ground and then put them on again, which seemed to reassure them. Being nervous, Tiago then lit a cigarette and proceeded to smoke. The creatures began to laugh, apparently very amused, so Tiago took the pack and laid it on the ground, pushing it toward the creatures with his foot. One of them extended his hand above the cigarette pack and it rose up into the air to his palm. He then made a quick motion toward his body and the pack disappeared.

The little men seemed to try to converse with Tiago by using sign language and Tiago responded in a likewise manner. The two raised their arms and made the outline of a sphere in the air, then indicated a motion which seemed to Tiago to denote a craft falling or drifting to the ground.

These events took only a very few minutes and soon the shouts of others who were approaching were heard. The little creatures began drifting up to the top of the disc and entered it through the lifted hatch which had opened when they first appeared. The last one to enter made a gesture to one of the crew inside, then pointed a pipe-shaped contraption at Tiago. He gave the handle a turn and it flashed a bluish-red ray at the boy's legs and he fell to the ground. The rim of the ship had been turning all the while that the creatures were on the ground and the central part, which rested on a tripod landing gear, remained still.

As soon as Tiago fell down, the object left the ground and disappeared into the sky at high speed. Others who were approaching saw the little men and the machine as it took off.

One additional detail which should be mentioned is that when the creatures laughed, Tiago noted that their teeth were dark. As our translator, Mrs. Irene Granchi, pointed out, we should note the similarity of the creatures in this incident as well as their apparent ability to fly, to the French Cussac Plateau case which is described in the chapter titled "Floating, Flying UFOnauts."

Anolaima, Colómbia, is the setting for our next occupant case. A total of eleven witnesses were involved and the incident took place at 8 P.M. on July 4, 1969. Mauricio Gnecco, thirteen, saw a yellow-red light moving from east to west. He was with a friend, Enrique Osorio, twelve, and they were outside watching for "shooting stars." Mauricio called to the other children, Andres Franco, thirteen, Marina Franco, eleven, Rosita N., ten, German N., fourteen, all of whom were playing inside the house. Also present in the house were Arcesio Bermudez, Lucrecia Bermudez, his sister; Rosa Ortiz, Luis Carbajal, the butler; and Evelia Carbajal, the butler's wife. Mauricio urged them to go outside and see the "flying saucer."

At first they would not go, then when Mauricio insisted they stepped out and watched the light which appeared to be at a distance of about 600 feet. Mauricio obtained a flashlight and began to turn it on and off as if to signal. At that moment the light source approached the house at considerable speed and remained suspended between two tall trees about 150 feet from the farmhouse where it hovered for about five seconds. When this occurred Mrs. Ortiz shouted to Mauricio: "That thing is coming down upon us—turn that flashlight off, Mauricio!"

The witnesses described the object as follows: Between 4 and 6 feet tall, yellow-orange in color with an apparent "arc of light" or halo surrounding it, and two luminous legs which were blue with green tips. It made no sound. It then flew to the right of the farmhouse and appeared to come low over a nearby hill. Mr. Bermudez, described as the only person in the group who was unafraid, took the flashlight from Mauricio and went running in the direction of the object. His sister, Lucrecia, followed him, but in the darkness she fell to the ground.

According to the testimony of the children and Mrs. Rosa Ortiz, Bermudez approached the area where the object was and began calling the butler who was the only other adult male present, saying, "Luis, come here. Look at this Martian." Mauricio and Andres watched the object from a nearby hill and reported that it "blinked on and off." Finally, they saw it rise high into the sky and fly away in the direction of Bogota.

Mr. Bermudez returned to the farmhouse and told the other witnesses that he had approached the object, which had landed on the ground, to within a distance of about 20 feet. The object, he said, "blinked out" momentarily and he shone the flashlight at it. He claimed that he saw a "person" inside and described the upper half of the entity as "normal," but from the waist down the anatomy of the "person" appeared to be like the letter "A" and was luminous. The object then blinked on, rose into the sky, and flew away. About five minutes later all of the witnesses saw an identical object crossing the sky at about 300 feet altitude. The speed was "slow" and constant as it flew toward Bogota and it also was soundless. Two other adults, Clemente Bolivar and Rosalba Prieto, who live about two miles from the Bermudez farm, reported a bright orange-yellow light flying slowly toward Bogota at approximately the same time.

Within two days of the observation, the principal witness, Mr. Arcesio Bermudez, was taken very ill; his temperature dropped to 95° and he had a "cold touch" although he claimed that he didn't feel cold. Within a few days his condition became far more serious; he had "black vomits" and diarrhea with blood. He was taken to Bogota and attended by Dr. Luis Borda at 10:00 A.M. on July 12 and later by Dr. Cesar Esmeral at 7:30 P.M. At 11:45 P.M. Mr. Bermudez passed away.

APRO has a copy of the medical report signed by Dr. Esmeral, diagnosing the cause of death as gastroenteritis. Neither of the two doctors knew of Mr. Bermudez's UFO experience which may or may not have some bearing on the case.

APRO Representative for Columbia, Mr. John Simhon, and Field Investigator Elias Nessim became aware of the UFO incident four days after Mr. Bermudez's death, on July 16. On the same day the children, Andres, Marina, Enrique, and Mauricio, were put into a hypnotic trance by Dr. Luis E. Martinez of the National University of Columbia. The session took place at 8:00 P.M. that night and both Simhon and Nessim were present. The hypnosis had been requested by relatives of the children.

The taped testimony of the children while under hypnosis is almost identical to the testimony already obtained and to the testimony of the adult witnesses (with the exception of Arcesio Bermudez, who was dead and consequently was never interviewed by APRO's representatives). The investigators considered all of the witnesses to be of unquestionable integrity and honesty. Drawings of the object made by the children depicted a spherical object with a ring at the midsection and two legs jutting down underneath.

The possibility of animal reaction to the object is also a part of this reported incident. A pet monkey named "Michin" commenced to screech loudly and persistently and several dogs around the farm began howling. This was reported by all of the witnesses. A visit to the farm by Simhon and Nessim yielded nothing more and they found no landing impressions.

Speculation began to grow about the possible relationship between Bermudez's approach to the UFO and his death so soon after. His clothing and wristwatch were sent to the Colombian Institute of Nuclear Affairs (CINA) and an official there told Mr. Simhon that the symptons of Bermudez's illness were similar to those caused by a lethal dose of gamma rays. However, examination of Bermudez's possessions yielded nothing.

Dr. Horace C. Dudley, Professor of Radiation Physics at the University of Illinois Medical Center, Chicago, Illinois, and Consultant to APRO in Radiation Physics, responded to our questions concerning the possibility of a link-up between Bermudez's encounter and his death and he wrote: "The illness and death of Mr. Bermudez may be due to radiation effects but there is not one bit of laboratory data to support such a conclusion without a complete autopsy and pathological (microscopic) study so a physician would not be warranted in giving a more specific cause of death."

Also consulted by APRO was Dr. Benjamin Sawyer, formerly an Air Force Flight Surgeon, and at the time in private practice in Middletown, Ohio. He wrote: "The symptoms of enteritis... are nearly identical to one of the three basic forms of (intestinal) illness from radiation exposure. There is nothing superficially apparent to distinguish the two illnesses." This, then, had to conclude our work on the case, for attempts to obtain permission to exhume the body and conduct an autopsy were met with considerable opposition from the family, which was understandable.

A year later the occupant action had switched back to Brazil, and this report detailed what three witnesses observed while they watched a water-going object. On June 21, 1970, at 11 A.M. Mr. Aristeo Machado, forty-nine, his wife Maria Nazare, and federal agent Aguiar, a friend of the family, were outside the Machado home which is perched high above Avenida Neimeyer and affords a sweeping view of the Atlantic Ocean. They saw an object about the size of a Ford Galaxie which landed on the surface of the ocean about 1 kilometer (3,280 feet or a little over a half mile) from the shore. When the object settled down onto the sea, spray was thrown out on all sides. The witnesses first thought it was a boat in trouble and went to the nearby hotel to telephone the Maritime Police. However, the object floated another 100 meters (about 350 feet) closer to the shore and the three people were able to discern that it had a transparent cupola, inside of which were clearly visible two beings in dark-gray coveralls, wearing helmets. Both appeared to be smallish and thickset.

At this point we should note that it is difficult to conceive of anyone thinking the object could have been a boat when it had been airborne and settled down onto the ocean. However, apparently the witnesses spotted it just as it settled on the water, giving the impression that it might have been a speedboat "skipping" across the water and occasionally speedboats do become airborne for a very few seconds.

Mrs. Irene Granchi, APRO's Field Investigator in Rio de Janeiro, investigated the report a week after it happened, at the same time of day and with the same lighting conditions. She took note that a motorboat going by at approximately the same distance from shore was easily seen, its passengers were noted, but no details were visible.

Other observations of the object, which was in view for between thirty and forty minutes, were that it had a bright rotating light which changed from red to green to yellow. Mrs. Machado said that while she waited for Mr. Aguiar to return from telephoning she saw the object "relieve itself" of a yellow ball which proceeded toward the shore but was not floating for it was moving against the current and seemed to be powered by something underneath it. Shortly thereafter the yellow ball relieved itself of another object which was bottle green in color and of indeterminate shape. She ran down the beach after the yellow object and pointed it out to some children but they all lost sight of it shortly.

The duration of the observation was forty minutes, after which the larger object took off quickly in a low, long flight out to sea.

The year 1971 brought more cases out of Brazil and the report by Paolo Caetano Silveira, twenty-seven, was enough to boggle the mind of even a veteran UFO researcher. He claimed that at 5 P.M. on Wednesday, September 22nd, he was driving home from Tombos when he noticed a light which appeared to be following his car. He stopped at a police station and reported it but the police did not appear disposed to investigate but rather suggested that he engage a room for the night and continue his journey in the morning. Silveira, however, was a typewriter mechanic and had worked all day at Tombos, and was anxious to get home to his family at Itaperuna, so he continued on his way.

At about 7:40 P.M. in an area near Itaperuna called Serraria he saw the same (or a similar) light again. It came to a stop in front of his car and its bluish rays turned to white and his car engine stopped. The car rolled to a halt and then two bright beams were focused on him and the two car doors popped open with no help from him.

Silveira said the two beams of light dragged him out of the car toward the large light, and he then became aware of three objects, man-shaped and about 50 centimeters (about 20 inches) tall, which moved toward him. He said they moved mechanically, holding their arms at right angles to their "bodies," but at no time did he refer to them as beings—always objects.

The objects did not touch Silveira; rather, the beams of light drew him to the large light and his legs were numb. He did not see the shape of the large light because of its brightness. Once inside the object, Silveira said he saw three beings, all of whom were dressed in blue "siren" (or jump) suits with a smooth covering over their heads which reminded him of Roman helmets. Their hands and faces were gray but he could discern no features. The hands, he said, appeared to him to be transparent.

While inside the object the beings moved around him and communicated with each other but he could not understand them. A sound like a turbine engine was heard all the while that he was aboard. The next thing he knew, he was lying on the ground a few meters from his car and Dr. Cirley Coutinho Crespo was talking to him. Dr. Crespo sent for help and Silveira was taken into Itaperuna where Dr. Bussade took over.

Dr. Bussade, who is Silveira's personal physician and knows him well, make the following observations: Silveira was highly excited but his blood pressure was normal; his face was very red, his eyes were bloodshot; he had scratches on his hands and arms which terminated at the elbows; and his clothing was torn and dirty as if he had been dragged. He had not been robbed, nor had his car been in an accident, and Dr. Bussade was very firm in asserting that Silveira *had not* been drinking.

Silveira's descriptions indicated that he might have been in a somnambulistic state for some of what he remembers is disjointed and not too clear. For instance, he said the inside of the UFO was very large and white, the "beings" inside were about six in number, and "there were a lot of little faces" everywhere. They were about 20 inches tall. He noticed some "buttons" in the ship, he said, but does not relate them to anything such as a control board.

After the experience Silveira complained of loss of appetite and a smarting sensation in his eyes. His wristwatch, which customarily lost about four minutes a week, was fifteen minutes slow when he was examined by Dr. Bussade at the First Aid Station in Itaperuna.

Before we attempt to compare Mr. Silveira's experience with another, let's take a look at another report which allegedly took place on September 25th, also in Brazil. Benedito Miranda, twenty-four, a truck driver from Cataguazes was on his way home from Itaperuna at 2 A.M. and was crossing the Carangola River bridge when he was drawn from his car by a beam of light and was held suspended at 50 to 100 meters (200-400 feet) above the ground. His legs were numb, he said, and he felt as though he was on a platform of some kind. He swayed in the air, he also said, and tried to call for help but his voice failed him. At this point a car was seen coming down the road and Miranda was gently lowered to the ground. He seemed unhurt and got into his truck and drove home.

To our knowledge, the Silveira incident had not been publicized by the time Miranda allegedly had his experience so it is not likely that Miranda had any knowledge of it. However, shortly after he made his report to authorities and the press, he retracted his statement and disappeared. At the time his sister was extremely upset and concerned about him but further news was not forthcoming about him or his claim.

In the latter case we can theorize that Miranda got sick of the attention and simply dropped out of sight, which quite often happens under these circumstances. Sometimes witnesses report their experiences and live to regret it because of the hounding they receive from the press. This could have been the case. If so, this is unfortunate for shortly thereafter the Silveira case was publicized and was corroborating testimony for Miranda's claims, because the reported happenings were similar.

Going back to Silveira, that report would have been much too heady material even for the Lorenzens, had it not been for the fact that when the report came in from Mrs. Granchi, we both recalled the Long Prairie, Minnesota, case of October, 1965, which is described in the chapter dealing with the occupants in the U.S. Except for the size, the "animated beer cans" in both cases are remarkably similar.

Although the foregoing does not include all landing cases involving strange or unusual creatures, it is a fairly representative group. There are the weird ones involving "green, wrinkled dwarfs," one-eyed and three-eyed humanoids, and stump-like or branch-like creatures, but they are a very small minority of the overall number recorded and so have not been included in this dissertation.

Even a cursory examination of the cases presented here indicates the presence of definite correlations: the "diminutives"—with dark or light skin; the nearly human-sized (average, that is) about 4½ to

5 feet in height—with dark or light skin and blond hair; the giants, the six-footers.

The "craft" follow a certain pattern also, including five-foot discs, egg-shapes, big discs, and huge discs.

In some instances an oily residue is found after a landing. Some landings indicate a concern for possible malfunction of the craft on the part of the operators. Others indicate a curiosity or concern about plant life on earth.

Exact sizes and facial characteristics are seldom included in such reports, probably because of the distances involved. Few of the foregoing listed cases involved close-up sightings. If an individual sees a completely strange type of ship in a field with no object near it with which to make a comparison for size, the margin of error is likely to be great. An example: a man of our acquaintance is six feet four inches tall, but does not seem so when standing by himself against a clear horizon. The reason: unlike most tall men, he is not slender and "tall looking." He has a large frame and is well-muscled, but his true size is only evident when he stands beside a familiar object such as a car or in a door frame.

It does seem, therefore, that the cases listed above do not all involve hoaxes. The witnesses have been checked out as serious, responsible, and honest.

Such cases, however, because of their bizarre and totally unfamiliar nature, cannot be evaluated on the basis of their very existence—a correlation with other reports must be sought. A thorough examination of those reports emanating from other countries and other continents, then, must be undertaken before a judgment can be made.

CHAPTER X

The Occupants in the United States

The first reported occupant case purportedly took place on August 19, 1949 in Death Valley, California. According to the story, two prospectors witnessed the crash landing of a disc-shaped flying object. Two small "men" jumped out of it and the prospectors gave chase. They lost the little fellows in the sand dunes and when they returned to what they thought was a landing site the craft was gone. This incident took place in the early years of the UFO mystery and as far as is known has not been thoroughly checked out, although it is mentioned often. It has not been exposed as a hoax, however.

Most researchers are familiar with Frank Scully's "little men," which he described in quite a bit of detail in his book, *Behind the Flying Saucers* (New York, Henry Holt & Co., Inc., 1950). Al though generally rejected by most researchers in the early years, subsequent incidents seem to indicate that Scully was either telling the truth or that he was a prophet. Small humanoids which generally answer the description given by Scully have been seen on several occasions since, as we shall see.

Another rather fragmentary report comes from Red Springs, North Carolina, where in December 1951, Mr. Sam Coley and his two children reported seeing a low-hovering disc-shaped aircraft with a "human-shaped" occupant inside. Coley was reportedly interviewed by the state's Director of Defense and the local police chief; the latter expressed his "loss of skepticism" after the talk. There was no detailed description of the "occupant" but the source material tends to accept Coley's story.

Probably the most frightening landing incident on record, considering the physical description of what was thought to be an occupant and its actions, is the Flatwoods, West Virginia, incident which took place on September 12, 1952. At sunset of that evening, a group of youngsters saw what appeared to be a "meteor" land on the top of a nearby hill. Similar observations of a low-flying "meteor" were made in that vicinity on the same night along with many others along the central Atlantic seaboard.

The boys decided to investigate and started toward the hill. Along the way they stopped at the home of Mrs. Kathleen May and she, her two sons, and a seventeen-year-old national guardsman, Gene Lemon, joined the group and they made their way to the top of the hill.

The first thing the crowd observed was a large globe or sphere beyond the crest of the hill. One of the boys said it was "as big as a house," another boy said he heard a "throbbing sound," and another said he heard a "hissing sound." At about this juncture in the sequence of events one of the group saw what was thought to be an animal's eyes in the branches of a tree and shone a flashlight beam toward it. The whole crowd then saw what appeared to be a huge figure just under the lower branches of the tree. It seemed to be about 10 or 15 feet tall, had a blood-red "face," and glowing greenish-orange "eyes." The lower part of the "thing" was in shadow, but Mrs. May thought she saw clothing-like folds. The whole apparition "floated" slowly toward the observers, who fled hysterically down the hillside in the direction from which they had come.

Some of the group were violently ill during the rest of the night, and this was verified by the editor of the local paper. He was one of several who searched the hill shortly afterward, but found nothing. On the following day, however, he and others found marks on the ground including two parallel skid marks and a large circular area of flattened grass. A strange and irritating odor lingered close to the ground.

The Flatwoods incident is one which was accepted by researchers, partly because of the large number of observers and supporting evidence, but we suspect that the non-human characteristics of the "entity" was a large factor. By and large, researchers in the United States have hesitated to accept, and even strongly resisted, the idea of humanoid UFO operators. It was generally felt that UFO occupants would not be likely to resemble human beings. The Flatwoods case is one of the few occupant cases involving a "monster."

"Little men" returned to the scene in 1953 when two goldminers working a claim near Brush Creek, California, reported to police that two midget-sized saucer pilots had been visiting the creek near their claim. The first incident took place on May 20, the second on June 20, and the two men expected that they would return on July 20.

The veracity of the miners, John Q. Black and John Van Allen, was attested to by the owner of the Brush Creek store, who said the two miners had a very good reputation and were not "drinking men." Both of the men unhesitatingly told their story to the sheriff's captain, Fred Preston, four days after the second encounter. Black had actually seen the little men, while Van Allen, his partner, had only seen the landing marks which he said were a foot wide and looked like the tracks of "elephant feet."

Black described the observed occupant as "about the size of a midget" and said he was very broad-shouldered. He wore "something like a parka" (a piece of clothing which covers the head as well as the trunk of the body) and his arms and legs were covered with a heavy, tweed-like cloth fastened at the wrists and ankles with "buckles or ties of some kind."

Some of the details were not included in press reports, and at that time APRO was only a year and a half old and did not have a member in that part of California who was willing to make the long trek into the brush country to interview Black and Van Allen. The available details, however, are as follows. In each instance, on May 20 and June 20, the object landed at almost exactly 6:30 P.M. The "little man" got out, scooped up a bucket of water in a shiny pail, and handed it to someone inside the craft. When the little man saw Black, he hurriedly jumped into the "saucer" and it took off at high speed, making a hissing sound which resembled the "sound of steam coming out of a boiler." The saucer, silver in color, appeared to be about 7 feet in diameter, 6 feet thick, with a tripod landing gear, and a "little dome" in front. It landed on a sand bar in Brush Creek and Black was within 50 yards of the saucer on each occasion.

The U.S. Air Force was notified of the incident, but it is not known whether or not an investigation was implemented. On July 20, however, Black and Van Allen were not the only ones at the site. Publicity brought huge crowds of people anxious to see the "little men." Snack bars were set up so that no one would go hungry during the vigil, and although the size of the reception committee would have warmed the heart of any ordinary person, the saucer pilots didn't show up. Perhaps they got wind of the fact that Black had asked permission of the sheriff to shoot one of them, and that bow hunters were present in force with blunted arrows with which to stun and capture the little fellows. As a result of all this hoopla, it was conjectured by some that perhaps Black and Van Allen and others had fabricated the story in order to publicize the area for reasons of commerce. This theory does not hold up very well for various reasons, mainly that the disappointment of not seeing the little men or their craft on July 20 precluded the appearance of any more sightseers later.

Coldwater, Kansas,was the site of the next "little man" appearance in September 1954. The exact date of the incident is not known, but the story appeared in a clipping from the Lincoln, Nebraska *Star* in late September. According to International News Service and the *Star* story, young John J. Swain, twelve, son of a farmer near Coldwater, had been returning to the farm from the fields at about 8 P.M. on his father's tractor, when he suddenly spotted a tiny man no more than 20 feet away behind a terrace in the field. The small figure had a very long nose and very long ears and when he moved he seemed to "fly." Young John watched as the little man "flew" over a small hill to a saucer-shaped object which was hovering about 5 feet above the ground. "It opened up," the story said, and the little man, "no bigger than a five-year-old child," then popped inside, the thing "lighted up," and then took off at a fast rate of speed.

The Swain boy went home and told his parents; they then called the Coldwater sheriff, who came out and questioned him. The sheriff cautioned them to stay away from the place where the boy reported seeing the "thing." He came back the next day, and with John and his parents, went out to examine the site of the landing. They found wedge-shaped tracks in the soft dirt which did not appear to be "human"—not made by ordinary shoes. Although it was not made clear, the possibility that the "tracks" were those of the object has not been discarded, but it does not seem likely for the boy was definite in his assertion that the craft was hovering about 5 feet off the ground.

Besides the clipping, which came to us via Reverend Albert Baller, an APRO member in Massachusetts, we have a copy of a letter written to Reverend Baller by John Swain, dated October 3, 1954, from which we quote: "You ask me about the saucer I saw. I was disking in the field when I saw it. We had tractor trouble. It was late when we got it finished. It cooled off some, so I worked till 8 P.M. Then I unhitched from the disk and came in. I met it about 400 feet, and didn't see it. I came on a (word not legible but believed to be "terrace"). He was crouched behind it. He jumped up and looked at me and kind of floated. He jumped in the saucer and it lighted up and it took off. It went out of sight. I told Mom and Dad about it. We talked over it. Then Mom called the sheriff. He came down that night and questioned me. He said he would come in the morning and look and see if there were any tracks around. There were. He sent the reports to Washington, D.C."

The letter adds a note of authenticity to this case, and the strange tracks indicate the presence of something out of the ordinary.

Although we have presented only five cases so far, we begin to see that there is a wide diversity of descriptions where occupants are concerned. We believe there are good and logical reasons for this, the main one being that individual interpretations of any observed thing differ simply because of the individualistic nature of man. The shorter the observation, however, the more diverse will be the descriptions. Also, different people observe and concentrate their attention on different details of a given subject.

The now defunct *Orbit,* official publication of the Civilian Research Interplanetary Flying Objects Organization (CRIFO) of Cincinnati, Ohio, contained a scantily detailed article about "little men" in the September 2, 1955 issue. Because of lack of names and other supporting evidence, we would not ordinarily include such a tale, but *Orbit*'s editor, Leonard Stringfield, is a highly reputable researcher and we are certainly very aware of the fact, that most people reporting strange men in conjunction with landed UFOs prefer not to be identified. Several weeks prior to September 2nd, according to Stringfield, a prominent businessman of Loveland, Ohio, saw four "strange little men about 3 feet tall" under a certain bridge near Cincinnati. He supposedly reported the observation to the police, whereupon a guard was placed at the bridge.

Because this case was dealt with rather briefly in *Orbit,* readers had to wait until Leonard Stringfield's book, *Inside Saucer Post 3-0 Blue* (Cincinnati, Ohio, Moeller Printing Co., 1957) came out to get any details, and other cases were also listed.

On July 3, 1955, Mrs. Wesley Symmonds of Cincinnati, Ohio, was driving through Stockton, Georgia, on her way to Florida. She claimed she saw four "bug-eyed" creatures near the road. The sketch of the creatures based on her description shows little bipeds with rather thin arms, large eyes, and pointed chins. Two, in the background, appeared to be turned away from the observer. One was bending over with what appeared to be a stick in its hand, and the other had its right arm raised and was facing the observer. This creature had large, bulging eyes, a caplike affair on its head (or what appeared to be a cap), no visible mouth, a long, pointed nose, and a chin that came to a sharp point. Its long, thin arms ended in claw-like appendages.

In attempting to track down the "under the bridge" case, Stringfield, with the help of Ted Bloecher of CSI (Civilian Saucer Investigations), New York, ferreted out a case which is probably more illuminating than the others with which he dealt. At about 4 A.M. on a morning in March 1955, Mr. R. H. of Loveland was driving through Branch Hill on his way to Loveland. His headlights suddenly illuminated what appeared to be three men kneeling at the right side of the road. He first thought that someone was hurt so he stopped his car to have a better look. He discovered that the figures were non-human, about 3 feet tall and grayish in color. Their clothing was also gray and seemed to be tight-fitting; it stretched over a "lop-sided" chest which appeared abnormally large on the right side, bulging from the shoulder to the armpit. Over this bulbous area hung a slender arm which appeared much longer than the opposite member. Legs and feet were not discernible because they were obscured by the vegetation in which the entities stood, but the observer got the impression of "something baggy."

The heads of these creatures, said R. H., reminded him of a "frog's face," mostly because of the appearance of the mouth: it was a thin line cutting across the smooth gray face. The eyes, which lacked brows, looked normal, the nose was indistinct, and the top of the head appeared to have a painted-on hair effect, comprised of what appeared to be rolls of fat running horizontally from above the eyes, over (or around) the whole head.

Mr. R. H. said the middle one of the three, who was the closest to him, was first seen with his arms raised about a foot above his head and appeared to be holding a dark-colored chain or stick which gave off blue-white sparks. As R. H. approached this entity lowered the object to about the area of the ankle. The observer said he wanted to approach closer to the creatures, but by the time he reached the area of the front fender of his car one of them made an "unnatural" move toward him as if motioning him not to move closer, so for about the next three minutes he just stood and looked, too amazed to be afraid. Stringfield closes this incident, before summing up, with the cryptic remark: "The next thing he knew he was on his way to Fritz's office (chief of police)."

Probably the granddaddy of all "occupant" sightings in the United States is that which occurred on August 22, 1955, near Hopkinsville, Kentucky. The basic details include the beginning of the episode when visiting relative Bill Taylor went out to the well for a drink and came back in to tell of a "spaceship" which had landed in a nearby field. Just a scant few minutes later the aroused household saw a small specter-like figure approaching the house. It appeared to be lit by an internal source, had a roundish head, huge elephantine ears, a slit-like mouth which extended from ear to ear. The eyes were huge and wide-set. Only about 3 or 3½ feet in height, the creature had no visible neck, and its arms were long and ended in clawed hands. Although it stood upright, it dropped to all fours when it ran.

According to the Frank Sutton family, several of these creatures roamed the area adjacent to the house, climbed trees, climbed up on the roof. At one point Sutton fired a shotgun through the screen door at one of the little men. Although struck and knocked over by the blast, the little fellow got up and scuttled away on his hands and feet. Later, Taylor walked out the same door, only to be confronted by one of the creatures on the roof, apparently grabbing for his head.

This weird sequence of events continued for the greater part of one night, and finally the family scrambled to the car and drove into town to report their plight. Deputy Sheriff George Batts and two Kentucky state police came to the house but found no evidence of the little men's presence or the "spaceship." However, researchers who interviewed the Suttons and carefully investigated the whole affair, including Isabel Davis of New York (Civilian Saucer Investigations), were inclined to believe the incident did take place. Local investigators, including Chief of Police Greenwell, said that "something scared those people—something beyond reason—nothing ordinary." One investigator with medical experience noted Sutton's rapid pulse beat of 140 per minute, which is about twice the normal rate.

Although generally discounted by UFO researchers, probably partly because of the ensuing publicity, the Kearney, Nebraska, "landing" and "contact" claim of Reinhold Schmidt is nevertheless interesting, for several reasons.

The gist of this story is that Schmidt, a grain buyer from Bakersfield, California, came to Sheriff Dave Drage's office late in the afternoon of November 5, 1957, seemed frightened, and asked to see a minister. (The sheriff's office is the wrong place to find one.) Schmidt then said he had been driving near Kearney when his car engine stopped. He found he was within about 20 yards of a silvery, blimp-shaped object about 100 feet in length, 30 feet wide, and about 14 feet high, which stood on four post-like legs.

Schmidt approached the object, whereupon a "staircase" came out and two "middle-aged" men searched him for weapons, then took him inside where he stayed for a half hour. They told him they would have to be there for a little while and he "might as well come inside." The people, two women and two men, all middle-aged and wearing ordinary clothing, were working on some "wiring." When they moved about they "slid" instead of walked. While there he was told nothing about the ship, its occupants, nor was he given any message as most contactees claim. Schmidt said they told him to tell the people they were doing no harm, and that in "a short time" he might "know all about it." He was then asked to leave, the ship lifted straight up, silently, and disappeared into the sky. After it left he found he could start his car again.

Most UFO enthusiasts are familiar with what transpired later. Schmidt was grilled for the better part of that night by Air Force and civilian law enforcement officers, eventually pronounced unstable, and "very ill" by psychiatrists and committed to an institution. Later, after release, he set about lecturing about his experience, other "contacts", and the poor way in which he was treated by authorities. It is generally felt that he later embroidered his original story and this tended to discredit him. During his incarceration another incident was related in the press which was quite similar but which was apparently unknown to officialdom or ignored.

At about 6:30 A.M. on the morning of November 6, 1957, twelve-year-old Everett Clark of Dante, Tennessee, got up to let his dog Frisky outside. He saw an object in the field about 100 yards from his home. He thought he was dreaming, he said, and went back inside. About twenty minutes later he went out to call his dog and found Frisky and other dogs across the road in the field by the object.

Outside the object were two men and two women, apparently normally dressed. One of the men grabbed at Frisky, who growled and backed away. He grabbed another dog who attempted to bite him, so he let it go.

During interviews later, Everett said the people talked like "German soldiers" he had seen in movies on television. When they got into the ship they looked as if they "walked right through the side, as if it were glass." The object took off straight up and made no sound. It was long and round, he said, and of no particular color. Asked if it could have been translucent, he said he guessed so.

Other information that bears on the incident is that one of the men had motioned to Everett to come to him but Everett declined. He was questioned by reporters to ascertain whether he had heard of the Schmidt incident, but he apparently hadn't. (The Schmidt story was just hitting news wires late on the preceding night and didn't appear in Knoxville papers until the 6th.)

His high school principals said Everett was a serious and honest boy. His parents said he was upset when they arrived home from work that morning (both worked at a nearby knitting mill), and his grandmother said that he called her after the incident and was "hysterical."

When reporter Carson Brewer went to the field with Everett and others he himself saw an oblong ring of pressed grass. He found he could not make a similar marking unless he walked round and round at least a dozen times. The impression was 24 feet by 5 feet. Everett said the object was considerably larger than that, however. His father remarked later: "I don't think he made it up, but I still don't believe it."

On November 7, 1957, a Tennessee truck driver for Cook Lines reported meeting three "little men" on the road about 15 miles northwest of Meridian, Mississippi, on State Highway 19. He was on his way to Meridian from Memphis, Tennessee.

The driver, Malvin Stevens, forty-eight, of Dyersburg, is described by his fellow workers and company officials as a "reliable family man not given to practical joking" and they stated they were inclined to believe that he saw what he said he had seen.

Stevens said he first thought the object, which was parked on the highway, was a weather balloon. He said it had a single propeller blade on each end and a third propeller on top. Stevens got out of his truck and was met by three "little men" who came out of the "thing." They were about 4½ feet tall, wore gray clothing, and had "pasty white faces." He said they seemed friendly and wanted to talk, but he couldn't understand their "chattering." "I stood there for what seemed like an eternity," he said. "They got back into the machine and it took off—straight up." When he first spotted the object it had no effect on his car engine as was the case in some stories of UFO landings. People to whom he talked upon arriving at Memphis said Stevens was visibly shaken and "white as a sheet." Although the experience lasted only about two minutes, Stevens said it seemed like an eternity.

Another "dog" story took place on the evening of November 6, if we can believe John Trasco, of Everittstown, New Jersey. He claimed he went outside at dusk to feed his dog and saw a brilliant egg-shaped object hovering in front of his barn. He was confronted by a 3-foot being with putty colored face. He had a nose and chin and large protruding frog-like eyes. Trasco said he thought he said, in broken English: "We are peaceful—people, we only want your dog." To which he, thoroughly frightened, replied: "Get the hell out of here." The creature then fled into the object which took off straight up.

Mrs. Trasco also claimed she saw the object from inside the house but did not see the "little man" due to some shrubbery near the house, although she heard the voice, and heard her husband's angry command. It is not known if certain details were ever cleared up, and were mentioned only nebulously in the *Delaware Valley News* on November 15. One of these questions involves whether there was more than one "entity," for Mrs. Trasco is quoted as saying that her husband tried to grab one of them, and got some green powder on his wrist which washed off. He also found some of the green powder under his fingernails the next day. The "little man" was dressed in a green suit with shiny buttons, with a green tam-o'-shanter-like cap, and gloves with a shiny object at the tip of each.

A strange story about stalled cars and little men was told to authorities and the press on the morning of November 6, 1957, when Richard Kehoe, an employee of the General Telephone Company of Santa Monica, related his early-morning experience. This is another tale which has fallen into ill repute because of the reluctance of researchers to accept human-like occupants as real, and the lack of corroborating witnesses.

Kehoe claimed that while driving along Vista del Mar at Playa del Rey in California (a beach area) at 5:40 A.M. his engine stopped as did the engines of two other cars. When the drivers got out to see what was wrong they saw an egg-shaped spaceship wrapped "in a blue haze" on the beach. Kehoe claimed two "little men" (about 5 feet 5 inches, which isn't really small) got out of the object and asked questions of him and the two other drivers, such as: "Where we were going? Who we were? What time it was? etc." He said their skin appeared to be yellowish-green in the early morning light, but that otherwise they looked normal. He said they were wearing black leather pants, white belts, and light-colored jerseys.

The two other drivers were identified as Ronald Burke of Redondo Beach and Joe Thomas of Torrance, and Kehoe claimed Thomas called the police. He said they sounded as though they were talking English but he couldn't understand them, and said simply that he had to go to work. The men got back into their ship and it disappeared into the sky, whereupon his car started up immediately. The ship was oval, tan or cream in color, with two metal rings around it upon which the object apparently rested, according to Kehoe.

The foregoing report faded into nothingness as other reports flowed out of news rooms across the United States in the ensuing days and months. The next incident took place at Old Saybrook, Connecticut, and was carefully investigated by Civilian Saucer Investigations, New York. Because of the reliability of the witness this is probably one of the most important of all of the "occupant" reports.

In the early morning of December 16, between 2 and 3 A.M. Mrs. Mary M. Starr, a resident of Old Saybrook and a holder of two degrees from Yale University, was awakened by bright lights passing by her bedroom window. The bedroom is located on the second floor of her cottage, the floor being 15 feet above ground level. She was looking north.

She saw an object just coming to a stop about 10 feet from her house. It appeared to be about 20 to 30 feet long, dark gray or black in color with brilliantly lighted portholes. The object remained motionless, about 5 feet above the ground, and had no protrusions of any kind.

Through the "windows" Mrs. Starr saw two forms which passed each other, going in opposite directions. What appeared to be their right arms were upraised, reminding her of stewards carrying trays, but no hands were visible. The wore a kind of jacket; their "heads" were square or rectangular, of a reddish-orange color, with what appeared to be a red bulb located at the middle of the "head." The feet were not visible. A third form entered from the left, and Mrs. Starr leaned forward in an attempt to see its face better and at that point the portholes faded and the entire shell of the object began to glow. Immediately a kind of antenna about 6 inches long rose from the top of the object at the end nearest to Mrs. Starr. It appeared to oscillate and sparkle. This "antenna" continued to glow and sparkle for about five minutes, and then the craft began to move to the right, back in the direction from which it had come. It made a very abrupt right angle turn, turned bluish-gray again, and small circular lights outlined the entire rim where the portholes had been. When it was over the nearby marsh it tilted steeply and shot up into the sky at the speed of a jet takeoff but without any sound.

Considering the fact that the object, while near the ground, was just above the clothesline yet below the upper part of the tool shed, according to Mrs. Starr's account, we can assume that the object was about 6 feet thick, and probably about 20 feet in diameter. Therefore, the "occupants" were no more than 4½ feet tall.

The Old Saybrook incident is the last 1957 "occupant" case, and it seems that the November-December time period was a popular one for landing incidents. Most people will recall that the November 1957 "flap" came close on the heels of the launching of the first space satellite by Russia. A few months earlier, however, according to the Milford, Pennsylvania *Dispatch*, Miss Francis Stichler observed a strange object and its occupants. Although no date is given, the December 19 issue of the *Dispatch* says the incident took place in May, as follows.

Miss Stichler, who lives on a farm near Milford, was doing chores in her barn at 6 A.M. when she heard a whirring sound and looked up. She said a flat, bowl-shaped object about 20 feet in diameter with a rim 3 to 4 feet wide came into view over the barn about 15 feet above the ground. When it stopped with one side tilted toward her, she saw a man clothed in a light-gray, tight-fitting helmet and loose, shiny, gray suit perched on the broad rim of the object. His feet and legs seemed to be concealed from view in the lower portion. His position was on the rim opposite Miss Stichler so that he was facing her. He seemed to be of average size, had deep-set eyes, a long face with a "quizzical expression," and looked quite tan. Just as Miss Stichler got over her initial shock, the object left toward the southeast, making a "spinning sound," and streaked out of sight. She claimed she said nothing about the sighting as she had no corroborating witnesses, and didn't think anyone would believe her. She eventually told about it after the other sightings of UFOs and occupants during the November-December "flap."

The "little men," or occupants, seem to have disappeared from the scene in the United States after December 1957, although there certainly may have been some which were not reported for fear of ridicule. Our next case deals with a "little man" although there is no craft involved.

A lady whom I know well and whose word I trust, reported the following incident to me, and I quote from her report verbatim.

"Joe and I and the two children were on our way to California on vacation in early June 1960. It was the night of the 9th, about midnight, when we were about fifteen minutes east of Globe, Arizona, heading west. Joe was asleep beside me and the kids were fast asleep in the back seat of the car. I was driving through the hills through which the road winds and dips. The Cadillac was performing beautifully and I kept a steady speed of about 65 miles per hour.

"At about 12:05 I began pulling around a right-hand turn and when I straightened out the car my headlights hit a small figure about 100 yards ahead on the right edge of the highway. It was facing to my left about to cross the road, it seemed. My immediate reaction was to let up on the accelerator, and the heavy car slowed immediately as we were on an upgrade. Simultaneously, the figure turned so that it was facing me, then turned again, and ran off into the wash out of range of my lights and off the road.

"The second I saw that thing my heart came up in my mouth and my stomach turned a flip-flop. When I got back my wits a few seconds later, I called out to Joe and tramped on the accelerator. He didn't respond right away, so I jostled him and he sat bolt upright. Then I told him what I had seen: the little figure, no more than twice the height of the posts which held the metallic reflecting road-guard (about 3 feet tall), small, broad-shouldered, with long arms, dark in color, and it had a head shaped like a somewhat flattened sphere—quite like a pumpkin. In this head were two yellowish-orange glowing 'eyes.' I recalled that when it was in side view there was light extending beyond the limits of the 'face.' I saw no nose, or mouth or ears. The body was not as well defined as the head, suggesting hair or fur.

"When Joe finally got the gist of what I was telling him, he told me to stop and we would go back. I told him that if he wanted to go back, we would go to Miami. He could drop us off, then go back by himself, but neither my children nor I were going back there on that lonely, dark road. By then I had pushed the Cad to 85 miles an hour, in a hurry to see lights and people again. He didn't insist so we kept on, stopped in Miami, then continued our trip."

The significant thing about this incident is, that besides the veracity of the observer and her husband's verification of her near-hysteria, the entity generally resembled the "little men" in Venezuela in 1954.

On April 18, 1961, at 11 A.M., Joe Simonton, a sixty-year-old chicken farmer of Eagle River, Wisconsin, allegedly witnessed the landing of a UFO in his yard. This is probably one of the most controversial cases we have ever investigated, and in the diverse spectrum of United States saucer groups it has aroused considerable suspicion, controversy, charges and countercharges, so that the truth seems almost indiscernible.

The original story is basically this. At 11 A.M. that morning, Simonton was startled by a strange loud noise outside and above his farmhouse. He stepped to the window and was surprised to see a silvery object coming down vertically in his yard. He approached the object (with no fear), whereupon a hatch in the upper portion opened and he saw three dark-skinned men inside. One of them handed him a silvery jug with two handles, made a motion like drinking, apparently indicating that he wanted water. Simonton took the jug, filled it and handed it back. Looking into the object, he saw a man "cooking" on some kind of flameless cooking appliance. There were several small, perforated, cookie-like objects beside the griddle and Simonton motioned that he wanted one, whereupon one of the men handed four of them to him. Then the object took off at a 45° angle and was gone in just a few seconds. As it left, pine trees near the takeoff path bowed over, apparently as a result of air turbulence as the object went over.

Although APRO had good representation in Wisconsin, we weren't fast enough to obtain one of the controversial "cookies," which Joe Simonton, who had eaten one, said tasted like cardboard. A UFO research group obtained one, as did Dr. J. Allen

Hynek, the Air Force's consulting astrophysicist.

After several days of much exploitation of the incident by news media, the UFO group announced that the affair had had too much publicity, and they did not intend to analyze the "cookie." On May 3 Simonton told United Press International that if "it happened again, I don't think I'd tell anybody about it." The same wire story quoted the UFO group statement which said that organization planned no further action and had more important things to investigate.

The most recent word on this affair comes from an APRO member in Minnesota who claims that one analysis with which he is familiar yielded the information that the cookie was made of corn and wheat flour as well as other well-known familiar ingredients, but that the exact origin of the certain type of wheat was not known. This is another case somewhat similar (where the occupants are concerned) to others, including the Playa del Rey Kehoe encounter.

The "men" involved were small, about 5 feet tall, had dark hair and skin, wore dark blue knit outfits with turtleneck tops, and knit helmets similar to those worn under headpieces. They had no beards or were clean-shaven. The whole episode lasted about five minutes and Simonton observed a few details of the inside of the craft. It was dull black, instrument panels included, he said, somewhat like wrought iron. One of the occupants appeared to be cooking, and stacked beside the appliance on which he "cooked" were some of the cookies. One man took care of getting the water, and the other stayed at the instrument board. The two who were cooking and watching the instruments did not look around. Just after Simonton obtained the cookies, the man hooked a line or belt into a hook in his clothing near the waist, the hatch closed and the object rose to 20 feet above the ground, then took off straight south.

The object itself appeared "like two washbowls turned face to face." The sound Simonton heard before coming out of his house was like "knobby tires on a wet pavement." The craft hovered a short distance (probably only a few inches) off the ground, all during the episode. The hatch was about 30 inches wide and about 6 feet high. All this, Simonton admitted, was guesswork.

Our next several occupant reports occurred during that historic period in the spring of 1964. On the morning of April 24, according to dairy farmer Gary T. Wilcox of Tioga City, New York, he was visited by the occupants of a flying saucer. Shortly before 10 A.M. he was spreading fertilizer in an open field and stopped to go and check a V-shaped field on another part of the farm which is almost completely surrounded by woods. As he approached the field, about a mile from his dairy barn, he saw a shiny object which he at first thought was a discarded refrigerator that had been there for a time. As he drew nearer he realized it was not, and thought it was a wing tank from an airplane which had fallen there. The object was about 20 feet long and 16 feet wide, shaped like an egg and made of a shiny metal which resembled aluminum. He saw no door or hatch, but two small men (approximately 4 feet tall) suddenly appeared, dressed in clothing without visible seams, and a hood which covered their faces completely. Each was carrying a tray of what appeared to be soil removed from the field. One of the men started to talk to Wilcox, informing him that they were from Mars, that he needn't be afraid, and that they had talked to people before. His English was very smooth and effortless. Wilcox said that he thought someone was playing a trick on him. One man stood by the craft, the other about 5 feet from Wilcox, and the voice seemed to come from the body rather than the head area.

The conversation then turned to a discussion of organic material, including fertilizers. They seemed to be interested in this facet of farming, and said that where they came from they grew food in the atmosphere. Among other things they said they could only travel to earth every two years and were currently using the western hemisphere (for a base?). They asked for fertilizer then, and when Wilcox went to get it, the craft took off. Wilcox got a bag of fertilizer, left it in the field, and the next day it was gone.

Another incident, which is similar to the Tioga County affair, allegedly took place on July 16, 1964, at Conklin, New York. Five young boys claimed they saw a spaceman and his craft just 2 miles from their homes. The field where the incident took place is favored by youngsters because of a proliferation of huckleberry bushes. When questioned closely and threatened with punishment for fibbing, they broke into tears but none of them would retract their original claims.

The boys were Edmund and Randy Travis, nine and seven years old, Floyd Moore, ten, Billy Dunlap, seven, and Gary Dunlap, five. Mrs. Travis said she first learned of the experience when three of the boys came running to her house shortly after 12:30 P.M. seeking a jar of water. "They said they were taking some water over to the spaceman," she said. "They said they couldn't understand what he said but it sounded like he needed water." An adult was sent after the other two boys and met them walking home from the field. They at first denied seeing the spaceman, afraid of a spanking because they didn't think anyone would believe them. They were separated from one another and questioned.

When Mrs. Travis finally convinced them they should tell what they had seen, this is what they told. They had come upon the creature in the field. He was about the size of a "little boy," had a human-looking face, and was wearing a black suit and black helmet. The helmet had antenna-like wires on top and white lettering (unidentified by the children) across the front. He was wearing a plastic or glass lens over his eyes and was making a peculiar noise which sounded like it came out of a pipe. They described it as similar to the noise made by a kazoo.

The spaceman walked toward the vehicle. Part of it was obscured by bushes, but what they saw was shiny "like a car bumper." He stepped up on top of it, and it was then that the children asked if he needed help or water. Then the creature seemed to "fall backward" from the top of the vehicle. At this point the children left the field and ran toward home. An observer who visited the field later noticed matted foliage where the boys said the vehicle had been. There were also three depressions around the matted area as though whatever had crushed the foliage was supported by columns or legs.

An industrial worker claimed he witnessed the landing of two noiseless, unlighted UFOs which came down in a wooded area in the vicinity of Lynchburg, Virginia, on January 23, 1964. The craft, he said, were 20 and 80 feet in diameter. Three creatures, 37 inches high, disembarked from the small ship and approached to within 12 yards of the observer, and he "froze" in his tracks. They were humanoid types except for their small stature and strange eyes "which looked through me," he said. The little fellows uttered unintelligible sounds, then turned around and walked back to the object from which they had emerged. A door opened, they entered, and the opening appeared to seal itself so there was no evidence of an opening when it was closed. The encounter purportedly lasted about thirty minutes, having begun at 5:40 P.M. The observer refuses to be identified publicly.

Most of us are familiar with the Brooksville, Florida, sighting of March 3, 1965, in which sixty-five-year-old John Reeves claimed he had watched a 5-foot spaceman and his craft near his home on the outskirts of Weeki-wachi Springs, Florida. Reeves claimed he came upon the object while out walking at about 2 P.M. He spotted the object some distance away, approached it by a circuitous route, then saw the "spaceman" who approached him and looked at him. The craft was 20 to 30 feet in diameter and about 8 feet thick. Around the circumference there was an arrangement of "slats" which resembled venetian blinds which opened and closed just before the object took off. The craft rested on four "legs," and a cylindrical affair with disc-shaped "steps" provided entry into the craft from underneath.

The "creature" in this instance was dressed in a silver-gray, tight-fitting, stiff-appearing suit, atop which was a helmet much like a glass bowl inverted over his head and resting on his shoulders. The head inside was covered by dark material which covered the hair area. The ears, mouth, and nose appeared normal but the eyes were large and very wide-set with a "flat" area between. The chin was very pointed. The hands were covered by mittens which appeared to be very pliable and the same color as the suit. Reeves did not notice the foot gear.

Reeves claimed that the creature, while approaching the saucer from some bushes, spotted him, came toward him, and just looked at him. Then he drew a small black box from "his left side," it "flashed," whereupon Reeves started to leave. He lost his hat, stooped to retrieve it, turned, and the box "flashed" again. He saw no flash attachment, doesn't know if it was a camera or not.

Footprints were later found, but unfortunately the photographer did not bother to take long-range shots of several sets and valuable information was lost. Reeves later claimed that the spaceman came very close to him, and knocked his helmet against his (Reeves') head, then conversed with him by mental telepathy. This latter has been discarded as embroidery of the basic story, for the assertion came a considerable time after the original story was told.

Reeves does not seem to be sufficiently knowledgeable about UFO lore to have concocted such a detailed story. Two pieces of tissue-thin paper containing strange marks, which Reeves claimed the spaceman dropped, were obtained and decoded by the Air Force and found to bear the trite message:

> PLANET MARS—ARE YOU COMING HOME SOON—WE MISS YOU VERY MUCH—WHY DID YOU STAY AWAY TOO LONG.

Other markings were not decoded. It has been hypothesized that if the landing and "contact" were real, it was a deliberate attempt to mislead humans, the paper and its message being a deliberate hoax by the "spaceman."

Three tiny "tin men" star in the case at Long Prairie, Minnesota, on October 23, 1965. According to his story, Jerry Townsend, nineteen, a fledgling radio announcer, was driving from Little Falls to Long Prairie at 7:40 P.M. on the night in question. At about four miles out of Long Prairie he rounded a curve; his engine, lights, and radio went dead, so he braked his car. Ahead of him was a rocket-shaped object, about 30 to 40 feet high and 10 feet in diameter, resting on three fins in the middle of the road. Townsend got out of his car, walked toward the front fender, then stopped at the sight of three little, beer-can shaped "objects" which came from under the ship and moved toward him. They were 6 inches high, walked on two "fins," and when they stopped, a third "fin" came down in the rear. He saw no faces, eyes, etc., and said they moved with a side-to-side waddling gait. They seemed to be watching him. After what seemed to be an eternity, he said, they went under the big "rocket," and disappeared into it. The object then took off. The "colorless" light which issued from the bottom of the "rocket" went out after it was airborne. The object's takeoff, Townsend said, looked like someone had "lifted a flashlight off a table."

The wrapup on this case included inquiries to teachers and friends. Townsend got a clean bill of health as far as his reputation for honesty was concerned. After the object left, he drove to Long Prairie where he told of his encounter at the sheriff's office. Sheriff Bain told us via telephone that Townsend had a good reputation, was not a drinker, and that he had been visibly frightened when he reported his experience. Bain and Long Prairie Police Officer Lavern Lubitz returned to the spot where the object was reportedly seen, and found three parallel strips of oil-like substance about 4 inches apart and a yard long, on the surface of the road. "I don't know what they were, but I've looked at a lot of roads and never saw anything like them before," Bain told reporters later.

A report out of the state of Washington in August 1965 told of three non-human-appearing men seen by two girls near Renton. According to the report, at 7:30 A.M. the two girls were in a bean field. The beings had white-domed heads and protruding eyes. The faces had no expression, the eyes were gray like stone, and the lower part of the faces appeared to be deeply tanned. They wore armless, V-necked jerseys of purple color with white shirts underneath. The frightened girls ran about 50 feet past the men and when they looked back the beings had disappeared. No craft was seen in connection with this incident.

One of the most unusual incidents involving occupants which has come into APRO Headquarters allegedly took place in the early morning hours of March 28, 1967. It is one of those extremely strange stories that one is prompted to completely disbelieve from the outset. However, after checking into the character and reputation of the witness, we were forced to conclude that he was telling what he saw and nothing else.

The witness, David Morris, who was twenty years old at the time, was a finish grinder at the Lamb Electric Company in Kent, Ohio. He usually worked from 5 P.M. to 2 or 4 A.M. and on the morning in question he left work at 2 A.M., drove out Rt. 5 to

Marsh Road, south to Munroe Falls Road which is a short cut to his home in Munroe Falls. Since that time, however, Morris takes the long way around and refuses to drive the route anymore.

It was about 2:20 A.M. when Morris spotted an orangish-red glow off to the left and on the other side of the hill on Munroe Falls Road. He was proceeding slowly because of a thick fog which had settled over the Kent area following an electrical storm.

Upon seeing the glow, Morris said he thought it might be a house on fire, and automatically slowed his 1964 Chevrolet. He thought perhaps a house had been struck by lightning. When he topped the crest of the hill he saw a glowing "wedge or cone-shaped" object 25 to 30 yards off to the left, south of the road, in a wheat field. It appeared to Morris to be about 25 feet tall and about 12 feet wide at the base. On top of the object where the triangular shape came to a point was what appeared to be a ball-shaped object.

Morris was non-plussed at the sight of the object but was more curious than frightened. His estimated speed was about 30 miles per hour. He pulled his eyes from the object and looked back at the highway, whereupon his curiosity turned to horror. About 45 to 50 feet in front of his car were four or five small figures about 3½ to 4 feet tall with oversized heads which gave off the same orangish-red glow as the object sitting in the wheat field. He said he didn't know if the little beings had headpieces on or not, but that their heads were abnormally large. The bodies appeared to be of stocky build and were humanoid in form. He could not distinguish any clothing or features but had the impression that they were wearing an all-emcompassing piece of clothing such as a coverall.

The small figures ran very quickly back and forth across the road with much more speed and agility than Morris felt he could accomplish. They seemed to be moving purposefully from a drainage ditch on the north side of the road to the south side and back again.

At first sight of the creatures, Morris slammed on his brakes. The figures had given no indication that they were aware of him, despite his headlights, and he did not stop his car in time. He heard a "thump" as the right front of the auto struck one of the figures as it was crossing the road. The car traveled another 8 to 10 feet before he could bring it to a complete stop. Almost instinctively, Morris put his hand on the door handle to open it, but stopped. He said he had no fear that he had struck down "an ordinary human," but the thought flashed through his mind: "If I killed them, they'll kill me." He then sped away as fast as he dared to in the fog. Looking into the rear view mirror he saw that the figures were standing in a group but could not discern whether or not one of them was lying in the road. When he reached home, Morris said, he simply sat in the living room for two hours. Then, finally having calmed down, had enough strength enough to climb the stairs and go to bed.

That afternoon, accompanied by a friend, he went back to the spot. The field where the cone-shaped object had been seen yielded no evidence of its presence there. They did find the skid marks on the road where Morris said he slammed on his brakes and struck the "figure." But there were no footprints or other indication of the presence of the little creatures, or that one had been struck down.

The front of Morris's car was dented in the chrome trim in three separate places and scratches were visible. He did not notify any authorities concerning the incident, fearing ridicule. What evidence there may have been on the chrome trim was destroyed that day, because being a meticulous individual who took good care of his car, he had washed and polished it that afternoon before going to work.

The foregoing is the basic information received at APRO shortly after the incident took place. Later, Morris was interviewed by Virgil E. Tarlton who learned the following. Morris got the impression that the cone-shaped object was hovering 2 or 3 feet above the ground and that its light came from the inside—it appeared to be translucent. It did not move nor did the glow change in intensity. He saw no markings, windows or doors, nor did he hear any sound. He did recall a smell (his window was rolled part way down) resembling the odor of hot brass. He admitted that it could have come from the car but didn't think so.

Morris's car was apparently not affected by the object; the lights and engine functioned perfectly. He felt no sensation of heat, but felt cold and clammy after the experience of seeing the figures. He was sure of the presence of four figures but said there could have been five. He could not discern that the figures were carrying anything and said that when his skidding car struck one of them it had been running across the road. At the point of impact he saw the figure's hand and there were no fingers that he could see.

Everyone who was questioned about Morris's honesty and reliability gave him high marks. It was the consensus of his friends, co-workers, and the investigator that he was describing an experience which he actually had.

Because of stepped-up UFO activity in 1967, when APRO published the Morris case we urged the membership to be doubly alert in the months ahead, for it was felt that more occupant cases would be reported, and our efforts bore fruit.

Two fourteen-year-old girls observed a strange tableau for quite a period of time on the night of September 15, 1967, near Winsted, Connecticut. Although they readily described what they saw, they refused to let their names be used. At 8:45 P.M. the two girls were in the bedroom (one was staying overnight with the other) and looking out the window when their attention was attracted by an egg-shaped glowing object which appeared to be about the size of a Volkswagen car. It was about 200 yards away in a field and looked as though it was over or beyond a barn complex. They watched the thing for at least thirty-five minutes while it moved back and forth, occasionally hovering. On occasion the color of the object would change from white to beige to pink to a deep red-orange in a continuous pattern, then reverse the procedure. This took place about ten times during the course of the observation.

After a period of time the girls heard a noise from the direction of the barn which sounded like a lawn mower starting up. Immediately following that two small figures emerged quickly from the barn and stood by the mailbox next to the road and appeared to be staring in the direction of the house. The girls could not get a good look at the two figures because the clouds repeatedly blocked out the moon. They said they had fleeting impressions more than anything else, but did judge the figures were less than 4 feet tall and appeared to be wearing similar outfits. One of the girls stated her impression that one of the figures which she could see more clearly than the other appeared to have an abnormally large head.

The figures were in the vicinity of the mailbox for about two minutes, then darted quickly across the road and stood under a large tree in its shadow. During this period the object in the field continued its maneuvers. The girls considered the possibility that the two small, dark figures might have been children but discounted it because they felt it would have been impossible for them not to have seen the object, and if they had been children they should have reacted to it, but they didn't.

The figures stood by the tree for a matter of moments until car headlights appeared down the road. Then they ran back across the street, where they were joined by a third figure, all three of whom ran across the lot by the side of the barn and disappeared in the darkness. The light went out on the object and stayed out until the car was out of sight up the road. The object stayed around, still maneuvering, for quite some time. The girls tired of watching, but later showed it to the mother who had been out shopping, but by this time it was very dim and a considerable distance away. A neighbor across the street watched the craft for a few minutes, became frightened, and went back into the house. She did not see the figures. Two adults in Winsted saw what apparently was the same or a similar object for a period of five minutes, within forty minutes of the sighting at the farm.

A little over a month later a report came in from a western state. Although we published the basic information we were limited to that only and no names or location. The witnesses were cognizant of the ridicule they might suffer if they made public what they had seen along with their identity.

A couple of campers watched a strange-appearing, glowing object on the side of a mountain twice during a week's camping outing. On both occasions they observed small lights which "danced" about as if the law of gravity had no effect on them whatsoever. Through binoculars the campers found that each of the lights had a tiny human form below it, giving the impression that the figures were being propelled through the air by some device with a light in the head area for illumination. Both sightings occurred during the week of October 22 to 28, 1967.

By the end of 1967 we had thought that the lag in sighting reports as well as the lack of occupant cases signalled the end of another UFO "flap" and we were right. But in the months and years ahead we were still receiving information on sightings for that particular year. A February 14, 1967, report did not reach the office until the fall of 1969 and again, because of the bizarre nature of the experience, the witness asked that his identity be kept a secret.

The location of the sighting was on a farm in Miller County, Missouri. At 7 A.M. the sky was clear and bright with no stars visible. Mr. X was walking toward a large barn located about 100 feet east of his house when he noticed one of his cows looking out into the field located east of the barn. He then saw an object on the ground some 335 feet from him. At this point he was looking through scattered trees and thought the object was a parachute. He walked to the northeast corner of the barn and could see the object and several smaller ones moving below it. They were moving quite rapidly and they seemed to have arms or levers which were also moving rapidly. The smaller "objects" appeared to have wide-set eyes but he could not see any legs. Mr. X had a bucket of feed which he placed inside the barn gate, then started toward the object, and as he reached a fence some 70 feet from the barn he stopped and picked up two rocks.

He said, "As I came through the first gate I picked up two rocks, pretty good size, one of them was, I got up to about 30 feet of it and it was sitting there kind of rocking slightly and I thought, boy, here goes. I'm going to knock a hole in that thing and see what the hell it is. I cut down on it and the rock stopped along about 15 feet from it and just hit the ground. The next rock I thought I would throw on top of it and it just hit something and bounced." As Mr. X neared the object the small objects started moving around, behind, and into a shaft which extended to the ground. The last smaller object was just going into the shaft when X was still about 80 feet from the UFO.

Mr. X's description of the object is quite interesting. "It just looked like a big shell, a grayish-green outfit, and underneath there were oblong holes where the lights were coming out. They were so bright you couldn't see when you got up close to it."

Concerning his progress toward the object, Mr. X told APRO's investigator: "I thought I was going right up to it; I got up to about here (about 15 feet from the object) and there it was. I just walked up against a wall; I couldn't see it at all; there was just a pressure."

He claimed that as he stood there, some 15 feet from the object, it started to rock slightly off the vertical about six times before it took off. "When it took off it just rocked back and moved real fast to the left of that ridge," he told the investigator, pointing to a hill nearby. He said it made no sound and he detected no odor and the "shaft was pulled up into it as it took off."

In this incident, there were clearly some sort of beings, whether living or robots, involved. Mr. X did not try to supply details which weren't there. He pointed out that the incident took place just before the sun broke above a large ridge in the east and the ground was well lighted. The sky was clear, the morning was cool with a light wind out of the east, the ground was muddy, and the largest object rested on a slight rise near the northeastern edge of the field.

The object was a disc, rounded at the top, flattened at the base. It appeared to be some 12 to 15 feet in diameter, about 6 feet thick, and sat on a shaft of some 2½ feet in height and about 18 inches in diameter, which was the same gray-green color. Mr. X compared the surface of the object to that of silk with no seams or rivets in evidence. Around the lower rim were located several oblong holes about 6 to 8 inches long and spaced about 1 foot apart. Extremely bright light emanated from the holes and the light changed colors. "They were all the colors of the rainbow," Mr. X said. There was no sound heard at any time and the whole incident lasted approximately five minutes and no ground markings were found after the object had left.

The smaller objects, which moved about in the vicinity of the larger one, were between ten or twelve in number and about 2 feet tall. The drawing made by Mr. X of the small "objects" or "humanoids" resembles generally a peanut with a proboscis-like protrusion near the top, an "eye," and what may have been a visor, and the "arms" (if such they were) were quite slim. No feet or legs were observed.

Weird as it seems, the foregoing incident was reported by a man who was as shocked by what he saw as the investigator who interviewed him. He would not embellish the details, but was adamant about what he had seen.

Another late-arriving report reached us in late December 1970 and related a strange nocturnal experience of a woman alone at night tending a sick child. Mrs. Adeline Davis initially contacted Mr. Walt Andrus, then a field investigator for APRO who was fairly well known in the states of Illinois and Missouri, and related her story to him. In June 1970 she attended the Midwest UFO Conference which was co-sponsored by APRO and APCCI of Peoria, Illinois. Because of the crowd she did not have the opportunity to talk with Mrs. Lorenzen who was one of the speakers at the conference so she wrote to her later. She was disappointed that, after having related her experience to one of our investigators, there had been no follow-up, and she wanted to know our decision regarding her report. Headquarters had not received the report and asked Field Investigators Allen Benz and Ted Phillips to go to Edina, Missouri, to interview her.

They learned the following. Mrs. Davis was in the northwest bedroom with her daughter, who was ill. She was not sleeping soundly because she was making regular temperature checks. The exact date is not remembered but the experience took place in the first or second week of January 1969.

She suddenly found herself sitting up in bed and looking at the window, although no sound was heard. She had no idea why she suddenly woke and sat up. At the window she saw an unusual looking object with an occupant in it who was looking in her direction. Unable to believe her eyes, she pinched herself, hit herself, jumped up and down, trying to make sure that she was awake. She even ran into the bathroom and bathed her face. After returning to the bedroom, she sat down in the middle of the edge of the bed by the window and once again peered at the entity outside the window. "He" seemed to be on a level with the window which would have placed him about 7 feet above the ground. When first seen, the occupant was about 6 feet from Mrs. Davis and seemed to be working on something below the window and looking downward.

Mrs. Davis said that the occupant suddenly raised his head, his mouth dropped open, and there was a definitely surprised look on his face. He continued to look at her for a brief time, then resumed his work below the level of the window. After a short time he looked up again and reached upward and to the right with his right hand for something which Mrs. Davis could not see. It seemed to her that he couldn't reach whatever he was after, for he turned slightly and reached with his left hand. He then turned and looked at Mrs. Davis, and the object in which he was located began to back slowly away from the house. As it moved away she could see a white light beam coming from the base of the object, projecting downward. It made a bend and illuminated a small cedar tree. This light was the only light observed by Mrs. Davis except for the light from the interior of the object. No sound was heard at any time.

The object then moved back about 10 to 12 feet, stopped, and the white light went out. After the object stopped it started turning slightly and moved to the northwest, and as it turned, Mrs. Davis could see that the windows were tinted blue. The back side of the object was identical to the front except for the window area. The frame around the window area was visible but a shield covered the window section, which was the same color of the object itself—army green. A dark, vertical marking was observed extending from the top edge of the window framing.

Mrs. Davis again went to bathe her face and when she returned to the window she noted that the leg on the far side of the object was about 3 feet off the ground and the near leg about 5 feet above the surface. She could only see about half of the back side as it turned and the object was last seen as it moved slowly northeast at very low altitude (just above the ground) and it disappeared behind the corner of the house.

After the object left, Mrs. Davis went into the living room and smoked a cigarette. It was at this time that she noted that the furnace fan (which is on automatic and runs constantly) was not operating. A minute or so after she sat down it started running again, indicating to her that the electricity had been off. The next morning, Mrs. Davis found that the electric clocks were twenty minutes slow. She checked with neighbors but they reported no electrical failure.

In their report, Benz and Phillips noted that at one point during its presence the object was in a position where it could have touched or pushed the power line to the Davis home. The power line is some 10 feet above the ground and tree branches which were pushed back by the object are about 9 feet above the ground. Mrs. Davis was not frightened by the episode and went to bed and slept soundly after the object left. The morning after the incident, Mrs. Davis felt extremely nervous, a condition which persisted throughout the entire day.

Mrs. Davis described the occupant as wearing dark clothing

with a cap resembling an army fatigue cap. No hair was noted and the eyes, rather slanted and wide-spread, had "fuzzy" or indefinite pupils. He wore a dark jacket with an opening down the front and a small upright collar with scalloped edges and a scarf.

This case raises many questions. If as most researchers tend to believe, these things are from outer space, why don't they contact leaders of governments instead of parking outside homes in the middle of the night? In this specific instance, we might recall that the "occupant" seemed to be doing something. Was he in fact effecting a repair of some kind? In the chapter titled "Are They Infallible?" we deal with some cases which indicate that at least some of the landings take place because of mechanical failure of some kind. If the entity in the Davis case was not repairing something, perhaps his preoccupation (even after becoming aware of her presence) was related to some kind of research. Unfortunately, this kind of case, although valuable from a statistical standpoint, leaves more questions unanswered than answered.

The craft and occupant described by Mrs. Davis amount to a "tame" report when compared to the alleged experience of Mrs. Lyndia Morel of Goffstown, New Hampshire, in the early morning of November 2, 1973. Although a one-witness incident, Mrs. Morel's hysterical condition when she began beating on the door of the Beaudoin residence on the outskirts of Goffstown, indicates she had a frightening experience of some kind. She had left her place of work in Manchester at 2:45 A.M., stopped for a cup of coffee with a friend, bought some gasoline for her car, and then proceeded home. During the trip she became aware of a strange, large, bright yellow light, which during the next few miles seemed to be following her.

Ultimately, on a deserted stretch of road the object came close enough so that she was able to observe its shape as well as the appearance of the sole occupant visible through an oval port on the front of the object. The thing itself was a sphere which was covered with what appeared to be six-sided facets all over the surface. Above midline was situated the oval-shaped window.

The occupant was only visible from about the waist up and the hands were out of sight below a dark portion which cut across the bottom of the oval, and which Mrs. Morel thought might have been an instrument panel. The occupant's body appeared darker than the face with small shoulders, but it was uncertain whether the body had clothing on or not. The rounded head was grayish (between a gray and flesh tone), except for a darker color on top, and the face bore wrinkles or loose skin like an elephant's hide. Angling upward across the forehead two large "egg-shaped" eyes with large, dark pupils gripped her attention so·much that she felt she was unable to look away. She said she received the impression or awareness that "told" her "don't be afraid." A mouth-slit turning down at the corners, completed the description of the face. No nose or ears were noted.

Panic-stricken, Mrs. Morel believed she was in imminent danger of being captured by the UFO, and after passing by a cemetery, she spotted a house ahead on the left. The globe had become so dazzling that she covered her eyes with an arm and simultaneously turned the wheel with the other hand, entering the driveway of the Beaudoin house at an angle and coming to a halt partly on the front lawn. She got out of the car, ran across the lawn where she began beating on the door and pleading for help. At this point the object changed position and moved away. When Mrs. Beaudoin opened the door two minutes later, Mrs. Morel began sinking to her knees in a faint but did not lose consciousness. Mrs. Beaudoin attested to the fact that the young woman was extremely frightened and hysterical when she saw her at the door.

In addition to the description of the occupant and the object, Mrs. Morel told Field Investigator Betty Hill and Astronomy Consultant Walter Webb that at one time before she came to the Beaudoin neighborhood she had the impression that she had lost control of her car and that the object had been accompanied by a high-pitched whine.

Investigators determined that Lyndia Morel was telling what she believed to be the truth about a very unnerving experience. But still it is one of the more weird encounters which puts a strain on the tolerance of even the most seasoned investigator or researcher.

In early 1974 Headquarters received a report from Field Investigator Kevin Randle who operates out of Des Moines, Iowa, and who has been an indefatigable researcher for many years. He had handing case, and although he eventually convinced the witness that he should submit to the interview, the man would not allow his name to be used and he refused to even fill out a report form.

Mr. T. claimed that he was working in the fields in a rural Iowa area where he operates a farm on the afternoon of June 6, 1972, when his attention was drawn to the sky by a flash of light. He didn't pay much attention to it at first because he thought it was an airplane but did note its silver color and the fact that it was approaching him. As it got closer, it was obvious that it was an unusual object, shaped like an egg and slowly descending into Mr. T's cornfield. Just prior to landing, legs or a type of landing gear "grew" out of the bottom and the strange craft landed gently in the field about 100 yards from the witness. A port of some sort opened on the side near the bottom and then "some people" got out. In Mr. T.'s words, "they messed around" in the corn for a while, then got back into the craft and it took off. As the object took off, a blue flame shot out of the bottom and the legs retracted. There was a slight roar as the ship shot into the sky. The corn shocks in that area of the field looked as though they had been caught in a whirlwind, but Mr. T. found no burned vegetation.

The "people" were thought by Mr. T. to be about 5 feet tall and seemed to be wearing one-piece "flying suits." From 100 yards distance the witness said he couldn't see much detail and he didn't attempt to get any closer. Mr. T. said the object cast a shadow when it was on the ground, was faster than a jet when he first saw it, but slowed as it approached the ground. When it left it was out of sight in a matter of seconds. He estimated its size to be about 15 to 20 feet tall.

In viewing the drawings made by Mr. T., one cannot help but note the similarities between this object and occupants and those observed by Patrolman Lonnie Zamora at Socorro, New Mexico, on April 24, 1964. Mr. T.'s drawing showed only three legs on the object (one may not have been visible to him) while Zamora reported four. On the other hand, while the blue flame was reported in both cases accompanied by a roaring sound, the Zamora object burned vegetation in the area while the only evidence of the landing in Mr. T.'s case was the swirled cornstalks, not unlike the so-called "saucer nests" reported before.

Another farmer, Mr. William Bosak, sixty-eight, of rural Frederic, Wisconsin, told the press of his encounter with an unusual-appearing entity on the night of December 2, 1974. At that time Wisconsin was just beginning to feel the effects of concentrated UFO activity throughout the state. Police officers as well as the average citizen were reporting strange, lighted objects in the skies.

Bosak was returning home from a Farmer's Co-op meeting in Frederic and was driving southeast when about a mile from his farm he spotted an object on the left side of the road ahead of him. He had been driving slowly because of patches of fog and his headlights reflected off the object so he slowed down as he approached it.

"It had a curved front of glass and inside I could see a figure with its arms raised above its head," Bosak told reporters. The object was standing still, he said, and appeared to be between 8 and 10 feet in height. The transparent "glass" area through which Bosak said he could view the occupant was bullet-shaped at the top, or tapered to a peak. He had slowed nearly to a stop when he came up to the object, but then fear took over and he stepped on the accelerator and left the object behind. He said that when he did so, the inside of his car became dark and he heard a swishing sound like branches of a tree brushing against the car.

The "human," as Bosak referred to it, had hair sticking out from the sides of its head with ears protruding out about 3 inches and they were shaped like a calf's ear. The creature had no collar or shirt with seam in front but appeared to be clothed in something tannish-brown in color and fitted (skin-tight) like a diver's suit. Both arms were extended above its head and hair stuck out from the outside of the arms. There was no beard, but there was hair or fur on the upper part of the body. The rest of it, from the waist down, was not visible because of the fog. The object itself was not lighted but reflected light from the headlights of Bosak's car.

Bosak said he returned to the location the next morning to search for marks or evidence of the object's presence, but found nothing. He said he was very frightened at the time but the look on the face of the occupant of the craft indicated that it was frightened too. Its eyes were very large and protruding.

Bosak, afraid of ridicule, kept the experience to himself for nearly a month, not even telling his wife and son. He admitted also that he was so frightened at the time that he was afraid to go out at night for a few days. Bosak admitted that prior to his own experience he had been very skeptical of UFO tales and said he realized that a lot of people wouldn't believe him and he would be willing to take a lie detector test to prove his honesty in the matter.

Mr. Bosak has operated a 450-acre farm east of Frederic for the past forty years and is considered to be honest and reliable by his fellow citizens in the area.

Another rural sighting incident which was of the late-blooming nature (not arriving at Headquarters until early 1975 while it had taken place in 1965), was a sighting of an object as well as a possible occupant in August of that year. Partially because of the way they were treated when they tried to get police to investigate, and partly because they fear ridicule, the parties involved will not allow their names to be used. Although the occupant was observed by only one of the trio, all three saw the landing or at least the descent of the main object.

D.G., his father, and sister were sitting in the yard of their rural home in Iowa at about 3 or 4 P.M. one day in late August 1965, when they heard a high-pitched whining sound. They looked around but didn't see anything at first, and then D.G. saw an unusual object descending in the southern part of the sky. The witnesses described it as looking like two saucers glued together, about 15 to 20 feet in diameter, and silver in color. In fact, D.G. told Field Investigator Kevin Randle that the surface looked like polished aluminum. The object descended at about the speed of a man on a parachute and finally disappeared behind a hill. The hill wasn't very far away and D.G. decided to try for a better look so he headed in that direction. The whining sound had faded away when the craft went out of sight.

At about 160 yards from the hill, D.G. spotted a being or some object standing behind a tree at the top of the hill. He watched it for only a very few seconds and started to walk faster. At that point he tripped and to keep his footing had to look down for an instant and when he looked up again the being was gone. A few minutes later he saw a blur, heard a sound like rushing air, and saw the object ascend into the air and disappear in a couple of seconds, going straight up.

D.G. ran to the tree where he had seen the being and, based on the size of the tree and the area where the being had shown its head and shoulders, guessed it to be approximately 3 or 3½ feet tall. The head had seemed to be bald but he was too far away to observe much else. He found no footprints so he continued over the hill to see if the object had left any evidence.

In an old quarry D.G. found a perfectly round, burned area. It was about 15 to 20 feet in diameter. (Note: Investigator Randle said he believes D.G. assumed the burned area would be the same size as the craft and therefore the estimate of the size of the object itself may be inaccurate.) All the grass in the circle was charred but at the edge it was green. There was a definite edge to the circle and inside it D.G. found three indentations about 1 inch deep, 5 inches wide, and 12 inches long. They were about 2 feet from the edge of the circle. The ground in the area was very firm.

D.G. ran back to his house and told his father. They set out for Cedar Falls where they stopped by the highway patrol office, but personnel there made fun of them and they received the same treatment when they reported the incident to the Waverly police. They told Randle they were bitter about the way they had been treated but were glad to talk to someone who would be willing to listen.

And so we bring up to date the occupant cases for the United States.

Although the facial features of the "little men" described in Ohio cases are anything but human-appearing, we can do little in the way of interpretation as is the case in most other entity episodes, because there is always the possibility of some kind of headpiece or mask being used. The surreptitiousness of the UFO entities in past years indicates an unwillingness to contact humans. Only in the past few years have we been confronted with cases coming from apparently credible and reliable witnesses relating to close-up contact and voice communication. This may be a simple matter of our "visitors" being ready for such contact. Some of us entertain the idea that the UFOs monitor our communications, and it seems if they have similar vocal chords, that they should be capable of learning our language given adequate time, which they certainly have had.

A certain segment of UFO researchers (which happen to be in the minority in our country, fortunately) resisted the idea of humanoid UFO occupants until the famous Socorro (Lonnie Zamora) case in 1964. To attempt to convince these people that their attitude is emotionally rooted would be a waste of time. Therefore, those of us who are deeply interested in every phase of the UFO mystery have been greatly hampered by our own colleagues. The modus operandi of these "researchers" is to gather every kind of report but to suppress those which are not personally acceptable—thus preventing others from the type of correlative work which needs to be done with all reports.

To sum up, it would seem that we are dealing, even at this juncture, only with a mass of reports involving various types of bipeds who apparently navigate or at least ride in unconventional aircraft. In order to be scientifically correct we cannot assume more than that.

Early on the morning of March 23, 1966, Mr. Eddie Laxton, fifty-six, of Temple, Oklahoma, came upon a fish-shaped silver object in the road on Highway 70 near the Texas-Oklahoma state line. Laxton is an experienced electronics instructor at Sheppard Air Force Base at Wichita Falls, Texas. He got out of his car, approached the object, and saw a man dressed in "GI fatigues" (work uniform) standing by the craft. He turned back to his car to get his camera and when he turned around the man was getting into the object via a ladder and the craft took off vertically. Laxton, familiar with aircraft, could not identify the object, although he got a good look at it. The letters and numbers TL41, arranged vertically, were easily visible on the ship. It was learned later that a truck driver approaching from the opposite direction saw the same object. Laxton is sure that the object is a "secret test vehicle," but if Anderson, the truck driver, is telling the truth when he says other drivers have seen similar things on the road in the same area in the near past, we have a ridiculous situation in which some U.S. government agency is flying test machines outside the confines of guarded test ranges. What else, then? Perhaps test vehicles from another country? Not likely—that would be too risky.

Our only possible answer, therefore, is that our "visitors" are modifying their own craft to look somewhat like earth aircraft and dressing their crews to resemble ours. Why? That's a good question. If we hypothesize that they are attempting to confuse us, we only come up with another question: Why?

Zamora sees the craft with humanoids several hundred feet away. (Chapter 2)

The craft takes off as Zamora approaches the wash. (Chapter 2)

Zamora returns to the patrol car as the craft proceeds into the southwest.

(Chapter 2)

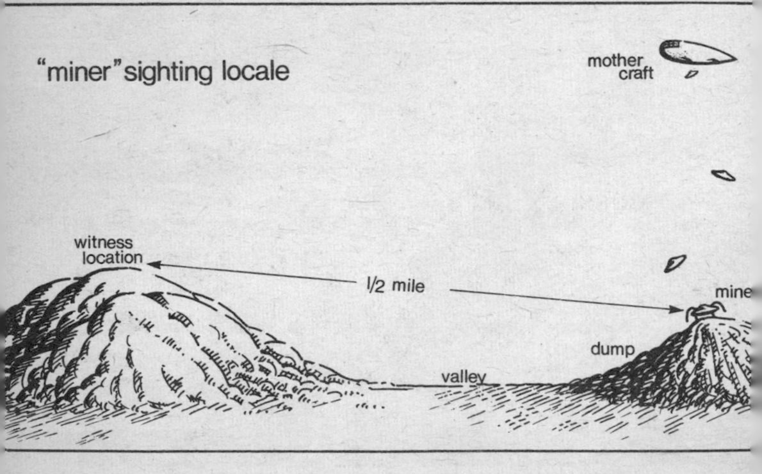

Long-range view of the Buzz Montague incident. (Chapter 2)

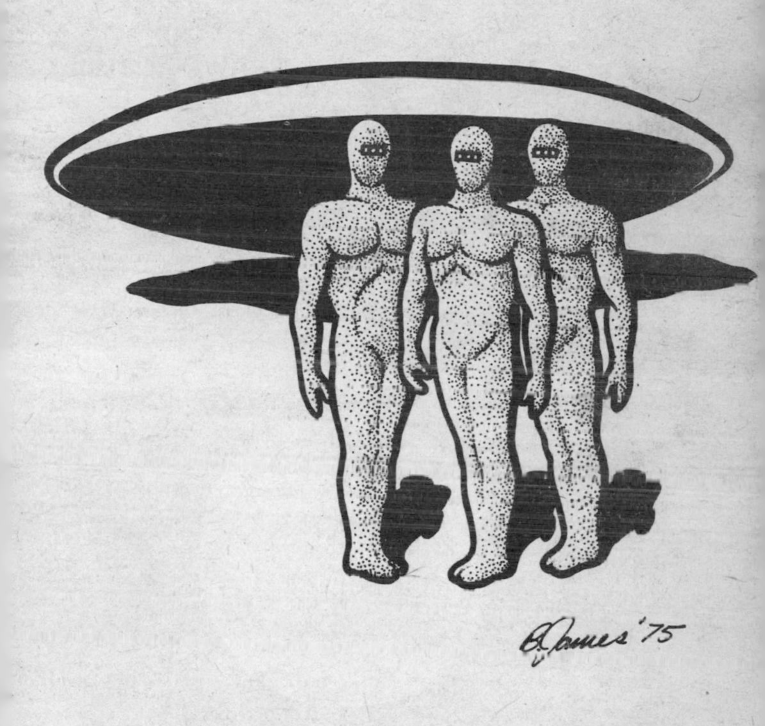

Creatures reported by C.A.V. near Lima, Peru. (Chapter 12)

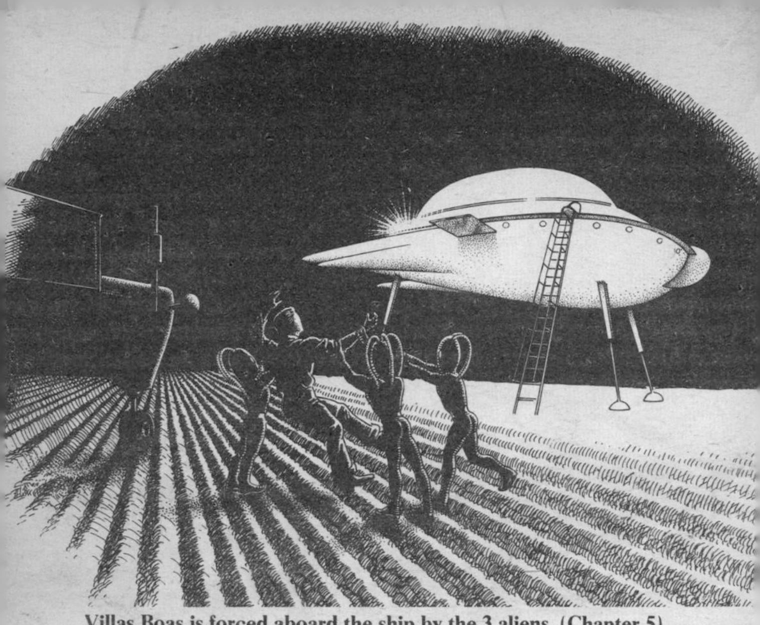

Villas Boas is forced aboard the ship by the 3 aliens. (Chapter 5)

The craft and occupant in the Lyndia Morel case. (Chapter 10)

The creature reported by William Bosak. (Chapter 10)

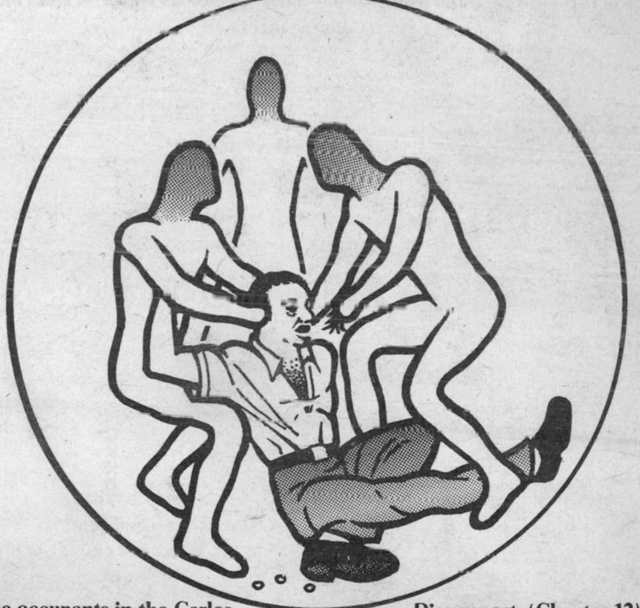

The occupants in the Carlos Diaz report. (Chapter 12)

The two glowing ships with glowing "men" as viewed by Reverend Gill.
(Chapter 16)

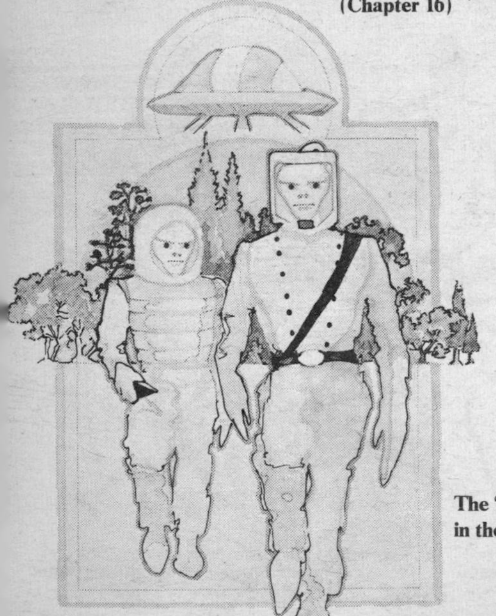

The "Twin-faced" entities
in the Warneton case. (Chapter 17)

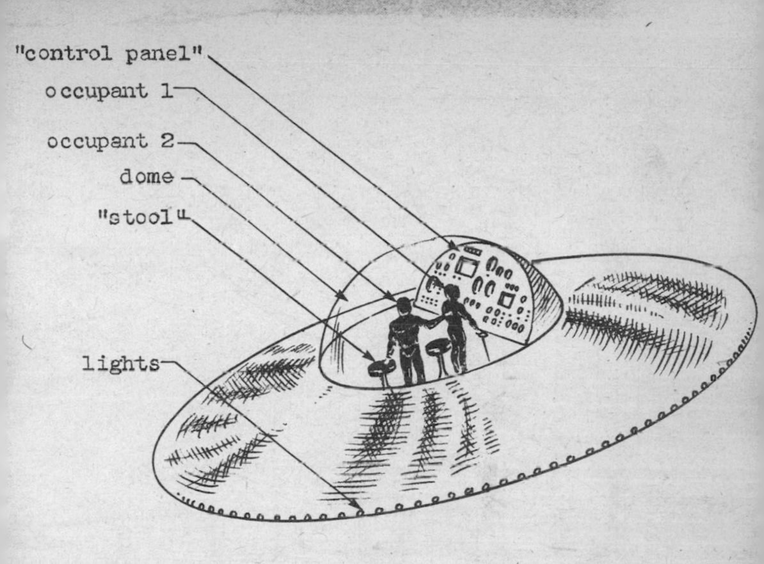

View of craft as seen by Coreen Kendall. (Chapter 19)

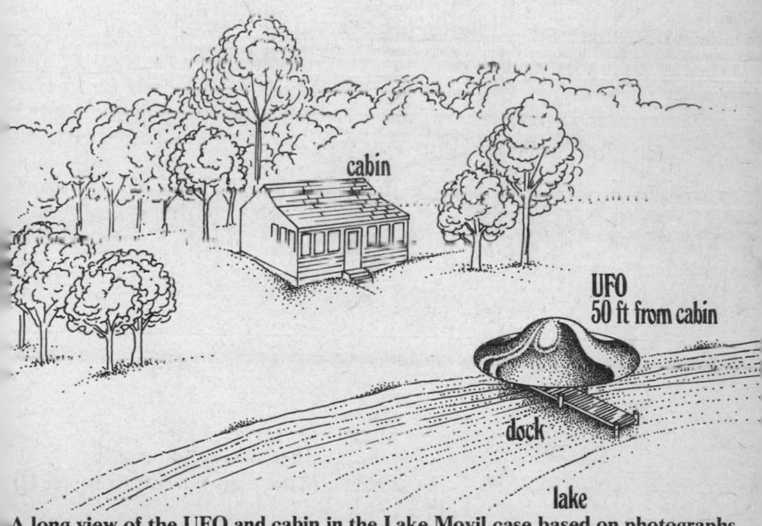

A long view of the UFO and cabin in the Lake Movil case based on photographs. (Chapter 19)

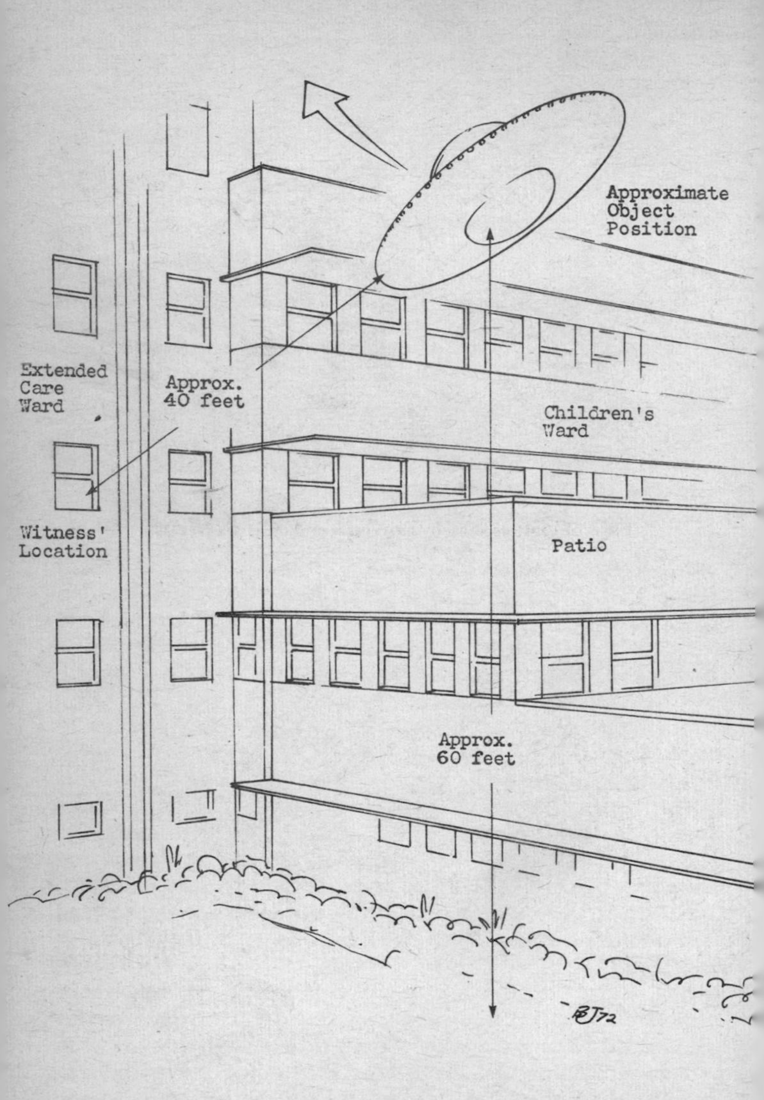

View of UFO from outside the Cowichan Station Hospital. (Chapter 19)

CHAPTER XI

Canada and Elsewhere

Because there were no occupant cases reported in Canada prior to 1965, it seemed as though they must have been confined largely to the United States and South America. There is always the possibility, however, that sightings were made but for some reason the witnesses did not report them. The first case to come to our attention allegedly occurred in 1965, but Field Investigator Louis J. Normandin did not learn of it until 1972 when he made his report to APRO. It should be noted that with seven years separating the actual incident and the interview by Normandin much detail was forgotten.

Mr. Harris and a lady friend were parked at the base of a water reservoir near the Carlington Heights Pumping Station near Ottawa, Ontario, on an August evening in 1965. At between 9:00 and 10:00 P.M. they saw an extremely bright light appear in the sky which lit up the whole area. When they looked out of the front window of the car and up toward the top of the reservoir they saw a glowing object approaching the reservoir. It had what appeared to be four searchlights on the underside which beamed down to the ground. Shortly after the craft stopped at an estimated 15 to 20 feet above the reservoir, what looked like a sliding door opened and a figure was standing in the doorway, joined shortly by two more figures. Harris did not recall if there was a ramp or anything of that nature, just that the figures, which appeared to be dark but shiny, stood there in the opening. His girl friend was very frightened and urged him to drive away so they left the area while the object was still there.

Harris did not recall any details of the figures, such as height or facial features, due to the fact that they were so far away from his location. Mr. Normandin asked if there were any other witnesses to the incident. Harris said that he had seen other cars in the area when they first arrived at the reservoir but did not speak to any others about the presence of the craft. He said that he was not frightened and that he thought that the Air Force must have been carrying out some experiments in the area which accounted for the craft and the figures.

Mr. Normandin pointed out that the top of the reservoir affords a good view of Ottawa, is located near a rock quarry, and that high tension electrical transmission lines run along the edge of the reservoir. All three of these features have figured in landed UFO incidents.

Our next case is reminiscent of the little men seen in a western state by campers in 1967 and mentioned briefly in Chapter X, "The Occupants In The United States."

At approximately 2:30 A.M. on Tuesday, June 13, 1967, Carmen Cuneo, a mine worker at Caledonia, Ontario, Canada, stepped outside briefly and saw two aircraft hovering about 12 feet above the ground near the lower part of the mine. One of the craft was cigar-shaped and estimated to be about 36 feet long with four small, evenly spaced windows along the side facing Cuneo. The other object was disc-shaped and appeared to be about 15 feet in diameter.

The most surprising thing, however, was the presence of three small men wearing hats similar to those worn by miners, who were moving about under a "boom" or aerial which protruded from one end of the cigar-shaped object. On top of each of the "helmets" were four amber lights. Cuneo stood and watched in fascination for about ten minutes, then decided that he should get someone to verify what he was seeing, so he went inside and called his friend, Merv Hannigan. The two men went outside, but the little men were nowhere in sight. However, they watched the two objects which continued to hover in the same spot, for a total of twenty minutes. At 3:05 the two craft took off toward the southwest with many colored, flashing lights in evidence. No noise was heard during the craft's presence at the mine nor during takeoff.

After the sun came up Cuneo went to the area to investigate and found a large gouge in the ground and an oil residue on the burdock leaves. The oil was analyzed and was found to have no unusual elements, but it was not an ordinary type of lubricating oil.

A single witness report of the silver-suited being type came out of Australia in August 1967 when attorney Peter Norris, APRO's representative, forwarded the report resulting from an interview with Ron Hydes of Kilda, Victoria.

Hydes claimed that at 5:00 P.M. on the 24th he had been enroute from Melbourne to Sydney when he found himself surrounded by a bright, bluish-white light. He said it was quite obviously coming from above him. As he slowed down to look up to see where it was coming from, he was blinded by the light and had to stop his cycle. He said the light was so bright that it obliterated the surrounding terrain so that all he could see was the light and a little bit of the road ahead of him. Hydes stopped the bike, left the engine running, and put it on the stand. Taking off his sunglasses he wiped his eyes and when he opened them he saw a disc-shaped craft about 100 feet away to his left and off the road. He surmised that this object was the source of the light above him a few seconds before when he had stopped his cycle, but he did not actually see the object land.

The craft gave the appearance of two plates joined together at the rim, the top half being silver "quite like high-polished silver and either a very dark gray or black underneath." No light emanated from the object as it rested on the ground.

After spotting the craft beside the road Hydes was amazed and continued to look at it for a minute or so until his eyesight came back to normal (it took a little time for his eyes to adjust after the blinding from the bright light source), whereupon he realized the object was not on the ground but was in actuality about 3 or 4 feet above it. He could see nothing supporting it. At about that time a car went by (Hydes wasn't sure it was a car, but at least some kind of vehicle passed), and Hydes turned away from the object to flag down the vehicle. When he turned back toward the craft there were two figures on the side of the object closest to him. They appeared to be about 5 feet tall, but he admits they could have been a bit taller as he was not precisely certain of the distance the object was from his location. The "persons" were dressed in "some sort of metallic coverall" which did not appear to have buttons or zippers or anything of that nature indicating a closing. Hydes said the clothing had the same sort of metallic sheen as the disc behind them. What he originally thought were abnormally sized heads he soon realized were actually helmets. These helmets were not clear—at least he could not see through them—but they were darker than the suits.

He described them in this manner: "They were obviously dark colored—just like a fish bowl popped on somebody's head but they weren't clear."

Hydes also said that he felt that the figures came from around the back of the object, or the side away from him, for he did not feel that he had looked away long enough for them to have opened a door, disembarked, then closed a door again. He assumed that as they stood there they were looking at him despite the fact that he couldn't see their faces for they were facing him. At this stage, although a little frightened, Hydes was still curious and he took a step forward to see what would happen and the two figures did the same and Hydes became even more frightened. The three stood and looked at each other for some time and then one of the figures —the one on the left—took another couple of steps toward Hydes and lifted his hand in a beckoning gesture—the same gesture one would use to call somebody across a street or something of that nature.

"It was at this stage that I panicked and I just dived on the bike and took off down the road," Hydes reported.

In response to questioning by Mr. Norris, Hydes said that he neither saw the persons get out of the disc nor get into it but that "quite obviously they belonged to it."

After getting on his bike, Hydes proceeded down the road at what he estimated to be 100 miles per hour. He shortly realized that the object was keeping company with him when he heard a humming sound and "knew straightaway what it was." He tried to flag down a couple of cars and point out the object to them but the people in them acted as though they had not seen anything out of the ordinary. Hydes felt that he had been on the road a minute or two before he noticed that the object was with him again, but admitted that it could have been following him from the moment that he left the area where the disc had been and he might not have known it. The craft preceded him down the road at a distance of between 100 and 200 feet and 100 to 200 feet altitude. He said he looked for a house or farm or something to pull up to but found nothing.

When he had first spotted the object he began to slow down and the object decreased its speed to correspond with his until he was nearly stopped. When he last observed the object he was at a standstill in the road. He had decided that there was nowhere to go so he had might as well stop, so he did. When he had left the original spot where the craft had been on the ground, he had been "flat out" —doing maximum speed for his cycle which was between 120 and 125 miles per hour. And when he slowed down the object did so correspondingly until his speed was 3 or 4 miles per hour.

It was then that the object tilted its base toward Hydes and "shot straight up into the air at about a 45° angle and vanished in two seconds," he said.

Hydes told Norris about the only structural detail he observed. When the craft was on the ground it had a bulge or cupola on the top and when it was in the air, when it "leapt" in front of his cycle as he made his escape, it was pinkish in color much as if it was reflecting a pink sunset. However, this was not the case for the sun was still above the horizon and also the whole of the craft had the same color.

Here we have a direct encounter between the UFOnauts and a human being in which the overt move is on the part of the aliens and in the first segment they seem intent upon luring Hydes into their ship. On the other hand, perhaps the initial move, when the blinding light was seen, was to panic Hydes into a highspeed dash down the highway. But when this didn't work, and Hydes stopped, we should consider the possibility that the entities disembarked and approached him hoping to frighten him into getting back on his cycle and performing as they wanted him to. Had they wanted to stop him, certainly they could have, as had been done many times with cars. And when he did slow down after realizing he couldn't get away, the disc abruptly left. Why? Because they had gotten what they wanted—the top speed of a motorcycle.

There have been many instances of UFOs chasing cars but to our knowledge this is the only reported instance in which a UFO has chased a motorcycle. In another chapter we discuss the case wherein a man on a motorcycle is stopped by two entities for what was apparently an entirely different purpose. From time to time the car encounters are used by those who oppose the extraterrestrial theory and their argument goes something like this: why would intelligent beings come all that way through space just to chase cars?

In the first place, there is no indication that a car encounter represents one single, deliberate trip through space. Considering everything else that the discs have been observed doing, such as drawing water out of ponds, hovering over high tension lines, and, most recently, abducting and examining human beings, it would seem that these airships (for the objects which we see in the sky are not spaceships—they are airships brought here by spaceships to operate within our atmosphere) have several purposes, and the encounters with cars serve only one of them. Those who use that sort of "reasoning" to support their emotional prejudices against interplanetary or interstellar visitors are guilty of fuzzy thinking.

But on to our next case which involves more of the "diminutives." This case is another which was published in the French UFO journal, *Lumières Dans la Nuit.* M. Luch Fontaine is considered to be a serious, hardworking, and entirely trustworthy man so when he reported his strange experience on the 31st of July, 1968, there was no reason to disbelieve him.

He said that he was at the kilometer 21 mark on the plain called La Plaine des Cafres, on the Island of Reunion (which is located in the Indian Ocean between Madagascar and Mauritius) at 9:00 A.M. picking grass for his rabbits when he saw a sort of oval-shaped object in a clearing about 25 meters away. The sides of it were dark blue in color while the middle was transparent and shaped somewhat like the windshield of a Peugeot 404 car. Above and below it had what appeared to be two glass "feet" of shiny metal.

In the center of the object were two individuals wearing what appeared to be divers suits replete with helmet through which Fontaine could catch a glimpse of their faces. They were standing with their backs to Fontaine, but then one turned around and looked directly at Fontaine, while the other (to his right) turned his head so that part of his face was visible through the faceplate of the helmet. The suits were segmented in appearance.

Fontaine said that then both of the figures turned their backs to him and there was a flash, similar to that made by an arc welder's torch, and everything went white around him. He felt a powerful heat and a blast of wind and a few seconds later there was nothing where the craft had stood.

When he approached the spot where the object had been, he found no marks. He had estimated its diameter to be 4 or 5 meters (13½ to 16⅔ feet) and about 2½ meters (9⅓ feet) from top to bottom. He told his wife about it, then the police, and the next day an enquiry began. At the scene a certain degree of radioactivity in a radius of from 5 to 6 meters (16⅔ to 20 feet) from the presumed scene of the near-landing and also on the clothing that M. Fontaine had worn that day was detected.

This case is one of those absolutely perplexing ones. Obviously the object was not *on the ground.* The suits worn by the "persons" are not unusual in UFO files, nor was their size (90 centimeters or just short of 36 inches), nor the shape of the machine. But the shiny "feet," one above and one below are most unusual. These "appendages" were white, it seemed, and closely resembled the broad, circular pedestal sometimes used on some tables, particularly patio tables, and in this instance, the upper one being flat side up and the lower one flat side down.

Four sightings of a small, Volkswagen-like "car" which could both move along the ground and fly through the air were reported to APRO by our representative in the Philippine Republic, Colonel Aderito de Leon. The four sightings, just hours apart, took place on November 1, 1968, near the communications satellite station (Philcomsat) some thirty miles east of Manila.

The first in this series of observations began at 4:00 A.M. local time when a farmer in an area north of the town of Baras saw an object descend, making a hissing sound like an electric welder. It had a red light on the front of it. The farmer took a flashlight and left his hut to get a better look at the craft, which he estimated to be about 100 yards distant. As he approached, he saw what he described to the investigators as a white vehicle "as big as a Volkswagen beetle car with two occupants." The vehicle had small wheels and six big exhaust tubes at the rear, each the size of which was comparable to the thickness of a man's leg.

The body of the vehicle was milky-white in color, the farmer said, and had a transparent canopy on the top through which he observed two occupants who were dressed in white overalls with earphones on their heads. He said they looked like "ordinary Caucasians," and one was taller than the other.

When the farmer approached the object, it emitted a loud roar, and he ran off in fright. He then observed it as it moved forward on the ground (on the wheels) until it reached a clearing, whereupon it took off. The roar made by the object was only apparent during its horizontal movement on the ground, and during its vertical ascent there was "not much noise." Colonel de Leon tried to determine if there had been a downward blast as the object rose but the farmer replied in the negative. He pointed out that the object's horizontal movement on the ground (accompanied by the roar) caused dust to fly but that there was no dust when the object took off in vertical flight.

The second observation occurred two hours later, at 6:00 A.M. Another farmer who was walking to Baras suddenly "felt" that something had landed behind him. He looked around and observed what he described as a strange, white car with two people in it. He ran as fast as he could and reported the incident to the mayor of Baras. This observation was not long or detailed but the description is of an object very similar to the one observed earlier.

At 8:00 A.M. a farmer plowing his field with his son observed a white object hovering silently over them. Colonel de Leon was not able to investigate this particular report because the farm in question was located in the middle of a mountain range and was very difficult to reach. Also, inasmuch as a detailed description was not given and no humanoids were viewed, it was not considered significant to the group of observations.

The fourth and last observation, however, occurred at 11:00 A.M. at the same place as the first sighting but involved another farmer who was riding his bicycle up an incline coming from Baras. Upon reaching the top of the grade he saw a strange "car" downhill from him. Although he felt undecided whether or not to continue, he let the cycle carry him downhill towards the object and he passed right by it. He told de Leon that he saw two men, one was inside and the other was outside "looking around". The latter, he said, was "very tall" and looked like a Caucasian. Both were wearing white coveralls with a head cover that had two black objects on the sides.

He continued cycling and stopped after about 20 yeards and looked back. The man who was outside the vehicle was watching him. He considered returning to speak with him but then the man climbed into the vehicle, which the farmer described as resembling a Volkswagen and was about the same size. There was a loud roar as the object moved up the hill from where the farmer had come, then took off vertically and silently.

When Colonel de Leon submitted his reports to APRO Headquarters he pointed out the similarity of the object and occupants to those observed by Lonnie Zamora at Socorro, New Mexico, four years earlier. In both cases the objects were white and at first Zamora thought the vehicle he saw was a car. Also, the occupants in both cases wore white clothing. But there the similarity ends, for the Zamora object had four wedge-shaped pads, whereas the objects described by the farmers near Baras described wheels. Also, the Zamora craft made a roar while landing or taking off and was silent during flight, whereas the Baras vehicle made a roar while running along the ground.

Animal reaction to the presence of a UFO figures in our next case—almost a common occurrence in UFO research. Investigated by William K. Allan, an indefatigable field investigator from Calgary, Alberta, Canada, this incident took place on June 9, 1971, at about 8:50 P.M. The witness, Miss Esther A. Clappison of Rosedale, Alberta, was attracted to a light that shone through a window of her house. She couldn't imagine what could have caused it, so she went out to the front porch of her house, accompanied by her dog George. Upon reaching the porch she was surprised to see a rectangular object which appeared to be on the ground at the intersection of two roads. At first shocked, she overcame the emotion and decided that she should try to observe as much as possible and because of the full moon did manage to observe many details.

At this point she became aware that three "men" were present, two inside the craft whom she could see through a window or port and another outside. One of those inside could be seen to make signs to the man on the outside to the right end of the craft. At the same time the man outside seemed to be trying to attract the attention of the men on the inside. During this interlude the man on the inside, who was gesticulating to the man on the outside, seemed to be attempting to conceal something with his body, which Miss Clappison took to be the instrument panel. She said that he kept looking backward as if to see if his arm was covering something. The man or humanoid located on the outside of the craft seemed to be picking up samples of something—objects or rocks—not dirt, she thought, because he was picking and not scooping.

Miss Clappison said that she tried to get closer but could not because the old dog wouldn't allow her to do so; he just pushed her back. He didn't bark, she said, but it was obvious that he was scared to death and would not let her go further. He was trembling and cowering and shoving against her to keep her back.

At this juncture, she decided to go inside the house, being afraid by now, and to tell her brother about the strange apparition. When she arrived inside the house, she looked out through a window and found that there was nothing where the craft had been seconds before. She then went outside again and found nothing.

Miss Clappison estimated that the craft was possibly between 10 and 13 feet in length, but the burned area which was found at the site where the object had hovered was just over 20 feet. In October of the same year when Mr. Allan investigated the case the grass was still blackened and had not grown.

Miss Clappison estimated that the height of the three humanoids could not have been over 5 feet tall and *their faces were covered.* But, she said, "their hands were the things that got me. They were like mittens, not exactly like a skidoo mitten, but the thumbs, very prominent thumbs going into points, but I gathered that was why he was having difficulty picking up the rocks. The hands were very obvious and the wrists were very obvious."

Their clothing, she said, was a kind of olive-green to drab green and all that she observed was seen by the light of the ship. However, the moon was full that night and it is possible that it added to the illumination.

Miss Clappison kept trying to describe what she called the "instrument panel" which she felt the humanoid aboard was trying to conceal. "It went right across the thing and was about 15 inches and straight down, but there seemed to be darker shapes on the down part." Her description here leaves much to be desired but her very inability to describe what she saw tends to lend credence to her story. However, we might here call attention to her difficulty in describing the "hands"—they seemed to be claw-like in the manner of those in several other reports in this book.

We are constantly being told how one should react while viewing a UFO or its occupants. The following case is one that is difficult for researchers to understand because obviously the witnesses were viewing something very strange but were not interested enough to take the time out from mundane chores to view and record the events in detail.

Our investigator in this case, Wido Hoville, is a very dedicated young man who has spent a great deal of time and effort in documenting the cases of UFO occupants, especially within the range of his ability to travel, and has done an outstanding job.

At 12:45 A.M. on October 6, 1974, Mr. and Mrs. R (names withheld upon request) of St. Matthias, Quebec, Canada, took a walk near their home to get some fresh air before retiring. Suddenly Mrs. R noticed a bright spotlight on their farmland about 1650 feet from their house. She pointed it out to her husband, saying, "Look over there—somebody seems to be searching for something." Her husband said it was probably the police chasing cattle thieves. Mr. Hoville pointed out that since the price of beef went up in 1973 there had been some cattle thievery in the area.

The next morning the Rs had workers at their home to install a new wrought-iron balustrade in the rear of their house. Mr. R was helping to install the connection of a welding machine in the basement and Mrs. R was busy washing clothes. At 11:45 A.M. Mrs. R took some laundry out to hang on the clothesline. While hanging the clothes, she noted heavy dark smoke rising into the sky from approximately the same location where they had seen the "spotlight" earlier that morning. Several neighbors later confirmed having seen the smoke in that area at that time. Mrs. R described the smoke as similar to that given off by burning rubber tires. Mr. Hoville doubts that the smoke had anything to do with the first sighting or what transpired later. The smoke lasted approximately thirty minutes. No fire was seen and Mrs. R was astonished because, to her knowledge, there was nothing in the field which could burn, as the ground was still wet from the rainfall the preceding Friday.

While watching the smoke, Mr. and Mrs. R suddenly saw what they described as a "dome-shaped" tent of orange-yellow color about the same distance (1650 feet) from their house as the "spotlight" seen earlier.

Out from this "tent" (which the Rs estimated to be 75 feet in diameter) came what the Rs described as a "bulldozer" which was approximately one quarter the size of the larger object. The smaller object moved 200 feet away from the large object, became stationary, then went out of sight toward a spring, disappearing from sight behind a slope. Before the smaller object left, out from the "big tent" emerged what Mr. and Mrs. R described as five "scouts" of small stature dressed in bright, yellow-colored clothing "much brighter than the clothing of highway workers." They appeared to be very busy running between the large object and the smaller one. Mrs. R said they had "some sort of helmets on their heads" and that because of the high grass only the upper part of their bodies could be seen. The movements of their arms were clearly observed, however. No windows or doors were noted on the objects, and the outlines were not sharp and were somewhat hazy.

Mr. Hoville notes: "It seems incredible but nobody asked himself what was going on." The workers installing the balustrade did not notice the UFO nor did the Rs call their attention to it. The witnesses continued their normal business, and after returning to the observation spot, found everything—the large object and the five "scouts"—gone. They wondered how this could have happened without the object and "scouts" passing close to the house.

Mr. and Mrs. R's daughter arrived home at noon, and upon hearing what her parents, saw, she immediately visited the area where the objects were seen and found a straight track of flattened grass about 6 inches wide leading to the spring. Where the largest UFO had been located, the grass was flattened and discolored, and three imprints arranged in a triangular pattern were found, each of which measured 1 foot 10 inches by 1 foot 3 inches. These impressions were exactly 34 feet apart.

On Sunday, November 4, 1973 and again on Sunday, November 11 Mr. Hoville visited the site and verified the existence of the 6-inch-wide track as well as the imprints which he interpreted as being from the landing gear. On the 11th Mr. Hoville discovered more flattened and discolored vegetation further back from the "landing" area—as well as broken bushes.

It is impossible to read a report such as this and not lament the fact that the Rs, though sufficiently interested in the events transpiring to occasionally glance over and notice the activity, made no attempt to investigate. This case involves unaccountable smoke which subsided, then two objects and five figures on the ground, but no one observed the arrival or departure of any of these phenomena. Therefore it can't be labeled a genuine UFO. However, the description of the two objects and the figures, as well as the colors displayed, correlate sufficiently with other cases so that we can assume that had the Rs investigated, or at least observed continually, they would have seen the occupants and smaller object reenter the large object which then would fly off, making it a case of an unidentified *flying* object or UFO. As things stand, this case involves an unidentified *landed* object. There was no evidence to indicate that any land-based vehicle had been in the vicinity of the site.

Our final case in this chapter seems very bizarre because it is one of the few cases involving what seem to be robots. Again Mr. Wido Hoville was the field investigator and submitted an excellent detailed report of the alleged event. And, as is very often the case, we must use only initials instead of the full name because the witnesses did not care to be identified.

Mr. and Mrs. L had come home from a holiday in Florida on the evening of July 22, 1974. Being tired from the trip, Mrs. L had gone to bed, and her husband was sitting up watching the late show on television. They live in a house trailer near St. Cyrille, Quebec. Other trailers on the lot had been installed but the Ls were the only occupants at the time.

Shortly after the end of the show, at about 1:15 A.M. on the 23rd, Mr. L was preparing to go to bed when he heard a strange sound like "bum bum bum" outside, much like something falling on the grass. He lifted the curtain in the living room and saw a reddish-orange, round object hovering over the field to the northeast side of his house trailer. He then went into the bedroom to wake his wife and while there heard another sound like buzzing. When he looked outside he saw what he described as a robot-like creature, about 6 feet tall within 15 feet of the trailer. Needless to say, Mr. L was shocked by what he saw and he and his wife then went into the living room where they looked out and observed three more "robots" (they described them as such because of their stiff manner of moving about as well as their appearance) close to an adjoining trailer and apparently examining the shaft and wheel assembly. From then on Mr. and Mrs. L only looked out occasionally to see if the "robots" were still there and because they were very frightened. During the observation, which lasted until 4:20 A.M., they both saw approximately fifteen of the robots together in one line close to the creek. The robots stood there for over five minutes and when they moved they did so as if they were one unit, giving the Ls the impression that they were remote-controlled.

During the following few days, the Ls learned that a farmer had had trouble with his dog on the morning after the incident. The dog, which usually barked wildly at the slightest provocation, had managed to slip out of his collar and was hiding.

Although only one object was seen, three of what could be described as landing traces were found. One was where the witnesses observed the object, the others on the other side of the creek hidden by high bushes, which would have screened anything from the L's view. Since the sighting, when Mr. Hoville's investigation was made, the grass had been cut on both sides of the creek but the landing marks were clearly seen because the grass had grown twice as high in the area of the marks as in the surrounding area. The grass in the landing area was not burned, but merely swirled as in the cases of other so called "saucer nests" around the world. According to the witnesses, they found a strange substance of whitish color where the robots were seen moving about, and close to their pre-fabricated shed.

The results of the analysis were that the whitish, chalkish substance was low-grade limestone and nothing out of the ordinary. In his final report to APRO Mr. Hoville pointed out that there was a limestone quarry in the area and that inasmuch as UFOs had repeatedly been observed over and in limestone quarries he assumed that the robots may have visited a quarry prior to their visit to the area of the R home.

In closing this chapter, we suggest that the reader compare the content here with other reports in this book. We have attempted to set down this information in chapters dealing with certain categories but at times categories overlap, and because of the wealth of material (unfortunately we have not been able to present *all* the cases—that would take ten books at least of this size) we have had to confine ourselves to the best cases and the most interesting ones without duplication.

CHAPTER XII

Floating, Flying UFOnauts

Now that the dust has cleared after the concentrated UFO activity in the U.S. in the fall of 1973, some very interesting data has presented itself. Although we had previously noted with interest several cases which involved UFO occupants with an apparent ability to fly, it was the fall "flap" which presented two outstanding cases of UFO occupants who either could fly or maneuvered about some distance above the ground.

The Pascagoula incident of October 11, 1973, has been described rather extensively in the press and various magazines as well as in at least one book. The "entities" were described as about 5 feet tall, grayish in color with wrinkled skin, a protuberance where the nose on a human being is located, and two additional protuberances where the ears would be. They did not walk as humans do and their legs appeared to be bound together and did not separate as they moved about. Also, their "hands" gave the appearance of "pincers" or of opposing two-digit members.

When we first learned of the Pascagoula incident early on the morning of Friday, October 12, we were intrigued by the description of "floating" entities and decided to contact the sheriff at Pascagoula and try to determine if the incident warranted sending in one or two of APRO's scientific consultants. After a conversation with the sheriff it was apparent that a full investigation should be undertaken and Mrs. Lorenzen called one psychologist and two psychiatrists on APRO's scientific consulting staff. She felt hypnotic regression would be helpful in extracting any information from the witnesses' subconscious minds which may have been suppressed due to fear or shock.

None of the three were available so she put in a call to APRO's Research Director, Dr. James A. Harder, who is a professor of civil engineering at the University of California at Berkeley. He also was impressed with the case as she disclosed it to him and when she noted that none of our psychologists or psychiatrists were available he reminded her that he was a certified hypnotist and had used the technique in past investigations, notably the Mr. S. (Cisco Grove) case described later.

After discussing the situation with Dr. Harder and Mr. Lorenzen, the decision was made to send Dr. Harder to Pascagoula and after we terminated our second conversation Dr. Harder booked his flight and there was nothing for us to do but wait.

The next morning, Saturday, October 13, Dr. Harder interviewed Hickson and Parker and called to make a preliminary report. The two men claimed that while fishing on an old abandoned pier at the Schaupeter shipyard they had seen a bright lighted object descend to the ground near them. Out of it came three strange-appearing creatures who approached them. Young Calvin Parker fainted when one of the things took hold of him with its pincer-like hands, but Hickson remained conscious throughout the ordeal. Two of the creatures took him, one on each side, into the ship. Hickson recalls that he was elevated above the floor of the inside of the ship and a round device which resembled an eye passed above, below, and all around his body. He estimated that he had been in the ship for about fifteen minutes when he was taken out side and placed on the pier. Parker was similarly deposited, the three entities went inside the object, and it took off. Calvin Parker and Charles Hickson could not give much more information than they did when interviewed while conscious. During the entire episode the creatures at no time touched the ground—they moved along a few inches above the ground.

The description of the entities who allegedly kidnapped and ex amined the two men closely resembled that of another "entities" case which had taken place twenty-six years before if we can believe the lone witness. It involved a Mr. C.A.V. of Lima, Peru, and he claimed it occurred six miles south of Lima in February or March 1947 and was investigated by Mr. Richard Greenwell in October 1967. Mr. Greenwell, APRO's representative for Peru at the time, had heard about the case through the Instituto Peruano de Relaciones Interplanetaris (Peruvian Institute of Interplanetary Relations) and had planned to obtain his name and address and interview him, but was approached by the witness himself. The man did and still does want his identity kept secret but inquiries into his background indicate that he is a reliable individual and APRO has found no motivation for a hoax.

C.A.V. claimed that he had been in Pucusana to attend to business concerning one of his trucks which had gone off the highway and into the sand dunes. On his way back to Lima he was six miles south of the city when he saw a disc-shaped object hovering about

6½ feet off the ground. He left his car and ran toward the object but found it was considerably farther away than he had initially thought. The object appeared to be the color of the sand, only very shiny. When the man was a few yards from the object three figures came out of it; he saw no door but the figures did appear to emerge.

C.A.V.'s description of the figures follows. "They didn't have a defined form. They looked like three mummies. They had a profile of human beings but the legs were joined. They did not have two legs but one "double" one—like twins. They had arms but their hands consisted of a group of four fingers stuck together and a separate thumb. They had a sort of strange skin, a sort of towely, sandy-colored skin."

C.A.V. further noted that the creatures had no exterior features except a transparent area where the eyes on a human are placed, which had a bubble that moved about.

For those interested in the whole story, which is quite long and involved, the entire interview between Mr. Greenwell and C.A.V. is contained in Chapter Eight of our book *UFOs Over the Americas* (New York, Signet, New American Library, 1968).

The important thing about this case is that the general physical characteristics of the entities closely match those of the Hickson-Parker incident, including the pincer-like appendages, "one" leg, and the manner of moving about.

The foregoing two incidents involve UFO occupants who "floated" above the ground, took place in two different countries, and the alleged times of the incidents are separated by many years. The similarities are striking, and when we note that neither Hickson nor Parker had any interest in UFOs prior to their experience, and the fact that the C.A.V. case was published only in our book and the APRO Bulletin, the odds against two such similar cases being happenstances begin to grow.

If, in both cases, the alleged incidents were hoaxes, one must wonder why these men selected that particular UFOnaut form as a basis for fabrication. Why not a more acceptable and more frequently reported type?

At about 6:00 P.M. on a mid-August evening in 1953 Salvador Villanueva was underneath his broken-down taxicab on the main highway near Ciudad Valley, Mexico. As he worked at repairing it, he became aware of a pair of legs encased in what appeared to be gray corduroy pants. Scrambling out from under the car he was confronted by two pleasant-appearing men about 4½ feet tall who were clad in one-piece garments from head to toe, wore wide shiny perforated belts, small black boxes on their backs, and metal collars around their necks. They carried helmets which Villanueva compared to those "worn by pilots or by American football players." He said he assumed at the time that they were pilots from another country.

Villanueva claimed that ultimately the men got into the car with him when it began to rain and they conversed at some length and they stayed in the car until dawn. One of the men spoke good Spanish, Villanueva said, only he seemed to "string the words together". They discussed the trouble he was having with the car, and Villanueva began to realize that there was something strange about the men when the speaker finally volunteered the information that they were from another world but that they knew much about the earth.

When dawn finally came, the strangers invited Villanueva to come to their craft which was parked about 1600 feet from the highway. To reach it they had to cross swampy terrain and Villanueva noted that the men's feet did not sink into the mire as his did, but that when they walked into the mire they touched their belts which began to glow and the mud seemed to spring away as if repelled by some force.

Another case involving reported floating UFO occupants took place on Labor Day weekend in 1964 when three men from the Sacramento area in California went bow hunting in the mountains near Cisco Grove. On the afternoon of September 4 the three men were hunting on a ridge some distance from their camp. As dusk approached they were separated from each other and one of the men ended up in a canyon with a granite outcropping, few trees, and sparse brush. He heard what he thought was a bear crashing through the brush and took refuge in a tree. After all became quiet and he was confident that the bear was gone he got down from the tree and, realizing he was lost, built three small signal fires hoping to attract the attention of rangers.

Shortly he saw a light below the horizon which he assumed was a lantern and concluded that it must be his friends searching for him. But when the light darted up and over a tree he realized it wasn't a lantern and thought perhaps a search and rescue helicopter was coming. When the light came in his direction, then stopped and hovered motionless without any sound, he realized that it was something out of the usual and he went back up into the tree.

The tree into which Mr. S (he still insists on anonymity) took shelter was 25 to 30 feet tall, big enough at the base so that it could not be circled by a man's arms, completely branchless up to 12 feet, and with sparse but sturdy limbs from there to the top. S climbed to the 12 foot mark and stayed for a time.

The light which S had seen appeared to be 8 to 10 inches in diameter and white in color. It appeared to be accompanied by two or three other objects which stayed at a regulated distance from it. It was dark and the moon was just rising so that S could only make out vague shapes.

The light then circled around the tree in which S had taken refuge, a flash was seen, and a dark object fell to the ground. Then S noticed a "dome-shaped affair" 400 to 500 yards away on or near the ground.

At this point noises like someone moving in the brush attracted S's attention and he saw a figure emerge from a patch of manzanita brush. It seemed to be examining the manzanita. Then another figure approached from a slightly different direction and the two came and stood at the base of the tree and looked up at him. He occasionally heard a "cooing" or "hooting" sound to which the two always reacted but didn't know if the sound came from them or from an owl in the area. The reaction from the entities might have been a simple curiosity about the noise. The only other noises he heard during the night was the sound of movement in the brush and once he heard a sound like that of a generator running.

The two figures at the bottom of the tree seemed to S to be approximately 5 feet 5 inches in height, clothed in silvery-gray material with a covering that went up over the head straight from the shoulder. This same characteristic was noted by Parker and Hickson in the Pascagoula entity case. He was not able to make out any facial features at any time.

Shortly after the two figures arrived at the base of the tree, S saw another figure come from the direction of the dome. It seemed to move in a different manner than the other two, making more noise, and seeming to run into bushes, going over or through them rather than around as the others did.

This third entity was gray, dark gray, or black. It had no discernible neck, but two reddish-orange "eyes" glowed and flickered where the "head" would be. It also had an opening where a mouth would be, which when it opened seemed to drop open, making a rectangular hole in the face. The mouth extended completely across the "face" area.

Mr. S saw the first two figures more clearly than the third as they had come toward him from an area bathed in moonlight while the other had come from an area still in shadow. The "eyes" of the latter appeared to S to be about 3 inches in diameter. The three entities attempted to get to S, the first two by boosting one another up the tree but apparently they didn't know anything about climbing trees. The third entity to whom S refers to as the "robot" seemed to be just watching and waiting at the base of the tree.

S climbed up past the 12 foot mark into the branches of the tree, and taking his belt which held his quiver and bow, belted himself to the tree because the third "entity" would float up toward him, open its "mouth" out of which issued smoke. When the smoke reached him he would become light-headed, and several different times between the time the entities arrived and dawn, he lost consciousness. He shot three arrows at the "robot's" chest and they apparently hit metal for they created a spark when they hit. This did no good and he resorted to tearing up his camouflage suit and setting bits of it on fire and tossing it at the figures below. All in all he destroyed his cap, the suit, and his jacket, and was left belted to the tree with nothing but shoes, socks, underclothing, T shirt, and levis. At dawn a second "robot" joined the first. The two stood chest to chest, sparks issued from them, and although he didn't know where the gas came from, another cloud of it hit him and he lost consciousness. When he woke up again they were gone.

A certain amount of corroboration was given S's story by his companions who came looking for him, and found him curled up some distance from where he had holed up in the tree, exhausted and suffering from exposure to the cold. They noted that on the night before they had seen a brilliant light come slowly down in the area where S had spent the night.

So far we have examined cases dealing with "floating" entities, but the number of reports which involve UFO occupants which actually seem to fly are more abundant.

A United States case of this nature came to our attention in early November 1973 when Mr. Donald Worley, one of APRO's field investigators for Indiana, submitted a lengthy report which related the details of a case in his state. Although no UFO had been seen on the occasion that the "flying men" were seen, there had been heavy UFO activity in the area. Based on past cases, it would be logical to assume that a UFO was in the area but not visible at the time.

At 9:45 P.M. on the evening of October 22, 1973, Mr. and Mrs. De Wayne (Donna) Donathan of Hartford, Indiana, were driving east on Indiana State Road 26 on their way home from a visit with Mrs. Donathan's mother. Donna was driving and De Wayne was holding their baby.

They were about one block from their home when the car rounded a slight curve and a small hill. On the road ahead they saw what they thought at first were two small children about 4 feet tall moving about on the road. Mrs. Donathan stopped the car about 30 feet from them, and with the headlights shining on them she decided they couldn't be children. She said they looked confused and they would hop up in the air. "Their feet would come up slowly, one at a time and the arms would flop funny. They moved slower than humans and their feet and arms would go up funny. Their feet came off the ground easy and they were bright silver in color," Mrs. Donathan told Mr. Worley.

Mrs. Donathan's description is of a figure with slight build, straight in form to the ground, and she doesn't remember a head. But her attention was attracted to the feet which appeared as boxes —square shoes, in other words. She did not detect any hands nor does she recall hearing any sounds, but she had the tape player going fairly loudly and the engine running, so she could not be certain that no noise was being made by the creatures.

When she realized that she was confronted by something quite out of the ordinary she became frightened and screamed; "Oh, my God!" and jammed the accelerator to the floor, swerved to the side of the road, and sped past the creatures. The little creatures had just begun to leave the center of the road and as she sped past them they seemed to be having difficulty getting off the road. They moved off in a slow, clumsy manner with feet apart and arms flopping.

Mr. Donathan's description of their experience closely parallels that of his wife except that he got the impression that the little fellows were "dancing." He at first thought they were little kids dressed in aluminum foil but wondered why they would be out on the road in the country at that time of the night. He said that when his wife panicked and sped toward them the entities seemed to have a problem getting off the road and "moved in a slow skipping motion with arms swinging slowly." When his wife screamed and veered around them, Mr. Donathan had turned to look at her and didn't therefore have the opportunity to get a really close look as the car passed them. However, he did look back after they had passed the creatures, and saw that the two were apparently over behind the fence on the edge of a cornfield.

Mr. Donathan described the creatures as straight and a little slight in build but in proportion to their heads. He did not recall the hands or feet but got the impression that they were wearing tight-fitting silvery suits.

Mrs. Donathan became so excited that she drove several blocks past their home, and when she stopped Mr. Donathan suggested that they go back to see the little fellows. He took over the wheel and they drove back but the creatures were nowhere about. They did see unidentified flashing or pulsating lights at a 45° elevation in the north but attached no significance to them after what they had just seen.

The Donathans went into Hartford City where they reported their experience to the sheriff's office. Deputy Sheriff Ed Townsend was on duty and with him was a friend, Gary Flatter, who is a wrecker driver and the owner of a service station in Hartford City. A state policeman, who did not wish to be identified, also was present when the report was made and when the Donathans finished their report he got into his car and went out to the area. Townsend and Flatter headed in the same direction in Townsend's patrol car. Flatter, in his report to APRO, said that when he and Townsend reached the intersection where the Donathans had allegedly encountered the little creatures, they heard a high frequency sound. They ultimately covered considerable territory looking for the "little men" but the sound was only heard in that one place.

It was getting late so the three men went back to Hartford City. Townsend remained in town but Flatter and the state policeman decided to go back out and check again. The policeman drove his cruiser and Flatter took his wrecker. When they reached the area where the Donathans had had their experience the policeman continued on further east, but Flatter drove up and down the road looking along both sides. The high frequency sound was still heard in the one particular area.

Going back west on Highway 26, Flatter decided to turn south on Highway 303 and check the area a half mile south, and turned on another road which runs east and west. Heading east again, he was forced to slow down to avoid hitting what appeared to be a virtual exodus of animals coming from the north side of the road to the south. He said there were six or seven rabbits, an opossum, a raccoon, and several cats. As he slowed down he began to watch both sides of the road carefully and finally spotted what he had been searching for, just as he became aware of the high frequency sound again.

On the north side of the road, in a field, were two human-shaped entities. They appeared to be about 4 feet tall and wearing tight-fitting silver suits. Flatter stopped his truck and backed up until he was about 75 feet short of them because he could see them best just in range of his headlights. When he was closer the light glared off the suits making viewing difficult. Flatter observed them for a while, then decided to use his spotlight. When he turned it on them, the two turned toward him. The glare of the silver suits was blinding so Flatter turned off the spotlight. The entire description included the following. The heads were egg-shaped, they appeared to be wearing masks which looked like a gas mask from which a hose about the size of an ordinary garden hose extended down to their lower chests. He saw no facial features or ears, the arms "just seemed to end," and no hands were evident. The feet appeared to be rectangular and box-like about 3 by 6 inches and about 2 inches thick.

After Flatter used the spotlight the two figures began to hop about. They moved much slower than humans do, Flatter said, and when they left the ground it was similar to the way a person jumps when jumping rope, but much slower. They left the ground three times, slowly coming back down, and the fourth time they rose into the air they continued to go and flew off into the darkness. Flatter said that he saw some red, tracer-like lights but that was all.

Because of Mrs. Lorenzen's early interest in reports involving alleged occupants, she has kept an extensive file of such cases. In August 1967 we and our son Larry, who served as interpreter, paid a twenty-one-day visit to South America, conferring with APRO's representatives and others who were actively engaged in UFO investigation. Our tour of that continent took us to Lima, Peru, where we visited APRO's Peruvian representative, Richard Greenwell. Two days later we emplaned for Santiago, Chile, where we conferred with our Chilean representative, Pablo Petrowitsch.

When we arrived in Buenos Aires a few days later we had the good fortune to make contact with Captain Omar Pagani who at the time was heading up the Argentinian Navy's investigation of UFO reports. He took us to his office in the Navy Ministry where he showed us the extensive files he had amassed. His investigatory techniques were very thorough and each case included an artist's rendering of the object or objects, and if such was the case, the occupants involved were drawn to the specifications of the witnesses.

Because of our time schedule we had no opportunity to obtain copies of the cases but we were able to read several good occupant reports. There were no "flying men" cases, however. After a prolonged visit and rest in Rio de Janeiro, where we talked with an Admiral in the Brazilian Navy and a Captain in Air Force Intelligence who were carrying out separate investigations of the UFO phenomena, we left for Caracas, Venezuela, where we really hit pay dirt.

On July 31 of that year Caracas was hit by a devastating earthquake which did millions of dollars of damage to its buildings. Within hours, close encounters with UFO's and sometimes their occupants were made. The late Mr. Horacio Gonzales G., APRO's representative in Venezuela at the time, was ready with clippings and reports which he had personally investigated.

We were frankly astounded with the number of cases and our son Larry was a bit chagrined because of the extent to which he was pressed into duty as interpreter. However, we did come away with some very unique cases, a few of which we shall discuss here.

One of them involved Pedro Riera who claimed that he was startled out of a sound sleep on the 7th of August at about 2 A.M. by the sudden and violent shaking of his bed. When he awoke he sat bolt upright and saw a creature by his bed which "flew" or "soared" out of the open window. It should be noted here that there are few if any flying insects in the Caracas area and that windows are left open without benefit of screens because of the lack of insects and because of the need of ventilation in the tropical heat.

When he realized what he had seen Riera went to the window to see what was happening, but was blinded by multi-colored beams of light which forced him to turn away. They seemed to come from the ground but beyond that he could not identify the source. By the time he was fully awake and dressed to go to investigate, a light rain had begun to fall and he decided to wait until later to look for the source.

On the next morning, however, Riera and several friends and neighbors found a semicircular scuff mark on the street below as well as small footprints which were composed of a reddish dust. The prints led from the scuff mark to the balcony where Riera had claimed the little man had "flown" out of the window.

Mrs. Betty Ruff, a neighbor in the area, was questioned about the incident and revealed that having known Riera since his boyhood she felt that she was qualified to comment on his reliable nature. Also, Riera's uncle, Civil Air Captain Gregorio Armando, questioned his nephew and was convinced that he had seen what he claimed to have seen.

Besides the corroboration concerning Riera's veracity, there was added testimony about a saucer-shaped device on the ground at 2 A.M. that morning in the same street by Carmen Ortega, Jose Andres Pasqual, and Javier Pascaul, who said that they had seen the object in front of Riera's building. They said they had been awakened by the lights and viewed the object from their window, which was situated a floor above street level.

On the 26th of August reports were made of "strange objects" in the vicinity of Puente del Rio Tigre. National Guardsmen who were questioned by newsmen would not elaborate, but it was known that they had been stationed on the highway to Maturin and that they had been stopping cars and warning the passengers that strange things were being reported in the area.

One man, an Arab national named Saki Macharechi, was driving between Barracas where he lived and Maturin, when he spotted a flying object which he at first thought was a wild heron. As he drew closer to the object, he realized that the thing he had seen *in flight* only seconds before was a dwarfish being about 3 feet tall, with huge eyes. When he got close enough to get a good look at it the creature was standing near a bridge. Macharechi was so frightened by the sight that he jammed the accelerator to the floor and sped away from the area. News accounts stated that other motorists had seen similar odd things but unfortunately none of the news offices kept records of incoming calls, reports, or names of witnesses.

During this same period "little flying men" were observed near the village of Cussac in France. On the 29th of August two children, a brother and sister aged nine and eleven, reported that they had seen three little black-clad men on the ground near a black sphere. The object was in a field near where the children were tending cows. Suddenly the little fellows soared up into the air, one by one, and entered the top of the sphere which then took off and flew out of sight. The case was thoroughly investigated by a French UFO investigative group which concluded the children were telling the truth.

Back in Caracas the situation was becoming critical. There were nightly sightings of unidentified flying objects, but there was also a proliferation of "little men" reports. Paula Valdez reported to police that she had had a very strange and unnerving experience on the evening of the 3rd of September.

She had come home from work with a severe headache and on advice of her mother she took two aspirins, drank some lemonade, and went to bed. Turning on her bedside radio, she soon lapsed into a half-sleep. She was shortly roused by a whistling sound and, thinking that her transistor radio was acting up, she turned toward her nightstand and began turning the knobs of the radio. At this moment she became aware of another presence in the room. At the side of her bed stood a small man leaning toward her. He had a large head and prominent eyes and said to her, "I want you to come with us so that you will know other worlds and you'll realize how small your world is."

As the significance of the creature's appearance and what he had said began to sink in, Miss Valdez began to scream loudly. At this noise the little man moved out of the room with a floating motion.

The girl continued to scream until her family came running to her room.

This claim was ready-made for sensational treatment by the news media. It was pointed out that Miss Valdez was a budding actress who attended classes in dramatics in the evening. But Miss Valdez did not act like someone interested in publicity—after the initial story hit the papers she went into hiding at a friend's house to escape the hounding from the press.

Another young lady had a similar experience a few days later, but fortunately for her, she had corroboration. Miss Alicia Rivas Aguilar, twenty-three, stated that at 2:30 A.M. on the 8th of September she was turning off her bed lamp when she saw a peculiar creature just outside her bedroom window, apparently gesticulating to her. She didn't get a good look because being very frightened she closed her eyes tightly and began screaming. When her parents ran into her room in response to her screams they saw the creature soaring over the rooftops surrounded by a bluish-yellow glow. Mrs. Aguilar said that the little man moved as if suspended by a balloon, and a strong smell which resembled that of hot iron was detected by all.

Alicia's brother-in-law, Gumersindo Neiro, probably got the best view of the little fellow from his own room. When Alicia first began screaming she yelled that something was outside her window, whereupon Gumersindo went to his own open window and looked toward Alicia's. There a little fellow was just "pushing off" from the window ledge outside Alicia's bedroom.

No one got a look at the little fellow's features, but all agreed that he was wearing silvery clothing with something on the shoulders which generally resembled epaulettes.

Still another "flying man" incident took place at 5:10 A.M. the next morning. Only one witness was involved but he happened to be a police officer of good repute. The location, however, was Valencia, in Carobobo state. Officer Porfirio Antonio Andrade was on duty in the City Hall of Valencia when he heard a humming sound and then the sound of light footsteps coming from the garage. As he gained the outdoors, he was confronted by a small man of about 4 feet in height, with a large head and bulging eyes which gave off a reddish light. "It" was wearing a silver-colored coverall.

Andrade pointed his gun at the creature, whereupon he heard a voice which seemed to come from the area of the roof, and speaking in Spanish, it said, "Don't do him any harm. We are here on a peaceful mission. He'll do you no harm."

Looking up, the officer noted that the voice seemed to come

from a disc-shaped object hovering in mid-air and wobbling from side to side. The little man on the ground then began talking to Andrade, repeating that he meant no harm, and that "they" wanted him to come as a guest to their world which was very distant and much larger than earth and which held many advantages for earthlings.

Thoroughly frightened, but nevertheless standing his ground, Andrade said that he couldn't leave because he was on watch. The little fellow then assured him, still in perfect Spanish, that they would bring him back. Andrade restated his position that he could not leave his post. At that juncture the "little man" lifted one foot, then the other, and somehow "flew" up into the air toward the object suspended above them. A door opened in the side of the disc and the creature sailed into it. The door then closed, white smoke with tongues of flame issued from the four exhaust tubes on the bottom, the humming noise started again, and the object left.

A detailed report of this incident was made to government authorities and it was classified and forwarded to the Ministry of the Interior.

Eighteen days later, on the 22nd of September, another "flying man" report came out of the Caracas area. A well-known television performer reported that he had been called in the middle of the night by a racetrack employee who stated that the performer's horse had been "attacked by a Martian." Upon questioning the fellow the man learned that the trainer was in bed and was awakened by a tug at his pillow. Then his arm was grasped tightly, and when he tried to sit up a very strong arm encircled his neck, almost choking him. He had given up hope of getting free when he heard the frantic neighing of one of the horses in the stable. Whatever or whoever had grabbed him released its hold suddenly. The trainer screamed for help and the creature left. The trainer was found only moments later by fellow employees and he had numerous scratches and nicks in the flesh on his back and chest where the creature had apparently raked him with its fingernails.

A half hour after the attack incident, another employee heard a mare kicking and prancing around in her stall and, thinking it was some pest hanging around the stable, he went to see what was going on. As he approached the stall, a "small man" about 3½ feet in height "zoomed" out of the stable and was out of sight within seconds. This employee described the creature as resembling an orangutan or monkey.

With rare exceptions, the UFO "occupant" cases of 1967 seemed to deal with quite human-appearing, hairless creatures as was apparently the case when four boys from Duncan, Oklahoma, beheld a strange sight while driving east out of the town on State Route 7 on the 21st of October.

At about 10 P.M. they saw something on the highway ahead but out of range of their dimmed headlights. When the driver turned on his bright lights, they said, they saw three small men who "almost flew off the road and disappeared." They estimated the size to be about 4 feet in height and the figures were either wearing tight-fitting shiny blue-green clothing or had skin of that color. From their location they said the faces of the creatures appeared human but that the ears were extremely large.

The four young men reported their experience to the police and Police Lt. Elmer McGill and Detective Pleasant Foster both said the boys appeared to be sincere. "They were really scared, and I think they must have seen something," McGill remarked.

The next morning, two of the boys, Ivan Ritter and Jerry Bennet, drove out to the spot and looked around for evidence. The only sign of anything unusual was a footprint about 100 yards from the road in the mud of the creek bed. It was so small that it resembled a baby's footprint except that the heel was too big and the arch appeared to come out past the heel on the sides and the foot had only four toes.

Our last two cases are real brain-teasers, not only because the featured players moved about above the ground with ease, but because of their bizarre appearance.

Carl Higdon of Rawlins, Wyoming, habitually takes to the wilds of the forests in his area every fall in search of game. Although an accomplished hunter, he does not hunt solely for the "sport" of bagging game; the animals he brings back from his expeditions are bound for the family table.

The Tuesday, October 29, 1974 issue of the Rawlins (Wyoming) *Daily Times* carried Mr. Carl Higdon's account of his strange experience while elk-hunting on the north boundary of the Medicine Bow National Forest on the 25th of October.

On Saturday, November 2, Dr. R. Leo Sprinkle, APRO's Consultant in Psychology, Mr. Rick Kenyon, art teacher in the Public Schools of Rawlins, and Mr. Robert Nantkes, vocational rehabilitation counselor at Riverton, Wyoming, spent four hours with Mr. and Mrs. Higdon, their children, and several relatives talking about Higdon's experience and their reactions to it. The pendulum technique and other hypnotic procedures were utilized to obtain more information from Mr. Higdon about his experience. Dr. Sprinkle was not satisfied with the results and decided to pursue the matter further at a future date. On November 17 another session was held and more information was obtained.

Mr. Higdon's experience is certainly strange. At about 4:00 P.M. he was hunting south of Rawlins when his "experience" began to unfold. "I walked over this hill and saw five elk," Higdon said. "I raised my rifle and fired, but the bullet only went about 50 feet and dropped." He went over, got the bullet and tucked it into a fold in his canteen pouch. "I heard a noise like a twig snapping, and looked over to my right and there in the shadow of the trees was this sort of man standing there."

The "man" was 6 feet 2 inches tall and approximately 180 pounds. He was dressed in a black suit and black shoes and wore a belt with a star in the middle and a yellow emblem below it. Higdon also said he was quite bow-legged, had a slanted head, and no chin. His hair was thin and stood straight up on his head.

The "man," Higdon said, asked if he was hungry, he replied that he was, and the man tossed him four pills, and he took one. The pills were in a container much like a "Dristan" package (apparently the cellophane type as he said it was transparent). He put the container in his pocket. Higdon also commented that he didn't understand why he took them because ordinarily he doesn't even like to take an aspirin. The "man" had told him that the pills were "four-day" pills, apparently to slake his hunger. Higdon said the man called himself "Ausso" and asked Mr. Higdon if he'd like to go with him and Higdon replied that he guessed so. The man pointed an appendage which came out of his sleeve and at this juncture Mr. Higdon said he found himself in a transparent cubicle along with Ausso. He was sitting in a chair with "bands" around his arms (apparently holding him in the chair which resembled a high-backed "bucket seat") and a helmet-like apparatus on his head—somewhat like a football helmet except that it had two wires on top and two on the sides leading to the back. On a sort of console opposite his chair Higdon said he saw three levers of different sizes which had letters on them and which "Ausso" manipulated.

Mr. Higdon was very unclear on the size of the cubicle. He said there was a mirror on the upper right in which he could see the reflection of the five elk which seemed to be behind him in a "cage" or corral. They were still, not moving, just as they had been when he first spotted them before he encountered "Ausso." He thought the cubicle was about 7 by 7 and couldn't account for the elk being there also.

When Ausso pointed his appendage at the largest lever it moved down and the cubicle felt as if it were moving. After they took off, Higdon said he saw a basketball-shaped object under the cubicle which he took to be the earth. There was another being in the cubicle who left, "just disappeared," when they landed. Ausso said that they had traveled "163,000 light miles."

Outside the cubicle, Higdon said, was a huge tower, perhaps 90 feet high with a brilliant, rotating light and he heard a sound like that made by an electric razor. The light bothered his eyes considerably and he put his hands over them.

Standing outside the tower were five human-appearing people —a gray-haired man of forty or fifty years old, a brown-haired girl of about ten or eleven, a blonde girl of thirteen or fourteen, and a young man of seventeen or eighteen with brown hair, and a blonde seventeen- or eighteen-year-old girl. They were dressed in ordinary clothing and appeared to be talking among themselves.

Ausso pointed his "hand" and they (Ausso and Higdon) moved into the tower and up an elevator to a room where he stood on a small platform and a "shield" moved out from the wall. Ausso was on the other side of it. The "shield" was "glassy" appearing, stayed in front of Higdon for what he estimated to be three or four minutes, then moved back in the wall.

Ausso then told Higdon he was not what they needed and they would take him back. The two moved out of the room to the elevator and then down to the main door. It seemed that all Ausso need ed to do was to point his "hand" and they moved effortlessly.

Next, Higdon found himself back in the cubicle with Ausso, who was holding his gun. He said the gun was primitive and he wanted to keep it but wasn't allowed to and he gave it back to Higdon. Then he pointed at the longest lever and Higdon found himself standing on a slope. His foot struck a loose rock and he fell, hurting his neck and head and shoulder.

At this point Higdon didn't know who or where he was and got up and walked past his pickup truck which was sitting in a wooded area on a road with deep ruts. He walked along the track about a mile past the truck, then came back to the truck and heard a woman's voice. As he regained a little of his senses, he used the citizen's band radio to call for help. He told the woman he didn't know who he was or where. Authorities were notified and Higdon was eventually found about 11:30 that night. He was dazed and confused and had difficulty recognizing his wife. The search party had a considerable problem getting Higdon's two-wheel drive vehicle out (it had to be towed as it could not navigate the rough road).

Higdon was brought to the Carbon County Memorial Hospital in Rawlins at 2:30 A.M. on the 26th. Besides the sore head, neck, and shoulder, his eyes were extremely bloodshot and teared constantly. He had no appetite on Saturday and his wife Margery had to force him to eat. On Sunday morning, however, he was ravenous and complained about the meager size of the hospital breakfast.

This, essentially, is Carl Higdon's account of his time from 4:15 P.M. on October 25, 1974, when he first spotted the five elk until he called in on the CB radio.

Some foundation for his story is found in the testimony of the search party who said Higdon's pickup truck could not have driven into or out of the area where it was found. Also, unidentified lights were seen near the area where Higdon was found before the searchers started driving out of the area so the lights of the vehicles could not have accounted for the unidentified lights.

The bullet, which was greatly mangled, was only the copper jacket; the lead slug was missing. This jacket was examined by Dr. Walter Walker, APRO's Consultant in Metallurgy, who could only say that it had struck something extremely hard with great force. Higdon points out that the 7 mm bullet is so powerful it can completely transit a standard telephone pole.

Other interesting details which Higdon recalled during hypnotic sessions are these. Before Higdon was returned to the ground, Ausso pointed at the pocket where Higdon had put the pills and they floated out and up and remained suspended in the air. Ausso had only six teeth—three above and three below. He said that on his planet there were no fish, that he could not tolerate the sun's rays as they burned him, and that he was exploring and searching for food. He said they took animals back with them for breeding purposes. Last but not least, when the cubicle first took off, Ausso pointed at Higdon's truck and it "just disappeared."

In conclusion we quote Dr. Sprinkle from his first (and preliminary) report: "Although the sighting of a single UFO witness often is difficult to evaluate, the indirect evidence supports the tentative conclusion that Carl Higdon is reporting sincerely the events which he experienced. Hopefully, further statements from other persons can be obtained to support the basic statement."

Doctor Sprinkle's comment about single witness UFO experiences is most appropriate and points up the difficulty researchers have in attempting to understand the descriptions of occupants and, indeed, the purported experiences in many of these reports.

In the case of the January 4, 1975, abduction of Carlos Alberto Diaz of Bahia Blanca, the circumstances are even more bizarre than those surrounding the Higdon experience and we are left with a puzzle which nevertheless tends to support Diaz' claims.

Carlos Alberto Diaz, a twenty-eight-year-old married man and father of one child, was born and lives in Ingeneiro White, a suburb of Bahia Blanca, which is located approximately 785 kilometers (423 miles) north of Buenos Aires, the capital of Argentina. Since becoming an adult he has been employed as a clerk, a laborer, and in 1974 to 1975 helped with the preparation of a football training school. To augment his income he frequently worked as a waiter at private parties.

At 3:30 A.M. on January 4 Diaz left the Holy Protective Society where he had spent several hours waiting on tables at a party, paused outside the building to buy a copy of *La Nueva Provencia* (The Province News), the morning newspaper, then boarded a bus to go home. The bus comes within several blocks of Diaz' home, and in order to save time and distance, it is his habit to take a short cut through a large and desolate railroad yard.

The sky was overcast, so when a brilliant flash lit up the area and momentarily blinded him, Diaz dismissed it as a flash of lightning from the approaching storm.

At 8:05 A.M. Diaz was found lying about 100 feet from a major highway in Buenos Aires; his valise with work clothes in it and the morning paper were beside him. He told a strange tale to a passing motorist who stopped because he thought Diaz had been struck by a car. He didn't believe the tale but because of Diaz' distraught condition, took him to the Railway Hospital where Diaz was admitted at 8:30 A.M.

Diaz' watch had stopped at 3:50 A.M., and it was when he noticed that fact, that Diaz became convinced that what he remembered of the past hours was true and he had been aboard an aircraft of unknown origin and in the company of extraterrestrials.

At 9:20 A.M. a call was put in to Diaz' family. Mrs. Diaz was by then frantic because Carlos seldom arrived home later than 4 or 4:30 A.M. The family set out by car and arrived in Buenos Aires at about midnight that same night.

For the next four days Diaz was confined to the Ferroviara Hospital in Buenos Aires where he was examined over and over again by no less than forty-six doctors. The hospital's director informed federal police who also questioned Diaz. Their examination revealed no physiological or psychological problems with the exception of dizziness, upset stomach, lack of appetite, and patches of hair missing from his head and chest. During the day of January 5 he had only one cup of milk which had to be fed to him forcibly.

During the course of the examinations by physicians and psychologists and interrogation by federal police Diaz' story came out. His alleged experience was even more strange than that of Higdon or any of the other UFO occupant witnesses whose accounts we have examined in this chapter.

Thunder did not follow the flash of light and he later described the light as not straight but "broken." After he regained his sight he was frightened and decided to run the rest of the way to his home which was now in sight, but he couldn't move—he seemed to have become paralyzed.

At that point Mr. Diaz heard a humming sound which he compared to the sound of rushing air or wind and his strange experience continued. Although he tried to resist, Diaz was pulled off the ground and went about 3 meters (about 8 feet) off the ground when he became unconscious. His vision faded before he fainted.

When Diaz regained consciousness he was inside a smooth, bright sphere which appeared to be semi-transparent plastic. There were no furniture or devices and the illumination seemed to come from the walls. Diaz said he was completely lucid and conscious, half kneeling and half lying on his side against several openings of about 3 centimeters in diameter (1¼ inches) in the bottom of the sphere through which issued air. He said he felt ill if he turned away from the openings and felt they served to keep him conscious. He estimated the "sphere" was 2½ to 3 meters (about 7 or 8 feet) in diameter.

Suddenly, Diaz reports, three creatures resembling humans came sliding into the sphere. They appeared to be 1.74 to 1.80 meters in height (approximately 5 feet 10 inches), their heads were half the size of a human head and completely devoid of features—no ears, nose, mouth, or eyes. The head was mossy green in color and the body, which was rather thin, was covered with something Diaz defined as rubber—light, cream-colored, and very soft, and the creatures were completely hairless. The arms were almost straight and very flexible and ended in "stumps" rather than hands and fingers.

When the creatures came into the sphere, they immediately began pulling tufts of hair from Diaz' head. He didn't know how they did it, at first, not having hands or fingers, but each time they would reach out, their arms would pull back and they had hair. They would then jump up and down and wave their arms.

Diaz tried to resist the creatures, but to no avail. During his struggles Diaz felt the softness of their bodies and ultimately noted they had "suckers" on their arms and assumed that was the method by which they removed the hair. One of them held him, another pulled his hair, and the third apparently only observed. Diaz noted the fact that he felt no pain as they pulled at his hair, both on his head and chest. The creatures moved slowly but were very strong and seemingly tireless, he said. After this ordeal was over, Diaz' sight began to wane gradually and he then fainted. He remembers nothing else of the experience.

Several hours went by and Diaz woke up and found himself lying on the grass and had to close his eyes as the sun was high and shining into them. He was fully recovered and conscious and near a large, busy highway. Diaz looked at his watch which had stopped at 3:50, the time he last noted before his experience began. Beside him was his bag containing his work clothes and the newspaper he had bought hours before. Diaz felt ill and this illness stayed with him throughout the day.

We are immediately struck by three similarities in the Higdon and Diaz cases, namely: in both instances, the "creatures" had no hands or fingers and in both cases the witness suffered a loss of appetite after the experience, and lastly, the entities in both cases "glided" rather than walked.

As we have pointed out in the *APRO Bulletin* in the past, we must consider the possibility of deliberate confusion in these cases of absolutely bizarre (to us) creatures and experiences. It seems likely in Higdon's case that he was under the influence (both he and his gun) of something when he went over the crest of that hill and saw the elk. In Diaz' case, he was rendered unconscious before his experience with the humanoids began. Was he also under some kind of influence? Obviously something unusual happened to him—the absence of hair in various spots on his head and chest attest to that. If we speculate that he pulled his own hair out, for whatever reason, we must then consider the fact that, outside of one interview with a magazine, he permitted no interviews with newspapers, radio or TV, and was questioned by only one civilian UFO investigator, Mr. Peter Romaniuk. He obviously did not thirst for publicity or notoriety. Then we have the problem of how he got from Bahia Blanca to Buenos Aires in a matter of four hours and ten minutes—a distance of 423 miles. In the United States, traveling on the best roads and breaking speed limits, the best that could be done would be something over five hours. Diaz does not own a car. We can rule out cars and, of course, buses. That leaves only air travel.

Diaz did not drive from Bahia Blanca to Buenos Aires. Nor did he fly; there was no record of a man of his description having booked passage on an airline on that date and actually the airlines do not have a schedule which would accommodate that time period.

So how did Diaz get there? It is established that he did indeed work at the Holy Protective Society until the hour he claims. He did ride the bus to his stop and he did get off. But what he did in the ensuing hours until he was found lying beside the road in Buenos Aires we can only learn from him. What he remembers *seems* unacceptable, but on the other hand, we have the problem of the missing hair. At this writing reports have not indicated whether or not hypnosis has been attempted but we will discuss that probability and its ramifications in another chapter.

With this last case, we have what appears to be a motley bunch of reports of impossible things—"flying men." Clearly, though, there is a correlation in the majority of the reports; they were small, wore some sort of clothing, had no visible means of locomotion, yet they could fly.

Of the four elements which has confronted man from the dawn of time, he has come to grips with three: he walks upon the face of the earth, he has learned to propel himself through the water without artificial help, and he has designed protective covering so that he can walk into fire if it should become necessary. But he has yet to devise a means by which to propel himself through the air without some mechanical aid.

Man has always wanted to "fly." There was the mythological Icarus who flew too close to the sun and his wax wings melted.

One of the many inventions of Leonardo da Vinci was the prototype of the modern helicopter.

On that historic day at Kitty Hawk, in North Carolina, the Wright brothers proved that it was possible for man to fly—with the help of a machine.

Since then man has gone on to improve upon the machine so that he can transport hundreds of people through the air in one machine at speeds approaching that of sound. Quite an accomplishment! Yet man has not been able to devise an instrument by which one individual can take off and easily fly through the air without benefit of large and cumbersome mechanical devices. But —the cases we have examined here indicate that *someone*, and usually someone associated with UFO's, has perfected a method by which they can do precisely that: fly without the benefit of a machine or device.

It is quite likely that some sort of device was used in all cases, but that the witness or witnesses were so surprised that they failed to make a careful, detailed observation. Or it may simply be that because most such cases take place at night, not much detail is readily discernible.

In summing up the cases of the flying, floating UFO "men," we should consider the advantages of free flight for an individual. UFOs have been seen in the air, going into and coming out of water, on the ground, and accompanied by occupants.

However, if they are carrying out some kind of research, it is difficult for them to obtain certain data, such as our mode of living and things of that nature, without close-up, close-encounter study.

If "they" have devised a means by which an individual can fly, then they can operate at will in urban areas where it would be somewhat difficult to park a flying machine and thence dispatch individuals to investigate on foot without fear of hindrance or capture.

Most UFO sightings, as the evidence shows, take place at night and the cases of UFOs landing in urban areas are very rare. Therefore, what would be more useful and appropriate than a device by which UFO occupants could gain easy access to places of interest which they otherwise would have to pass by?

Man may not yet have learned to fly without cumbersome mechanical means, but *someone* or *something* has!

CHAPTER XIII

Technological Aspects

Among the most mystifying aspects of UFO reports from the standpoint of contemporary physical science is the repetitive appearance of descriptions of right-angle turns and (less often) accounts of UFOs that disappear abruptly.

If such accounts appeared only in cases with obvious psychic content, they would of course present no problem, for there is no reason to expect psychic projections to obey physical laws. But this is not the case. Many reports which appear substantial from every other physical standpoint record one or both of these mystifying attributes.

If we ascribe the sudden disappearances to instant acceleration (i.e., the object speeds away so abruptly that the eye cannot follow) a common characteristic suggests itself—that of masslessness.

Some writers have suggested that the 90° turns could be accounted for by assuming an anti-gravity system, but we suggest that, even if earth gravity could be nullified in some manner with the craft producing its own gravity field, there would still be *mass* to contend with in the form of inertia.

We have all experienced the discomfort of being thrown to one side while rounding a turn in an automobile. This effect is due not to our weight, but to our inertia—the tendency for a moving body to keep moving in a straight line and for a stationary body to remain stationary. As far as we know, weight and inertia both depend on the existence of mass.

The proponents of the anti-gravity idea propose that some system is utilized by the UFOs which is able to nullify the gravitational field of the earth and produce its own field which it carries with it—a field within a field, so to speak. This theory, however, appears to take care of only half the problem. We have no basis for the assumption that eliminating the weight of an object eliminates its inertia.

To illustrate: It seems that we on this earth, which manifests its own gravity field inside that of the sun, would have a long walk home if this earth should abruptly change direction. Since both weight and inertia seem to depend on the existence of mass, it would seem that some UFOs have found a way to negate the effects of mass (i.e., both weight and inertia)—a concept which is untenable within the framework of current physical knowledge. If so, this would explain why they are able to accomplish right-angle turns with apparent ease.

To say that we do not know how to accomplish a particular effect is not the same as saying it cannot be done.

To say either that such a thing is ultimately impossible or that such a thing is ultimately possible requires that one drop the mantle of the scientist and don that of the fortune-teller.

Circumstantial evidence in the form of UFO reports, however, advocates slightly the assumption of the idea that we are dealing with possibilities. Science, however grudgingly, is constantly converting the impossible to the possible.

In our technology the servo system is the indispensable component of all automated systems.

A servo system in a simplified definition can be described as being composed of three basic parts: (1) A means of accepting an instruction; (2) a means of carrying out the instruction; (3) a monitor to determine when the instruction has been carried out.

A common example of a servo system is a household all-weather air-conditioning system. The three components, as outlined above, are: (1) the thermostat, which is set to instruct the system as to the desired room temperature; (2) the heating and refrigerating units, one or the other of which is engaged as required by the instruction of the thermostat; (3) a temperature-monitoring device which shuts off the engaged system when the instruction has been fulfilled (i.e., the desired room temperature has been reached). For practical considerations there is a "dead zone," a narrow range of temperature wherein neither the cooling system nor the heating system is required to operate. The room temperature is allowed to float or fluctuate within this range. This is to avoid system oscillation, a situation where the heating system, before disengaging, would operate to a point which would engage the cooling system, which in turn would immediately cause the heating system to re-engage, and so on.

An ideal system would, of course, hold the room temperature at an absolutely stable preselected temperature but practical limitations make this impossible. A form of this limitation extends into all practical applications of the servo technique—that is, we always have a dead zone of sorts.

Let's move our area of discussion now to encompass one servo loop in an automatic pilot system—the one which controls aircraft altitude. Here again we must have an altitude dead zone.

In this case it is a range of altitude within which the aircraft may fluctuate without bringing about any corrective action of the aircraft control surfaces. The result is generally as follows. The craft gains slightly in altitude until the upper edge of the dead zone is reached. This causes a slight corrective action of the control surfaces, causing the plane to lose altitude slightly until the lower limit of the dead zone is reached. This causes a slight upward correction to take place, and so on.

With conventional aircraft this effect is not pronounced enough to be readily visible to an observer on the ground or in another plane, for it is largely damped out and absorbed by the elasticity of the air and/or electronic damping equipment built into the control system. However, a craft which did not depend on conventional aerodynamic lift to maintain altitude—especially one which was designed to travel at excessive speed—might well find the tendency to wander from limit to limit of the dead zone intensified. Increased speed would mean a tendency to overcorrect unless the dead zone limits were more lenient. It is quite probable that a degree of wandering easily apparent to the average observer would be a characteristic of the kind of craft the UFO seems to be.

As previously stated, the servo system is the indispensable component of all automated systems. It is used to perform tasks where human senses and reactions are too slow, where matters cannot be left to human judgment, in areas where human senses do not operate. Presumably it could serve our visitors in like manner.

They deal basically with the same physical problems that we do. It should be expected that their solutions to at least some of them would be subject to the same limitations.

The term "flying saucer" originated when Kenneth Arnold attempted to describe the flight paths of the group of objects he saw near Mt. Rainier in June 1947.

Arnold said, "They definitely flew in formation, but erratically, in a weaving motion. Their movement was comparable to speedboats on rough water or a formation of geese.... *They flew like a saucer would if you skipped it across the water.*" Arnold's description is not unique; in fact it has become typical. The path of the famous Trindade Island UFO (Brazil, 1958) was described as "like the flight of a bat."

Again and again we read accounts of UFOs which move through the air with an undulatory or skipping motion.

The skipping motion often attributed to UFOs which are traveling at a fair rate of speed can be the result of a servo system operating to keep the craft on a programmed course as the craft brushes alternately the limits of the dead zone assigned by the current program.

If this is true, we should also find that: (1) The skipping motion is not noticeable in the case of a UFO which crosses our vision at a very high rate of speed as in the case of the "fly overs." The vast distance covered in one "skip" would render comparison with stable points of reference nonfeasible to such a degree that the skipping action would not be detectable. And (2) a wobbling or fibrillation would be evident in cases of hovering UFOs, since the looseness of a servo system designed for rapid flight would be easily visible in the hovering craft.

We do, in fact, find both of the above symptoms. In connection with the second, another commonly reported maneuver should be mentioned—the so-called falling leaf pattern which can be described as a series of gliding falls separated by momentary pauses. Here we can assume that the UFO is hovering for a specific purpose when the operator desires to make a closer inspection of some surface feature. He, therefore, takes over manual control of the craft's altitude and "punches" a series of adjustments into the altitude control system until he arrives at a level satisfactory to his purpose. The craft, due to its aerodynamic characteristics, does not "drop like a rock," but concurrent with each correction, "slides" in a direction probably controlled by the instantaneous altitude of the fibrillating craft.

If the idea of an otherwise highly sophisticated craft behaving in so clumsy a manner offends your judgment, consider that any engineering design represents a compromise or combination of compromises.

In our own experience, planes which are built for speed and/or extended cruising range are pretty clumsy getting on and off the ground. The ocean liner which crosses the ocean in stately grandeur needs help getting up to the dock.

It has been quite popular in the past, in order to discount the physical reality of the UFO, to call attention to reported characteristics that are not understandable in the light of current physical theory. It would seem, then, equally valid to call attention to characteristics that are understandable in that same light, in order to advocate their reality.

CHAPTER XIV

UFO and CIA

In *Flying Saucer Occupants* we presented the dual hypothesis (1) that the CIA was conducting an undercover intelligence-gathering program relating to the UFO phenomenon, and (2) that, for intelligence reasons, it had been the architect of Project Blue Book (the Air Force investigation project on UFOs) and general Air Force public information policy—the latter being a "cover" program designed to hide the fact that the former existed.

We supported this hypothesis by pointing out that, among other things:

A. The Robertson Panel, made up of five prominent physical scientists who met in early 1953 to study the UFO problem, was CIA sponsored.[1]

B. The study conducted by the Robertson Panel was not a bona fide unbiased scientific study since the panel members were only given a small group of cases (selected by ATIC) from Blue Book files for consideration.

C. The study conducted by the Robertson Panel was not a bona fide unbiased scientific study since they spent only three days on the complex problem.

D. Although the panel, by and large, was made up of physical scientists with *little or no experience in military matters,* it was being asked to make what amounted to *tactical* decisions in the area of national *defense.*

E. The Panel's recommendation to expand Project Blue Book was ignored.

F. The Panel's recommendation to "debunk" acceptance of flying saucers through public-relations techniques was classified (and followed).

G. Blue Book never was a research project in any true sense of the word.

H. Those UFO incidents of prime importance from a national defense standpoint—that is, those involving airborne vehicles which occur under military jurisdiction, including instrument documentation—are classified Top Secret as a matter of standard operating procedure.

I. Such incidents are of high priority interest to the CIA.

Correspondence resulting from the publication of these ideas, together with subsequent research and events, points up the need for further development of this theme. Response from various individuals who could speak from experience was very encouraging. For example, the following, from a retired Air Force officer:

> "I just finished reading your recent book *Occupants*—most significant and enthralling reading.
>
> Your explanation of what seems to be unjustified secrecy of the federal military services and those of all the rest of the world is quite remarkable. Any higher echelon officer in any of the services would draw these conclusions automatically. All of the staff schools of every military service teach military intelligence procedures. It is a significant part of the courses taught the staff officer concerning intelligence as related to a potential military threat.
>
> Your dissertation is so close as to be nearly textbook."

Our purpose in pursuing this matter is not to malign the CIA, or to insinuate that it is doing an improper job, but rather to throw light on what are otherwise some rather confusing paradoxes. It is our view that the nature of the UFO problem is such that open communication between the Defense Department and the public is prevented by standard national security practices. We maintain that the claim of many that a *special* conspiracy of silence is applied where UFOs are concerned is unsubstantiated. Simply stated, we feel that UFO information is withheld *through the application of normal national security procedures since there is no reason why these procedures should be set aside in the case of the UFO!*

Within this frame of reference, then, Blue Book appears as a key agency in a long term "deception" maneuver—a standard intelligence tool.

According to "Mr. CIA" himself, Allen Dulles: "In Intelligence, the term 'deception' covers a wide variety of maneuvers by which a state attempts to mislead another state, generally a potential or actual enemy, as to its own capabilities and intentions."[2]

It should be remembered that the CIA's existence springs from a chain of events leading back to the tragedy at Pearl Harbor. Therefore, it is to be expected that it would be exceptionally sensitive concerning reports of unauthorized vehicles entering our air space—that is precisely the sort of problem that the CIA was created to cope with. In intelligence circles, actions such as UFOs demonstrate can only be interpreted as those of a potential enemy and it is, of course, the CIA's job to collect as much intelligence concerning potential enemies as possible.

What is intelligence? The Second Hoover Commission's Task Force on Intelligence Activities summed it up as follows: "Intelligence deals with all the things that should be known in advance of initiating a course of action."

What is the CIA's position in the total United States Intelligence picture?

According to Allen Dulles:

> "Between these three agencies (i.e., the State Department, the Defense Department, and the CIA) there is an immediate and often automatic exchange of important intelligence data. Of course, someone has to decide what "important" means and determine priorities. The sender of an intelligence report (who may be any one of our many officials abroad—diplomatic, military or intelligence) will often label it as being of a certain importance but the question of priority is generally decided on the receiving end. If a report is of a particularly critical character, touching on the danger of hostilities or some major threat to our national security, the sender will place his message in channels that provide for automatic dissemination to the intelligence officers in the State and Defense Departments and the CIA. The latter, as coordinator of foreign intelligence, has the right of access to all intelligence that comes to any department of the government. This is provided for by law."

From the foregoing we note, among other things, two important points: all United States Intelligence information is available to the CIA, and anything touching a threat to national security is automatically brought to the attention of the CIA and the Defense and State Departments.

Do UFO cases fall into this classification? It is likely that some do and some do not. It is to be noted that this decision is partly left to the initiator of the report. The authors have had, over the course of many years, repeated opportunities to converse with various initiators of these reports and we have been able to establish to our own satisfaction that numerous reports exist which the initiators felt "touched on matters of national security." And, apparently, the receiving end concurred, since the reports in question never showed up in the unclassified files of Project Blue Book.

For example: in early 1956 we were both employed at Holloman Air Force Base, New Mexico—Mr. Lorenzen in the Data Reduction Facility and Mrs. Lorenzen in the Range Scheduling Office. Captain Buchanan, project officer for the Falcon air-to-air missile test project, was aloft one morning piloting an F 102 equipped as a Falcon launch aircraft. His mission was a simple one—to launch a Falcon at a small, remote-controlled, jet target aircraft. As he approached the launch area, his APG-30 series radar, operating in automatic mode, showed "lock on." Since there was supposed to be nothing in the area except the target aircraft, there was no reason to assume he had locked onto anything else. Therefore, he did not bother to check the acquisition visually. At this point the mission controller at King One called as follows: "Hey, Buck, you're on the wrong target—yours is at about one-o'clock-low."

A skilled test pilot, Buchanan reacted quickly and surely; he verified the controller's report visually and simultaneously switched the radar to manual mode—to unlock from the false target—and put the F-102 into a power drive in an attempt to get it into proper attitude for a successful missile launch. In his haste he broke through the sound barrier. There were two sonic booms as he accelerated and then decelerated past the speed of sound. Alerted by these sonic booms, individuals working outside at various locations around the base looked up and saw a bright ovoid object move downrange in a rapid zigzag course, and disappear in the distance in a matter of seconds. It did not produce a sonic boom.

It was part of Mrs. Lorenzen's responsibility as secretary of the Range Scheduling Office to write the Daily Mission Summary Report. This report, as the name implies, summarized the accomplishments of all missions conducted on the Holloman test range for a given day. Normally, Mission Control submitted a form outlining its daily accomplishment late in the day, and the Summary Report was written the following morning.

Under ordinary circumstances, the commanding general (Leighton I. Davis) would have been on the phone making inquiries had the report not reached his desk by 9:00 A.M. On the day following Captain Buchanan's experience there was no Range Summary Report. The notes from individual project officers which provided the basis for the Summary Report were not forthcoming. These notes, or rather a crude fascimile thereof, arrived twenty-three hours late, all pencilled in the same handwriting, their content plainly indicating a rather inept forgery. When she received them Mrs. Lorenzen called General Davis' office to inform him that the material for the report was late, and obviously false; she was merely encouraged to do the best she could. Nowhere in the spurious notes was Captain Buchanan's UFO mentioned. There is little doubt as to the priority selected by the initiator in this case.

During our (APRO) investigation of the Socorro, New Mexico case, Blue Book's Sergeant Moody told us bluntly, "You get lots of cases that we don't get."

We had been aware for some years that many UFO cases of a rather startling nature never seemed to find their way to the Blue Book files. The Socorro case served to reinforce our memories in this area.

One of Sergeant Chavez' first moves after a preliminary inspection of the landing site was to call Captain Holder, commanding officer of Stallion Site on the White Sands Missile Range and an Army intelligence officer. Holder lived in Socorro, he was at home and arrived at the landing site within a matter of minutes. An intelligent and competent young officer, Holder proceeded to make a thorough investigation and eventually to write a complete and comprehensive report based partly on evidence which had been obscured by the idle curious who had flocked in to mill around and speculate by the time other investigators could arrive.

In spite of this, Sergeant Moody showed up two days later to conduct his own investigation. It was as though the right hand didn't know what the left hand was doing.

One would expect that Captain Holder's report would be routed to Blue Book as a matter of course. Not so. According to Holder, it would be routed to "the UFO board in Washington."

At our insistence, before leaving Socorro Sergeant Moody agreed to request a copy of Holder's report. I assume that he did. But for some reason, comments on the Socorro incident, for instance those of John Lear who quoted the Air Force report in the *Saturday Review,* made no mention of Holder's excellent treatise.

A few days after the Socorro incident, a B-57 pilot on a simulated bombing mission over an area which included the north range extension (a section of ranchland lying north and east of Socorro) reported to Mission Control that he "had a UFO."

In answer to queries he reported that the UFO was landing or landed and was shaped and marked "like the one at Socorro."

On May 22, 1964, a radar instrumentation station on the White Sands Missile Range, an Army installation, tracked a UFO. Its path was recorded automatically by means of a special device which places the range, azimuth, and elevation in digital form on tape.

Seven days earlier two objects moving leisurely across the range were acquired on radar. Their appearance when acquired visually was described as brown and football-shaped. And—they were "transponding" in response to the standard Federal Aviation Agency's recognition signals, alternating between two frequencies reserved for that purpose where normally an aircraft would utilize one or the other.

Here again we have no indication that reports of the foregoing cases were routed to Blue Book. They were filed with the base commander at White Sands Missile Range.

When these cases appeared in the *APRO Bulletin*, Major Hector Quintanilla, Blue Book officer in charge, queried the Foreign Technology office at Holloman Air Force Base and was informed that the office was unaware of any such incidents. This is as far as the investigation went.

In the two days following the Socorro incident, "landings" were reported at La Madera, New Mexico, and Canyon Ferry, Montana. In each of these cases "landing gear tracks" were found that were identical to those at Socorro. They had not been described in the press in sufficient detail to support the probability of imitation. Yet this circumstantial support for the Socorro case is not mentioned in the Blue Book report. It was not called to Hynek's (the chief author of the Blue Book report) attention. As far as we can determine, these other two cases were investigated by local Air Force people and the reports filed with local base commanders.

Over the Davis-Monthan Air Force Base at Tucson, Arizona, in early 1952 (exact date not recalled by witnesses) two UFOs appeared at noon. Since most employees were on their lunch hour, there were many witnesses including the control tower operator. An intelligence officer and a sergeant obtained cameras and began to photograph the action. One UFO stayed "near the sun" and was therefore relatively unphotographable, but the other maneuvered over the base for a considerable period of time allowing each of the photographers the opportunity to expose in the neighborhood of forty plates of excellent fine-grained 4X5 film.

On the developed film some of the images displayed a diameter of ¼ inch. Obviously, blowups of such images on fine-grained film can be expected to disclose considerable detail. However, it was discovered on development that even though the discs seemed metallic to the naked eye, their film images were black ovoid blobs—as though they had emitted some form of radiation that had caused their images to be overexposed.

Also in the spring of 1952, over Davis-Monthan Air Force Base, in broad daylight a cruising B-36 suddenly acquired company. A disc-shaped object moved into a position which from the ground appeared to nearly fill the space behind the right wing and in front of the right horizontal stabilizer. Crew members aboard the plane looking through the observation port on the right side of the fuselage could see that the object was slightly below the plane of the horizontal stabilizer. Simultaneously another, identical, UFO had appeared off the left wing tip. After a few minutes the disc on the right moved over to join the one off the left wing and they flew away together.

It is worthy of note that this case was not one of those shown to the Robertson Panel for it was not in the Blue Book files at the time the panel convened about nine months later.

Man reacts to a given situation on the basis of habit, previous experience, and precedent. If this is true of man as an individual, it is also true of man collectively and it is equally true of military organizations. Therefore military reaction in many situations is, to a high degree, predictable.

A new problem does not automatically evoke new techniques. It has always been a policy of the military to classify any occurrence which reflects in any manner on the total efficacy of the service. There is no reason to think that this traditional policy would be breached in the case of the UFO. It is worthy of note in this connection that no UFO case occurring under exclusive military cognizance has ever been volunteered to the public via the press.

With a little thought it can be accepted that an authority in the area of physical science might reject the whole UFO phenomena as "utter bilge" because of the inherent emotional obstacles. The idea has connotations which chop away at some of the basic building blocks of our scientific edifice. Rejection comes more easily if the authority concerned has been only fleetingly exposed to limited parcels of the total evidence. On the other hand, we cannot visualize trained and experienced intelligence personnel succumbing to similar pitfalls. The Cold War has made them especially sensitive to such pitfalls and it is difficult to believe that the lesson of Pearl Harbor has been so swiftly forgotten.

From a military intelligence standpoint, the surreptitious penetration of our air space by alien vehicles can be treated in only one way. It must be assumed to be the act of an unknown enemy until proven otherwise.

Operating on this assumption, all information concerning the unknown enemy, including the very fact of his existence, must be withheld from the public, since it cannot be known with any certainty what intelligence facilities the enemy has at his disposal. It may be easier to divine his intentions if he does not know we are aware of him and does not, therefore, become more secretive.

If the public, uninformed, becomes apprehensive concerning those incidents which become a matter of public record, the problem becomes double-edged.

In addition, it can easily be seen that any official endorsement of the invaders' existence would merely open a Pandora's box of further questions.

Where are they from? What are their intentions? Etc.... As long as the answers to these questions remain largely in the dark it is better to leave the box closed if possible. Time may bring illumination.

Early in the game, then, it would seem that the problem presented (again from the standpoint of military intelligence) two major aspects: (1) an unknown (possible) enemy who had to be treated as though he were not there while a concerted effort was made to divine his intent; (2) an apprehensive public which had to be reassured lest it upset the intelligence applecart.

When a deception maneuver is employed it often results, unfortunately, in the deception of our allies as well as our adversaries. Dulles says, "When one deliberately misleads, sometimes friend as well as foe is misled. And later the deceiver may not be believed when he wishes to be." Apparently such a situation developed in the air force in the post-Robertson Report years. That is to say, individual officers were so impressed by public UFO-debunking techniques that they became lax in reporting UFO incidents. The now notorious "Flying Saucers Serious Business"[3] memo was issued to rectify this situation.

The intelligence officer cannot afford to take anything for granted or to be lulled into apathy. If the first UFO must be viewed as a tool of either a known or an unknown potential enemy, no less so must the second or third or the thousandth or the ten thousandth. If these vehicles prove evasive and surreptitious, all the more reason to suspect them. For to the intelligence-oriented, the probability looms large that the minds behind these vehicles may well be gathering intelligence of their own.

The fact that wide variations and inconsistencies exist between individual reports is considered by many scientists and laymen as reason enough to dismiss the possibility of the problem having real substance. However, the trained intelligence officer will realize that even ignoring variations resulting from individual interpretation, there may be a deliberate attempt on the part of the alien to confuse our intelligence system—that is, the intruders may indeed be applying their own "deception" techniques.

Another reason for our government indulging in intelligence activities in connection with UFOs lies in the hope of acquiring specific knowledge concerning advanced propulsion methods and systems. To fulfill this hope it is necessary to amass as many as possible of these details in thousands of reports which may relate to propulsion techniques. In amassing and evaluating these data we must avoid tipping off, if possible, the potential enemy (as well as our cold-war adversaries), for if there *is* something to be gained in the area of physical knowledge, we stand to gain the additional advantage of time if our efforts go undetected. During our trip to South America in August 1967, we found more than one government-sponsored agency engaged in an effort to solve the secret of UFO propulsion. Such endeavors, which proceed on the assumption that "flying saucers are real," could hardly have come into being without a certain amount of preliminary intelligence gathering.

APRO is also an intelligence-gathering organization. Our efforts are directed toward providing the public with information, unlike the CIA, whose efforts are directed toward providing secret estimates on which the government may base courses of action. Over the years, however, our paths have crossed occasionally in a rather startling manner.

In the late 1950's an agent of ours in Canada, tracing down UFO reports, uncovered the fact that high-flying reconnaissance planes were over-flying parts of Russia from a secret base in Canada—this was years before the general public was apprised of the existence of the U-2 via the Gary Powers mishap. In the immediate pre-Bay of Pigs era, another of our agents, while checking out reports of repeated landings of UFOs in the Florida everglades, discovered a complete military airbase equipped with unmarked (United States manufactured) vehicles and planes. In the above cases we decided immediately that we had acquired information beyond our area of interest, to say the least, and promptly consigned the relevant reports to flames.

The above incidents represent accidental encounters. There are other cross involvements, however, which can only be considered deliberate, as we shall see.

In 1951 Mrs. Lorenzen, then a feature writer for the Green Bay (Wis.) *Press-Gazette*, did a series of articles on the UFO situation, based on information she had been collecting since 1947, when Kenneth Arnold's report brought the matter to public attention. The series drew an unusual quantity of mail. This local interest, together with the fact that a sizable correspondence had already developed with interested individuals around the country, led us gradually to the decision to form APRO.

One of our first, most energetic supporters was a gentleman

from Green Bay. He helped with minor donations and many suggestions for organizing. He claimed to have a background in intelligence work. In retrospect, we can see that he made several attempts to lead us into metaphysical areas—which would naturally detract from an objective study—attempts which were gently parried.

Many typists employ a simple device of using a sheet of stationery as a platen (pad); that is, they insert two sheets of paper in the typewriter, and when the typing of the first page is complete it is removed, and a new sheet of paper is inserted behind the remaining sheet. This sheet is then typed on, while the new sheet serves as *its* platen, and so on. Our benefactor had this habit—a rather serious one for an agent (if agent he was). After reading a letter from him dated February 22, 1953, Mrs. Lorenzen flipped it into the file basket on her desk. It caught the light in such a way that she saw her name embossed across the top of the page. A closer examination, with the aid of a soft lead pencil, disclosed not only her name, but the beginning of an abbreviated intelligence report, apparently inadvertently impressed into the paper through its use as a platen.

The report began with a short history of her residences, then moved on to list impressions of her personal habits and character.

When confronted with the evidence, our benefactor stated that this was merely a routine he used to formalize his feelings about people he met and to define his impressions and that it was strictly a report for his own files. On the face of it this was a rather flimsy excuse, but taken in conjunction with other things we knew about the fellow, we felt it could be genuine.

In 1953 the CIA-Robertson Panel Report made a curious statement: "The Panel took cognizance of the existence of such groups as the 'Civilian Flying Saucer Investigators' (Los Angeles) and the 'Aerial Phenomena Research Organization' (Wisconsin). It was believed that such organizations should be watched because of their potentially great influence on mass thinking if widespread sighting should occur. The apparent irresponsibility and the possible use of such groups for subversive purposes should be kept in mind."

How could the CIA-Robertson Panel have drawn any conclusions concerning APRO at this point? When the report was written, we had been in operation barely a year. We do not plead guilty to the charge of irresponsibility, and we doubt that the report writer was himself entirely irresponsible in making the statement; in all fairness it must be admitted that any intelligence estimate concerning APRO at that time would have had to have been tentative due to the extreme youth of the organization. Whether or not our Green Bay benefactor's report had any connection with this appraisal and recommendation will probably never be known for certain.

J. Allen Hynek, who as Project Blue Book's scientific advisor monitored the Robertson Panel discussion, does not recall that APRO was discussed other than in a possible passing mention. Since this idea was apparently not a product of the panel, we are left with the alternative that it was a product of the sponsor. Since nowhere in the panel minutes do we find mention that unofficial investigating groups were disucssed we can fairly assume that this particular admonition was not the fruit of panel deliberation. How, then, did it get into the report? The Wednesday morning minutes furnish a clue.

According to the minutes, CIA interest in the subject was reviewed; "...and (three letter deletion) concern over potential dangers to national security indirectly related to the sightings. Mr. (deletion) *enumerated these potential dangers.*" (Italics ours.) One of these dangers was apparently considered to lie in the nature of private groups such as APRO.

It should not surprise us to find a group of college professors (the Robertson Panel) "taking cognizance" of potential dangers as enumerated by a national security expert (the deleted CIA agent above) to the point where they would restate them in their final report.

When we consider that the sponsor, the CIA, was already involved in a "deception" action designed to influence mass thinking through the subversion of a group of prominent scientists, the matter becomes more clear. The pointing out of apparently fertile fields for the continuance of and expansion (if necessary) of the program would be a logical and desirable part of the report with respect to its value as a "deception" tool.

Certainly APRO has been watched and probably other UFO groups as well. During the summer of 1952, the first year of our existence, two men called on Mrs. Lorenzen on a bright afternoon. She observed them first driving slowly up Memorial Drive as though looking for an address. They passed our house before stopping. One man alighted and walked back to our door. He told Mrs. Lorenzen that he was a painting contractor and would like to bid on a paint job for the house. When it was explained that we were renters, he attempted to engage Mrs. Lorenzen in conversation, but expressed no interest in obtaining the landlord's name. When he rejoined his friend, they drove to the next street and turned left without stopping at any other house on the street. A few minutes later Mrs. Lorenzen went out the back door and noted that after turning the corner they had proceeded down the block and stopped at a point where a clear area afforded them a view of the back of our home. In relating this incident later we were surprised to find that on the same day APRO's treasurer and secretary each received similar visits from the same two men. The story in each case was essentially the same—a paint contractor soliciting business—even though the treasurer's home was newly painted and the secretary lived in an apartment. In each case an attempt was made at lengthy conversation and no other homes in the neighborhood were visited. Perhaps they were painting contractors, but if so, they certainly were not very enterprising ones.

An associate of Mrs. Lorenzen whose husband worked in OSI (Office of Special Investigation) told her that the local office (of OSI) had a sizable dossier on APRO and the Lorenzens. Apparently its content was favorable since it prevented neither of us from obtaining the high-level clearance our jobs required.

When we were preparing to move from Alamogordo to Tucson in 1960, FBI Agent Ray Kissiah called Mrs. Lorenzen to obtain our Tucson address. His excuse was that he, personally, was interested in the UFO problem and would like to start receiving our publication. We sent Mr. Kissiah the proper material for joining—and have not heard from him since.

On our third day in Tucson we were visited by an "exterminator" who offered to inspect the premises (for termites) free of charge. He was not discouraged on being informed that since we were renting he would have to speak with the landlord on such matters, but drew Mrs. Lorenzen into a lengthy conversation disucssing, among other things, our reasons for moving, where Mr. Lorenzen was employed, and UFOs. Once again we were confronted with a picture of a rather inept businessman. He was dressed in new white coveralls, wore freshly polished dress shoes, and had well-manicured fingernails. Although he invested a good hour of his time in probing conversation, he did not once mention the firm he represented or present a business card or inquire as to the identity of our landlord.

The foregoing examples, only a few of many similar incidents, are not intended specifically to prove anything; they are, at best, only circumstantial evidence. The same cannot be said for the following, however. In the fall of 1966, Olavo T. Fontes, a member of APRO's advisory staff and our special representative in Brazil, visited the United States briefly on medical business. Fontes was director emeritus of the gastroenterological branch of the National School of Medicine of Brazil and co-sponsor of one of the world's most modern clinics practicing internal medicine. While in the Chicago area, he met with Dr. J. Allen Hynek to discuss their common interest—UFOs.

During the course of this meeting, Hynek, knowing that Fontes had good connections with the Brazilian Defense Community, asked if it would be possible for Fontes to obtain UFO cases from the Brazilian Air Force and send them to him. Fontes promised to find out.

When Fontes, in due time, relayed the request to his Air Force "connection" he did not receive an immediate answer. Before responding, the Brazilian officer had decided to request a security check on Dr. Hynek. Fontes' friend was able to state eventually that the check was favorable, and that Fontes' own name had actually appeared in the report on Dr. Hynek obtained from an unnamed United States intelligence agency.

Dr. Hynek, the report said, had on at least two occasions visited at the home of a prominent writer on the subject of UFOS, Mrs. Lorenzen of Tucson, Arizona. Furthermore, the report continued, Dr. Fontes of Brazil had visited this same person and had been seen dining alone with her on at least one occasion.

Dr. Hynek and Mrs. Lorenzen have been acquainted since 1953; they met while she was in Milwaukee, Wisconsin, to address the Milwaukee Astronomical Society.

Hynek's visits to the Lorenzen home were not particularly significant, being in line with his stated policy of "monitoring the noise level," but lest they be misinterpreted, they were made unannounced while he was in the area on other business. Therefore, since they are mentioned in the report, we must conclude that someone was watching the Lorenzens, or watching Hynek, or both.

The statement about Fontes is more revealing. Dr. and Mrs. Fontes visited us in 1963, bringing with them their two oldest children. We reserved an apartment for them at the Tucson Inn since there was not enough room for the four of them at our home. On the evening of the day they arrived, Mr. Lorenzen had an engagement (he is the inventor of various electronic devices for musicians and at that time would occasionally accept engagements with dance combos in order to verify the efficacy of current design under actual playing conditions). He left Mrs. Lorenzen and Dr. and Mrs. Fontes at the Tucson Inn at about 8:30 P.M.

Mrs. Fontes, who was in poor health at the time, wished to retire early, as did the children. Mrs. Lorenzen and Dr. Fontes who had much to talk about in connection with UFOs, not wishing to disturb the sleepers, walked a block to Sambo's Restaurant where they conversed over coffee from 11:00 P.M. until about midnight.

Since this was the only occasion on which these two appeared together at a restaurant it must be the "dining" incident referred to in the report; establishing rather conclusively that on at least this one occasion a member of the Unted States intelligence community was tailing APRO officers.

Whether the Robertson-CIA recommendation to watch UFO groups was followed in the case of other organizations, we cannot say, but there is no reason to assume otherwise. There is an indication also that "the possible use of such groups for subversive purposes" *was* "kept in mind."

James Moseley, publisher of a fan magazine which dates back to the mid-1950's, claimed stoutly that he had been privileged to see a classified government document which established definitely that UFOs were not extraterrestrial. There is no reason to doubt Mr. Moseley's honesty in initially making this claim, but at this late date it seems worthwhile to consider the fact that the "leaking" of information through forged documents is a favorite trick of the CIA and other intelligence organizations.[4]

Probably, the CIA's main concern with the activities of private groups is that should these groups become too influential, they could well upset the intelligence applecart, making the public aware of UFO reality long before enough intelligence has been gathered on which to base a clear course of national action. The greatest threat to the intelligence mission would be a situation in which public confidence became so invested in a private organization (or organizations) that individuals preferred to report directly to the private group(s) rather than to government agencies.

An expression which appears frequently in official UFO writings is "signal-to-noise ratio." This expression describes a comparison between the total of the relatively few hard cases from which, presumably, some firm conclusions could be drawn (i.e., the "signal") and the majority of inconclusive and incomplete reports (i.e., the "noise" or static).

Using this frame of reference, it is the goal of the objective researcher to increase the signal-to-noise ratio by increasing the number of hard cases and reducing the number of false cases. The goal of the CIA's "deception" maneuver would be the opposite—that is, publicly to decrease the signal-to-noise ratio. (Privately, presumably, their goal would be the same as that of any objective group bent on obtaining the truth.)

To implement such a program, using standard techniques, it would be necessary to neutralize as many hard cases as possible through the confiscation and/or destruction of evidence and the discrediting or silencing of witnesses. Mail watches and phone taps could be used to obtain information being reported confidentially to private groups. It seems likely to the authors that such measures are being undertaken at the present time.

The Richardson-auto-UFO-collision incident is a case in point. Richardson had discussed the fact that he had physical evidence of the encounter with no one except our investigator, Mr. Nils Paquette, and with APRO headquarters by telephone.

Yet someone knew about it, and called on him in an attempt to seize the evidence. Altogether, four individuals were involved in the attempt. The first pair were fairly young men who tried to talk him out of his evidence. They were driving an automobile with an Ohio license plate, bearing what proved to be an *unissued number.* The second pair were older men. They tried to talk Richardson into getting the evidence back from APRO. When this failed, they left after threatening; "You've got a pretty nice wife, it would be a shame if something happened to her." To his everlasting credit, Richardson stood his ground. The attempt to neutralize this particular case failed, but one cannot help but wonder how many times such attempts have succeeded.

Another case of which we have first-hand knowledge runs as follows: an APRO member in Minnesota, whose work consists partly of inspecting power lines in remote areas, called to say that he had found two circular patches of so-called "angel's hair." Since this material, occasionally reported as dropping from UFOs, is reputed to be of delicate constitution, tending to dissolve or sublimate when touched by human hands, the investigator had telephoned APRO headquarters for instructions as to how to proceed. We suggested that he take such precautions as using refrigerated and sterile containers, etc., for sample collection.

It was two days before the investigator could return to the location due to time restrictions imposed by his job. When he arrived at the scene once more, he found that a truck had entered the area in his absence and had dumped fuel oil over the entire site, ruining the evidence.

APRO's investigator had discussed the matter only with four fellow employees, and with Mr. Lorenzen on the telephone. How the evidence-destroyer knew of its existence and location is not certain, but it is suggested that an exceedingly thorough surveillance is being carried out for the purpose of detecting "hard" evidence UFO cases and nipping them in the bud. There is no way of knowing now if this particular case was UFO-connected or not. Had the evidence been left in an untampered-with state it might have become part of the signal. As it stands, the case can only contribute to the noise level.

We use the above cases for purposes of illustration, since they embody facts to which we can testify as matters of personal experience. These cases, however, constitute only a minute part of the total evidence for the existence of a far-flung concerted effort to keep the signal low and the noise high. During 1966 APRO members who investigated cases in the Ohio Valley and in the New England area encountered a veritable rash of instances involving the coercion of witnesses and the compromising of evidence. Cases of operatives posing as air force officers became so numerous that the Air Force Chief of Staff felt compelled to issue a directive requesting military and civilian personnel to refer rumors of such cases to their local OSI officer.[5] From the wording of the order it is impossible to tell whether it constitutes an attempt to apprehend the impersonators or is merely a means of warning the operatives to be more careful.

1. See Appendix A
2. All quotes in this chapter attributed to Allen Dulles are from his book *The Craft of Intelligence*, Harper & Row, 1963.
3. Actually, "UFO's Serious Business." See Appendix B
4. Allen Dulles, op. cit.
5. See Appendix C

CHAPTER XV

Hypnotic and Psychic Implications in the Investigation of UFO Reports

By R. Leo Sprinkle, Ph.D.
University of Wyoming
APRO Consultant in Psychology

INTRODUCTION

Since 1947 there has been an increasing number of persons who have reported observations of "flying saucers" or unidentified flying objects (UFOs). Serious investigations of UFO sightings have been conducted by many persons and agencies throughout the world. In the USA there are many organizations which collect, analyze, and disseminate information about UFO reports, including the Aerial Phenomena Research Organization (APRO), the Center for UFO Studies, Mutual UFO Network (MUFON), and the National Investigations Committee on Aerial Phenomena (NICAP).* In 1968, a symposium on UFOs was conducted by the U.S. House of Representatives Committee on Science and Astronautics (Roush, 1968). The *Condon Report* (UFO Project, University of Colorado) was released in January 1969; many persons were hopeful that the report of the *UFO Project* (Condon and Gillmor, 1969) would settle the issue. However, the activities and conclusions of the *UFO Project* (Saunders and Harkins, 1968) also were controversial, especially in the views of experienced UFO investigators (Bowen, 1969; Hynek, 1969; Keel, 1969a).

The complexity of the history of UFO research may be seen by reading the excellent book by Jacobs (1975); in a scholarly and insightful manner, Dr. Jacobs has described the UFO controversy as experienced in the USA. The controversy has developed over the questions of various hypotheses (Salisbury, 1967) to account for UFO reports; the positions taken by investigators (Sprinkle, 1967) in regard to the significance of UFO reports; the explanations of

* See References at end of chapter.

UFO reports (Fowler, 1974; Klass, 1974); and the social and political implication of UFO reports (Lorenzen and Lorenzen, 1969; Hobana and Weverbergh, 1975).

In recent years, more scientists and professional persons have expressed interest in the physical (McCampbell, 1973; Vallee, 1965; Vallee and Vallee, 1966), biological (Sanderson, 1967; Salisbury, 1974), psychological (Jung, 1959; Saunders and Harkins, 1968), and religious (Downing, 1968; Blumrich, 1974) implications of UFO phenomena.

The rising interest in the investigation of UFO reports by members of the scientific community can be attributed, in large part, to the influence of Hynek (1972). Dr. Hynek served for over twenty years as the Consultant in Astronomy for the USAF Project Blue Book, and his book (J. Allen Hynek, *The UFO Experience,* Chicago, Henry Regnery, 1972) has called for an objective appraisal of the UFO problem. At first, the early investigators (Lorenzen and Lorenzen, 1967; Lorenzen, 1967; Keyhoe, 1973) had little help from the scientific community; however, with the efforts of persons like Michel (1958) of France, Fontes (Lorenzen and Lorenzen, 1967) of Brazil, and McDonald (1969) of the USA, more attention was directed toward the patterns of UFO reports. With the recognition that many reports of objects also involved claims of occupants (Bowen, 1966; Hynek, 1970; Lorenzen and Lorenzen, 1967), investigations were widened to include psychological, as well as physical, aspects of UFO reports. Salisbury (1974) has suggested a fascinating hypothesis: the UFO experience is a "display" to the UFO witness.

There are noted authorities whose views and/or findings raise doubts about the reality of the claimed UFO observations (Festinger, Riecken, and Schachter, 1964; Markowitz, 1967; Menzel and Boyd, 1963; Klass, 1974). Nevertheless, unless there is sufficient evidence to reject the hypothesis, the writer believes that it is appropriate to use the hypothesis that the UFO observer is submitting reliable information. This approach is based upon the practical (and scientific) notion that the best hypothesis is the one which will lead to further results which will lead to further hypotheses, etc.

For many years, the "flying saucer psychosis" was a highly visible hypothesis; however, it also was an untested hypothesis. Because of the "strange" claims of UFO observers, many persons assumed that UFO reports were being submitted by "strange" persons.

Schwarz (1968) made an important contribution by conducting psychiatric studies of observers in four New Jersey UFO cases;

Dr. Schwarz concluded that there was no evidence of psychopathology in the personality patterns of the UFO observers. Thus, the strange claims of those persons probably should be explained on some other basis than the hypothesis of "flying saucer psychosis."

Studies of various problems of UFO research through established avenues of psychological investigation have been conducted by many persons, including Hall (1968), Hartmann (1969), Lee (1969), Rhine (1969), Saunders (1968a, 1968b), Shepard (1968), Sprinkle (1969a, 1975), Vallee (1966), and Wertheimer (1969). In the opinion of this writer, the work of Dr. Saunders is most important in continuing the investigation of psychological implications of UFO sightings.

However, there are questions which go beyond the present "boundaries" of psychological research. The general question is this: are there relationships between UFO phenomena and hypnotic processes and *psi* processes (psychical phenomena, or extrasensory perception and psychokinesis)?

Because of the minor limitations of space, and because of the major limitation of his knowledge, the writer is unable to deal with all of the questions about the possible relationships of these complex phenomena. For the sake of simplicity, this chapter is organized into four general sections, followed by a section of References.

I. THE PROBLEM, including a review of related literature.
II. SOME USES OF HYPNOSIS IN UFO RESEARCH, including a report of an interview with a UFO observer, Herbert Schirmer.
III. PSYCHIC IMPRESSIONS OF UFO PHENOMENA, a survey of some persons who claim to experience various impressions of UFO phenomena.
IV. SUMMARY AND CONCLUSIONS.

Before continuing, however, the writer should point out that there is another important limitation which may affect his ability to deal appropriately with the questions posed by these unusual UFO reports. The limitation is the personal bias of this writer: I believe that there is sufficient evidence to accept the hypothesis that the earth is being surveyed by spacecraft which are controlled by intelligent entities or beings from an alien civilization or civilizations; apparently, the purposes and powers of these beings are not known, but I believe that investigations should be continued in the hope of gaining more information and knowledge about UFO entities or UFO occupants.

I.
THE PROBLEM

Some UFO reports present statements by persons who claim that they have experienced "loss of time," "hypnosis," or "trance-like" states of awareness during UFO sightings. In some cases, UFO observers claim to see UFO occupants or UFO entities and claim to experience "mental communication" with the UFO entities (Fuller, 1966; Lorenzen and Lorenzen, 1967). Investigation of these events and of the personal characteristics of these persons might provide further information which may tend to support or reject these claims of "trance states," "mental communication," or other psychic impressions of UFO entities.

Before dealing with the literature of these unusual UFO reports, a brief review of professional literature on ESP (extrasensory perception) and hypnosis is presented. Thus, the interested reader may be able to compare his or her views of these phenomena with the findings of professional investigators.

ESP Literature: Psychical research, often called parapsychology ("beyond psychology"), is a subject of scientific controversy (Murphy, 1969; McConnell, 1969). Parapsychologists have been aware that their findings (not their methods) have been inconsistent with the main body of current scientific knowledge. However, in December of 1969, the American Association for the Advancement of Science (AAAS) officially accepted the Parapsychological Association as an affiliate organization; now, the study of ESP is "scientifically acceptable." At present, one major alternate hypothesis to account for positive results is that of fraud (Hansel, 1966); however, the "fraud" hypothesis has less evidence for its support than does the hypothesis that ESP processes "exist." Of course, there are disagreements among authorities about the theoretical interpretation of empirical findings. For example, Persinger (1974) has suggested that ESP experiences may be explained on the basis of physical, biological, and psychological mechanisms. However, experimental results provide sufficient evidence to indicate that, using "normal" psychological processes, there are many persons who produce or who experience unusual space-time processes or paranormal events, e.g., telepathy, clairvoyance, precognition, and psychokinesis.

The careful reader will be impressed by the scope and significance of results obtained in parapsychological research. The beginning reader is referred to the paperback book by Ashby (1972); the sophisticated reader is referred to the source book by White and

Dale (1973). There are many excellent sources for a review of scientific studies, including the books by Broad (1962), Eisenbud (1967), Murphy (1961), Rao (1966), Rhine and Pratt (1962), Smythies (1967), and Vasiliev (1963). Two well-known journals in the USA are: *Journal of the American Society of Psychical Research* (ASPR), 5 West 73rd Street, New York, N.Y. 10023; and the *Journal of Parapsychology* (Parapsychological Association), the Parapsychology Press, College Station, Durham, N.C. 27708. Two other informative publications are: *Parapsychology Review*, Parapsychology Foundation, Inc., 29 West 157th Street, New York, N.Y. 10019; and *Psychic*, P.O. Box 26289, San Francisco, Cal. 94126. Three other well-known USA foundations are: The Association for Research and Enlightenment (ARE) of Virginia Beach, Va.; the Foundation for Research on the Nature of Man (FRNM); and the Psychical Research Foundation (PRF); both of Durham, North Carolina. There are many current topics of interest to some parapsychologists, including: acupuncture and Kirlian photography (Moss, 1974; Krippner and Rubin, 1973); astral projection or out-of-the-body-experience (Crookall, 1970; Munroe, 1971; Swann, 1975); psychological and psychiatric implications (Eisenbud, 1970; Rhine, 1961; Schmeidler, 1969; Tart, 1969); reincarnation (Head and Cranston, 1967; Stevenson, 1966); psychics and physicists (Koestler, 1972; LeShan, 1969); time and precognition (Dunne, 1958; Fraser, 1966; Vaughan, 1973); and healing (LeShan, 1974; Moss, 1974).

Hypnosis Literature: The topic of hypnosis also has been noted for controversy and misunderstanding. However, the scientific study and application of hypnotic techniques has gained impetus from the approval for medical use by the British Medical Association and the American Medical Association. There are professional practitioners in many fields, including dentistry, medicine, psychiatry, and psychology. Two well-known professional organizations in the USA are: The American Society of Clinical Hypnosis (ASCH), 2400 East Devon Avenue, Suite 218, Des Plaines, IL 60018; and the Society for Clinical and Experimental Hypnosis, Inc. (SCEH), 205 West End Avenue, New York, NY 10023. The ASCH publishes *The American Journal of Clinical Hypnosis*, and the SCEH publishes *The International Journal of Clinical and Experimental Hypnosis.*

Clinical and Experimental Hypnosis.

The interested reader will note that there are many theoretical positions which provide an explanation for hypnotic effects (Weitzenhoffer, 1963), including the view that there is no such "state" as hypnosis (Barber, 1969). However, most authorities are in agreement that unusual phenomena can be produced by some persons while they follow hypnotic procedures (Cheek and LeCron, 1968; Cooper and Erickson, 1959; Erickson, Hershman, and Secter, 1961; Gordon, 1967; Haley, 1969; Kroger, 1963). An excellent laboratory study is offered by E.R. Hilgard (1965) and an excellent field study is offered by Josephine Hilgard (1970). Professional and public interest in the USA for study of hypnotic procedures was increased by the work of Leslie LeCron (1952), including his emphasis upon the uses of self-hypnotism (LeCron, 1964).

ESP, HYPNOSIS, AND UFO REPORTS: A REVIEW OF LITERATURE

In the opinion of the writer, there is sufficient evidence in the literature of hypnosis and parapsychology to accept the view that *psi* processes (ESP) and hypnotic phenomena occur. The questions arise: are there relationships between the reports of UFO experiences and the process of hypnosis and ESP? Are UFO percipients, or observers, experiencing *psychic* events only, or are they experiencing both physically "real" and psychically "real" events? Are UFO occupants or UFO entities using hypnotic and psychic phenomena in their "display" or their communications with UFO percipients?

Extraterrestrial Communication: These questions assume greater importance in light of the work which is being conducted to deal with the question of radio communication with extraterrestrial intelligence (ETI). Several authors have dealt with the difficulties —and challenges—of possible interstellar or intergalactic communications (Bracewell, 1974; Sagan, 1973a, 1973b; and Sullivan, 1964), including a proposed system (Oliver, 1975).

If the general public becomes enthusiastic about the possibility of radio communications with ETI, perhaps the scientific community may be willing to focus attention upon the claims made by persons who believe that "communication" is continuing between earth people and representatives of other civilizations. The scholars of religious history might be talking, once again, with other scientists and philosophers, who gaze skyward and wonder about the number of inhabited planets.

Ray Fowler (1974, pp. 276-284) summarizes a September 1965 conference on military electronics, dealing with the topic of communication with extraterrestrial intelligence. He quotes the speculations of one physicist, Dr. William O. Davis (p. 283), as follows:

> ...I strongly suspect that the first communication is very likely to be telepathic; perhaps it will just involve a sense of being friendly....
>
> The problem of language is that you require some kind of a cultural reference. In just learning to speak a European language, for example, you may know all the words and be able to translate them into English, but if you know nothing of the culture of the country, you will not really understand the subtleties of what you are saying. This sort of problem will be incredibly more complicated in communication with an alien race. In fact, I suspect that language communication will be almost the last thing to take place.
>
> In summary, I would say that the most probable case of communication with extraterrestrial beings is an encounter with a race more advanced than we; therefore, the problem would be primarily psychological on our part. We would undoubtedly be deeply upset by this state of affairs. Thus these beings, if they are really advanced and subtle, would know this and would approach us in such a way as not to frighten us. If I were on their staff, I think I would use my advanced knowledge to learn the languages of the human race through one means or another, imitate human structure and appearance, and send representatives down to mingle with the earth's people. Gradually I would begin to understand the earth's culture and develop means of communication to a point at which at a later time communication could be established in the proper verbal manner. Thus, it is entirely possible and maybe even probable that *extraterrestrial races are already amongst us!* (Italics are mine).

Some readers, who view themselves as "scientific minded," may consider as absurd the speculation that extraterrestrial races are among us. However, the contemporary view of the "scientific" mind is shifting: more and more investigators recognize that the frontiers of the mind are expanding. Singer (1975) has discussed the implications of studies on daydreaming; Tart (1969) has edited a collection of studies on altered states of awareness; Greeley and McCready (1975) have surveyed the "widespread" incidence of "mystical" experiences among "normal" USA adults.

One need not necessarily agree with Rimmer (1969) that the UFO is an anti-scientific symbol; however, the results of opinion polls about extraterrestrial life (Sprinkle, 1975, pp. 38-39) are indications that a majority of persons in the general public do not agree with the denials by traditionally-minded scientists about the reality and significance of UFO sightings.

In the opinion of the writer, the results of the public opinion polls are an encouraging sign that most adults are ready for further information about possible communication with extraterrestrial life. There are many unresolved questions, including these. Would there be widespread panic or social disruption if public statements by trusted officials announced the arrival (Cantril, 1966) of an alien race or races? Were we ignorant in our willingness to ridicule those writers who claimed verbal communication (e.g., Adamski, G. *Inside the Space Ships.* N.Y. Abelard-Schuman, 1955; Foreman, L.W. *Passport To Eternity.* Lawrence W. Foreman, Publisher, 1970, 334½ West 33rd Street, Los Angeles, CA.) with highly intelligent beings? Is the Fatima Prophecy (Culligan, 1967; Stanford, 1973) an example of communication between mankind and beings from extraterrestrial or extradimensional sources? Does the Fatima Prophecy represent the "final solution" (Wilson, 1971) to the UFO mystery?

One need not necessarily agree with the predictions of the effects of a destructive world war (Lindzey, 1970) or cyclic cataclysms (Thomas, 1965) to recognize the possibility that mankind could learn much through continued contact with representatives of extraterrestrial civilizations. Perhaps, some day, there may be available evidence to compare *The Urantia Book* (1965) with other publications which purport to describe the historical relationships between mankind and "star man" (Flint and Binder, 1974; Von Daniken, 1968) or the contemporary relationships between mankind and representatives of other civilizations (Nada-Yolanda, 1974; Wannall, 1963). Until that day arrives, the writer believes that the best approach is two-fold in nature: (1) continue to catalogue each UFO report (Bloecher, 1967; Sable, 1967; Saunders and Harkins, 1968) through empirical investigations; and (2) continue to explore the paraphysical and parapsychological implications of UFO phenomena. For example, Eisenbud (1975) has discussed the "mind-matter interface"; Keel (1970, 1975) has offered views about purposes and powers of "elementals" or "ultraterrestrials"; Puharich (1974) has provided a journal of Uri Geller and his fantastic experiences with representatives of another civilization; Steiger (1973) has described interviews with persons claiming to obtain spiritual revelations from other intelligences, and he has suggested (1974) that the UFO phenomenon is interwined with the "reality game": the ability of each person to effect, to some extent, his or her perceptions of reality; Clark and Coleman (1975) explore the UFO phenomenon as a kind of "planetary poltergeist"; Vallee (1969) has compared the occult literature of goblins, fairies, and "little people" with the reports of UFO landings and UFO occupants, and he has suggested (1974) that there is an important link between psychic phenomena and UFO phenomena.

These writers, and others, seem to be pointing to the inescapable conclusion: the continuing reports from UFO percipients are an indication of important relationships between ESP, hypnosis, and UFO phenomena.

In the opinion of the writer, much of the literature on the relationships of ESP, hypnosis, and UFO reports can be found in the *Flying Saucer Review*. (FSR Publications Ltd., P.O. Box 25, Barnet Herts, EN5, 2NR, England.) The writer is not well-acquainted with UFO literature from Asia, Europe, and South America; thus, his opinion refers to the books and journals which are printed in English.

Flying Saucer Review: Charles Bowen, FSR editor, and his colleagues, continue to publish an excellent journal, and they encourage research into all phases of UFO research: physical, biological, psychological, and psychical. The *Flying Saucer Review* (FSR) has provided a variety of articles on the general relationship of ESP and UFO phenomena: Bowen (1969a, 1969b); Cade (1967, 1968); Creighton (1971); Edwards (1970); Keel (1968); and Mackay (1970a, and 1970b, with a bibliography on ESP literature).

Articles about the use of hypnosis (either by UFO investigators or by alleged UFO entities) have been written by Allan (1975); Creighton (1970); Edwards (1973); and Sprinkle (1969b).

References to cases of apparent teleportation have been submitted by Buhler (1973); Galíndez (1968, 1973); and Creighton (1970b, 1971).

Suggestions for the use of mediums, or for the use of other methods of psychical research, have been advanced by Chibbett (1969); Druffel (1972); and Michel (1972).

Theoretical speculations about a "parallel" universe, or UFOs as "psychic projections," have been offered by Bowen (1969); Caplan (1974); Lemâitre (1969); and Schonherr (1968). Comments about the "time factor" in cycles of UFO reports, and the "reflective" quality of the UFO phenomenon (the apparent adjustment of the UFO experience to the individual beliefs and attitudes of the witness), have come from Keel (1969).

Views on UFO phenomena and psychical phenomena have been expressed by Bord (1972); Bowen (1968); Creighton (1970a,

1972a, 1974); LeGarde (1975); and Mackay (1973). Descriptions of individual UFO cases, which involved apparent psychic phenomena, have come from Bowen (1967); Creighton (1973); Hugill (1968); Keel (1968a); Schwarz (1972, 1973, 1975); and Simonsen (1968).

A puzzling—but fascinating—aspect of some UFO reports is that of "healing." Bowen (1971) explored the possible link between psychic surgery and healing during the UFO experience. Creighton (1969, 1972b) discussed the questions of electro-magnetic radiation and healing from UFOs. Fontes (1967) described the claim by a woman who said she watched two small humanoids, who communicated telepathically to the master of the woman, while they performed a half-hour operation on the master's young daughter who was ill with stomach cancer; according to the story, the operation, plus thirty small white capsules (which were taken at the rate of one each day), led to a cure of the young girl's illness. Michel (1969, 1971) reported the strange case of Dr. "X," a French physician who witnessed a UFO sighting and, shortly thereafter, experienced the healing of a recent leg wound, plus the remission of the aftereffects of an old wound from the Algerian War; the physician was able, once again, to play the piano, a hobby which he had not been able to pursue for many years because of the war wound effects.

Romaniuk (1973a, 1973b) investigated the UFO experience of a seventy-three-year-old "gaucho" (rustic) of Tres Arroyos in Argentina; medical (clinical and psychiatric) examinations revealed some startling changes, e.g., new teeth, new intellectual knowledge, parapsychological symptoms, etc. In discussing some aspect of this unusual UFO case, Jane Thomas (1973, p. 16) presented an interesting suggestion: "...all investigatory groups (should) start their own register of 'incredible' or 'crazy' cases which, for precisely that reason are not considered suitable for publication. How would it be if they were all made known, and a comparative study undertaken of the statements uttered by these contactees? Maybe corroborating details would be found which would help us fit together a few more pieces of this immense jigsaw puzzle."

In the spirit of the suggestion by Jane Thomas, the next section, II. "Some Uses of Hypnosis in UFO Research," is presented. Perhaps the publication of an "incredible" case (Condon and Gillmor, 1969, Case 42, pp. 389-391) can be of assistance to UFO investigators who are looking for the *patterns* of UFO reports, and the significance of the UFO "display" to the UFO observer.

II.
Some Uses of Hypnosis in UFO Research

The writer accepts the "spacecraft hypothesis" as tenable; this acceptance does not mean, necessarily, that the writer believes that all UFO sightings are of "spacecraft" from an alien civilization or civilizations. However, it does mean that the writer believes that the available evidence ought to be gathered and analyzed, in the hope that the evidence can be used to support or reject the hypothesis.

One aspect of this approach is to raise the question: can the use of hypnotic techniques with UFO observers provide further information about their UFO experiences?

Of course, any reader can recognize that there are possible disadvantages in using hypnotic techniques, including the possibility that a UFO observer may not respond to hypnotic suggestions, or the UFO observer may distort or fabricate information. Also, there is the difficulty that arises from the general misconceptions about hypnosis, which may increase the doubts and fears of UFO observers who are not familiar with the nature and use of hypnosis.

Despite the possible disadvantages, there are possible advantages in using hypnotic procedures in studying UFO phenomena. The primary advantage seems to be the facilitation of physiological and psychological relaxation, and the possible release of "subconscious" information (Cheek and LeCron, 1968).

A list of some uses of hypnosis in UFO research might include the following:

1. Assisting UFO observers to relax and to reduce anxiety which may be associated with their UFO observations.
2. Interviewing UFO observers, eliciting ideomotor responses, and using other techniques for gaining more information about their UFO sightings.
3. Checking the reliability of previous information from UFO observers about their UFO sightings.
4. Releasing repressed subconscious information from UFO observers about apparent "loss of time" experiences.
5. Possible training of persons to gain "out-of-body-experiences" and "project" themselves mentally into UFO locations.
6. Possible training of persons to gain psychic impressions; e.g., clairvoyant impressions of and/or telepathic communication with UFO occupants or UFO entities.

In summary, hypnotic techniques could be used in a variety of ways, based upon the interests and needs of the observer and the investigator, and their particular relationship. The procedures could be conducted in the hope that the obtained information might reduce the effects of investigator bias (Rosenthal, 1966) and tend to confirm or disconfirm other information about the UFO experience.

THE HILL CASE

The classic case of using hypnosis to investigate a UFO observation has been reported by Fuller (1966), *The Interrupted Journey*, the story of Mr. and Mrs. Barney Hill, of Portsmouth, New Hampshire, and their hypnotherapeutic treatment by Dr. Benjamin Simon, Boston psychiatrist. This writer has had the pleasure of meeting and talking with Mr. and Mrs. Hill, and he has been impressed with their honesty, intelligence, and psychological openness; furthermore, he tends to accept their story, as revealed under hypnosis, as a description of events which probably occurred. (This writer was saddened to learn from Mrs. Hill that Mr. Hill suddenly became ill and died on February 25, 1969. Their dog, Delsey, died December 24, 1968; now, Mrs. Hill is the "sole survivor" of their UFO sighting of September 19, 1961.)

However, the investigator is aware that noted authorities have expressed serious doubts about the validity of the story. Greenwald (1967) had discussed some of the possible interpretations of the revealed information. Simon (1967) has discussed the four hypotheses which might account for the descriptions by Betty and Barney Hill. 1. "The Hills were psychotic and suffered a *folie à deux*" (joint psychosis). 2. "This is a fraud." 3. "The entire story is fundamentally true." 4. "The Dream Hypothesis." Simon rejected hypotheses 1 and 2, and he considered hypothesis 3 to be a "remote possibility." He considered the most tenable hypothesis to be "The Dream Hypothesis": Betty Hill, as a result of their UFO observation, experienced several terrifying dreams which she related to her friends in the presence of her husband; somehow, the information of Betty's dreams was transferred to Barney so that he presented similar information during the hypnotherapeutic interviews.

Despite the weight of authoritative views which raise doubts about the authenticity of the stories, this investigator tends to accept the view that the events probably occurred. To some extent, this acceptance is based upon the similarities between this case and other UFO reports: the descriptions of UFO occupants; the claim of bodily examinations of UFO observers by UFO occupants; the claim of "mental communication" by UFO occupants and suggestions that the UFO observers will not remember their experiences (Lorenzen, J. and Coral, E., 1967; Bowen, 1966). Also, "The Dream Hypothesis" presents certain difficulties, including the fact that Betty did not claim to see the UFO occupants during the initial sighting. Barney claimed that he walked out onto a field and used binoculars to view the UFO. Betty claimed only that she saw an object with lights; Barney claimed that he saw the object with "men" standing at the "control panel." In using "The Dream Hypothesis," an investigator is faced with these questions: how did Barney "transfer" his perceptions of UFO occupants to Betty so that she dreamed of an examination in a landed "flying saucer?" Then, how did Betty "transfer" her perceptions to Barney so that he also dreamed of an examination in a landed "flying saucer?" Even if an investigator accepts the evidence for extrasensory perception (ESP), he or she is faced with difficult questions about the complex array of "transferred" information. For further information about the "star map" drawn by Betty Hill, see the evaluation by Webb (1974) of the model by Ms. Marjorie Fish.

THE SCHIRMER CASE

The writer was pleased by the opportunity, early in 1968, to discuss his views about the possible uses of hypnosis in UFO research with members of the "Condon Committee" (*UFO Project*, University of Colorado). During that initial meeting, several UFO cases were considered as possible choices for a demonstration. In the opinion of the writer, the UFO cases with multiple witnesses were most interesting; however, the committee selected the Schirmer case because of the possible "loss of time" during the UFO experience.

On February 13, 1968, the writer was invited to the Boulder Campus to participate in an interview with Sergeant Herbert Schirmer, a policeman from Ashland, Nebraska. The interview was conducted in the hope that hypnotic procedures could be used to assist Sgt. Herb Schirmer to obtain more information about the events which occurred during the 15 to 20 minutes of "lost time" during his UFO experience of December 3, 1967.

The Condon Committee report stated that new information about the UFO experience was obtained; however, the information was based upon the impressions of the 15 to 20 minutes of "lost time" which was claimed by Sgt. Schirmer. From the viewpoint of some committee members, there was no "physical evidence" to support the claims. Also, there was a question about the reliability of the witness because of the statements of some acquaintances and because of the results of the battery of psychological instruments which had been administered.

The writer was not provided with any copy of results of the psychological tests and inventories. However, he was asked to provide the Condon Committee with a report of his observations and evaluations of the interview with Herb Schirmer. In March 1968, the writer presented the following report to the Condon Committee.

Impressions of the February 13, 1968, Interview With Sergeant Herbert Schirmer

A Report Presented to
The Condon Committee
UFO Project
University of Colorado
Boulder, Colorado

by
R. Leo Sprinkle, Ph.D.
University of Wyoming
Laramie, Wyoming

March, 1968

Introduction

This report presents, for your consideration, the personal impressions of the writer which have resulted from the February 13, 1968, interview with Sergeant Herbert Schirmer, policeman from Ashland, Nebraska. The report is concerned with personal impressions for two main reasons: (1) the biases of the writer; and (2) the purpose of the writer.

Biases. The writer believes that there is sufficient empirical evidence to support the views that the following phenomena exist: hypnotic processes or varying levels of awareness; extrasensory perception and psychokinetic processes (ESP or *psi* processes); and spacecraft ("flying saucers") from extraterrestrial sources which are controlled by intelligent beings who seem to be conducting an intensive survey of the earth.

Because these views are different from those of many persons in contemporary society, the writer offers his impressions with the recognition that other observers may have obtained different, and even conflicting, impressions of the interview with Sgt. Schirmer.

Purpose. The purpose of the writer is to present a subjective evaluation of the information obtained during the interview. The writer recognizes that he was only one of many observers and that the recordings of the interview can serve as much more reliable indicators of the events which transpired.

Hopefully, the tone of the report is non-technical, personal, and subjective, so that the reader may compare this one point of view with the many other kinds of information: interview recordings, personality assessment and evaluation, observations and conclusions of other observers, and previous testimony from other persons.

Impressions of Sgt. Schirmer

My first impression of Sgt. Schirmer was similar to that which I have received from other persons who report UFO sightings: an uncertainty on their part about whether their story will be believed or whether they will be viewed by a psychologist as being "confused" or "crazy." After initial introductions, a short discussion was held in the Woodbury Hall offices. Those who were present included: Ahrens, Craig, Schirmer, Sprinkle, Wadsworth, and Wlaskin. (Later, Dr. Hallack McCord, psychologist from Denver, appeared as an observer.)

Verbal and Non-Verbal Behavior. Sgt. Schirmer gave the appearance of being pleasant and cooperative, aware of the possible significance of his role in the proceedings, and willing to submit himself to questions about the UFO sighting.

At times, he seemed to have some hesitation in choosing the words he wished to use. (E.g., he changed from "craft" to "object" on some occasions, as if to mimic the terminology of others who were present at the morning introductory meeting.)

I considered him to be of average or above-average intelligence, with an average educational background. He presented himself as a conscientious policeman who had a sixth sense or intuition about crime detection; he also seemed to gain satisfaction from the occasional need for violence in his work, although he spoke favorably about the use of "mace." He seemed fairly relaxed, although he and Chief Wlaskin said they were tired from two days and nights of police duty.

Relationship with Chief Bill Wlaskin. I viewed the relationship of the two policemen as being close and comfortable. It seemed that Chief Wlaskin took a special interest in the proceedings, as if he wanted to be certain that his sergeant would be treated fairly and considerately. Sgt. Schirmer gave the impression that he was a trustworthy observer and an excellent policeman, and he seemed to be pleased with the supporting comments which he received from his superior officer. They were friendly with one another, and they seemed pleased with the "first name" basis established among the UFO Project personnel and themselves.

Description of the UFO Sighting. During the initial discussion, Herb was willing to sketch a diagram on the blackboard to represent the Ashland community and the location of the UFO sighting. The information he submitted seemed consistent with what had been told to me by Roy Craig and Jim Wadsworth. Herb seemed to gain confidence from the general acceptance of his story, and he seemed to become less apprehensive about the proceedings planned for the afternoon.

Reaction to Setting and Participants. I saw Sgt. Schirmer's reactions as an indication that he wished to consider himself courageous but was not confident enough to admit his own doubts and fears. Just prior to the afternoon session, which was to be conducted in the Counseling Center of the Student Personnel Services, I learned from John Ahrens that Herb was very doubtful about whether he would undergo hypnotic techniques.

Looking back upon the events, I believe it would have been better to utilize hypnotic techniques with Herb during the morning session; these procedures could have been used to relax him and to orient him to the procedures, as well as to facilitate trance introduction in the afternoon. However, because of his fatigue—and because I judged our rapport to be sufficient—I decided to wait until the afternoon interview, so that all observers could see what might develop "from scratch." (Of course, experts in the use of hypnosis believe that the total relationship is a factor in the ease and productivity of using hypnotic techniques so that the morning discussion undoubtedly influenced the events of the afternoon session.)

Sgt. Schirmer seemed to be faced with conflicting wishes: the desire to be seen as a competent observer and courageous policeman versus the desire to be considered "his own man" rather than a puppet which could be controlled through suggestion or hypnosis.

Reaction to Interview and Interviewer. The crux of the apparent conflict occurred when I handed Sgt. Schirmer the copy of the release form* for him to sign. His hesitation appeared to stem from his wish to be cautious and prudent as well as from anxiety and doubt about the use of hypnotic techniques.

Because his concern was so evident, and because I did not wish to jeopardize the entire session by allowing him to discontinue the interview, I decided to utilize the pendulum technique. Although there is disagreement among experts about the reliability of subconscious information obtained by the pendulum technique, there is general agreement that it can be utilized as a method of obtaining concentration, relaxation, and preparation for deeper levels of awareness.

Herb seemed willing to use the pendulum, and he expressed

amazement at his reactions and at the signals which seemed to be related to the questions being asked.

Impressions of Information Obtained from The Interview

Those attending the afternoon session included Ahrens, Condon, Craig, Hallack McCord, Schirmer, Sprinkle, Wadsworth, Wlaskin, and the psychologist, Bob Fenner, who was to administer personality tests to Sgt. Schirmer on Wednesday, February 14. Although I assumed that a tape recording (and perhaps video tape recording) of the interview was being conducted, I took brief notes to use as a basis for conducting the interview. (See Appendix.)

Information From Pendulum Techniques. The responses obtained from the pendulum technique suggested that Sgt. Schirmer was aware, at a deeper level of consciousness, of further information about the UFO sighting. However, information also indicated that there was subconscious uncertainty about divulging those memories.

Techniques were used to "placate" the subconscious resistance and to "persuade" Herb that he could obtain further information from these levels of awareness. When it was obvious that Herb was deepening the trance state, suggestions were offered that he could relax, go deeper into the trance state, recall and describe the events which took place during the UFO sighting.

Information From Hypnotic Session Although there was apparent effort involved, Herb responded to the suggestions that he could describe the events that took place during the UFO sighting. He stated that a bright light had shone from the object upon the car and that he saw a "white blurred object" which came toward the car. He said that he felt he was in communication with someone in the object, and that he also felt the communication was in effect during the interview.

When Sgt. Schirmer said that he felt it would be "wrong" to say anything else until the "proper time and proper place," I had the distinct impression that nothing more could be done to change his attitude. Nevertheless, I offered suggestions to see if he might "imagine" the proper time and place. Because of his resistance, I

* A form which contained a statement that the University of Colorado would be released from legal responsibility for any bothersome effects of the hypnotic procedures.

believed it best to discontinue the hypnotic session and allow him to return to the normal state of awareness.

During the post-hypnotic session, Herb offered many comments in response to questions from the observers. Although his statements had a "ring of truth" to them, he did not seem to know how or where he had received the information which he was submitting to us.

Comparison of "Old" and "New" Information. The information which was obtained during the interview did not seem to be inconsistent with information which had been obtained from previous investigation of Herb's story. However, the "new" information certainly seemed unusual by most standards of comparison. The references to "sister ships," "electrical-magnetic force," "force of gravity," "from another galaxy," "friendly intentions" of beings whose "purpose is to prevent earth people from destroying the earth" were different from the earlier descriptions of the UFO sighting.

Although these terms are not unfamiliar to anyone who is interested in UFO reports, the "new" information raises many questions about the UFO sighting and the UFO observer.

Interpretations About the "New" Information. I believe that there are four general interpretations which might be made in regard to the obtained information:

1. The information comes from a person who is emotionally disturbed and in need of psychological evaluation and psychotherapeutic treatement. This interpretation suggests that the additional information resulted from hallucinatory and/or other pathological reactions. A clinical psychologist or psychiatrist might utilize various approaches to determine if this interpretation is the more likely explanation.
2. The information comes from a person who is deliberately lying. This interpretation suggests that the additional information was offered to perpetrate a hoax. A polygraph test might be utilized to determine if this interpretation is the more likely explanation.
3. The information comes from a person who is responding to the conscious or subconscious wishes of the interviewer to submit certain information. This interpretation suggests that the information resulted from the interviewer-interviewee relationship. Another interviewer or interviewers might be utilized to see if the information is reliably obtained or whether other information might be submitted.
4. The information comes from a person who is reliably report-

ing events which he perceives as a part of his experience. This interpretation suggests that the information is "reliable." (It is "true," in the experience of the observer.)

In my opinion, the fourth or last interpretation is more likely to be an adequate explanation of all of the impressions I received during my observations and interactions with Herb Schirmer. However, the latter interpretation raises more questions than it answers. How did he obtain the information? Why did he obtain the information? From whom did he obtain the information? For what purpose might the information be used by Sgt. Schirmer? For what purpose might the information be used by UFO investigators? Are there methods or techniques which can be used to verify the obtained information?

Summary and Conclusions

In summary, the use of the pendulum technique and hypnotic techniques resulted in additional information from Sgt. Schirmer about the experiences which he reports in regard to his UFO sighting. The information indicates that Sgt. Schirmer not only claims to have observed a low-level, hovering UFO, but that he also claims to have experienced the following events.

(A) Observation of a bright light which was emitted from the object and which shone upon the police squad car.

(B) Observation of a white, blurred object, apparently an intelligent organism, which came from the object and approached the car.

(C) "Conversation" with the white, blurred object by some means of mental communication.

(D) Apparent mental contact, during the interview, with the person or being with whom he communicated during the UFO sighting, including a description of the activities and purposes of the UFO occupants.

(E) Apparent mental contact, during the interview, with the UFO occupants and the resultant belief that further information could be obtained at the "proper time and proper place."

(F) Apparent conviction that the additional information is valid, but with no supporting evidence of the source or validity of the additional information.

In conclusion, I believe that the interview demonstrated that hypnotic techniques can be utilized for the purpose of obtaining further information about UFO sightings from UFO observers. Also, in Sgt. Schirmer's case, I believe that the additional information serves as a basis for explaining the apparent "loss of time" which was reported in the original description of the UFO sighting. However, the additional information also raises further questions about the source, method, and purpose of communicating the additional information.

In my opinion, the events described by Sgt. Schirmer are "true" in his experience; however, I believe that the present evidence does not answer the questions regarding the source, method, and purpose of communicating the additional information.

Appendix:

Notes on the February 13, 1968 Interview With Sgt. Schirmer

Although the following statements are only an approximation of the actual interview, they serve as the basis for many of the interpretive comments of the report.

Use of the Pendulum Technique

The following signals were elicited for interpretations of the ideomotor responses:

1 Yes	(Cf. LeCron, L. M. *Self-Hypnotism*. Englewood Cliffs, NJ, 1964. Pp. 33-36.)
— No	
I don't know	
I don't want to say	

INTER-PRETATIONS	RESPONSES	QUESTIONS
Yes	1	1. Did I experience a UFO sighting on December 3, 1967?
Yes	1	2. Is there more information available?
Yes	1	3. Is there more subconscious information?
Yes	1	4. Are the recollections of the event accurate?
No	—	5. Are there some details which are not accurate?

INTER-PRETATIONS	RESPONSES	QUESTIONS
Yes	1	6. Is there a discrepancy in "time" between the sighting and the end of the sighting?
Yes	1	7. Am I aware of what happened?
Yes	1	8. Did I place my cap in the rear of the car?
Yes	1	9. Did I put my cap to my side?
No	—	12. Am I willing to go into a deeper level?
No	—	13. Is this concern because of what I might find out?
No	—	14. Did I turn off the ignition switch of the car?
Yes	1	15. Did the car engine stall or stop?
Yes	1	16. Do I believe there is a relationship between the object and the engine failure?
No	—	17. Did I turn off the headlights?
Yes	1	18. Did the headlights go off during the sighting?
Yes	1	19. Did I remember having an impulse to take my gun out (of the holster)?
No	—	20. Did I take the gun out?
Yes	1	21. Was I prevented from taking the gun out?
Yes	1	22. If I had not been prevented, would I have taken the gun out?
Yes	1	23. Do I believe I was prevented (from taking the gun out of the holster) by someone in the object?
Yes	1	24. Do I believe I was in communication with someone in the object?
Yes	1	25. Do I believe a light was shown to me from the object?

INTER-PRETATIONS	RESPONSES	QUESTIONS
Yes	1	26. Do I believe the light has something to do with the welt on my neck?
Yes	1	27. Do I believe the welt was associated with my being in a trance state?
No	—	28. Do I believe I entered the object?
No	—	29. Do I believe someone approached me from the object?
Yes	1	30. Do I believe my mind was being searched from something or someone in the object?
Yes	1	31. Do I believe I communicated with someone in the object?
No	—	32. Do I remember the communication or conversation?
No	—	33. If I went deeper, could I remember?
Yes	1	34. Do I believe that someday someone might communicate with me again?
Yes	1	35. If another object were to come, would I be willing to communicate with someone?
No	—	36. Was there a feeling of fear during the sighting?
I don't know		37. Was there a feeling of fear after the sighting?

BREAK IN QUESTIONING

Sgt. Schirmer described some of his reactions after the sighting: he said that he drank two cups of hot, steaming coffee "like it was water"; he claimed that he often experienced a "ringing," "numbness," "buzzing" in his ears before going to sleep (around 1:30 A.M. or 2:00 A.M.); he believed he had experienced precognitive dreams (e.g., he dreamed about the death of a man he had visited; and after the dream, he found the man was dead); he said he felt concern and "hurt" since the UFO sighting; he described disturbances in his sleep, including incidents in which he awoke and found that he was "choking" his wife and "handcuffing" his wife's ankle and wrist; he said that his wife sometimes woke up during the night and placed his gun elsewhere so that it was not in his boots beside his bed where he had been keeping it.

INTER-PRETATIONS	RESPONSES	QUESTIONS
Yes	1	38. When I first saw the object, did I have an impulse to get the mike (microphone of the police car radio)?
Yes	1	39. Did I reach for the mike?
Yes	1	40. Did I take hold of the mike?
I don't know		41. Did I press the mike button?
No	—	42. Did I attempt to speak over the radio?
Yes	1	43. Do I believe I was prevented from speaking?
Yes	1	44. Do I believe I was prevented from pressing the mike button?
Yes	1	45. Do I believe I was prevented (from pressing the mike button) by something or someone in the object?
No	—	46. Do I remember anything which was said to me during the sighting?
I don't want to say		47. Do I remember seeing anything or anyone emerge from the object?
Yes	1	48. If I did want to say, would I say that I saw something emerge from the object?
I don't want to say		49. Was it a physical object?
Yes	1	50. Was it a light from the object?
Yes	1	51. Did a figure or person emerge from the object?
I don't know		52. Did the figure or person come to the car?

INTER-PRETATIONS	RESPONSES	QUESTIONS
I don't know		53. Was there more than one figure or person?
No	—	54. Did I have my eyes closed (at the time)?

Because Sgt. Schirmer obviously was going deeper into a trance state, at this point in the interview it was suggested to him that he could relax, go deeper into the trance state; then it was suggested that he could "go back" in memory to the experiences of the UFO sighting and to talk about these events.

After several minutes of apparent effort, Sgt. Schirmer began to speak and to describe what he said were his reactions to the events of the UFO sighting

A Summary of Sgt. Schirmer's Statements During the Hypnotic Session

Sgt. Schirmer claimed that the following events were among those that occurred: a bright light came from the object and shone upon the car; a "white, blurred object" approached the car and then faded away; then the craft moved upward, back and forth; a weird sound came from the object; a bright red-orange glow came from beneath the object; and then the object "shot" straight up and out of sight.

Sgt. Schirmer then stated that he felt it would be "wrong" to say more until the "proper time and proper place." (Suggestions were given that he might consider, in imagination, what could be the proper time and place; however, he did not accept the suggestions, and it was decided to discontinue the questioning in the trance state. Suggestions were given to Sgt. Schirmer that he could remember the events of the UFO sighting and that he could return comfortably to the normal state without any ill effects from the trance state.)

Summary of Sgt. Schirmer's Statements After the Hypnotic Session

Sgt. Schirmer responded to various questions from those present, and he offered comments about his reactions to the trance state.

Chief Wlaskin discussed the events related to a visit by Dr. Gerald Brewster, a psychiatrist who expressed his interest in the question of whether any of the three officers would have fired his gun at an UFO.

Questions from those present led to comments from Sgt. Schirmer, including these: the white, blurred object seemed to be a living object, although he didn't remember anything about the object until the hypnotic session; communication with someone in the craft occurred at the time of the UFO sighting and the feeling of direct mental contact with someone was occurring at the time of the interview; information was obtained (but which had not been mentioned previously to Chief Wlaskin or John Ahrens) which indicated that the craft was propelled by some type of electrical and magnetic force which could control the force of gravity; the craft was obtaining a power supply from nearby power lines in order to assist in communications; someone or something told Sgt. Schirmer that he was "doing a good job," that he should not talk further during the interview, but he could talk later this year and tell more about the events of the UFO sighting. Information given to Sgt. Schirmer indicated the following: the craft belonged to a "sister ship" which was like an aircraft carrier; the occupants of the craft were based on Venus or Saturn but were from another galaxy; the intentions of these beings were friendly, and their purpose was to prevent earth people from destroying the earth.

Sgt. Schirmer was unable to offer evidence or opinions about how he had obtained this information or whether the information was valid; nevertheless, he claimed that this information was given to him and that he believed it to be true as it was given to him.

(End of Report to the Condon Committee)

EVALUATION OF THE SCHIRMER CASE

According to rumors, many changes have taken place in the life of Herbert Schirmer during the passing years. Some of these rumors concern his personal and vocational activities, and his relation with the members of the Ashland community. These rumors raise doubts about the reliability of the story which Herb Schirmer offers about his UFO sighting.

On the other hand, some UFO investigators believe that the UFO experience of Herb Schirmer is an important clue to the UFO mystery (Norman, 1970).

The writer attempted to follow the subsequent activities of Herb Schirmer; due to the efforts of "Hub" Ogden, reporter for the *Omaha World Herald*, information was obtained about the changes in Herb's address and occupation. Herb seems to have experienced similar difficulties to those of other UFO percipients or "contactees"; however, he seems to have tolerated the difficulties and hopes to build a good life for himself.

With the passing years, the questions continue. Did Herb Schirmer perceive a "real" object, or were his perceptions of "real" psychological events? Did Herb perceive psychological events which were "personal" or were his perceptions of events which were being "transmitted" to him by other persons or UFO entities? If other persons or other entities were communicating the UFO experience to Herb, what was the purpose or what were the purposes of the communications?

The writer is unable to answer the "larger" questions about Herb Schirmer's experience. In fact, the writer is unable to answer some "smaller" questions about the case. Did the Condon Committee hope to find "physical evidence" from Herb Schirmer, based upon the information from hypnotic procedures and from a battery of psychological instruments? Did the Condon Committee deemphasize the "new information" because it was so unusual, or because the "new information" came from a UFO observer who, in their views, exhibited some of the characteristics of an unreliable witness? Did the Condon Committee wish to confuse, or mislead, the reader by describing Case #42 as that of a "state trooper" with military experience in the marines?

When the *Scientific Study of Unidentified Flying Objects* was published, the writer corresponded with Dr. Condon about the release of the report of the interview with Herb Schirmer. (See the letters of February 17, 1969 and February 19, 1969.)

In the opinion of the writer, the letter from Dr. Condon is puzzling. Did he mean to encourage, or discourage, the release of the report? Did he wish to prevent the writer from "making a fool of himself," or did he wish to prevent the writer from informing other UFO investigators about the interview with Herb Schirmer?

include his report to the Condon Committee in a manuscript; the manuscript was to be submitted as a chapter in a book manuscript, written by consultants to APRO (Aerial Phenomena Research Organization) and edited by Richard Greenwell. However, at that time, the public interest (or the publisher interest) in books on UFO research was at a low ebb; the manuscript was reviewed by many publishers but accepted by none. Now, thanks to Mrs. Coral Lorenzen, and other UFO investigators who have expressed an interest in the case, the report is submitted as an example of the use of hypnosis in UFO investigation.

The writer is unable to state absolutely whether Herb Schirmer experienced a UFO sighting or not; however, the writer believes that Herb Schirmer is convinced of his experience. As usual, the UFO witness seems to be the key to the UFO experience; the writer believes that UFO investigation should be based upon the hypothesis suggested by Salisbury (1973, p. 220): "...the UFOs seemed to be putting on a show, a display *aimed specifically at the witnesses.*"

If the UFO experience of Herb Schirmer is viewed through the "Salisbury Hypothesis," then several questions emerge. Was Sgt. Herb Schirmer exposed to a situation in which he was unable to use his military and police training for violence? Was he exposed to an experience which was designed to change his ethical and social values? Was he exposed to an experience which was designed to change his personal and vocational interests?

The writer is unable to answer these questions. His wish is that further investigation of UFO experiences may lead to a *pattern* of reports; perhaps the pattern of reports may reveal the answers to the questions about the reliability of UFO observers and the meaning of their UFO experiences.

The following section, III. "Psychic Impressions of UFO Phenomena," presents the results of a small survey of persons who claim such experiences. The writer expresses appreciation to the Research Coordination Committee, Graduate School, University of Wyoming, for a grant to support the research study.

THE UNIVERSITY OF WYOMING

DIVISION OF COUNSELING AND TESTING

BOX 3708, UNIVERSITY STATION

LARAMIE, WYOMING 82070

February 17, 1969

Dr. E. U. Condon
Department of Physics
University of Colorado
Boulder, Colorado

Dear Dr. Condon:

Greetings! I hope that your personal and professional life is less hectic, with the completion of the *Scientific Study of Unidentified Flying Objects.* However, I suppose there is little reason to expect that hope to materialize—given your history of dealing with scientific and social issues, and the history of the UFO controversy!

This letter represents a request for information: is there any objection to my releasing to interested persons a copy of the report I submitted to you about the interview with Patrolman Herbert Schirmer? Thank you for your attention to this request. Best wishes to you.

Sincerely,

R. Leo Sprinkle

R. Leo Sprinkle, Ph.D.
Counselor and Associate
Professor of Psychology

RLS/hd

UNIVERSITY OF COLORADO

BOULDER, COLORADO 80302

DEPARTMENT OF PHYSICS AND ASTROPHYSICS

1006 JILA Bldg.

19 February 1969
Prof. R. Leo Sprinkle
Division of Counseling and Testing
University of Wyoming
Box 3708 University Station
Laramie, Wyoming 82070

Dear Prof. Sprinkle:

Replying to yours of 17 February.

I have no personal objections to your releasing your report on Herbert Schirmer with this proviso that you or the University of Wyoming must assume all legal liability in case of actions of any kind growing out of your distribution of that material.

Look in last Saturday's (15 Feb.) N.Y. Times which prints in full the Sirhan defense attorney's opening statement in his trial for the murder of Robert Kennedy. The attorney seems to me to be saying that Sirhan, by mystic mental powers, could cause a weight suspended from a fixed support to start swinging!

Sincerely,

E U Condon

E. U. Condon

EUC:kes

III.
PSYCHIC IMPRESSIONS OF UFO PHENOMENA*

Because of the strangeness of UFO reports, and because of the question about the psychological characteristics of persons who claim these UFO experiences, it can be hypothesized that there are significant differences between two groups of people: persons who claim to experience UFO dreams, or other psychic impressions of UFO phenomena, and those persons who claim to experience observations of UFOs and communication with UFO occupants. The present investigation was conducted in an attempt to test this general hypothesis. Further, it was hoped that information could be obtained about the vocational interests and personality characteristics of persons who experience psychic impressions of UFO phenomena. This information might shed some light on the question of possible relationships between ESP processes and "mental communication" with UFO occupants.

METHOD OF STUDY

In 1968 a questionnaire survey was begun in an attempt to obtain information from persons who were interested in describing their psychic impressions of UFO phenomena. In the initial phase, 63 persons participated, including 56 USA citizens, 3 Canadian citizens, 2 English citizens, 1 Norwegian citizen, and a USA citizen living in Hong Kong. Generous cooperation in publicizing the survey was extended by the following persons and organizations: Mr. and Mrs. L.J. Lorenzen, Aerial Phenomena Research Organization (APRO); Mr. C. Bowen, *Flying Saucer Review* (FSR); Mrs. Laura Mundo, The Interplanetary Center; and Dr. J.B. Rhine, Foundation for Research on the Nature of Man (FRNM).

The National Investigations Committee on Aerial Phenomena (NICAP) denied the request that notice of the survey be published.

The questionnaire survey included the following materials: "Adjective Check List (ACL), a personality inventory; "Strong Vocational Interest Blank"—Male or Female (SVIB—M or F), a vocational interest inventory; and a questionnaire form (see the following UFO Report Form) which requested personal information about each participant, including interest and experience in

(continued on page 295)

* Adapted from a paper which was presented at the APRO UFO Symposium, Denver, Col., July 13, 1974.

Aerial Phenomena Research Organization
3910 East Kleindale Road
Tucson, AZ 85712

UFO Report Form
(*Unusual UFO Observations and Impressions*)

This questionnaire is designed to gain information in several specific areas: self-information about each participant; a self-description of each participant's views about his psychic abilities; a self-description of each participant's views about UFO phenomena; "loss of time" experiences, observation of UFO occupants, or other unusual UFO events; and impressions obtained by each participant about the possible origins, powers, and purposes of those who control UFO phenomena.

PLEASE NOTE: On the last page, there is a section for your signature and the date of completing the questionnaire. Also, each participant is asked to indicate whether his or her name may be used in connection with any publication of results from this study. The personal information will be handled in a confidential manner, and no names of participants will be used in any publication unless participants permit their names to be used.

Thank you very much for your cooperation and your willingness to complete this questionnaire.

I. Self Information (Please complete the following items.)

1. Name (Please Print): ______________________________

2. Address: ______________________________

3. Age: ____________ Date of Birth: ____________

4. Check one: Male ______ Female ______

5. Please encircle the number which represents the total number of years of your formal education or its equivalent:

   1 2 3 4 5 6 7 8 9 10 11 12 13 14 15 16 17 18 19 20

6. Please list any special diploma, certificate, degree, or educational award or achievement: ______________________

____

7. Check one: Single ______, Married ______, Divorced ______, Remarried ______, Spouse is deceased ______.
8. Title of present occupational position: ________________
____
9. General duties of present position: ________________
____
____
____
____
10. Other occupational positions which have been held prior to present position: ________________________
____
____
____
____
____
____

II. Psychic Interests and Abilities (Please complete the following items. If you wish, you may use the back of the page for additional comments.)

1. Do you believe you have some ability to gain extra-sensory perceptions (ESP) of thoughts and feelings of other people (telepathy)?
   Yes ______ No ______ Not Sure ______
2. Do you believe you have some ability to gain impressions of events or objects which are outside your usual environment (clairvoyance)?
   Yes ______ No ______ Not Sure ______
3. Do you believe you have some ability to gain impressions of future events (pre-cognition)?
   Yes ______ No ______ Not Sure ______
4. Do you believe you have some ability to influence the physical environment around you (psycho-kinesis or "mind over matter")?
   Yes ______ No ______ Not Sure ______
5. Have you ever participated in a scientific investigation of your ESP abilities?
   Yes ______ No ______

6. Have you ever participated in a seance or a group meditation to demonstrate your ESP abilities?
Yes ______ No ______

7. Do you gain some of your psychic impressions through any of these processes?
Dreams Yes____ No____ Communion with other persons Yes______ No______
Visions Yes____ No____ Communion with other spirits Yes______ No______
Prayers Yes____ No____ Other Processes: __________
Meditations Yes____ No____

8. Through what process do you gain most of your psychic impressions? ____
____

9. Have you ever experienced a spiritual event or a religious "rebirth"?
Yes ______ No ______

10. Do you consider your knowledge of parapsychology (study of ESP) to consist mainly (check one or more) in the areas of: personal interest in ESP events of everyday life ______; magazine and newspaper accounts of ESP events ______; empirical investigations of alleged ESP events ______; experimental investigations in the laboratory of ESP processes ______.

III. UFO Phenomena. (Please complete the following items. If you wish, you may use the back of the page for additional comments.)

1. Have you seen a UFO (Unidentified Flying Object)? Yes ______ No ______

2. If you have seen a UFO, please give the date, location, number of objects seen, and your opinion of what you saw: ______
____
____
____
____
____
____

3. Are you a member of any organization which gathers information about UFO reports? Yes ______ No ______ If "yes," please list the organization(s):

   ____

4. Do you believe that most "Unknown" sightings can be explained by the hypothesis of "Misinterpretation of Known Phenomena"? Yes ______ No ______

5. Do you believe that most "Unknown" sightings can be explained by the hypothesis of "Psychological Phenomena"? Yes ______ No ______

6. Do you believe that most "Unknown" sightings can be explained by the hypothesis of "Lies or Hoaxes"? Yes ______ No ______

7. Do you believe that most "Unknown" sightings can be explained by the hypothesis of "Governmental Secret Weapons"? Yes ____ No ______

8. Do you believe that most "Unknown" sightings can be explained by the hypothesis of "Extraterrestrial Space Craft"? Yes ______ No ______

9. Have you observed a UFO sighting during which you experienced a "loss of time"? If so, are you now aware of the possible events which occurred during that "loss of time" experience? Please describe your impressions of the event and possible association with a UFO observation:

   ____
   ____
   ____
   ____
   ____
   ____
   ____
   ____
   ____
   ____
   ____
   ____

10. Are you interested in the possible use of hypnotic techniques to help remember the "loss of time" events? Yes ______ No ______

IV. *UFO Occupants* (Please complete the following items.):

1. Have you observed a UFO sighting which included the observation of a humanoid or UFO Occupant? Yes ______ No ______. If yes, please give the date, location, number of UFO Occupants seen, and your opinion of what you saw: ______

______

______

______

______

______

______

______

______

2. On the back of this page, please draw a figure or figures to rep resent the UFO Occupants seen.

3. Have you communicated, directly or indirectly, with UFO Occupants? Yes ______ No ______. If "yes," have you communicated through writing ______, speech ______, or through "mental communication" ______?

4. If you communicated by speech, could you notice lip movement of the UFO Occupant(s)? Yes ______ No ______

5. Was the speech conducted in English? Yes ______ No ______ Other language ______

6. If you communicated by writing, do you have any written material given to you? Yes ______ No ______

7. If you communicated through "mental communication," were you told by UFO Occupant(s) how this process was conducted? Yes ______ No ______

8. Were any apparent devices (microphones, earphones, etc.) used in the communication by UFO Occupant(s)? Yes ______ No ______

9. What information did you give? ______

______

______

______

______

______

______

10. What information did you receive? ____________________

____

____

____

____

____

____

V. Additional Comments. (Please use this page to describe in more detail, your own psychic impressions of UFO phenomena, including your own impressions of the possible origins, powers, and purposes of UFO Occupants or those who control UFOs.)

Signature ______________ Date ____________________

☐ You may use my name in connection with any publication of these results.

☐ You may use these results, but do not use my name in connection with any publication of these results.

ESP processes, UFO observations, and impressions of possible communication with UFO occupants. Data were tabulated and submitted to the Computer Center, University of Wyoming, for analysis. Then, results were summarized in a short statement, and copies were sent to each participant in the survey.

There are several limitations to the study, including the following: the difficulties of obtaining reliable and valid information by a questionnaire survey; the questions about the generalizations of results from a small sample of participants; and the influence of personal biases on the part of the investigator: the view that the "spacecraft" hypothesis is the best hypothesis (tentatively) to account for the "unknown" cases of UFO reports; the view that UFO sightings include, on some occasions, the observation of UFO entities or UFO occupants; the view that some UFO reports indicate the possibility that hypnotic and ESP phenomena are being used by UFO occupants to observe and communicate with UFO observers.

RESULTS OF INITIAL STUDY

Results of the *Adjective Check List* (ACL) profiles indicate that the scores of the 63 participants were similar to those scores of USA men and women, with the highest average score on the Intraception Scale (expressed need for psychological awareness) and the lowest average score on the Succorance Scale (expressed need for assistance). See Table 1 for further information about the ACL results.

Results of the *Strong Vocational Interest Blank* (SVIB) indicate that, as a group, male participants scored higher on the scales of Group VI (Esthetic occupations), Group I (Biological Sciences and Professional occupations), and Group X (Verbal occupations); and they scored lower on the scales of Group XIII (Business Detail and Office occupations) and Group III (Production and Military Occupations). Also, male participants scored lower than most men score on the Masculinity-Femininity Scale (MF), and they scored higher than most men score on the Occupational Level (OL) Scale and the Academic Achievement (AACH) Scale. See Table 2 for further information about SVIB-M results.

Results of the SVIB profiles indicate that, as a group, female participants scored higher on the scales of Group I (Music occupations), Group VII (Nurses and Physical Education Teachers), and Group VIII (Medical occupations), and they scored lower on the scales of Group IV (Life Insurance Saleswoman) and Group V (Business occupations). Female participants scored similarly to most USA women on the Femininity-Masculinity (FM) Scale, and on the Academic Achievement (AACH) Scale they scored similarly to women college graduates. See Table 3 for further information about the SVIB-F results.

The results of the completed questionnaires were based upon the self-descriptions of the participants. Male participants claimed an average of 13.8 years of education; female participants claimed an average of 14.3 years of education; as a group, participants claimed an average of 14.0 years of education (SD-3.12).

TABLE 1

*Mean Scores on the Adjective Check List**

#	*Name of ACL Scale*		*Males*	*Females*	*Total*
1	Number Checked	(No Ckd)	52.21	58.17	54.48
2	Defensiveness	(Df)	49.85	52.83	50.98
3	Favorable Items	(Fav)	49.10	57.25	52.21
4	Unfavorable Items	(Unfav)	49.08	44.08	47.17
5	Self Confidence	(S Cfd)	50.10	56.04	52.37
6	Self Control	(S Cr)	48.23	52.92	50.02
7	Lability	(Lab)	52.82	53.17	52.95
8	Personal Adjustment	(Per Adj)	47.69	53.71	49.98
9	Achievement	(Ach)	52.36	54.00	52.98
10	Dominance	(Dom)	49.79	53.54	51.22
11	Endurance	(End)	53.25	52.54	52.98
12	Order	(Ord)	53.05	52.88	52.98
13	Intraception	(Int)	55.89	57.13	56.37
14	Nurturance	(Nur)	50.07	53.42	51.35
15	Affiliation	(Aff)	47.46	50.67	48.68
16	Heterosexuality	(Het)	46.07	50.92	47.92
17	Exhibition	(Exh)	49.59	50.25	49.84
18	Autonomy	(Aut)	51.33	51.88	51.44
19	Aggression	(Agg)	49.21	49.88	49.46
20	Change	(Cha)	49.26	51.00	49.92
21	Succorance	(Suc)	47.10	43.75	45.83
22	Abasement	(Aba)	48.03	45.83	47.19
23	Deference	(Def)	47.46	46.92	47.25
24	Counseling Readiness	(Crs)	52.05	50.54	51.48
	Number of Participants		39	24	63

* These obtained scores are based upon standard scores, with an average (mean score) of 50 and a standard deviation (SD) of 10.

TABLE 2

*Mean Scores on the SVIB-Male Profiles**
(N=39)

Group	*Description of Occupational Group*	*Scores*
I	Biological Sciences and Professional	35.87
II	Physical Sciences	31.44
III	Production and Military Officer	22.03
IV	Technical and Outdoor	23.82
V	Personnel Services	26.21
VI	Esthetic Occupations	37.36
VIII	Business Detail & Office Work	19.44
IX	Sales and Business Contact	24.62
X	Verbal Occupations	36.10
SL	Specialization Level	47.10
OL	Occupational Level	57.23
MF	Masculinity-Femininity	40.18
AACH	Academic Achievement	56.03

TABLE 3

*Mean Scores on the SVIB-Female Profiles**
(N-24)

Group	*Description of Occupational Group*	*Scores*
I	Music Occupations	32.00
II	Artistic and Verbal Occupations	29.13
III	Professional and Social Services	27.88
IV	Life Insurance Saleswoman	20.63
V	Business Occupations	26.54
VI	Teacher and Housewife	28.33
VII	Nurse and PE Teacher	31.25
VIII	Medical Occupations	29.67
IX	Math, Science, and Engineering	30.17
FM	Femininity-Masculinity	50.79
AACH	Academic Achievement	52.17

* These obtained scores are based upon standard scores, with an average (mean score) of 50 and a standard deviation (SD) of 10.

About three-fourths of the participants (26 males and 20 females) described themselves as having "some" ability for extrasensory perception (ESP). Only 17 participants (13 males and 4 females) described themselves as having "no" ESP abilities. About one-half of the participants (15 males and 16 females) described themselves as having a high interest in the study of ESP, including participation in scientific investigation or group demonstration of their ESP abilities; 32 participants (24 males and 8 females) described themselves as persons who are not interested in the study of ESP and have not participated in scientific investigations or group demonstrations of their ESP abilities. See Table 4 for summary information about the self-descriptions of the participants.

TABLE 4

Classification of Claims of ESP Interests and Abilities

	Males	*Females*	*Total*
Average Years of Education	13.82 (SD=3.23)	14.29 (SD=2.97)	14.00 (SD=3.12)
Have "no ability" for ESP (telepathy, clairvoyance, precognition, or psycho-kinesis)	13	4	17
Have "some ability" for ESP (telepathy, clairvoyance, precognition, or psycho-kinesis)	26	20	46
Have "high interest" in ESP, including participation in scientific investigation and/or group demonstration.	15	16	31
Have "no interest" in ESP, including no participation in scientific investigation or group demonstration of abilities.	24	8	32
Total Number of Participants	39	24	63

TABLE 5

Classification of Claims of UFO Observations

	Self-Description of UFO Observation	*Males*	*Females*	*Total*
A	Has not seen a UFO	8	4	12
B	Has seen "nocturnal wandering light" (V)*	1	0	1
C	Has seen "unusual object" moving continuously through sky (IV)*	3	1	4
D	Has seen "unusual object" stationary or with discontinuous flight (III)*	8	3	11
E	Has seen "cloud cigar" in the sky (II)*	0	0	0
F	Has seen "unusual object" on or near the ground (I)*	8	4	12
G	Has not seen a UFO but has experienced communication with UFO occupants	4	5	9
H	Has seen a UFO and has experienced communication with UFO occupants	5	6	11
I	Has seen UFO occupants and has experienced communication with UFO occupants	1	0	1
J	Has seen UFO, been inside UFO, and has experienced communication with UFO occupants	1	1	2
	Total Number of Participants	39	24	63

* An attempt was made to classify the statements of UFO observations within the system presented by Vallee, J. and Janine. *Challenge to Science: the UFO Enigma*. N.Y.: Ace Star Book, 1966. Pp. 225-226.

Two-thirds of the participants (27 males and 15 females) claim to have seen a UFO, while 21 participants (12 males and 9 females) claim that they have not seen a UFO. Approximately one-third of the participants (11 males and 12 females) claim to have experienced some kind of communication with UFO occupants, while 40 participants (28 males and 12 females) claim they have not experienced communication with UFO occupants. Of the 42 participants who claim to have seen a UFO, 14 participants (7 males and 7 females) claim to have experienced communication with UFO occupants. Of the 21 participants who claim they have not seen a UFO, 9 participants (4 males and 5 females) claim to have experienced communication with UFO occupants. See Tables 5 and 6 for further information about self-descriptions of UFO observation and communication with UFO occupants.

TABLE 6

Classifications of Claims of UFO Observations and Communications

Classifications of Claim	*Males*	*Females*	*Total*
Has seen a UFO or UFOs	27	15	42
Has not seen a UFO or UFOs	12	9	21
Has experienced communication with UFO occupants	11	12	23
Has not experienced communication with UFO occupants	28	12	40
Has seen a UFO but has not experienced communication with UFO occupants	20	8	28
Has seen a UFO or UFOs and experienced communication with UFO occupants	7	7	14
Has experienced communication but has not seen a UFO	4	5	9
Total Number of Participants	39	24	63

TABLE 7

Classifications of Psychic Impressions of Possible Motives of UFO Occupants

	Possible Motives of UFO Occupants	*Males*	*Females*	*Total*
A	*Hostile*, to invade the earth or destroy mankind	1	0	1
B	*Alien*, unknown extra-dimensional mind	0	0	0
C	*Curious*, to study mankind	23	6	29
D	*Prevenient*, to prevent destruction of the earth	2	2	4
E	*Nurturant*, to assist development of mankind	2	4	6
F	*Hostile* (see above)	0	0	0
G	*Alien* (see above)	2	1	3
H	*Curious* (see above)	8	6	14
I	*Prevenient* (see above)	0	3	3
J	*Nurturant* (see above)	1	2	3
	Total Number of Participants	39	24	63

Has experienced communication with UFO occupants: F, G, H, I, J

Most of the participants were willing to describe their impressions of possible motives of UFO occupants. Classification by the investigator indicates that the impressions of participants range between "hostile," "alien," "curious," "prevenient," and "nurturant" motives. (If a participant did not specify his or her impression of the motives of UFO occupants, his or her response was classified in the category labeled "curious.") Of the 40 participants who claim that they have not experienced communication with UFO occupants, 29 participants (23 males and 6 females) describe impressions which suggest a "curious" motive on the part of UFO occupants. Of the 23 participants who claim that they have experienced communication with UFO occupants, 14 participants (8 males and 6 females) describe impressions which suggest a "curious" motive on the part of UFO occupants. Thus, 43 participants (31 males and 12 females) describe impressions which suggest a "curious" motive on the part of UFO occupants. See Table 7

TABLE 8

Selected Correlations of Participant Characteristics

#	*Variables*	*Males*	*Females*	*Total*
1 and 37	Years of Education and SL (Specialization Level) of the SVIB-Male	+ .430		
2 and 3	Survey of UFO Observations and Level of Psychic Impressions	+ .705		
2 and 3	Survey of UFO Observations and Level of Psychic Impressions		+ .534	
1 and 19	Years of Education and Heterosexuality Scale of ACL		—.426	
1 and 30	Years of Education and Group III, Professional Occupations of SVIB-Female		+ .528	
1 and 38	Years of Education and Academic Achievement Scale of SVIB-Female		+ .565	
2 and 3	Survey of UFO Observations and Level of Psychic Impressions			+ .635
3 and 6	Level of Psychic Impressions and Favorable Items Scale of ACL			+ .352
	Number of Participants	39	24	63

for information on the impressions of possible motives of UFO occupants.

Table 8 presents selected correlations which indicate significant statistical relationships between certain variables of the inventory scores and self-descriptions of participants. These correlations are of interest to the extent that they reflect some expected relationships; however, none of the correlations is so high that it could be used with confidence to predict the relationships which might be obtained through future observations. In general, the higher correlations probably are obtained because of similarity of items or overlapping characteristics of the participants.

RESULTS OF SECOND SURVEY

Since the completion of the initial study, the investigator has attempted to learn about other persons who have experienced psychic impressions of UFO phenomena. During the past few years, another 19 persons have responded to the request that they complete the questionnaire and inventories. Most of these persons also completed two other psychological inventories: the 16 PF Test *(Sixteen Personality Factors Test)* and the MMPI *(Minnesota Multiphasic Personality Inventory).*

These persons usually became known to APRO investigators because of unusual UFO sightings, including experiences which suggested that the participants had experienced "mental communication" with UFO occupants. In some cases, the participants claimed that they were engaged in a continuing series of telepathic communications with UFO occupants.

The limitations of this phase of investigation were similar to those of the initial study: the questionnaire method of obtaining data; the question of representativeness of the sample of respondents; and the biases of the investigator.

Results of the *Adjective Check List* (ACL) indicated that the obtained scores were similar to those of USA men and women, with higher group scores on the Scales entitled Number Checked, Self-Confidence, and Intraception (expressed interest in psychological awareness); lower group scores were obtained on the Succorance Scale (expressed need for assistance). See Table 9 for further information.

TABLE 9

*Group Scores on the Adjective Check List**
(Group II)

#	*Name of ACL Scale*		*Males* (II)	*Females* (II)	Total (II)
1	Number Checked	(No Ckd)	55.00	62.84	61.00
2	Defensiveness	(Df)	51.50	55.30	54.41
3	Favorable Items	(Fav)	56.00	59.38	58.58
4	Unfavorable Items	(Unfav)	45.00	45.84	45.64
5	Self Confidence	(S Cfd)	60.50	59.69	59.88
6	Self Control	(S Cr)	50.50	55.00	53.94
7	Lability	(Lab)	60.00	48.77	51.54
8	Personal Adjustment	(Per Adj)	47.75	54.92	53.23
9	Achievement	(Ach)	59.25	58.54	58.71
10	Dominance	(Dom)	59.00	56.77	57.29
11	Endurance	(End)	54.00	58.38	57.35
12	Order	(Ord)	54.25	59.54	58.30
13	Intraception	(Int)	64.00	58.31	59.65
14	Nurturance	(Nur)	55.25	51.54	52.41
15	Affiliation	(Aff)	52.00	52.69	52.53
16	Heterosexuality	(Het)	41.75	45.23	44.41
17	Exhibition	(Exh)	52.00	52.48	52.37
18	Autonomy	(Aut)	55.00	54.31	54.47
19	Aggression	(Agg)	48.25	48.77	48.65
20	Change	(Cha)	62.50	47.00	50.65
21	Succorance	(Suc)	41.00	41.92	41.70
22	Abasement	(Aba)	46.50	42.92	43.76
23	Deference	(Def)	41.75	46.08	45.06
24	Counseling Readiness	(Crs)	41.75	56.23	53.76
	Number of Participants		4	13	17

* These obtained scores are based upon standard scores, with an average (mean score) of 50 and a standard deviation (SD) of 10.

Results of the Strong Vocational Interest Blank (SVIB-M) indicated that, as a group, the male participants scored higher on the scales of Group I (Biological Sciences and Professional Interests) and Group VI (Esthetic Occupations), and they scored lower on the scales of Group VIII (Business Detail and Office Work) and Group IV (Technical and Outdoor Occupations). See Table 10 for further information about the Occupational Scale scores. The results of the Basic Interest Scales (SVIB-M) indicated that male participants scored like those men who score significantly high on the scales of Science, Adventure, Medical Service, Social Service, Religious Ac-

TABLE 10

*Group Scores on the SVIB-Male Profiles**
(Group II)

Occupational Group	*Description of Occupational Group*	*Scores*
I	Biological Sciences and Professional	40.40
II	Physical Sciences	30.00
III	Production and Military Officer	26.40
IV	Technical and Outdoor	18.20
V	Personnel Services	32.20
VI	Esthetic Occupations	39.80
VII	CPA Owner	25.00
VIII	Business Detail and Office Work	15.60
IX	Sales and Business Contact	22.20
X	Verbal Occupations	34.40
SL	Specialization Level	53.40
OL	Occupational Level	64.40
MF	Masculinity-Feminity	39.20
AACH	Academic Achievement	70.00

Number of Participants = 5

* These obtained scores are based upon standard scores, with an average (mean score) of 50 and a standard deviation (SD) of 10.

tivities, Teaching, Music, Art, and Writing. See Table 11 for further information.

The results of the Occupational Scales of the *Strong Vocational Interest Blank* (SVIB-F) indicated that the female participants scored highest on Group V (Professional Group, including Psychologist, Librarian, Speech Pathologist, Translator) and lowest on Group VIII (Lawyer and Business Group). See Table 12.

TABLE 11

*Group Scores on the Basic Interest Scales (SVIB-M)**
(Group II)

#	*Name of Basic Interest Scale*	*Scores*
1	Public Speaking	59.0
2	Law/Politics	52.2
3	Business Management	44.0
4	Sales	46.2
5	Merchandising	42.8
6	Office Practices	40.8
7	Military Activities	46.2
8	Technical Supervision	42.0
9	Mathematics	53.8
10	Science	61.6
11	Mechanical	49.4
12	Nature	56.0
13	Agriculture	49.0
14	Adventure	59.8
15	Recreational Leadership	46.2
16	Medical Service	59.6
17	Social Service	60.2
18	Religious Activities	58.8
19	Teaching	64.2
20	Music	65.6
21	Art	63.6
22	Writing	63.2

Number of SVIB Profiles = 5

* These obtained scores are based upon standard scores, with an average (mean score) of 50 and a standard deviation (SD) of 10.

The results of the Basic Interest Scales of the SVIB-F indicated that female participants scored significantly higher than USA women on the Physical Science Scale. See Table 13 for further information.

The results of the *Sixteen Personality Factors Test* (16 PF) may not be useful, since only 2 males and 5 females have completed the test; perhaps, with other participants, the profile scores can be useful for comparison with adult norms. See Table 14 for obtained scores.

TABLE 12

*Group Scores on the SVIB-Female Profiles**
(Group II)

Occupational Group	*Description of Occupational Group*	*Scores*
I	Music and Entertainment Occupations	25.71
II	Artistic Occupations	27.21
III	Verbal Occupations	30.35
IV	Social Services	25.21
V	Professional Group	36.28
VI	Medical and Engineering Group	32.50
VII	Military Group	33.71
VIII	Lawyer and Business Group	22.35
IX	Home Economist and Dietitian	27.92
X	Therapists and Nurses	32.00
XI	Teacher, Saleswoman, and Operators	25.71
AACH	Academic Achievement	53.60
DIV	Diversity of Interests	47.10
FM	Feminity-Masculinity	49.00
OIE	Occupational Introversion-Extroversion	51.3

Number of Participants # 14

* These obtained scores are based upon standard scores, with an average (mean score) of 50 and a standard deviation (SD) of 10.

The results of the *Minnesota Multiphasic Personality Inventory* (MMPI) indicated that the male participants scored highest on Scale 5 (Masculine-Feminine Interests) and lowest on Scale 0 (Social Introversion); the average profile is similar to that of a man who is seen as having many interests, including artistic and literary (or "feminine" interests), with a high level of ego strength and psy-

TABLE 13

*Group Scores on the Basic Interest Scales (SVIB-F)**
(Group II)

#	*Name of Basic Interest Scale*	*Scores*
1	Public Speaking	49.35
2	Law/Politics	46.92
3	Merchandising	48.92
4	Office Practices	50.28
5	Numbers	52.35
6	Physical Science	60.64
7	Mechanical	56.57
8	Outdoors	54.00
9	Biological Science	53.85
10	Medical Service	54.21
11	Teaching	50.78
12	Social Service	48.64
13	Sports	45.00
14	Homemaking	47.00
15	Religious Activities	49.35
16	Music	49.21
17	Art	52.64
18	Performing Arts	51.92
19	Writing	54.35

Number of Participants = 14

* These obtained scores are based upon standard scores, with an average (mean score) of 50, and a standard deviation (SD) of 10.

chological energy, with an interest in social activities and interpersonal relationships, and a tendency toward critical or rational objectivity and personal sensitivity (a profile of a "creative person"). However, the small number of profiles is a major limitation for any general interpretation of the results. The female participants scored highest on Scale 3 (Hysteria) and Scale 4 (Psychopathic Deviancy) and lowest on Scale 5 (M-F Interests). The average profile is similar to that of a woman with "normal" scores, with a tendency toward

TABLE 14

*Group Scores on the 16 Personality Factors Test (16 PF)**
(Group II)

#	*Name of 16 PF Scale*	*Males*	*Females*	*Total*
A	Reserved: Outgoing	5.0	4.2	4.4
B	Less Intelligent: More Intelligent	9.0	6.4	7.2
C	Affected by Feelings: Emotionally Stable	6.0	5.8	5.9
E	Humble: Assertive	8.0	5.6	6.3
F	Sober: Happy-Go-Lucky	6.0	4.4	4.9
G	Expedient: Conscientious	5.5	5.6	5.6
H	Shy: Venturesome	6.0	5.2	5.4
I	Tough-Minded: Tender-Minded	6.0	7.2	6.0
L	Trusting: Suspicious	5.5	5.2	5.3
M	Practical: Imaginative	8.0	7.2	7.4
N	Forthright: Shrewd	2.0	4.8	4.0
O	Self-Assured: Apprehensive	4.5	4.6	4.6
Q	Conservative: Experimenting	9.5	6.4	7.4
Q	Group-Dependent: Self-Sufficient	6.0	8.2	7.6
Q	Undisciplined Self-Conflict: Controlled	6.0	4.8	5.2
Q	Relaxed: Tense	5.0	4.6	4.4
	Number of Participants	2	5	7

* These obtained scores are based upon standard scores, with an average (mean score) of 5

psychosomatic complaints and with a tendency toward "rational thinking." See Table 15.

In summary, the results of the vocational interest inventory and psychological inventories indicated that, "on paper," the participants as a group showed no unusual psychological and professional activities than in technical or business detail occupations.

TABLE 15

*Group Scores on the Minnesota Multiphasic Personality Inventory (MMPI)**
(Group II)

#	*Name of MMPI Scale*	*Males* Raw Score (+K)	*Males* T Score	*Females* Raw Score (+K)	*Females* T Scores
?	Number of Unanswered Items†	0.00	—	4.78	—
L	Lie Scale†	4.50	52	5.64	56
F	Validity Scale†	5.50	57	5.07	56
K	Ego Functioning Scale†	14.00	53	17.28	60
1	Hypochondriasis (Hs)	9.00	44	13.93	52
2	Depression (D)	15.25	52	17.35	52
3	Hysteria (Hy)	19.75	56	23.43	61
4	Psychopathic Deviancy (Pd)	24.25	63	22.92	60
5	Masculine-Feminine Interests (MF)	30.25	70	38.85	45
6	Paranoia (Pa)	12.50	64	10.14	56
7	Psychasthenia (Pt)	23.75	52	23.64	52
8	Schizophrenia (Sc)	23.75	53	24.50	53
9	Hypomania (Ma)	23.00	65	19.64	58
0	Social Introversion (Si)	13.75	39	22.71	48
ES	Ego Strength (ES)	53.50	65	40.14	50
	Number of MMPI Profiles	5		14	

* These obtained scores can be compared with standard scores (T scores), with an average (mean score) of 50 and a standard deviation (SD) of 10.

†Non-clinical Scales: ?, L, F, K

The responses to the questionnaire items indicated that the respondents of Group II claim an average of 14.6 years of education; and a majority (16 of 19) claim to have "some ability" for ESP processes, yet a majority (12 of 19) claim to have "little" interest in formal study of ESP. See Table 16.

TABLE 16

Classification of Claims of ESP Interests and Abilities (Group II)

	Males	*Females*	*Total*
Average Years of Education	15.60	14.49	14.63
Have "no ability" for ESP (telepathy, clairvoyance, precognition, or psychokinesis)	0	3	3
Have "some ability" for ESP (telepathy, clairvoyance, precognition, or psychokinesis)	5	11	16
Have "high interest" in ESP, including participation in scientific investigation and/or group demonstration.	2	5	7
Have "no interest" in ESP, including no participation in scientific investigation or group demonstration of abilities	3	9	12
Total number of participants	5	14	19

TABLE 17

Classifications of Claims of UFO Observations (Group II)

	Self-Description of UFO Observation	*Males*	*Females*	*Total*
A	Has not seen a UFO	0	1	1
B	Has seen "nocturnal wandering light" (V)*	0	0	0
C	Has seen "unusual object" moving continuously through sky (IV)*	0	0	0
D	Has seen "unusual object" stationary or with discontinuous flight (III)*	0	0	0
E	Has seen "cloud cigar" in the sky (II)*	0	0	0
F	Has seen "unusal object" on or near the ground (I)*	2	2	4
G	Has not seen an "unusual object" but has experienced communication with UFO occupants	0	3	3
H	Has seen an "unusual object" and has experienced communication with UFO occupants	3	5	8
I	Has seen UFO occupants and has experienced communication with UFO occupants	0	3	3
J	Has seen UFO, been inside UFO, and has experienced communication with UFO occupants	0	0	0
	Total Number of Participants	5	14	19

* An attempt was made to classify the statements of UFO observations within the system presented by Vallee, J. and Janine. *Challenge to Science: the UFO Enigma*. New York, NY: Ace Star Book, 1966. Pp. 225-226.

The majority of respondents (16 of 19) claimed to have experienced communication with UFO occupants, although the experience may or may not have occurred at the time of a UFO sighting. In some cases, participants claimed that they had not seen UFO occupants and yet they had the distinct impression that they "visited" or were "visited" by UFO occupants and given certain information. See Tables 17 and 18 for further information on the classification of claims of UFO observations and claims of communications.

TABLE 18

Classifications of Claims of UFO Observations and Communications
(Group II)

Classifications of Claim	*Males*	*Females*	*Total*
Has seen a UFO or UFOs	5	10	15
Has not seen a UFO or UFOs	0	4	4
Has experienced communication with UFO occupants	4	12	16
Has not experienced communication with UFO occupants	1	2	3
Has seen a UFO but has not experienced communication with UFO occupants	1	2	3
Has seen a UFO or UFO and experienced communication with UFO occupants	4	8	12
Has experienced communication but has not seen a UFO	0	3	3
Has not seen a UFO and has not experienced communication with UFO occupants	0	1	1
Total Number of Participants	5	14	19

As would be expected, the majority of respondents who claimed to experience "mental communication" with UFO occupants also offered statements which were interpreted as "positive," rather than "negative," views of the possible motives of UFO occupants. Most of these respondents claim to receive information, sometimes on a continuing basis, of the relationship between mankind and a Galactic Federation, or "Space Brothers." See Table 19 for further information.

TABLE 19

Classifications of Psychic Impressions of Possible Motives of UFO Occupants (Group II)

	Possible Motives of UFO Occupants	*Males*	*Females*	*Total*
A	*Hostile*, to invade the earth or destroy mankind	0	0	0
B	*Alien*, unknown extra-dimensional mind	0	0	0
C	*Curious*, to study mankind	1	1	2
D	*Prevenient*, to prevent destruction of the Earth	0	0	0
E	*Nurturant*, to assist development of mankind	0	1	1
F	*Hostile* (see above)*	0	0	0
G	*Alien* (see above)*	0	0	0
H	*Curious* (see above)*	2	3	5
I	*Prevenient* (see above)*	0	2	2
J	*Nurturant* (see above)*	2	7	9
	Total Number of Participants	5	14	19

* Has experienced communication with UFO occupants: F, G, A, I, J

In some cases, participants received information about impending destruction from earthquakes or floods to the possibility of nuclear war or a natural catastrophe. In some cases, participants received messages which profess a great love for mankind and a desire to assist the development of earth's civilization.

For example, a respondent, LM, claims to be sixty-five years old, claims to have eleven years of education; claims to have seen UFOs, to have seen UFO occupants, and to have received "mental communication from UFO occupants." In response to the question about her "impressions of the possible origins, powers, and purposes of UFO occupants or those who control UFOs," she provided this statement:

> "I feel that some UFOs come from other planets in our universe, or galaxy, and some may have bases (not stationary) in submarine-type Mother Ships under seas, and in very remote areas on our planet and Mother Ships in the higher Earth spectrum.
>
> "I sense UFO crews volunteer to come to help us save ourselves from prevalent chaos, and a possible holocaust. I sense their craft operates with natural ether-ized energy that they use, and 'it' is forever recharged. I sense UFO crews are thousands (longer?) of years ahead of Earthman's knowledge in every area.
>
> "I think that UFOs monitor Earth inhabitants' collective percentage of evolvement by the degree of 'Light' (enlightenment) they evaluate in man's composite body.
>
> "I believe there may be a few soul-less UFO crews to try and harm us, but I'm impressed that they are in the minority, and chased out by 'Aerial Scout Crews.'"

Another person, CF, has received "mental communications" for several years; the materials, dealing with scientific and spiritual topics, have been cross-indexed for reference by interested researchers.

Similar messages have been catalogued by another person, JOS. A description of the materials, and the recipient, follows.

Argent—Another World

Transmission Transcribed by JOS 11/27/74

This set of volumes is a longhand transcription of communications received by JOS since early 1974. The senders claim to be space travelers from the planet Argent (of another solar system) who are now exploring earth by means of skimmer boats (flying saucers).

Transmission started after JOS had a "UFO experience" with a light ray on September 4, 1970, in a Pittsburgh, Pennsylvania, suburb. Transmission was brief and intermittent until late April, 1974; however, in the following fifteen months, about 1,300 longhand pages have been transcribed, with one hundred fifty to two hundred words per page; it is continuing. For convenience, the the transcript is divided into two hundred-page volumes. The first volume starts on January 29, 1974, about the time the communications first indicated that they were transmitted by people from another planet. Earlier communications (as later explained) were supposed to be a testing period. No reason has been given for the selection of JOS as the recipient of the messages; it was stated that she was selected by computer, and that there are other recipients for other information.

About half of the material is "language lessons," interlanguage vocabulary (they claim to understand English and numerous other languages), interspersed with encyclopedia-type information and people names. Described are the people, the home planet, ways (space stations), space ships, skimmer boats (flying saucers), religion, customs, etc. Precise predictions have not been made to date.

According to the information received, these people started building ways over 500 years ago, and have established at least six between Argent and Earth. The ways are practically self-sustaining and hold about 12,000 people each. They have also established a base on Uranus. Space ships transport about 1,200 people each. Skimmer boats hold three, seven, or eleven people, depending upon the size and shape. They do not claim to be responsible for all "flying saucers"—only those of certain described shapes.

JOS transcribes the messages as she receives them. Messages may be lengthy, or a series of short bursts with considerable time between. Furthermore, different individuals may transmit. They have reported that a team of twelve people is assigned to carry on transmission with JOS. It appears that the team is assigned to the task of communicating language lessons and some technical information to JOS, but also they add comments and other information about themselves, and sometimes "small talk." Thus, the transcript may jump from one subject to another. However, it is apparent that the transmission is overall a highly organized and intelligent effort.

Communication between JOS and the Argent people appears to

be through a form of thought transference or radial hearing (clairaudience?), reported to be triggered by the light ray (as a catalyst). She appears to be awake and alert during the message reception; there is no trance. During the first month or two after September 4, 1970, JOS had several visual or externally auditory experiences, but none since.

JOS is a woman in her late fifties, a semi-invalid due to arthritis and related ailments; she has been a housewife most of her life, and has displayed little interest in science, or science fiction. Her husband, a recently retired electrical engineer with fifty-eight U.S. patents, most of which are in use, has rather broad interests in the natural sciences, particularly physics. Neither previously has had more than a casual (skeptical) interest in paranormal phenomena.

CONCLUSIONS OF SURVEY

If an investigator accepted the questionnaire and inventory results as reliable, he or she could conclude (tentatively) that the scores were obtained from a sample of persons of average or above average education, with professional and academic interests, with an interest in human behavior, and with no obvious psychoneurotic or psychotic reactions. The results are similar to those of the "upper middle class" who are viewed as intellectual, creative, and productive; sometimes, these people are viewed as "pace setters" and leaders. Yet, the statements of the participants suggest that they have been observers of strange phenomena which defy explanation through any single body of knowledge.

In conclusion, the results of this survey indicate that most of the participants believe that they have observed UFO phenomena. The statements of many participants suggest that they have experienced direct or indirect communication with UFO occupants. Some participants claim to have experienced "mental communication" with UFO entities.

If further investigations were conducted and revealed similar findings, then many puzzling questions would face UFO investigators: how do UFO observers obtain these impressions of communication with UFO entities? If hypnotic and ESP processes are involved, for what purposes are these phenomena used by UFO entities?

The physical, biological, psycho-social, and spiritual implications of these questions should serve as a challenge and perhaps as a spur to further investigation of these interesting experiences of unusual phenomena.

IV.
SUMMARY AND CONCLUSIONS

Summary. This chapter has presented some information and some views regarding the hypnotic and psychic implications in the investigation of UFO reports. An attempt was made to deal with some of the questions which arise from the claims of some UFO observers, or UFO percipients, who state that they have experienced "loss of time," "hypnosis," or "trance-like" states of altered awareness, and/or "mental communication" with UFO occupants or UFO entities.

The chapter was organized into four parts: "The Problem"; "Some Uses of Hypnosis," including a report of an interview with a UFO observer (Case 42, Condon and Gillmor, 1969, 389-391); "Psychic Impressions of UFO Phenomena," including a survey of some characteristics of persons who claim to experience various psychic impressions of UFO phenomena; and "Summary and Conclusions."

References were cited from books and professional journals which deal with the study of hypnosis and psychic phenomena (ESP and psychokinesis). Possible advantages and disadvantages of hypnotic procedures were considered for obtaining and evaluating information from UFO observers. Parapsychological research methods and findings were questioned as a means of investigating the claims of "mental communication" with UFO occupants.

Despite the difficult questions of methodology, analysis, and interpretation of results, the writer believes that the investigation of UFO reports proceed on all levels of scientific concern: physical, biological, psycho-social, and spiritual or psychic phenomena. Evidently, a single UFO report will not "make or break" the UFO puzzle; the accumulation of evidence is more likely to be meaningful if there is an emphasis upon the patterns of reports. Also, the *reliability* of these patterns is likely to be a more important question, in the present stage of investigation, than the *validity* of the obtained information. (This opinion would tend to support the claim that the hypnotic and psychic experiences of UFO observers are "true" or "real" experiences but that the obtained information from UFO entities may or may not be "true" or "valid" information.)

Conclusions. In conclusion, the writer believes that both a tenderminded "Yeasay" attitude and a toughminded "Naysay" attitude are important for investigation of UFO reports: as Aimé Michel has stated (Bowen, 1966, p. 68), "...in Ufology the rule is to think of everything and to believe nothing." The UFO investigator can be very "open-minded" to new hypotheses as well as very "closed-minded" to any conclusion which is not based upon the available evidence.

This writer, because of his own UFO sightings and because of his investigations with many cooperative persons, accepts (tentatively) the available evidence as support for these hypotheses:

1. The earth is being surveyed by spacecraft which are piloted or controlled by intelligent beings from an alien civilization(s).
2. Hypnotic and psychic phenomena are being used by UFO entities to study and/or communicate with UFO observers or UFO percipients.
3. Further investigation of UFO reports and UFO observers may lead to more knowledge about the powers of UFO entities and the purposes of their "display" or their communications with UFO percipients.

REFERENCES

ACL. Gough, H., and Heilbrun, A. B. *Adjective Check List Manual.* Palo Alto, California, Consulting Psychologists Press, 1965.

Allan, W. K. "Crocodile skinned Entities at Calgary." *Flying Saucer Review.* April 1975, *20,* No. 6, 25-26.

APRO, *APRO Bulletin.* Aerial Phenomena Research Organization, 3910 East Kleindale Road, Tucson, Arizona 85712.

Ashby, R. H., *The Guide Book For the Study of Psychical Research.* New York, Samuel Weiser, 1972.

Barber, T.X., *A Scientific Approach to 'Hypnosis'* NY, Van Nostrand, 1969.

Bloecher, T., *Report on the UFO Wave of 1947.* Private printing, 1967.

Blumrich, J. F., *The Spaceships of Ezekiel.* New York, Bantam Books, 1974.

Bord, C. "Angels and UFOs." *Flying Saucer Review,* Sept.-Oct. 1972, *18,* No. 5, 17-19.

Bord, Janet. "Are Psychic People More Likely To See UFOs?" *Flying Saucer Review,* May-June 1972, *18,* No. 3, 20-22.

Bowen, C. "Comments on Condon." *Flying Saucer Review,*

March-April 1969, *15*, No. 2, 31.

Bowen, C. "Fantasy or Truth? A new look at an old contact claim." *Flying Saucer Review*, July-Aug. 1967, *13*, No. 4, 11-14.

Bowen, C. (Ed.) "The Humanoids." Special Issue, *Flying Saucer Review*, 1966.

Bowen, C. "Psychic Surgery and Healing by UFOs—Is There a Link?" *Flying Saucer Review*, July-Aug. 1971, *17*, No. 4, 23.

Bowen, C. "Strangers About the House" *Flying Saucer Review*, Sept.-Oct. 1968, *14*, No. 5, 10-12.

Bowen, C. "Thinking Aloud." *Flying Saucer Review*, Nov.-Dec. 1969, *15*, No. 6, 22-24. (b)

Bowen, C. "UFOs and Psychic Phenomena." *Flying Saucer Review*. July-Aug. 1969, *15*, No. 4, 22-25.

Bracewell, R. N. *Intelligent Life in Outer Space*. San Francisco, W. H. Freeman, 1974.

Broad, C. D. *Lectures on Psychical Research*. New York, Humanities Press, 1962.

Buhler, W. "More Teleportations and Levitations." Flying Saucer Review, Jan.-Feb. 1973, *19*, No. 1, 28-29, iii.

Cade, C. M. "A Long Cool Look at Alien Intelligence," Part IV. Possible significance of parapsychology. *Flying Saucer Review*, Nov.-Dec. 1967, *13*, No. 6, 13-15.

Cade, C. M. "A Long Cool Look at Alien Intelligence," Part V. "It's all in the mind." *Flying Saucer Review*, Mar.-Apr. 1968, *14*, No. 2, 7-9.

Cantril, H. *The Invasion from Mars: a study in the psychology of panic*. NY: Harper Torchbooks, 1966.

Caplan, J. M. "Parallelism" as a terminology. *Flying Saucer Review*, Dec. 1974, *20*, No. 3, 22-23, 27.

Catoe, Lynne E. *UFOs and Related Subject: an annotated bibliography*. U.S. Government Printing Office, Washington, DC 20402, 1969.

Center for UFO Studies. P. O. Box 11, Northfield, IL 60093.

Cheek, D. B., and LeCron, L. M. *Clinical Hypnotherapy*. NY: Grune and Stratton, 1968.

Chibbett, H. S. W. "UFOs and Parapsychology." *UFO Percipients, Special Edition No. 3, Flying Saucer Review*, Aug. 1969, 33-38.

Clark, J., and Coleman, L. *The Unidentified*. New York, Warner Paperback, 1975.

Condon, E. U., and Gillmor, D. S. (Eds.) *Scientific Study of Unidentified Flying Objects*. NY: Bantam Books, 1969.

Cooper, L. F., and Erickson, M. H. *Time Distortion in Hypnosis*. (2nd edition). Baltimore, Williams and Wilkins, 1959.

Creighton, G. "Curioser and Curioser." *Flying Saucer Review.* Oct. 1974, *20*, No. 2, 5-8.

Creighton, G. "The Extraordinary Happenings at Casa Blanca." *Flying Saucer Review,* Sept.-Oct. 1967, *13*, No. 5, 16-18.

Creighton, G. "The Healing of Wounds by Electromagnetic Radiation." *Flying Saucer Review,* Nov.-Dec. 1972, *18*, No. 6, 8-9, 27. (b)

Creighton, G. "Healing from UFOs." *Flying Saucer Review,* Sept.-Oct. 1969, *15*, No. 5, 20-23.

Creighton, G. "More Teleportations." *Flying Saucer Review,* Sept-Oct. 1970, *16*, No. 5, 11-13, 32. (b)

Creighton, G. "Parapsychology—Some Facts." *Flying Saucer Review,* July-Aug. 1970, *16*, No. 4, 19. (a)

Creighton, G. "Some Thoughts on 'Thinking Globes.'" *Flying Saucer Review,* May-June 1972, *18*, No. 3, 23-24. (a)

Creighton, G. "Another Teleportation and Its Sequel." *Flying Saucer Review,* Sept.-Oct. 1971, *17*, No. 5, 15-17, 19.

Creighton, G. "Uri Geller; The Man Who Bends Science." *Flying Saucer Review,* Jan.-Feb. 1973, *19*, No. 1, 8-11.

Crookall, R. *Out-of-the-body Experiences: A Fourth Analysis.* NY University Books, 1970.

Culligan, E. *The 1960 Fatima Secret.* Box 5396, San Bernardino, CA: Culligan Publications, 1967.

Downing, B.H. *The Bible and Flying Saucers.* NY: Lippincott, 1968.

Druffel, Ann. "An Experiment to Obtain Information by Psychic Means." *Flying Saucer Review,* July-Aug. 1972, *18*, No. 4, 18-19.

Dunne, J.W. *An Experiment with Time.* 24 Russell Square, London, Faber and Faber, Ltd., 1958.

Edwards, P.M.H. "UFOs and ESP." *Flying Saucer Review,* Nov.-Dec. 1970, *16*, No. 6, 18-20, 26.

Edwards, P.M.H. "A Few Coincidences, and Two Postscripts." *Flying Saucer Review,* May-June 1973, *19*, No. 3, 23-26.

Eisenbud, J. "The Mind-Matter Interface." *The Journal of the American Society for Psychical Research,* April 1975, *69*, No. 2, 115-126.

Eisenbud, J. *Psi and Psychoanalysis.* New York, Grune and Stratton, 1970.

Eisenbud, J., *The World of Ted Serios: 'thoughtographic' studies of an extraordinary mind.* New York, William Morrow, 1967. (Pocketbook, 1968).

Erickson, M.H., Hershman, S., and Secter, I.I. *The Practical Application of Medical and Dental Hypnosis.* New York, Julian Press, 1961.

Festinger, L., Riecken, H.W., and Schachter, S. *When Prophecy Fails*. New York, Harper Torchbooks, 1964.
Flint, M.H., and Binder, O.O. *Mankind—Child of the Stars*. Greenwich, Connecticut, Fawcett, 1974.
Flying Saucer Review. FSR Publications, Ltd., P.O. Box 25, Barnet, Herts, EN5 2NR ENGLAND.
Fontes, O.T. "Dying Girl Saved by Humanoid Surgeons." *Flying Saucer Review*, Sept.-Oct. 1967, *13*, No. 5, 5-6.
Foundation for Research on the Nature of Man. Box 6847, College Station, Durham, N.C. 27708.
Fowler, R. *UFOs: Interplanetary Visitors*. Jericho, NY, Exposition Press, 1974.
Frazer, J. T, (Ed.) *The Voices of Time*. NY: George Braziller, 1966.
Fuller, J. G. *The Interrupted Journey*. New York, Dial Press, 1966.
Galindez, O. A. "Teleportation from Chascomús." *Flying Saucer Review*, Sept.-Oct. 1968, *14*, No. 5, 3-4.
Galindez, O. A. "A New Teleportation near Córdoba." *Flying Saucer Review*, May-June 1973, *19*, No. 3, 6-12.
Gordon, J. E. (Ed.) *Handbook of Clinical and Experimental Hypnosis*. NY: Macmillan, 1967.
Greeley, A. M., and McCready, W. C. " 'Mystical' Episodes Widespread," *The Denver Post*, Feb. 28, 1975, 5BB-6BB.
Greenwald, H. "Forgotten Visit to a Flying Saucer." *Saturday Review*, Dec. 31, 1966, 22-23.
Haley, J. (Ed.) *Advanced Techniques of Hypnosis and Therapy*. New York, Grune and Stratton, 1968. (Papers by M. H. Erickson).
Hall, R. L. Statement of Dr. Robert L. Hall. In Roush, J. E. (Ed.) *Symposium on Unidentified Flying Objects*. Hearings before the Committee on Science and Astronautics, U.S. House of Representatives, 90th Congress, 2nd Session, July 29, 1968. (No. 7). Pp. 100-112.
Hanzel, C. E. M. *ESP: A Scientific Evaluation*. NY: Charles Scribner's Sons, 1966.
Hartmann, W. K. "Process of Perception, Conception, and Reporting." In Condon, E. U., and Gillmor, D. S. (Eds.) *Scientific Study of Unidentified Flying Objects*. NY: Bantam Books, 1969, Pp. 567-590.
Head, J., and Cranston, S. L. (Eds.) *Reincarnation in World Thought*. NY: Julian Press, 1967.

Hilgard, E. R. *Hypnotic Susceptibility.* NY: Harcourt, Brace, and World, 1965.

Hilgard, Josephine. *Personality and Hypnosis.* Chicago, University of Chicago Press, 1970.

Hobana, I., and Weverbergh, J. *UFOs From Behind the Iron Curtain.* NY: Bantam Books, 1975.

Hugill, Joanna. "A Tube of Light," *Flying Saucer Review,* July-Aug. 1968, *14,* No. 4, 15-16.

Hynek, J. A. "The Condon Report and UFOs," *Bulletin of the Atomic Scientists.* April 1969, *25,* No. 4, 39-42.

Hynek, J. A. "Twenty-one Years of UFO Reports—2," *Flying Saucer Review,* Mar.-Apr. 1970, *16,* No. 2, 6-8, 22.

Hynek, J. A. *The UFO Experience: a scientific inquiry.* Chicago, Henry Regnery, 1972.

Interplanetary Center, 27328 Cranford Court, Dearborn Heights, MI 48127, USA Earth! (Now disbanded, founded by Mrs. Laura Mundo) (For further information: *The Mundo Monitor,* 23084 Brookfront Road, Novi, MI 48050.)

Jacobs, D. M. *The UFO Controversy in America.* Bloomington, IN: Indiana University Press, 1975.

Journal of the American Society for Psychical Research. (ASPR) 5 West 73rd Street, New York, N.Y. 10023.

Journal of Parapsychology. (Parapsychological Association) College Station, Durham, NC (27708): Parapsychology Press.

Jung, C. G. *Flying Saucers.* NY, Harcourt, Brace, and Co., 1959.

Keel, J. A. *The Mothman Prophecies.* NY, Saturday Review Press (E. P. Dutton), 1975.

Keel, J. A. "A New Approach to UFO Witnesses," *Flying Saucer Review,* May-June 1968, *14,* No. 3, 23-24. (b)

Keel, J. A. "Review of the Final Report of Dr. Edward U. Condon," *Flying Saucer Review,* Mar.-Apr. 1969, *15,* No. 2, 31-32 and iii-iv. (a)

Keel, J. A. "An Unusual Contact Claim from Ohio," *Flying Saucer Review,* Jan.-Feb. 1968, *14,* No. 1, 25-26. (a)

Keel, J. A. *UFOs: Operation Trojan Horse.* NY, G. P. Putnam's Sons, 1970.

Keel, J. A. "The Time Factor," *Flying Saucer Review,* May-June 1969, *15,* No. 3, 9-13. (b)

Keyhoe, D. E. "*Aliens From Space... the real story of unidentified flying objects,*" Garden City, NY, Doubleday, 1973.

Klass, P. J. *UFOs Explained.* NY, Random House, 1974.

Koestler, A. *The Roots of Coincidence.* NY, Random House, 1972.

Krippner, S., and Rubin, D. *Galaxies of Life.* NY, Gordon and Breach, 1973.

Kroger, W. S. *Clinical and Experimental Hypnosis.* Philadelphia, Lippincott, 1963.

LeCron, L. M. (Ed.) *Experimental Hypnosis.* NY, Macmillan, 1952.

LeCron, L. M. *Self-hypnotism.* Englewood Cliffs, NJ, Prentice-Hall, 1964. (Signet Book, 1970).

Lee, Aldora. "Public Attitudes Toward UFO Phenomena," In Condon, E. U., and Gillmor, D. S. (Eds.) *Scientific Study of Unidentified Flying Objects.* NY, Bantam Books (YZ 4747), 1969. Pp. 209-243.

Lemaître, J. "The Parallel Universe Myth," *Flying Saucer Review,* Nov.-Dec. 1969, *15,* No. 6, 22-24.

LeShan, L. *The Medium, the Vystic, and the Physicist.* NY, Viking Press, 1974.

LeShan, L. *Toward a General Theory of the Paranormal.* 29 West 57th Street, New York, NY 10019, Parapsychology Foundation, 1969.

Lindsey, H. *The Late Great Planet Earth.* NY, Bantam Books, 1970.

Logarde, F. "The Other Side of the Coin." *Flying Saucer Review,* April 1975, *20,* No. 6, 26.

Lorenzen, Coral E. *Flying Saucers: the startling evidence of the invasion from outer space.* NY, Signet, 1966.

Lorenzen, Coral, and Lorenzen, L. J. *UFO: the whole story.* NY, Signet, 1969.

Lorenzen, L. J., and Coral E. *Flying Saucer Occupants.* NY, Signet, 1967.

Mackay, E. A. I. "UFO Entities: Occult and Physical," *Flying Saucer Review,* Mar.-Apr. 1973, *19,* No. 2, 26-29.

Mackay, I. "UFOs and the Occult—2," *Flying Saucer Review,* Sept.-Oct. 1970, *16,* No. 5, 24-26.

Markowitz, W. "The Physics and Metaphysics of Unidentified Flying Objects," *Science,* 1967, *157,* 1274-1279.

McCampbell, J. M. *UFOLOGY: new insights from science and common sense.* Belmont, CA, Jaymac Co., 1973.

McConnell, K. A. "ESP and Credibility in Science," *American Psychologist.* 1969, *24,* No. 5, 531-538.

McDonald, J. E. *A Very Credible Effort?* Presented to the

Sacramento Section, American Institute of Aeronautics and Astronautics, May 28, 1969.

Menzel, D. H., and Boyd, Lyle G. *The World of Flying Saucers.* Garden City, NY, Doubleday, 1963.

Michel, A. *Flying Saucers and the Straight Line Mystery.* NY, Criterion Books, 1958.

Michel, A. "The Strange Case of Dr. X," *UFO Percipients,* Special Edition, No. 3, *Flying Saucer Review,* Aug. 1969, 3-16.

Michel, A. "The Strange Case of Dr. 'X'. Part 2," *Flying Saucer Review,* Nov.-Dec. 1971, *17,* No. 6, 3-9.

Michel, A. "The UFOs and History: Reflections On a Programme of Possible Research," *Flying Saucer Review,* May-June 1972, *18,* No. 3, 3.

MMPI. Hathaway, S. R., and McKinley, J. C. *Minnesota Multiphasic Personality Inventory Manual.* NY, Psychological Corporation, 1967.

Moss, Thelma. *The Probability of the Impossible.* Los Angeles, J. P. Tarcher, 1974.

Munroe, R. A. *Journeys Out of the Body.* Garden City, NY, Doubleday, 1971.

MUFON. Mutual UFO Network, 103 Oldtowne Road, Sequin, TX 78155.

Murphy, G. *Challenge of Psychical Research: A Primer of Parapsychology.* NY, Harper and Brothers, 1961.

Murphy, G. "Psychology in the Year 2000." *American Psychologist,* 1969, *24,* No. 5, 523-530.

Nada-Yolanda. *Visitors from Other Planets.* Miami, FL, Mark-Age Meta Center, Inc., 1974.

NICAP, *The UFO Investigator.* National Investigations Committee on Aerial Phenomena, 3536 University Boulevard West, Suite 23, Kensington, MD 20795.

Norman, E. *Gods, Demons, and UFOs.* NY, Lancer Books, 1970.

Oliver, B. M. (Co-director). *Project Cyclops: a design study of a system for detecting extraterrestrial life.* Prepared under Stanford/NASA/Ames Research Center, Moffett Field, CA 94035. (1975).

Parapsychology Review. (Parapsychology Foundation) 29 West 57th Street, New York, NY 10019.

Persinger, M. A. *The Paranormal: Part II, Mechanisms and models.* 655 Madison Avenue, New York, NY 10021: MSS Information Corp., 1974.

Psychic. P. O. Box 26289, San Francisco, CA 94126.

Puharich, A. *URI: a Journal of the Mystery of Uri Geller.* Garden City, NY, Anchor Press (Doubleday), 1974.

Rao, K. R. *Experimental Parapsychology: A Review and Interpretation.* Springfield, IL, Charles C. Thomas, 1966.

Rhine, J. B., and Pratt, J. G. *Parapsychology: Frontier Science of the Mind.* (Revised 2nd printing) Springfield, IL, Charles C. Thomas, 1962.

Rhine, Louisa. *Hidden Channels of the Mind.* NY, William Sloan Associates, 1961.

Rhine, M. W. "Psychological Aspects of UFO Reports," In Condon, E. U., and Gillmor, D. S. (Eds.) *Scientific Study of Unidentified Flying Objects.* NY, Bantam Books, 1969. Pp. 590-598.

Rimmer, J. A. "The UFO As An Anti-Scientific Symbol," *Merseyside UFO Bulletin,* July-Aug. 1969, *2,* No. 4, 41-43.

Romaniuk, P. "Rejuvenation Follows Close Encounter With UFO," *Flying Saucer Review,* July-Aug. 1973, *19,* No. 4, 10-14.

Romaniuk, P. "The Extraordinary Case of Rejuvenation," *Flying Saucer Review,* Sept.-Oct. 1973, *19,* No. 5, 14-15.

Rosenthal, R. *Experimenter Effects in Behavioral Research.* NY, Appleton-Century-Crofts, 1966.

Roush, J. E. (Ed.) *Symposium on Unidentified Flying Objects.* Hearings before the Committee on Science and Astronautics, U.S. House of Representatives, 90th Congress, 2nd Session, July 29, 1968. (No. 7). Clearing House for Federal Scientific and Technical Information. 5285 Port Royal Road, Springfield, VA 22151. (PB 17941, $3.00).

Sable, M. H. *UFO Guide: 1947-1967.* Rainbow Press Co., P. O. Box 937, Beverly Hills, CA 90312, 1967.

Sagan, C. (Ed.) *Communication With Extraterrestrial Intelligence.* Cambridge, MA, The MIT Press, 1973. (a).

Sagan, C. *Cosmic Connection: an extraordinary perspective.* Garden City, NY, Anchor Press (Doubleday), 1973. (b)

Salisbury, F. B. "The Scientist and the UFO," *Bio-Science,* Jan. 1967, 15-24.

Salisbury, F. B. *The Utah UFO Display: A Biologist's Report.* Old Greenwich, CN, The Devin Adair Co., 1974.

Sanderson, I. *Uninvited Visitors: A Biologist Looks at UFOs.* NY, A Cowles Book, 1967.

Saunders, D. R. "Studies of UFO Attitudes," *Perceptual and Motor Skills,* 1968, *27,* 1207-1218, and 1219-1239.

Saunders, D. R., and Harkins, R. R. *UFOs? YES!: Where the Condon Committee Went Wrong*. NY, Signet Books, 1968.

Saunders, D. R., and Van Arsdale, P. "Points of View About UFOs: A Multi-Dimensional Scale," *Perceptual and Motor Skills*, 1968, *27*, 1207-1208.

Schmeidler, Gertrude (Ed.) *Extrasensory Perception*. NY, Atherton Press, 1969.

Schonherr, L. "UFOs and the Fourth Dimension," *Flying Saucer Review*, Nov.-Dec. 1968, *14*, No. 6, 12-13, 15.

Schwarz, B. E. "Stella Lansing's Clocklike UFO Patterns," *Flying Saucer Review*, Part 1, Jan. 1975, *20*, No. 4, 3-9; Part 2, Mar. 1975, *20*, No. 5, 20-27; Part 3, April 1975, *20*, No. 6, 18-22.

Schwarz, B. E. "Stella Lansing's UFO Motion Picture," *Flying Saucer Review*, Jan.-Feb. 1972, *18*, No. 1, 3-12, 19.

Schwarz, B. E. "UFOs: Delusion or dilemma?" *Medical Times*, Oct. 1968, *96*, No. 10, 967-981.

Schwarz, B. E. "Woodstock UFO Festival, 1966—2," *Flying Saucer Review*, Mar.-Apr. 1973, *19*, No. 2, 18-23.

Shepard, R. N. "Some psychologically oriented techniques for the scientific investigation of unidentified aerial phenomena." In Roush, J. E. (Ed.) *Symposium on Unidentified Flying Objects*. Hearings before the Committee on Science and Astronautics, U.S. House of Representatives; 90th Congress, 2nd Session, July 29, 1968. (No. 7). Clearing House for Federal Scientific and Technical Information, 5285 Port Royal Road, Springfield, VA 22151. (PB 179541, $3.00) Pp. 223-235.

Simon, B. *Personal Communications*. Jan. 16, 1967, and Jan. 31, 1967.

Simonsen, W. S. "An Invisible Speaking UFO?" *Flying Saucer Review*, May-June 1968, *14*, No. 3, 27.

Singer, J. L. "Navigating the Stream of Consciousness: Research in Daydreaming and Related Inner Experience," *American Psychologist*, 1975, *30*, 7, 727-738.

16 PF. Cattell, R. B., and Eber, H. W. *Manual for the Sixteen Personality Factor Questionnaire*. Champaign, IL, Institute for Personality and Ability Testing, 1962.

Smythies, J. R. (Ed.) *Science and ESP*. NY, Humanities Press, 1967.

Sprinkle, R. L. "Psychological Implications in the Investigation of UFO Reports" In Lorenzen, L. J., and Coral E. *Flying Saucer Occupants*. NY, Signet Book, 1967. Pp. 160-168.

Sprinkle, R. L. "Personal and Scientific Attitudes: A Study of Persons Interested in UFO Reports." In "Beyond Condon," Special Issue, No. 2, *Flying Saucer Review*, June 1969. Pp. 6-10. (a)

Sprinkle, R. L. "Some Uses of Hypnosis in UFO Research." In "UFO Percipients," Special Issue, No. 3, *Flying Saucer Review*, Sept. 1969, 17-19. (b)

Sprinkle, R. L. "UFO Research: Problem or Predicament?" *Proceedings of the MUFON Symposium*, Des Moines, IA, July 1975. Pp. 37-49.

Stanford, R. *Fatima Prophecy: Days of Darkness, Promise of Light*. Box 5310, Austin, TX. Association for the Understanding of Man, 1972.

Steiger, B. *The Divine Fire: Revelation*. (An investigation of men and women who claim to be in spiritual communication with a higher intelligence.) Englewood Cliffs, NJ, Prentice-Hall, 1973.

Steiger, B. *Mysteries of Time and Space*. Englewood Cliffs, NJ, Prentice-Hall, 1974.

Stevenson, I. *Twenty Cases Suggestive of Reincarnation*. NY, American Society for Psychical Research, 1966.

SVIB. Strong, E. K., Jr. (Revised by Campbell, D. P.) *Strong Vocational Interest Blank*. Stanford, CA, Stanford University Press, 1966.

Sullivan, W. *We Are Not Alone: The Search for Intelligent Life on Other Worlds*. NY, McGraw-Hill, 1964.

Swann, I. *To Kiss Earth Goodbye*. NY, Hawthorn, 1975.

Tart, C. *Altered States of Consciousness*. NY, John Wiley and Sons, 1969.

Thomas, C. *The Adam and Eve Story*. Los Angeles, CA, Emerson House, 1965.

Thomas, Jane. "The Contactee of Tres Arroyos: Some Thoughts," *Flying Saucer Review*, Sept.-Oct. 1973, *19*, No. 5, 16, 21.

Urantia Foundation (Eds.) *The Urantia Book*. Chicago, IL, Urantia Foundation, 1955.

Vallee, J. *Passport to Magonia*. Chicago, Henry Regnery, 1969.

Vallee, J. "UFOs: the psychic component." *Psychic*, Jan.-Feb. 1974, *5*, No. 3, 12-17.

Vallee, J. "The Pattern Behind the UFO Landings." In "The Humanoids," Special Issue, No. 1, *Flying Saucer Review*, Oct.-Nov. 1966, 8-27.

Vallee, J. *Anatomy of a Phenomenon*. NY, Ace Books, 1965.

Vallee, J., and Janine. *Challenge to Science*. NY, Ace Star Books, 1966.

Vasiliev. L. L. *Experiments in Mental Suggestion*. Translated and published by the Institute for the Study of Mental Images, Church Crookham, Hampshire, England, 1963.

Vaughan, A. *Patterns of Prophecy*. NY, Hawthorn, 1973.

Von Däniken, E. *Gods from Outer Space.* NY, Bantam Books, 1968.

Wannall, W. L. *Wheels Within Wheels and Points Beyond.* LITRONICS (3702-A Waialae Avenue, Honolulu, HI 96816), 1963.

Webb, W. N. "An Analysis of the Fish Model." *APRO Bulletin,* Sept.-Oct. 1974, *23,* No. 2, 8-9; Nov.-Dec. 1974, *23,* No. 3, 3-7.

Weitzenhoffer, A. *Hypnotism.* NY. Science Editors (John Wiley), 1963.

Wertheimer, M. "Perceptual problems." In Condon, E. U., and Gillmor, D. S. (Eds.) *Scientific Study of Unidentified Flying Objects.* NY, Bantam Books (YZ 4747), 1969. Pp. 559-567.

White, Rhea A., and Dale, Laura A. (Eds.) *Parapsychology: Sources of Information.* Metuchen, NJ, Scarecrow Press, 1973.

Wilson, G. C. *The Final Solution to the UFO Problem.* Unpublished manuscript, June 3, 1971.

CHAPTER XVI

Are They Infallible?

One of the most frequently asked and derisive questions from the skeptics is: "If they're real machines why hasn't one of them crashed?" The insinuation is that even if the UFOs are real and interplanetary they must, like earth aircraft, occasionally suffer a mechanical failure of some kind which would force them to the earth. Actually, one would expect a technology which can span space to have perfected both its spacecraft and aircraft to a point of nearly zero failure factor.

There is, in fact, a good indication that on several occasions some of the UFOs have been forced to land to effect repairs. But considering the number of UFO reports on file, and the probability that there are millions of unreported sightings, there has been a tidy number of UFO fly-overs in the atmosphere of this planet without mishap. And, in looking at the following cases, we can show that although man has yet to capture and retrieve a (supposedly) crashed UFO, "they" do have their problems.

In chronological order, we begin with the now famous Ubatuba, Brazil, magnesium fragments which were retrieved by a fisherman when a small disc dived toward the sea, pulled up abruptly, then exploded into hundreds or perhaps thousands of tiny fragments. Those which were retrieved and eventually reached the hands of Dr. Fontes, APRO's Brazilian representative, were tested, and found to be an unusually pure grade of magnesium. The finder of the fragments definitely stated that it appeared that the object was going to crash into the sea and seemed to have been out of control. The complete case, along with test results, was contained in our 1966 book, *Flying Saucers—the Startling Evidence of the Invasion from Outer Space* (Signet, T-3058, New American Library, 1966). We mention it here only to illustrate the point, and the entire report is too lengthy to include.

Another case, which took place two years later at the Anglican mission at Boinai, New Guinea, followed a series of sightings by natives, medical personnel, and mission helpers on June 21, 1959. Again, this is a lengthy report but the general gist is important to this correlation.

On Friday, June 26 at 6:45 P.M. a bright light came in from the northwest and at 6:50 Father William Gill called others to observe the object which was approaching rapidly. At 6:55 an object on top of the disc-shaped thing began to move and what appeared to be three glowing men began moving about on top of the craft; then they disappeared from sight. At seven o'clock two of the men appeared again, only to disappear at 7:04. Gill said that at 7:10 a cloud ceiling covered the sky at about 2,000 feet. Four men showed up at 7:10, then a thin, blue, electric spotlight appeared and the men disappeared again. Two minutes later two of the human-appearing creatures reappeared in the blue light. At 7:20 the spotlight and the men disappeared again and the craft entered a cloud. At 8:20 the same or another object appeared and Father Gill called to others as the object appeared to approach; it was not as large as the first object but it seemed closer. During the next hour and a half no less than four separate objects were seen approaching the Mission, coming in and out of the clouds, all apparently proceeding in an orderly fashion. One was the large, manned craft with elaborate superstructure, the others were smaller, disc-shaped, with no apparent protuberances.

The sighting on Saturday, June 27, proved to be the most important of the Boinai sequence of reports. At 6:00 P.M. a large object was sighted by one of the mission workers, and he called Father Gill who in turn called other personnel outdoors to observe the craft. After sundown there was sufficient light so that the observers could clearly see four men who appeared shortly after the object was spotted. Two of the smaller objects were hovering near—one was overhead and the other one above the hills to the west. On the larger object two of the figures were bending over and raising their arms as though adjusting or setting up something which was not visible to the witnesses below.

Father Gill impulsively raised his arm and waved in the direction of the object. To his surprise one of the figures reciprocated. Then Ananias, one of the native mission workers, raised both arms and waved them above his head, whereupon the two figures on the craft did likewise. Both Father Gill and Ananias continued to wave and all four of the figures appeared to return their salutation.

By then darkness had begun to close in and Gill sent another native, Eric Kodawara, for a flashlight. With it he directed a series of long dashes toward the UFO and after a minute or two the object made several wavering motions back and forth. They continued to send light flashes and to wave, and the object seemed to grow larger as though approaching the group on the ground. After about half a minute the object ceased the approach and came no closer. Two or three minutes later they apparently lost interest in the party on the ground. They went back to work at what they had been doing and then shortly disappeared "below deck."

At about 6:25 two figures reappeared and appeared, to carry on what they had been engaged in before, and the blue spotlight came on twice in succession for just a few seconds. During this time the other, smaller UFOs remained stationary at high altitude. At 6:30 Father Gill and the others went in to dinner and when they came out again at seven o'clock the large object was still visible but seemed to be a considerable distance away. Father Gill then left to attend evensong and when he returned at 7:45 the sky was overcast and visibility was severely limited and the UFOs had apparently gone.

At this juncture we must deal with the treatment of the case afforded by Philip J. Klass (*UFOs Explained*), Random House, 1974. Very carefully, by questioning Father Gill's judgment in leaving the UFO to attend first dinner, then church services, and by comparing his behavior with what he, Philip Klass, would have done under the same circumstances, he insinuates that the whole thing was a hoax. But he does not prove a thing by this sort of tactic. We recently discussed the reverend's behavior with a native Australian who is well versed in the tradition of the Anglican church. She pointed out that the Anglican priesthood is extremely tradition-bound and that the priests are very self-controlled and adhere to the rules. It was Reverend Gill's duty to go to dinner as he would on any night, and to evensong as well. After all, there was no emergency; the short-lived social contact with the airborne strangers was over and they obviously wanted to get back to their business and had no further interest in the group below them. Also, food was ready in the dining hall and like any other normal human beings Father Gill and his flock were hungry. Quite simple and nothing strange about that behavior at all.

We go now, briefly, to the Socorro landing incident of April 24, 1964. This is another case in which it is quite likely that the craft landed at the place and time that it did in order to effect some minor repair. Certainly there was nothing of interest in that wash other than some scrub chaparral and cacti. Unfortunately we can only guess in most of these instances but this speculation fits the Socorro incident as well as any other. According to Lonnie Zamora, the figures seemed to be surprised to see him come upon the scene when he first viewed them, and by the time he reached the top of the mesa in a position from which he could observe them, the two figures were gone. The apparatus immediately took to the air with a loud roar (something which is not often associated with UFOs, by the way—their audible sound usually is described as a high-pitched whine or a buzzing sound).

Another, most impressive, two-witness acount of what surely was an emergency landing, during which some sort of repair took place, became public only recently and a full account is needed to get the flavor of the report. It first appeared in the Volume 20, No. 2 issue of the British publication *Flying Saucer Review*. The investigation was ably carried out by Mr. Ted Bloecher, a New York investigator and researcher of much experience and dedication. The report is detailed and very revealing. To wit: On the morning of November 25, 1964, Mrs. Mary Merryweather (a pseudonym) and her mother-in-law watched the landing of two strange crafts and what appeared to be repair of same by several humanoids.

Mrs. Merryweather's husband and father-in-law had gone hunting so Mrs. M was staying with her mother-in-law so that she would not be alone in the rural home north of New Berlin, New York. At about 12:30 A.M., Mrs. M discovered she couldn't sleep so she turned on the television. An old movie she had seen several times before was being shown so she turned the set off and got a glass of ginger ale and decided to have a look outside.

It was a cold but clear night and Mrs. M went back to get a coat. After she returned to the outdoors she saw a "falling star," and then another one; but the second one, instead of arcing along the horizon, came straight down, and leveled off. She described it as an unusually bright light of a brightness and intensity which she had never seen before, even brighter than a mercury vapor lamp. Also, she began to hear a low, humming sound which she compared to a water pump which is running laboriously. The pitch did not change. Shortly, her mother-in-law got up to use the bathroom, and when she came through the living room to go back to bed, Mrs. M called to her to come and look.

At this point a car came along the road between her and the creek bed where the object was traveling. This car went on, but a second car which followed it about a minute and a half later slowed down and pulled off onto the shoulder of the road. At this time the light also slowed practically to a stop, then it stopped, hovered for a moment, then started back toward Mrs. M's position past the car, and at the same time the car took off down the road at high speed.

When the object started back in the direction of Mrs. M, the mother-in-law had come to the door, opened it, and was about to step out but upon seeing the object's motion she stepped back in, then urged Mary to come in also. Mary, until that time, had been standing on a rise in the middle of the driveway, but although she didn't go back inside, she did retreat to the porch. At this time, she estimated, the object had come to a stop at a point several hundred feet across the road from the house and hovered there. Mrs. M said she felt as though she was being observed. She then tried to persuade her husband's English Springer to come out, but the dog, who ordinarily would have been outside at that time, refused to come out. The dog stayed close to the mother-in-law's legs and shivered.

At this point another car came along the road and slowed down and the lighted object started to go along the road at the same speed. The people in the car appeared to have become frightened because they speeded up and left the area. The object then traveled along the creek bed, up the side of the mountain about 3,800 feet distant (according to the topographical map), then settled just below the ridge of the hill. The droning sound was no longer in evidence and the mother-in-law again urged Mrs. M to come in, but she refused and asked for the binoculars which were shortly produced.

After she got the binoculars, the mother-in-law went back into the house, then called to Mary saying that there was a better view out of the corner dining room window and she was worried that Mary was getting cold. She was, so she re-entered the house and went to the window designated. At this point it was about 1:00 A.M.

When she lifted the binoculars to her face and looked through them, she discerned movement at the base of the object, which lighted up the ground below. She said she couldn't tell the shape of the object, except that the "men" (who were tall—6½ to 8 feet), when moving around the object, gave the appearance of going around a round object. The object was hovering or supported by legs, for the men could crawl around underneath and would lie down on the ground much like a mechanic does when working on a car, although they had much more room. The "men" brought large boxes—at least two, and perhaps three—large enough so that it took two men to carry them. Mrs. M passed the binoculars to her mother-in-law, who also observed the men, but passed the glasses back to her because she didn't want to watch them, asking her to watch and tell her what she saw.

The "men" were dressed in something like a diver's wet suit

which was a darker color than their skin. She based their height on the sizes of bushes she could see in the lower portion of the field on the hillside.

There were at least five "men" in all and the only time she could see them clearly was when they were on the side of the object close to where the light shone on them. They went in under the vehicle and took something from the center of the vehicle and laid it down gently with their hands. Sometime before the thing was removed and the "work" started on the vehicle, the mother-in-law called to her that there was another object coming. Mrs. M took the glasses away from her face and could see that another object was coming in from the west southwest, going east northeast and settled down on the crest of the ridge just above the place where the first vehicle had landed.

Four or five more "men" went over to where the first group was working and joined them in their efforts. She could see some of the men standing together down the hill a little way and they appeared to be cutting cable, which was dark in color, and she could see it falling in an arc or loop as they worked with it. They appeared to be cutting it in exact lengths and working quite hard at it.

The thing that was taken from the center of the vehicle was left on the ground under the place where it was dislodged, Mrs. M said. At the time that they left it there and went to work on it, her mother-in-law informed her that the time was 1:15 A.M. The men would kneel, sit, half lie down, leaning on an elbow or walking around. In all, she estimated that there were between ten and twelve "men" involved in this endeavor. She was able to observe the "men" only with the binoculars—without them she could only see the two lights from the two objects resting on the hill. The light situated at the higher elevation on the hill was not as large as the other.

Mrs. M's mother-in-law decided to stay up because she said she couldn't sleep anyway until they left and also she didn't want to leave Mary alone. Also, the dog was terribly frightened. Mrs. M said she wasn't particularly frightened. They debated as to whether they should notify a governmental agency or police but decided not to. Mary felt that people would come with guns and bother them and she felt that the "men" merely wanted to get their machine fixed and leave. She also said she felt that they knew she wouldn't call anyone; that when the light had first come toward her she had the impression of being watched by many eyes.

At exactly 4:30 A.M. by the kitchen clock, the men got together in a team and raised up the object which had been on the ground and proceeded to put it up into the vehicle. One man who seemed to be the leader was gesturing with his hands as if instructing the others. They raised the thing up about 8 inches, then off at an angle; they maneuvered it but it didn't seem to fit. They tried this again and again, stopped to cut more cable and work with the mechanism. It became obvious to Mrs. Merryweather that they were hurrying and getting exasperated. It was six minutes to five when they finally got the thing fitted up into the vehicle and they seemed to be pleased.

At that point they went about picking up things, and the men from the vehicle above on the hill took their equipment up there, running as if carrying something extremely heavy. A minute later, at five minutes to five, the second vehicle left, going straight up, then shooting off in the direction from which it had come. Mrs. M said it was almost like an instantaneous disappearance. A minute later the first vehicle took off also, going up to the crest of the hill, rising a little further again, and then shooting off in the same direction as the other.

The next afternoon after Mrs. M arose, she decided to examine the area where she had seen the objects the night before. Her mother-in-law did not accompany her, as she is quite heavy and suffers from arthritis and bursitis. She had to ask a neighbor if she could go through their property to the top of the hill, not explaining why. They looked at her rather oddly, so she assumed that they hadn't seen anything.

Upon searching the hill, Mrs. M found three places where something cone-shaped and round at the bottom, very heavy, and spaced in a triangle about 15 to 20 feet to a side, had pressed into the ground. She felt that whatever had been there had been very heavy, as one of the impressions had a broken rock where something had broken it and gone down a little ways into the ground to more rock. The impressions on the bare ground were about 14 inches wide and up to 18 inches deep, and the shallowest hole was about 4 inches deep. There were two sets of these impressions, one where the first vehicle apparently had been, and the other where the second was located. They were in the form of an equilateral triangle.

As she searched the ground, Mrs. M recalled the "men" cutting the cable and went on down the hill where there was a lot of tall grass and looked there. She doesn't recall if she found the artifact that day or later when she went up there with her husband, but on the ground some 50 or 60 feet below the lowest set of impressions, she found a 3 inch piece of what looked like a cable. The outer part of it looked as if it was wrapped in dark brown paper towel, but it was nothing like our paper toweling. The inside was made up of what appeared to be very finely shredded aluminum. Aluminum will crumple, Mrs. M pointed out, but this material wouldn't crumple nor could it be creased. The inside could be removed from the paper outside and had been cut along the entire 3 inch length of the piece, but it all hung together.

Mrs. M was interviewed several times both personally and by telephone but as of Mr. Bloecher's writing (December 15, 1973), the artifact had not been found. Mrs. M said that they had meant to "put it up" so that it would not get lost but apparently it did get lost. It had practically no weight at all. This strange, cylindrical piece of material might very well have supplied some very valuable scientific clues.

One question immediately comes to mind concerning the detail observed. One APRO member raised the objection that it would not be likely that so much detail could be observed with binoculars from such a distance. During a conversation with Mr. Bloecher in July of 1975 Mrs. Lorenzen brought up this objection, but pointed out that we can observe considerable detail three-quarters of a mile from our house looking up at the foothills of the Catalina Mountains which lie just across the Rillito River from our home in Tucson, Arizona. Considering that Mrs. M said that light from the object spilled out from underneath it and illuminated the ground for from 40 to 50 feet around, it is not strange that she could make out figures moving about. She did not say that she discerned features or things of that nature but that she could see the figures, that they were humanoid in form, and she could easily observe their actions. Mr. Bloecher also rather disappointedly told us that an extensive search had not produced the artifact and it is assumed that it was accidentally thrown out.

The last apparent "repair job" took place on the night of March 13, 1975, near the small town of Mellen in northern Wisconsin. The Philip Baker family was engaged in various pastimes and occupations in and around their rural home outside of Mellen. Mr. Baker was sitting in the living room with his shoes off watching television and it was time for fifteen-year-old Jane to take the family cats out to the garage for the night. The Bakers are sure of the time—9:00 P.M., for the adventure series "Harry-O" had just started on the television.

Jane got nearly to the garage door when she heard "strange high-toned noises," and turning around, looked up at the hill to the north and saw an object apparently sitting on the road into Mellen.

The whole hill was lit up, she said, and she described the object as a silvery, disc-shaped object with a domed top which gave off a yellow-white glow. Around its midsection were located alternating red and green lights which blinked on and off.

Jane put the cats in the garage and then went back into the house to get her father. She said, "There's a thing on the hill up the road." Mr. Baker hurriedly put on his shoes and they both went outside to look at it. At this point the glow was subsiding and the flashing red and green lights were no longer in evidence. There was no noise at this time but there was a square lighted area with rounded corners in the middle of the object. This area, which appeared to be an opening, had the same yellow-white glow that the top of the object had had earlier when Jane viewed it alone.

The two then walked to a position beyond the garage where they were able to hear a metal-on-metal banging sound coming from the direction of the object. Partly because it was cold, and partly because Mr. Baker wanted to call authorities, the two went back into the house and he made a telephone call to the under-sheriff. While he was talking on the phone they heard a loud boom and when Jane looked out again the object was gone.

When Jane initially came into the house to get her father she pointed out the object to Mrs. Baker as well as three other members of the family, eleven-year-old Jeff, twelve-year-old John and sixteen-year-old Montgomery, so that they also viewed the object.

The next morning Jane went outside to see if she could find any traces from the previous night. She looked over toward the swamp near her home and saw the same or a similar object again—only this time there were no flashing lights or glow. The shape and color were the same, however, and it was hovering over some evergreen trees. She went back into the house to put on heavier clothing and when she came back outside she brought the family dog with her. She was starting toward the evergreens when the dog gave a big yelp and started to whine and paw at her ears, and then became completely still. Jane said that she could hear nothing and carried the dog back into the house because it refused to move. When she came back out again the object was gone.

Later in the morning she and Monty and John walked to the spot where the object had been seen the night before. They found a round area on the road where the snow was "fluffed up." There were tire tracks over the area where a car had passed after the object had left, but there were also bicycle tracks leading up to it, then taking up again on the other side. These tracks made by one of the boys riding his bicycle the morning before. The "fluffed up" area where the object had been sitting apparently obliterated parts of the bicycle tracks.

This "fluffed-up" condition of the snow is a new phenomenon where UFO landings are concerned, and while we can easily understand how a jet of flame can burn vegetation or an antigravity propulsion system could partially dislodge bits of earth when a UFO takes off, it is hard to understand how the snow condition relates to the UFO. It did occur to us that had that really been a repair-service stop, possibly the repair/servicemen "fluffed" the snow up in order to cover their tracks and destroy any evidence of their presence there.

The New Berlin, New York, and the Mellen case seemed to be the most solid evidence that the UFOs sometimes suffer mechanical breakdown and need repair but the other cases discussed in this chapter should be considered also, and of course the Ubatuba explosion could be called the first UFO fatality on record.

We are almost sure that when this book is published we will receive a good number of letters asking "what about the crashed disc that the government has with the twelve little bodies?" etc. This was most recently publicized in the fall of 1974 but the same old story has been making the rounds since the early 1950's and to date we have yet to find any substantial evidence that such an occurrence really did take place. All of these claims have several things in common. However, in all cases the ship is a disc, the bodies are small humanoids, the crash took place in a southwestern state, and the craft and the bodies were spirited away by the U.S. Air Force to some air base where they haven't been heard from since except for the occasional rumor that somehow surfaces periodically and gets good press play.

We suggest that when the day comes that someone gets some good, solid information about such a happening it will be impossible for anyone, even the U.S. Government, to cover up the facts. Meanwhile, UFO researchers have their hands full with the never-ending flow of reports which yield sparse, hard evidence that a phenomenon does exist and deserves our attention.

CHAPTER XVII

Terror in the Night

In July 1975 two cases came to our attention, which if considered separately are extremely interesting, but when studied in tandem indicate that we at last have two occupant reports which seem to involve the identical type of entity.

Our first knowledge of what I shall call the Utah case came from Field Investigator Kevin Randle who had been contacted by Martin Singer of *Saga* magazine relative to a letter he had received from a woman in Utah. She said she thought that she and her children may have had a UFO experience, and went on to write that she remembered a strange being in her house and also had memory of going up steps into some kind of vehicle.

Randle contacted us because he needed advice on how to proceed as well as someone with expertise in hypnotic techniques. The logical person was Dr. Sprinkle who was relatively near, being located in Wyoming, but we knew that he had been on vacation; with speaking engagements and an overload at the university, we hesitated to ask him. We then called Dr. Harder and asked him if he could make the trip, which he did, and after spending two days with the witness and her children, reported back. Eventually we obtained transcripts of the hypnotic sessions as well as sketches made by the woman and her children. The information we received is bizarre but nonetheless believable. In the following description of the alleged happenings pseudonyms will be used to protect these people from the curious, the sensation-seekers, and the skeptics as well.

On October 17, 1973, at approximately 11:00 P.M. Mrs. P woke from a sound sleep with the hysterical cries of her young son ringing in her ears. He was saying that there was a "skeleton" in the house. He had been sleeping next to her on the davenport where she had fallen asleep earlier. In short order the night became a nightmare. Looking over at the bookcase where the boy was pointing she saw a strange figure, about 4 feet 8 inches tall, dressed in a phosphorescent blue suit from head to toe, and with a helmet encasing his head. Shortly, she and four of her seven children were taken aboard a craft where they were herded into a large, bright, round-shaped room.

Mrs. P was then separated from the rest and taken into another room where she was given a complete physical examination, including a gynecological examination by a strange-appearing humanoid. "He" was about 4 feet 8 inches tall, wore a bluish, phosphorescent uniform with a segmented "Sam Brown" belt which crossed his torso from the left shoulder to the right hip where a small black box was located. The creature had no ears and there was a dark skullcap affair which came down over his forehead. The "hands" were pincer-like affairs and did not function as the hands of a human do. There appeared to be a rudimentary thumb, quite small, where a human thumb joins the wrist. His feet were rounded and shaped like a "clubfoot," and Mrs. P was quite certain that he as well as the others was wearing a mask which was painted to look human. She said that the eyes, which were very large (about the size of a quarter), moved a lot and were clearly visible behind the cut-out holes of the masks. There were several of these entities and all had the same facial appearance, mask, and clothing.

Probably one of the most startling things learned about this experience was that Mrs. P said that she and her two eldest children, Barbara, twelve, and Terry, ten, were put under hypnosis by a very human-appearing individual who was of medium height, middle-aged, wore horn-rimmed glasses, and was bald on the top of his head. After the hypnosis she was able to observe events taking place around her but was completely immobilized, numb, and unable to resist.

Mrs. P is an intelligent, very strong-minded, and stable woman. Although she was frightened, her main emotion during the whole episode was that of concern about what they were doing to her children and she was extremely indignant at the treatment she was given. She repeated several times her feeling that they had no feeling for humans and she and her children were treated like animals. She is also sure that they have been doing this (capturing and examining humans) for a long time and that it is an ongoing thing. When asked why she felt this way she said that they seemed to have a system worked out and that they knew exactly what step to take next—in other words—a routine operation.

In addition to the physical examination, Mrs. P said that needles were inserted in her head and she was asked many questions and she insists that they were "taking her thoughts." There were instruments on the walls which were lighted and blinked on and off, she said.

The youngsters did not respond to hypnosis by Dr. Harder too well, seeming to be resistant because what had happened to them was so frightening or repugnant that they did not want to remember. Therefore considerable more work will have to be done on this case, but this preliminary information is included in this chapter because of its possible relationship to the other cases which we will review.

After thoroughly perusing the report on the Utah case, Mrs. Lorenzen was sure that she had seen a sketch and read a description of the same type of similar type of entity, but because of the huge volume of mail and periodicals coming into headquarters she couldn't pinpoint the source. She recalled that there had been a drawing or two accompanying the other report and seemed to recall that it was a French language periodical and began a search of the periodical files. It was finally located in No. 139 of *Lumierès Dans La Nuit* published in November 1974. When going through material which had been set aside as source material for this book she came across the same report in the Volume 20, No. 5 issue of *Flying Saucer Review*, an English publication, with translation by Gordon Creighton. It is from that article that the information was obtained.

At 8:40 P.M. on January 7, 1974, less than three months after the Utah case, Monsieur X (again identity is withheld to protect the witness) was driving from Comines to Warneton (which is located on the Franco-Belgian frontier) in his Ami 6 automobile. There had been rain earlier and the road surface was wet, but the sky was clear with stars, and there was no wind. The moon was nearly full (it was full the next night). Mr. X was traveling at a moderate speed of 60 to 70 kilometers per hour (37 to 44 miles per hour) and his car radio-cassette player was on.

Suddenly the car's headlights went out and almost simultaneously, after a few misfires, the car's engine cut out, and the radio as well. Surprised, X put the car into neutral gear and the car coasted for about 100 meters (330 feet). He was on a slight downhill grade. Being a mechanic, he immediately assumed that a fuse had blown, so when the car stopped he was ready to step out and check the car over. He had his left hand on the door handle and with the other pressed down lightly on the passenger seat to aid himself in getting out. But X got no further, for turning his head slightly to the right, he could see through the front door window something about 150 meters (500 feet) away in the field bordering the road. The field stands slightly higher than the road at that particular spot. X thought at first that what he was observing was a load of hay, but then he noticed areas of orangish-white light on the object, and then perceived that it was standing on three legs. After further inspection he realized that he was not looking at hay but at an unknown object, the shape of which was reminiscent of the type of battle helmet worn by British soldiers in World War I. Then something else caught his attention....

Through the windshield he saw two figures which he first thought to be a farmer and his son as one was shorter than the other, were about 30 meters (100 feet) distant, and walking toward the car in a slow, rigid fashion. He realized they were not farmers, and they continued to proceed toward him, finally stopping about 15 meters (50 feet) away. At this distance he was able to get a better look at them and noted the following details. The smaller being was dressed in a suit with an appearance of "rings" around the torso and was wearing a round helmet on its head with a large "window" or glass area in the front. This "window" afforded a good view of the face. In its right hand the creature was holding a strange object which had the appearance of a thick ruler with a pointed, pyramidal tip. He held it much the same as one would hold a gun, and pointed it at the car.

The second entity was slightly taller than his companion who was approximately 1.20 meter to 1.30 meter (4 feet 8 to 5 feet) and walked slightly ahead of number one. The clothing of the number two "man" was different; his helmet was box-like, opaque on the sides but transparent like glass in front and revealed a very weird face. The shape of the head was much like an inverted pear, of a uniform, faintly greyish shade, with two perfectly round eyes like "marbles" which were slightly sunken in "eye sockets" resembling those of humans. There was a slight arch to the eyebrows, the nose was small and showed up only faintly, the mouth was a horizontal slit with no apparent lips. When at one moment the being opened its mouth Mr. X could see neither teeth nor tongue. The faces of the two were the same, like twins.

Inside the helmet, beneath the chin, was a small black rectangular box. The overall suit was a dull, metallic, grey in color and seemed to have been one piece, encompassing the hands and feet as well as the body. The boots that the men wore appeared heavy and pointed. Atop the cube-shaped helmet was what appeared to be a sort of tube which Mr. X thought might have been associated with a breathing device of some kind or perhaps a handle.

The suit of the number two creature was considerably different from that of number one, in that although he also had an athletic sort of build with broad shoulders and narrow hips, what looked like a row of black buttons ran from the shoulders down to the black belt which had a luminous, or phosphorescent, nearly circular spot at the point where the buckle of a belt is located. A sort of oblique "Sam Brown" strap ran from the belt to the left shoulder. The arms of both of the creatures were very long, their hands reaching down to just slightly below the knees. Mr. X pointed out that he was able to observe the face detail because a soft light inside the helmets illuminated them although it did not seem to radiate to the exterior at all. The nature of this light appeared to be the same as the lighted oval on the belt.

The two creatures began to approach even closer and shortly stopped at the ditch by the side of the road. Mr. X was sitting rooted to his seat in fear and amazement. When the two creatures had stopped, Mr. X felt a faint shock in the back part of his skull, at about the location of the cerebellum, then immediately heard (but not with his ears, he emphasizes, because all of the car doors were closed) a low-pitched, modulated sound which grew noticeably louder and louder. Just before X felt the shock on the back of his head and heard the sound, the entity with the box-shaped helmet had opened its mouth as though to speak. But Mr. X heard no sound from it at that moment and the shock at the back of the head came a few seconds later, followed by the sound. By that time the mouth had closed again.

At the beginning of the experience with the beings Mr. X had also seen a third being which seemed identical in appearance to the first entity, but this one remained close to the object in the field as though on guard duty.

During the time that Mr. X and the two beings confronted one another there on the roadway, a small object, oval in shape and shiny or luminous, fell from the left side at about the level of the belt of the entity in the box-shaped helmet, who did not appear to notice it or at least didn't seem concerned about it. (The witness remained silent about his experience for some time and it was not made known to the investigators until two and a half months later, so it was not possible to make an effort to retrieve the item which fell from the creature's belt. The farmer who owns the field had in the meantime plowed it.)

Suddenly the two beings turned their heads in a perfectly synchronized movement to their left, and appeared to look behind the witness's car. The low-pitched modulated sound stopped without any accompanying shock to the witness's head, and then in another perfectly synchronized movement the two creatures executed a half turn to their left, appearing to pivot on one leg, turned their backs on the witness, and set off at a fast pace toward the object in the field. Their movement seemed almost human, with their knees bending and legs moving normally, except for one detail—they did not seen to be hampered by the wet, muddy soil of the field. In fact, they seemed to be walking effortlessly and smoothly across hard ground.

The witness no longer remembers in what manner the beings entered the object but does recall that the legs vanished, then the object rose about 50 centimeters (20 inches) off the ground and then, after remaining stationary in that position for a few seconds, it began to climb horizontally, in a trajectory at an angle of 60 to 70°, and eventually vanished from sight.

Just as the machine was about to take off, after the tripod legs had retracted, Mr. X noticed the lights of a car approaching from behind, in his rear view mirror. Overcome by the sudden release from tension and nervousness, he rested on the steering wheel for a few minutes, wondering all the while whether he had been dreaming or having a hallucination.

When the car behind him drew up, the driver, a Belgian, got out and came over and opened the door to find X slumped over the wheel, still holding the door handle. Mr. X straightened up and the Belgian asked him, "Have they hurt you?" to which the witness replied, "Did you see them too?" The Belgian said he had, and said that his engine had faltered a few times but his lights had not failed. The Belgian then left and drove on. The witness, whose headlights and radio were now functioning again, got his engine going after several tries with the starter, and then he headed for home as fast as he could go.

The Belgian had told the witness that he would return with some friends to look for any traces of the object's presence in the field and if they found any he would see that the matter got plenty of publicity. If nothing was found they would drop the whole matter. He took the witness's address and having heard no more of the matter, Mr. X assumes that nothing was found.

Some details of the nature of the UFO follow. The estimated height of the object was 2.5 to 3 meters (7.5 to 10 feet, calculated from the ground, including the legs) and the width between 7 and 10 meters (23 to 33 feet). There were no structural details except for the bulge on the upper part of the object. The sequence of the color changes, which began when the entities started back toward it, were observed on the two surfaces as an orange-tinged white at the start of the observation. They changed from orange-white to blue to reddish (dirty garnet) to electric blue which was the last color before the take-off. X described the pulsating of the blue as similar to that of a strobe light of a police car. The variable luminosities did not diffuse themselves outward toward the exterior and the only light that actually furnished illumination to the outside came from beneath the object and appeared to come from the interior, lit up an area between the three legs of the object, and vanished upon the object's take-off.

The object did not move during the whole sighting. X estimated the duration of the sighting at about twenty minutes but could not be more certain for he had no watch and had to base his estimation on the amount of time by which he was late arriving home.

Some interesting added details follow. Although there were several houses in the area and some of the residents were watching television, none could recall if there had been television disturbance on that night. Mr. X's radio-cassette remained defective after the incident, despite the fact that it had been new and had not given any trouble prior to the experience.

Although Mr. X's story is improbable enough, the fact that a similar occurence later took place makes it all the more curious. Nearly five months later, on June 6, 1974, at the very same spot where he had had the initial encounter, X saw the entities again.

In the first experience, X had been on his way home from a business refresher course, and in the second incident it was the same way, except that Thursday, July 6, was the first day he resumed attendance at the course, having had an accident at work during February.

However, this time being summer, it was still broad daylight. He was driving along, everything apparently normal, when he saw the two beings (apparently the same two he had seen in January) standing on the edge of the road like a couple of hitchhikers. As on the first occasion the engine sputtered a bit, but there was no effect on the lights because they were not on, but the cassette player, which, despite the fact that it didn't play well, he had turned on, also fell silent. X stopped the car, pulled up level with the two beings which were so close they could have touched the car. But he made no attempt to get out of the car, being afraid to do so. Again he felt the shock, then heard the sound, which lasted perhaps two or three minutes, and the beings vanished without a sound. A few seconds later the cassette player started playing again and he had no problem restarting the car. He drove home, shaken by the experience but not nearly as much as he had been by the first one.

X did note that there was no object in the field this time. Shortly before the experience began he had been overtaken by a Ford with a Belgian registration which was about a kilometer ahead of him when the experience was over, and which did not seem to have any trouble with its engine. There was no indication that the occupants of the Ford had seen the entities either.

The joint investigation of this case was undertaken by Messrs. Bazin, Sr. and Jr., Monsieur Bigorne, and Monsieur Boidin of the Lumièrs dans la Nuit investigation network. In their report to that journal, they said that they had conducted a most thorough investigation of the witness and that his good faith could not be doubted.

The journal report goes on to say that they would make no attempt to interpret the strange case and one can scarcely blame them. We would not ordinarily attempt to interpret the events in this incident, but in the light of the details which came out of the Utah case, we feel that at least we should pose some questions in the hope that the readers might have some suggestions or some answers, as well as make suggestions of our own.

But before we go into that aspect, we feel it necessary to examine two more cases. These cases do not involve humanoids per se, but the indication is very strong that the witnesses experienced some kind of mental block about a certain period of time about which they could learn nothing.

* * *

The young man on the hospital bed stirred fitfully and mumbled. The attending nurse slipped quietly out and returned almost immediately with a doctor. Together they watched the troubled limbs struggle through the molasses of a nightmare—the face contorted with the effort. Once more he mumbled: "Jacket on the bush," then lapsed into incoherency.

The nurse pulled her attention away from the man in the bed and addressed the doctor. "Do you think he's coming out of it?"

"I hope so—he's been out for over twenty-three hours now," the doctor said. Then to the man in bed he said, "Take it easy, Irwin, you're safe and you're among friends."

Irwin opened his eyes slowly, winced at the bedside light, squinted until his eyes had adjusted to it, and surveyed the room in utter disbelief.

* * *

On February 28, 1959, PFC Gerry Irwin, returning from military leave, rolled south toward Cedar City, Utah—destination Ft.

Bliss, El Paso, Texas. As his headlights pushed back the lowering dusk he thought of his mother, brothers, and sisters. More and more they seemed like strangers. He had enjoyed his visit but the small town routine had been boring and he would be glad to be back at work.

At Cedar City he turned left (southeast on Route 14) without hesitation. Though little traveled, it afforded a convenient link between highways 91 and 89. It was a timesaving route which had become an habitual part of his returns to Ft. Bliss from Nampa, Idaho. Recalling the wild beauty of this mountain country he found himself wishing that he had been able to accomplish this leg of the trip in daylight.

Anticipating the lonely drive ahead, he checked the indicators on his dashboard just to be sure. The army had taught him to be thorough. A Nike missile technician was trained never to be slipshod—never to depend on luck.

About six miles from the turn-off Irwin was suddenly aware of a brightening of the landscape and almost at once the cause became apparent. A glowing object of indefinite shape moved into his field of vision from the right, crossing over the roadway ahead in a shallow glide path. Bringing his car to an abrupt halt at the edge of the roadway, Irwin alighted and watched the strange object continue on to his left until obscured by a nearby ridge. At the point of disappearing, light flared up brightly against the night sky, subsided and was gone.

During the next twenty minutes, Irwin debated. What had he seen? The glide path and speed were that of a landing plane—still, he had been able to discern no shape—only a glowing mass. Was it an aircraft in trouble; on fire and making a forced landing in the mountains? If so what of possible survivors? He could return to Cedar City for help but that would take time and there was no time to spare.

Jumping back into his car, Irwin turned around, pulled down the road briefly to a point which seemed to him to be opposite the "plane's" disappearance. He pulled a notebook from his pocket and wrote: "Have gone to investigate possible plane crash. Please call law enforcement officers." Tearing the page out, he placed it on the steering wheel. He pulled his army overcoat from where it had been lying on the seat beside him and put it on over the sports jacket he had been wearing while driving. There was a decided nip in the night air. He picked up the flashlight, also lying on the car seat, and started across the road. Then he stopped and looked back. Something bothered him. People don't usually investigate cars pulled off the road at night—they usually assume that a tired driver has pulled over to "catch a few winks." How would anyone find his note?

He returned to the car, rummaged through a zippered bag, and came up with a container of shoe polish. Using the dauber he printed S T O P in large letters on the side of his car, returned the shoe polish to its place, slammed the car door, and flashlight in hand, set off up the hill.

Half an hour later, a fish and game inspector found the car, read the note and drove to Cedar City to inform the sheriff. Approximately one and a half hours from the time Irwin had started up the hill, Sheriff Otto Pfief, accompanied by volunteer searchers, found him face down in the mud—unconscious. His temperature and respiration seemed normal but he did not respond to any attempt to rouse him. There was no sign of a plane or wreckage to be seen. A ground and air search conducted the following day disclosed nothing unusual.

Irwin was taken directly to the Cedar City Hospital for emergency treatment. One of the searchers drove his car into town. During the next few days as it sat unattended on a Cedar City street, the cooling system froze and the engine block cracked.

At the hospital Irwin's condition proved to be an insoluble puzzle. His unconsciousness could not be accounted for from a physical standpoint. He merely seemed to be a man who was normally asleep but could not be awakened. His condition was finally diagnosed by Dr. Broadbent as hysteria.

Meanwhile, Irwin had been identified through personal effects and his Commanding Officer at Ft. Bliss notified. Attempts to revive him were stopped and a bedside vigil established to watch for any change.

* * *

Irwin looked around the room—obviously he was in a hospital. He turned to the doctor with a troubled expression. "Were there any survivors?" he asked.

The doctor ignored his question. "How do you feel, Irwin? Do you have any pain or discomfort?"

"Not a bit," Irwin replied. "In fact, I feel fine. Were there any survivors?"

Gerry Irwin listened skeptically as he was reassured first by Dr. Broadbent and then by the sheriff that there had been no plane crash. What, then, had he seen? No one knew.

In gathering together his personal effects to depart, he turned up another mystery. His sports jacket was nowhere to be found. Hospital attendants assured him that when he was brought to the hospital he was not wearing a jacket—only an army overcoat. The searching party which found him in the mud came up with the same report—no jacket. Gerry entertained a private opinion on the matter but held his peace. Thirty dollars in bills which he had been carrying in his shirt pocket was also missing. One of the volunteer searchers had sticky fingers, he thought, and dismissed the matter. The general's plane was being flown to St. George to take him back to Ft. Bliss and there was no time to bicker. Best to forget the whole thing.

Once back at Ft. Bliss Irwin was hustled immediately to William Beaumont Army Hospital. After some preliminary questioning he was assigned to Ward 30 (known as the "psycho ward"). Here he was held four days for observation and returned to duty with a clean bill of health. Meanwhile however, his security clearance had been revoked. He was reassigned to work as a file clerk.

One evening after work several days later, SP/4C Irwin (he had received a promotion while on leave) fainted. As near as he could remember later, it was not brought on by anything specific. He was just walking in the company area near his barracks when he fainted. He had no history of fainting and he seemed to recover rapidly with no ill effects.

On March 11 he was contacted by telephone by Mrs. Lorenzen who was investigating the case for APRO. On the phone he was self-assured and rational. Yes, he was the guy. Yes, it had happened but it was over and he would like to forget it. Furthermore, said SP/4C Irwin, he was a career man, he liked his job, and didn't want to do anything to spoil it.

Mrs. Lorenzen listened sympathetically and agreed. She assured him that it was not APRO's intent to pester him but rather to document his case for the files. She quoted similar incidents to him.

Irwin had a natural curiosity and desire for learning. He made no secret of the fact that his experience had aroused his curiosity toward the general subject of UFOs. He finally agreed to meet APRO representatives at his barracks after work on Friday, March 13th. Accordingly, the Lorenzens and another member were in front of his orderly room at 3:30 P.M. The others waited in the car and Mr. Lorenzen went in to get Irwin. Irwin was not there. He had been at work that day but he was not around the barracks area. We waited an hour and then left.

Late that night Irwin was again contacted by phone. He apologized for breaking the appointment. Having received word during the day to report to the hospital, he had tried to call APRO headquarters but had received no answer. Then he recounted the events of the day in more detail. A lieutenant had questioned him at length, apparently as a result of the recent fainting incident, and made arrangements to get together soon.

On Sunday, March 15th at about 10 P.M. SP/4C Irwin was

walking down the street in downtown El Paso when he fainted. Someone called an ambulance which transported him to Southwest General Hospital for emergency treatment. At the hospital no physical reason was found for his unconscious condition. He seemed to be a man who was merely asleep but he could not be wakened. He was placed in a bed and a vigil kept to watch for any change. At about 2:00 A.M. Monday he stirred and opened his eyes. Gathering his wits he looked around and turning an anxious expression to the attendant at his bedside, he inquired softly: "Were there any survivors?"

* * *

After the initial confusion had subsided, Irwin was made to understand that he was not in Utah but in El Paso, Texas. That the date was March 16th, not February 28th. He accepted these statements with considerable skepticism for his last conscious memory consisted of hurrying up a hillside in Utah, flashlight in hand, to investigate an airplane crash. His doubts were dispersed, however, when a G.I. ambulance arrived to transport him to William Beaumont Hospital, and Ward 30. In this way he kept an appointment of which he was completely unaware, arriving several hours early besides.

* * *

They kept him thirty-two days this time. In answer to questions he was told that he was there for observation.

He was administered several tests including the Rorschach ink blot test and several dealing with word association. Capt. Valentine told him that the results of these tests indicated that he was normal and cooperative and: "Didn't seem to be holding anything back."

Then, abruptly after about thirty days of confinement, he was told: "We're going to try sodium amytal."

The drug was administered by Captain Valentine with an enlisted man assisting. Strangely enough, Irwin remembered nothing of what occurred while he was under influence of the anesthetic. When completely recovered he asked Valentine what he had found out. "It didn't work," was the doctor's terse reply. He added that Irwin could be expected to be held for observation for some time.

Two days later, again with no warning, Irwin was notified that he was to be returned to duty. In discharging him, Valentine told him that he could find no indications of any known psychological disease—that he appeared to be normal in every respect and in good health. To account for Irwin's strange experience, which now included (from the doctor's viewpoint) hallucination, hysteria, amnesia, and fainting spells, he suggested, rather ambiguously, that Irwin might have something bothering him at a sub-conscious level which was causing him to "do these things."

On this curious note SP/4C Irwin was discharged from Ward 30 of the William Beaumont Army Hospital on Friday afternoon April 17, 1959.

The next morning began a series of events of which Irwin said later, "I felt an urge to return to the location of my original experience and I proceeded to follow this urge. Although I can remember everything that happened, it all seems more like a dream than an actual memory. I just seemed to know that I was going back—I didn't know why and I didn't question it. That's why I say that it seemed like a dream. In a normal state of mind I would certainly have questioned my motives."

Boarding a Greyhound bus in El Paso sometime Saturday, Irwin arrived at Cedar City, Utah, slightly after noon on Sunday. He got off at the intersection of State route 14, walked along this road for five or six miles, then left it abruptly and walked up into the hills directly to where his jacket was hanging on a bush. In one buttonhole was a piece of paper wound tightly around the hexagonal shaft of a lead pencil. Methodically, he removed pencil and paper from the buttonhole, paper from the pencil. He took out his cigarette lighter, set the paper afire, dropped it to the ground, and watched until the flames had consumed it and expired. The last wisp of smoke floating upward seemed to jolt him back to reality.

The seriousness of the situation in which he found himself pressed upon him: SP/4C Irwin, A.W.O.L., on foot, lightly dressed, six miles from town, the pitiless spring night fast approaching, on an errand which he could not understand, much less explain.

The Utah winter had not been kind to his jacket; he dropped it on the ground near the bush where he had found it and began to search for the highway. He had walked in without hesitation, as one who knows exactly where he is going, but now he had to search for the road out. Hiking toward Cedar City he wondered why he had burned the note (for there was no doubt in his mind that it was a note) and what was the source of the strange urge that had brought him back?

How had he known where to go?

And he had other, more immediate problems.

He was A.W.O.L. (away without official leave). Should he attempt to get back to Ft. Bliss undetected? No, he decided, best get this incident on record. Maybe it would help the medics find out what was wrong with him.

At Cedar City he turned himself in to the local police and spent the night in jail. Monday morning he contacted the sheriff, Otto Pfief.

Pfief recognized Irwin and filled him in on many of the details of the original incident and little by little Irwin felt the memory of certain events return rather hastily. Irwin, however, did not remember Pfief and had to constantly remind him of this fact as Pfief referred to previous conversations and incidents.

But Pfief had an A.W.O.L. to dispose of. He consulted a local recruiting sergeant and was advised to notify Ft. Ord, California. Ft. Ord responded with two M.P.s who escorted Irwin to Ft. Ord where he was held for three days awaiting military escort from Ft. Bliss. During this period he contacted a military doctor and appointments were made to examine him and provide psychological consultation, but his Ft. Bliss escorts arrived before the appointments could be kept.

At Ft. Bliss, Irwin was called before his commanding officer for administration of company punishment under "Article 15." After hearing Irwin's story, the C.O. decided to check with Captain Valentine. Valentine ventured the opinion that Irwin was normal and therefore responsible for his actions.

Thus SP/4C Irwin once again became P.F.C. Irwin. But upon his insistence that his recent A.W.O.L. was the result of some strange compulsion, and that Valentine's opinion seemed to fluctuate, his C.O. decided to request that Irwin be examined by another doctor—just to make sure. He was sent to a psychological clinic which is located at Ft. Bliss but is not part of the William Beaumont Army Hospital. The officer in charge was Captain Nissen—a man of prompt and decisive action. He sent a P.F.C. to interview Irwin, armed with a little book full of questions. He read the questions to Gerry and noted his answers carefully on a piece of paper.

When he finished, he retired to the inner sanctum from which shortly emerged the good Captain Nissen with his duly considered diagnosis: "Quit gold-bricking, soldier, and get back to work," said he. Gerry remained a P.F.C.

We had kept track of Gerry during his thirty-two-day hospitalization by calling his orderly room periodically (non-relatives were not allowed to visit Ward 30). We were eventually able to reach him by phone and after a good deal of explaining (he did not recall our previous conversations due to the memory lapse previously mentioned) set up another appointment. We had in the meantime made arrangements with an El Paso M.D., skilled in the use of hypnosis, to treat Irwin—if he was willing, of course. We picked Gerry up at his orderly room and took him to dinner. We explained our ideas to him and he was quite receptive. Much of the story which you have read so far came out of a preliminary meeting with the doctor. Regular appointments were set up for hypnoanalysis and it looked as though everything was working out fine.

The first appointment was on a Wednesday evening after duty hours. As the date approached Gerry found himself on a barrack cleaning detail. The usual procedure in such a situation would be to "trade duty" with a buddy and this is what Gerry did—or attempted to do. He found a willing buddy and then asked the NCOIC for approval. To his surprise the sergeant began to cross-question him. Why did he need Wednesday night off? Who did he have an appointment with? Why? Before he hardly knew what was happening, he was in front of his commanding officer again.

"Listen, Irwin, you've had a good record up until now. Why spoil it? We're willing to let bygones be bygones, but you've got to toe the line. Forget about this thing and tend to business and we'll forget about it, too," the C.O. said. "If you insist on keeping things stirred up we can make it plenty rough on you—you know that. Please don't force us to do it that way."

For the next fifteen days Gerry found himself on a detail of some sort nearly every night. "They" were showing him how rough they could be if they had to. Gerry was convinced—he kept no appointments with the civilian M.D.—but he was not through stirring things up. He went to see the Inspector General.

The I.G. proved to be the most sympathetic ear that Gerry was to find in the army. He shared Gerry's feeling that he had been treated unfairly. He volunteered: "If these (Army) doctors had anything on the ball they'd be out in civilian life practicing medicine."

The last time we saw Gerry Irwin was May 30, 1959. He spent the weekend at our home in Alamogordo, New Mexico.

A memo from the I.G. had rattled down the chain of command and he was scheduled to re-enter William Beaumont Army Hospital on July 10th.

We never saw him again. He had agreed to keep us informed but we heard no more from him. Some months later we checked with his orderly room. From August 1, 1959, he had failed to report for duty. On August 30, 1959, he was dropped as a deserter.

In evaluating this case, we can fairly assume first of all that Irwin had a real experience—the twenty-three-hour period of unconsciousness seems to confirm this.

Reconstructing the incident, we can say that somewhere over that ridge he saw something which prompted him to leave another note. He removed his jacket, left the note in the buttonhole, and hung the jacket on a bush to attract the attention of eventual searchers.

Amnesia is often brought on by an experience which the subject for some reason cannot face or accept. What did Irwin see? He had climbed the ridge thinking he was investigating a plane crash; presumably the second note furnished additional information; its very existence suggests a fear on Irwin's part that he might no longer be around when help arrived. We have the distinct feeling that Gerry somehow came under some bizarre influence which caused his hysteria—and later, amnesia.

If we accept the foregoing cause for his amnesia, it would follow that the ensuing fainting spells and progressive amnesia were triggered by attempts to get at the cause of his original hysterical condition. Possibly his eventual desertion was subconsciously brought on by the continued probing of the army medics. In all fairness we must point out that Gerry's conscious attitude was quite another thing. On the conscious level he was quite anxious to find out what had happened and what was wrong with him.

Now what about the trek back to the scene of the original incident to burn the crucial note? It shouts post-hypnotic suggestion, or should we say post-amytal suggestion. Our first reaction was to suspect the army of deliberately sending Gerry back to destroy the evidence but we now feel that there are many things wrong with this idea. It's too messy and unpredictable for one thing and it's just not the army way. Under amytal, suggestion can be given inadvertently. For instance, a suggestion that he eliminate things that were bothering him if carelessly worded, could conceivably produce this result.

The army way would be to detail a group of men to search the area. We can imagine Army Intelligence resorting to post-amytal suggestion but we find that Irwin went into the truth drug session with only the doctor and a regular medic present. And only these two were present when he came out of it.

It is our opinion that the army did not take the Irwin case seriously during any phase of its development. The men in the barracks generally considered that Gerry was "bucking for a discharge." The approach of the medics seemed to be "What makes this guy tell these ridiculous stories and have these fainting spells?" It may have been this attitude that drove him eventually to desertion—or possibly further probing by the medics brought on another amnesia seizure and an excursion from which he never returned.

In a report to APRO, Dr. Olavo Fontes, special Brazilian representative to APRO, cited several cases in which children disappeared concurrently with the reporting of UFO activity in the vicinity. The children returned unharmed—in some cases days later—with no memory of what had happened in the interim.

Suppose the influence which we mentioned earlier had placed memory blocks to prevent Gerry's remembering anything of his original experience? (We propose that the note and jacket had already been placed when this happened.) And suppose that every time he began to pry at these blocks a mental mechanism was set in motion to enhance his amnesia or otherwise complicate matters to prevent a solution.

The second of the non-humanoid cases which nevertheless indicates a time-loss and possible kidnapping, was investigated by Dr. Max Berezovsky and translated by Mrs. Irene Granchi, a brilliant and dedicated instructor of English at the Cultura Inglesa in Rio de Janeiro, Brazil. Mrs. Granchi, a master of the Italian, French, German, Spanish, Portuguese, and English languages, is one of the few women who have distinguished themselves in the field of UFO research. It is because of her untiring efforts and dedication to the subject that we have the details of this report.

Onilson Patero is a Brazilian, forty-one years of age, married, with two daughters. He has completed secondary schooling and his occupation at the time of his experience was Organizer of Public Libraries for the townships in the state of Sao Paulo.

On his way home after his day's work on May 22, 1973, in his blue Opala (Chevrolet), the witness had left behind him the town of Oswaldo Cruz on his way to Sao Jose do Rio Preto. After crossing the Tiete River at a place called "Salto do Avanhanduva" (Avanhanduva Falls) he gave a lift to a young man who was standing by the police patrol station. He took him to Itajobi, 18 kilometers (11 miles) beyond Catanduva.

Driving back to Catanduva, where he resides, he was traveling at a rate of between 90 and 100 kilometers per hour (56 to 62 miles per hour). It was raining and he turned on his car radio in order to listen to Radio Record, a Sao Paulo broadcasting station.

At an upward slope of the hill, about 7 kilometers (4 3/4 miles) from the Catanduva crossing, Patero noticed a persistent fading of the radio program and he turned off the radio. Then the car's engine began coughing and missing so he shifted into second gear.

At this point a bright blue, luminous circle about 20 centimeters (6 inches) across, now appeared to the left and moved across his instrument panel, moved slowly right, turned left again, moved over the seat and suitcase lying there, the car floor, and the driver's legs. He had the distinct impression of being able to see the very engin of his car right through the instrument panel as the blue circle passed over it. At the time he wondered how the moon could cause such a strange optical effect and then remembered that it was a moonless night and the sky was overcast and it was raining.

At this point there appeared, facing Patero, close to the upward curve of the road, a kind of luminous line of the same brilliant blue as the circle, which grew brighter and brighter. Its focal point was also growing, directed at the witness. Because the Opala engine kept on missing, he shifted into first gear.

Patero first thought the "line of light" was coming from some powerful truck headlight headed toward him so he brought the car to the shoulder of the road, blinking his lights on and off to signal the oncoming vehicle. He found that was no use as the light kept growing and approaching so he finally took off his glasses, bent down onto the instrument panel protecting his head with his hands and arms, all the while hoping the "truck" would pass by.

After about a minute had passed with nothing happening the witness lifted his head and, looking up, noticed a "vehicle" hovering up above in the sky. Through the windshield he saw it at a distance of about 15 meters (50 feet) and about 10 meters (40 feet) above the road. He thought it might have been a helicopter trying to land using his lights to guide it. He also thought of his gun which he had left at home and which might have proved useful at the time. Patero was beginning to feel very hot and the lack of air in the car led him to open the door. But the heat and sensation of lack of air persisted after he stepped out into the road.

He noticed then the buzzing sound and noted that the "helicopter" had no propellor and realized that the object was a so-called "flying disc." The object had the shape of two upside-down soup plates 7 meters thick and about 10 meters (40 feet) wide. No structural details were noticed but the object was a dull, dark gray with no luminosity of its own. All around him everything he saw was brightly lit, yet he could see no specific source for this light. Also, he still suffered from the sensation of great heat and lack of air.

Something like a "transparent curtain", which seemed to issue from the right side of the object, encircled it little by little. After it completed its round Patero noticed that the heat and lack of air had vanished. The size of this "curtain" seemed to equal the "thickness" it covered. While this was happening a tube came out of the bottom of the object, stretching towards the ground. When it reached a point approximately 2 meters from the ground the thought struck Patero that the "thing" might well want to kidnap him and he began to run. He realized that if he headed for town he would have to cross under the "thing" so the wisest choice would be to run in the opposite direction and then hide in the woods.

After running for about 30 or 40 meters (100 to 130 feet) Patero noticed an odd power putting a stop to him like a brake or "rubber lasso" thrown over him. He tried to get loose from it by sweeping his hands across his back but there was nothing there.

Patero then turned around to see what it was and saw a blue, tubelike, torch of light about the size of the span of his hand coming from the underside of the brim of the UFO. It struck his car which seemed to become transparent. From where he was standing, to the right of and behind the vehicle, he said he could see the engine, seats, and every detail of the interior of his Opala. At that point he lamented the possibility that his car might be melted away and that he had several installments yet to pay on it. It was at this juncture that he fainted.

About one hour later a Volkswagen stationwagon arrived on the scene, having proceeded from Itajobi. Two young men, Valdomiro Barcoso, twenty-one, and Celso Aparecido Piu, twenty, were in the car. They saw a man lying still on the road, stretched out in the torrent of water, and a few meters away stood the Opala with its headlights on and the door on the driver's side open. Thinking there had been an assault or a murder committed there, the two drove straight on to the crossing for Catanduva where they advised the Police Patrol of what they had just seen.

The sentry on duty at the patrol station requested them to go along with him to show him where it was, and they did not reach it until about 4:50 A.M. Their information, as given to the sentry, proved correct. A Brazilian road map was found on the ground, soaked through. It was illuminated by the lights of the car, which were still burning. The map showed the northern region of Brazil. Inside the car, on the seat, lay the witness's open suitcase, its contents spread around as though it had been searched. There were several papers including checks and large photographs.

Seeing that the body lay face down and apparently without wounds, the sentry turned it over, whereupon Patero regained consciousness. He was very startled and began to fight his rescuers, apparently thinking they were kidnappers.

The sentry, who was known to Patero by sight, managed to calm him down after some time and asked him to reconstruct the events. Onilson confirmed that the map had in fact been in his suitcase, as well as the checks and papers, and it had been locked. Though the key was still in his pocket, the suitcase was inexplicably open. Nothing whatsoever was missing and the car was working too.

It was 6:45 A.M. when Patero arrived at the Padre Albino Hospital in Catanduva in a police car. Later on the Opala was removed by a member of Patero's family. He, Patero, spent the rest of that day in the hospital under the supervision of Dr. Aziz Chedieck, who not discovering any physical or psychic alteration in his patient, prescribed a sedative injection and sent him home at 7:30 P.M.

That same day, however, while lying face down in the bed, the patient started suffering from a slight itch that spread around his body from the lumbar and abdominal region. This started at 2:00 P.M. The next day, and from then on, he noticed some changes in the appearance of his skin, spreading from his abdomen and the lumbar region. They were purplish-blue spots of various sizes, irregular in contour, smooth and painless, larger in number and more visible near the buttocks and hips. Although they were painless they produced a slight itch at first. As time went by, the spots changed from purplish-blue to yellowish, the same as ordinary bruises.

At a later date the patient was directed to Sao Paulo where he underwent a complete series of medical tests.

The following is Dr. Max Berezovski's medical report.

"The patient revealed good orientation in space and time. He was well related to his surroundings and with those to whom he spoke. His replies were coherent with the questions addressed to him and no clinical complaint could be observed. The physical examination revealed nothing of an abnormal nature.

"After we had submitted him to laboratory tests to check his biochemical state of health, this was found to be normal, no disturbance being noted. The tests employed were glucose-count, potassium, sodium, urea, bilirubin, phosphorus, calcium, hemogram, coagulating-period and bloodletting.

"Nothing of any account appeared in the pathological-anatomical test of the material drawn by biopsy of the skin in the region where the spots had appeared.

"An electro-encephalogram was employed as well as two regressive hypnotic sessions and the results were good. The last revealed information regarding the period during which the patient had been unconscious."

Since the publication of the information about the Hill case (see Chapter VI) we have suspected that there may have been similar abductions before and since. After all, only thousands of UFO sightings have been reported, yet fully 5 per cent of the American population claim to have seen UFOs. If we take only a fraction of a percentage point and apply it to the kidnap-examination type case, we find there may have been possibly hundreds of such cases which have not been reported because the witnesses, having been "programmed," do not know they had an experience in the first place, or are simply afraid to report for fear of ridicule.

As the state-of-the-art of UFO research has progressed, we have learned how to deal with such offensive cases as the Hill case, the Utah report and the claims of Onilson Patero. How many other similar reports are lying dormant simply because the general public is ignorant of the facts, docilely accepting authoritative dogma which declares that UFOs are not a scientific problem and indeed, do not need to be investigated?

We have spoken of the emotionalism quite often displayed when the UFO subject is broached, but it is nothing compared to the feelings evoked when it is suggested that intelligent beings from elsewhere are here, can come and go as they please, and we can't do a thing about it.

In Chapter 10 of his book, *The UFO Experience—a Scientific Inquiry*, titled "Close Encounters of the Third Kind" (a scientific designation for sightings involving humanoids), Dr. J. Allen Hynek confesses that he has a prejudice which he "finds hard to explain." He writes about fears of competition for territory, loss of planetary hegemony, etc. What he apparently has not yet come to grips with is another, more strident fear—that we, the human race, are possibly only one civilization (if you can really call it that) among many in the universe and, technologically speaking, we are what is popularly called "low man on the totem pole."

If the Utah case is a true account of a real happening, we must face squarely the possibility that one is not safe from "them" even in one's own home. Even the fellow who'd had an experience (See Chapter IV "UFO-Car Encounters") with a UFO while driving, and swears that he'll never again drive on a lonely road at night, is taking a chance if he lives in a house at the edge of a small town as Mrs. P did.

In the case of Monsieur X—had not the car come along—what might have happened to him? Might he have been just another specimen to be observed, examined, and probed?

And what really happened to Gerry Irwin? Did he really only see something which shocked him into unconscious but voluntary amnesia? Or was he captured and subjected to mind-probing examination? What might have been learned had the army engaged a competent psychiatrist skilled in the administration of hypnotic techniques? Irwin was a Nike missile technician—what could aliens have learned about our national defense effort? Some readers may assume that the army might have pulled Irwin's security clearance because they suspected a UFO-connected experience. Not necessarily so. By military tradition a man not considered to be emotionally or mentally competent is automatically taken out of a sensitive position.

In Onilson Patero's case we have a real conundrum. Since his experience he has been a confused man and on two occasions he has unaccountably disappeared from his job and home to be found hours or days later at great distances from his point of origin. Why?

Some favor the idea that Onilson Patero actually concocted a story and that his whole alleged experience is a hoax, but then there are equally fervent defenders of his story.

In the middle of August, after a conversation with Bernard O'Connor, editor of the New York-based *Official UFO Report* magazine, he forwarded a letter which he had received from a young serviceman who claimed to have had a strange experience in the early hours of August 13, 1975. In the beginning of the letter he identified himself, his service, the location of his service base, as well as describing his job, family, and home. He made a point of the fact that prior to his experience he had never seen any type of UFO and really didn't care much about them except to "crack a joke about or make fun of someone who says they have seen a UFO."

He then went on to detail what had happened to him. He was working a late shift and upon arriving home was not tired, so he changed out of his military clothing and settled down to watch television until half past midnight. He had heard about the meteor shower (Perseid) which was supposed to be a spectacular event at 1 A.M., so he got into his car and drove out into the country to get away from the city lights. Parking his car just off a dirt road, he got out and sat on his left front fender and observed eight or nine bright meteors. Then things really got exciting.

At 1:15 A.M. a dull, metallic object "seemed to drop out of the sky" and started to hover with a wobbling motion approximately 100 feet in front of the car and 10 to 15 feet off the ground. The witness became very frightened, jumped off the fender, and got into the car and tried to start it. But, he said, it was as though there was no battery at all—it would not start, wouldn't even "turn over"—and neither the dome light nor the courtesy light came on. He was at a loss at this because his car, a late model, is kept in top-notch condition at all times.

At this point the disc had stopped dead still in the air and he observed it closely. It appeared to be approximately 50 feet in diameter and 18 to 20 feet thick at the center and was now giving off a high-pitched sound "something like a dental drill might make at high speed." Just to the right of the center of the object he saw what appeared to be an oblong-shaped window, 4 to 5 feet long and about 2 or 3 feet wide.

In describing the following the witness wrote: "Sirs, this part that I will tell you now is very hard for me to tell, so please keep an open mind. At the window there were shadows of what looked to be human forms." He said there were two or three of the forms and at this time the high-pitched sound stopped and a feeling of numbness came over his body. The fear that he had felt before left him and he felt a very peaceful calmness which he compared to "floating on a cloud." Then he saw the object lift up very fast, making no sound and glowing slightly.

The witness went on to say that the time of the sighting was 0120 hours (1:20 A.M.) and after the object left his car started with no trouble. When he drove off he looked at his watch which read 0245 (2:45 A.M.) and when he arrived home he checked again with the wall clock which read 3 A.M. He told his wife about the object but not about the time loss. That same day he sat down and wrote the long letter to Official UFO Report which was in turn forwarded to us at APRO.

We have deliberately avoided giving any information which might lead to the identification of this man. He is well aware of the treatment he might receive should he report it to authorities, and has asked us to handle his case. Because of certain physical symptoms which showed up the next day, he decided to have a complete physical. Some physical evidence of the landing at the scene of the incident was photographed for the record. In the ensuing months we will first have a polygraph examination performed, and from there will go to hypnotic trance questioning. Although it is a single witness case, added to the other information gleaned from other abduction cases it may well be a turning of the road for UFO research.

In the chapter "Speculation," we will have some suggestions as to the answers to the questions posed in this chapter.

CHAPTER XVIII

Interpretation and Evaluation

The greatest single difficulty in attempting to evaluate the reports of UFO occupants is the observer himself. Because of the individualistic nature of man his observations must be carefully studied before any headway can be made.

No two people are exactly alike—they see, smell, and hear differently. Two witnesses to one single happening invariably produce two separate and distinct descriptions of the incident observed. Similarity of description may exist but there still remains the inevitable dissimilarity.

These tendencies have to be considered in any analysis, and particular care must be taken with such a controversial and bizarre subject as the occupants of the UFOs.

Interpretation of UFO evidence, and especially that concerning the occupants, depends to a great extent on the emotional tendencies of the investigator and also the researcher. Fortunately it has not happened too often, but occasionally we have undertaken an investigation and found that various observations by the witness or witnesses have been altered or left out entirely because the interviewer unconsciously discounted some information which did not appeal to him, all the while completely unaware that he was altering the evidence.

As we have mentioned before, this omission of evidence has occurred on a large scale among some researchers who have discounted stories about occupants, and therefore either discarded or filed them without bringing them to the attention of those who were willing to deal with the *entire* problem. Whether or not the incidents described by witnesses actually took place or not, the reports exist and should be considered in that context.

Any attempt to interpret the reports of occupants of UFOs should take into consideration the possible motivations of witnesses who concoct stories. It is obvious that there are those who will manufacture a report for the sake of the attention it generates. There are also those who have legitimate psychic experiences, examples of which were cited in an earlier chapter. After eliminating these two possibilities as motivations for a given report, we must face squarely the possibility that a report is generated because an incident actually occurred.

One single factor has stood out where witnesses of occupant sightings are concerned—and that is their obvious emotional distress during and after the experience. In many instances the observer is so impressed by what was seen that he or she is greatly disturbed by it for days and even weeks afterward. Therefore, in the interpretation of such an incident, we must attempt to determine the ability of the witness to simulate emotion (in other words, act).

In the instance where emotional stress precedes a UFO experience, it can be fairly assumed that the incident may be one of psychic projection. When emotional upset follows a UFO experience, we have two possibilities: (1) that the incident was a real one and caused the upset; or (2) that the emotion is merely feigned and the incident is a hoax. The difficulty lies in differentiating between the two. Other considerations are: the witness' ability to perceive color, the characteristics which most interest him and therefore impress him, such as facial features, clothing, etc. It is a fact that different people are attracted to different things for different reasons.

Let's examine a hypothetical case. Three people observe a UFO on the ground. In the vicinity of the UFO are two human-shaped forms. During the course of the investigation we find that the three witnesses agree on those three facts: an object is seen, it is on the ground, and there are two shapes near it. There the similarity of description ends.

Witness number one recalls little about the "entities." He paid more attention to the object, and reports a cupola of transparent material, three legs, flashing lights around the circumference, and the colors of the lights.

Witness number two notices that there are two entities, that they were small, and he says they were wearing blue clothing. He recalls little about the craft except that it was there and that it was generally round and flat.

Witness number three notices the craft but thereafter pays no attention to it. He says the two entities are small, compares their size to familiar surroundings, estimates their size as about 3 feet tall. He also says they had large heads and thin bodies. Their clothing, he observes, is green.

In this hypothetical case we have all the ingredients of confusion.

It would seem, to the casual observer, that the case is not a real one because no one can agree on one specific element. The fact of the matter is, the very disagreement between the three lends credence to their report and precludes the possibility that it is a concocted story in which the three collaborated. Further probing and questioning indicate that witness number one is mechanically inclined, interested in machines of any kind, and specifically aircraft. It is natural that he noticed what he did.

Witness number two turned out to be a nervous individual who spent practically all the observation time in a state of fright. He observed little.

Witness number three, a good observer who paid close attention to detail, gave a good description of what he riveted his attention on: the "shapes."

It is these considerations of differing interest and ability to observe which must ultimately play a large part in the evaluation of the "occupant" cases, even more so than in the more mundane observations of the UFOs in the air.

Another factor to be considered, of course, is the emotional reactions of the individuals involved. An unstable person who becomes badly frightened is more likely to give a warped or inadequate description of what he sees than one who has his feelings under control.

On the other hand, even a stable person who is confronted with a very bizarre and unusual situation is likely to misinterpret what is actually visible out of fear and repugnance. He might tend to magnify certain features of the observation. There can be no doubt that even in the reports of humanoids, who closely resemble man, there is sufficent indication that they are sufficiently "different" (alien might be a better word) to arouse in the observer a kind of panic which might color his judgment and impressions.

In rare instances we may examine a report of UFO occupants which involves an observer who is sound of mind, has a stable emotional structure, an artist's eye for observation, and whose experience takes place under ideal lighting conditions. The Villas-Boas case may be one of these. This type of observation would make our task of interpretation and analysis much easier, but unfortunately reports of this type are few and far between.

The whole subject of UFOs is tinged with emotion and this is evidenced by the fact that nineteen years of reports was required before orthodox science and the general public began to face the implications of the sightings. It may take a comparable period of time before there is general acceptance of the existence of reports of occupants. That the acceptance or rejection of UFO occupant reports is emotionally inspired is demonstrated by UFO researchers themselves; the same reasoning concerning the circumstantial evidence of UFO reports which leads most UFO buffs to the conclusion that UFOs are interplanetary can be applied to the UFO occupants reports with the result that the observed humanoid occupants are real entities. However, a substantial portion of UFO researchers still reject that conclusion.

A little simple arithmetic and a big IF are quite revealing. IF the UFOs are real physical objects and not mere psychic projections, the hard core of evidence indicates that they are intelligently controlled physical objects. IF they are real and intelligently controlled, it logically follows that they are controlled by *something.*

IF the UFOs are real and intelligently controlled by something, what would the something consist of? Strange-looking, vegetable-like creatures with antennae? Or robots? If robots, some living intelligence should logically be in control of them.

IF we allow the evidence to speak for itself, we are confronted with the logical possibility that the reported observations of humanoid occupants in the vicinity of strange landed objects (which have also been seen in the air) are real.

Man is the ultimate creation among animals on earth. According to the theory of evolution his roots are in the sea and his life "began" in the sea millions of years ago. Eons were required for him to evolve from the simple sea creature he was at one time.

But, we are told, *all* life sprang from the sea, and man is the one unique animal with an upright stance and a large brain mass.

Dr. George Wald, professor of biology at Harvard University, was quoted in *The New York Times,* November 13, 1960, concerning the elements of life. He stated that life existing elsewhere in the universe is likely to be the same as life on earth. Living organisms everywhere would be constructed primarily of the same four elements: carbon, oxygen, nitrogen, and hydrogen, not because of their abundance but because of their appropriate qualities. Wald said that it was doubtful that life could arise apart from water or go very far without oxygen, nor could it thrive without access to radiation, and specifically in the wave-length range of 300 to 1100 microns which excites molecules electronically and so activates photochemical reactions.

There are certain advantages in the specific physical attributes of man. It is most advantageous for man to walk upright, have three-dimensional vision, his mouth, nose, eyes, and ears a considerable distance from the ground. An opposing thumb for grasping is important as is the arrangement of certain organs such as the anus which is located in a very convenient position considering where its contents ultimately are deposited.

The brain mass and posture of man set him apart from other animals who generally have the same number and type of organs.

In other words, man, considered only from the standpoint of the sequence of his evolutionary trend, is quite a "successful experiment."

Does it follow, then, that life elsewhere would be likely to follow the same general trends? The observable physical universe certainly demonstrates some order—stars are made up of the same general combination of elements and many have planets which in turn have satellites, indicating that the structure of our solar system is not necessarily unique.

Science, and specifically the field of astronomy, has found in the last fifty years that our planetary system is not as unique as we once thought. Once-cherished and stoutly defended theories concerning the physical makeup of planets in our solar system have been replaced by new ones based on evidence gathered by space probes. In view of the tendency of science to formulate theories and treat them as fact, it may be that there will be considerable difficulty in obtaining a scientific study and evaluation of UFO occupants, which is the next logical step.

The efforts of "amateurs" and non-academic researchers is constantly lamented while most academically qualified people refuse to study the observational data such as that presented here.

Since the spring of 1964 and the classic case at Socorro, New Mexico, even the reactionaries of UFO research in the United States have turned their attention, albeit grudgingly, to the occupants to a limited degree. Prior to that time it seemed apparent that most American UFO buffs discounted the testimony of "foreigners" concerning the reports of occupants which dated as far back as 1954, and could only be persuaded concerning their reality after the humanoids were seen in the United States.

At that time, APRO's office asked its members to redouble their efforts to collect, investigate, and submit all reports of UFO occupants to the central office for study. An incident which took place in Brazil in the fall of 1965 pointed to a startling correlation with the Masse report of July 1 of the same year. That the observers in the new case had been influenced by press reports out of France is not likely for they were fragmentary and gave little detail.

For several nights during late October and early November

1965, strange objects were seen in the sky and seemed to be reconnoitering the huge farm complex of industrialist-chemist Dario Anhaua Filho near Mogi-Guacu, Brazil. During the course of one incident, on November 11, Mrs. Filho and her grandson watched a lighted object land in an adjacent field and saw small men alight from the craft and walk around the field. The small figures picked up twigs and branches and appeared to examine a mare which was standing by the fence. They seemed unaware of their observers. Mr. Filho was in town on business and when he returned his wife told him of the event. The next day he went back into town where he contacted and invited friends, including the bank manager, to come and watch for the return of the object and its occupants.

The vigil was rewarded on the night of the 13th. As darkness settled over the countryside the object came in and landed about 400 feet from the fence separating the yard and the field. At about this time the local sheriff and a police clerk who had been driving to Catagua drove by on a highway near the farm and saw the object hovering prior to landing.

The bank manager became so excited when the craft came down that he stumbled and dropped his camera and could not find it in the dark.

The beings observed by the Filhos and the bank executive were small, about the size of seven-year-olds. One was wearing overalls, the other chocolate-colored pants and a gray collarless shirt. The third being had a squarish, flat head and was wearing what appeared to be a surgeon's apron. All three, including the ship, glowed brightly. They set about the tasks of the preceding night—uprooting plants and plucking leaves and twigs from bushes.

When the object first landed, Filho called a neighboring farm, and before the little men had departed some guards and the local parish priest, Longino Vartbinden, arrived at the farm and witnessed the tableau in the field. When the little creatures were finished with whatever they were doing, they got into the object which took off at high speed. The area apparently was not visited again.

This particular incident correlates with others in which the entities showed interest in plants and bushes, and the size of the creatures fits that of the ones reported in the Masse incident in France.

The call for reexamination of all occupant sightings brought immediate response from the late Dr. Fontes, APRO's representative for Brazil, who had been one of the few researchers to face the problem of the "little men" squarely from the beginning of their injection into the UFO puzzle. He submitted several cases which had not received widespread attention, among which is the following.

The location of this incident is Ceres, State of Goias, which is 300 miles in a straight line from Sao Francisco de Salles, the home of Antonio Villas-Boas. The date is October 10, 1957. The entities involved in this report, it will be noted, closely resemble those of the Villas-Boas case, but as Dr. Fontes pointed out, there is no possibility that one case was the cause for the other. The Ceres case was first reported in the Brazilian press on November 30 and the first letter from Villas-Boas concerning his experience to reporter Joao Martins had been received on November 15. At the time that Villas-Boas contacted Martins, no mention of his experience had been published.

On the night in question, Miguel Navarrete Fernandez, thirty-five, and a friend identified only as Guido, arrived in Ceres. Both men were obviously very frightened and shortly related their weird experience with a huge flying machine. They were initially questioned by the proprietor of the local hotel, who noticed their extreme agitation. They told their story.

Fernandez, an agent for the coffee company Exportacao e Importacao Planalto Ltda., with his friend Guido, had come to Ceres to pick up some merchandise. They went to a farm in the vicinity where they carried out the business, loading merchandise into the truck. They then headed back to Ceres at 6:00 P.M. The trip was uneventful until about 8:00 P.M. when they were in an area called "Quebra Coco." Guido called the attention of Fernandez to a brilliant light ahead. Fernandez thought it was the lights of another truck and said so.

It was soon obvious that the light was not that of a truck, for the light took shape—resembling the "body of a helicopter"—and was very large. It was not on the road as they thought, but was moving above the ground. Their truck moved under it; then the object, now behind them, made a turn, came back, and hovered about 150 feet in the air ahead of them. About two minutes later, it began to move toward them. Guido, very upset, lost control of the truck and it ran off the road. The motor stalled and the truck's lights went out.

Both men were terrified. Guido shouted, "My God, that ball is going to hit the truck!" The object appeared to be at least 420 feet wide and 120 feet high. It seemed to have stopped about 120 feet in front of the truck and hung about 18 feet off the ground.

The dazzling violet-colored light went off suddenly and only a bright red antenna could still be seen. Then a door opened from top to bottom, forming a sort of bridge (like the door of a Convair plane, Fernandez said). Six slim and apparently normal people appeared in the doorway and looked silently at the two men. Then a seventh appeared and stood with them. All were of small stature, had long hair, but otherwise appeared to be human. All of them had a phosphorescent or glowing red badge on their chests which made it difficult to discern their features.

For about three minutes the group of creatures watched the two men in the truck, then the door was pulled up, the machine climbed until it was at about 1500 feet altitude and a small disc-shaped object appeared through another opening and moved away in the direction from which the big object had approached. At this point the truck's lights came back on and the engine began to function normally. The two terrified men drove as fast as they dared toward Ceres.

Fernandez said that all the while the men were looking at him and Guido he felt as though he was in a trance, and had a strange feeling that they were talking to him and saying that they had come on a peaceful mission, although he heard no sounds.

A few weeks later Mr. Gabriel Barbosa de Andrade, the Judge of Ceres, forwarded a report to the Secretary of Interior and Justice for the state of Goias giving the foregoing details.

The small stature of the "creatures," the red glowing area on their chests, and the way the "door" opened all resemble those three features in the Villas-Boas case, yet there is no indication that Villas-Boas knew of this incident, nor that Fernandez and his friend could have heard about the Villas-Boas case later and concocted the story. They were questioned by the hotel manager on the night of the experience and shortly thereafter by Judge de Andrade. In February 1958, Fernandez was questioned in Rio by Dr. Fontes. All of the interrogators noted the agitation with which Fernandez told his story. His friend Guido confirmed the details.

Another early occupant story to come to light in 1967 was reported to Colonel Adil de Oliveira in January 1955. At that time de Oliveira was Chief of the Brazilian Air Force Intelligence Service. The witness, who was vacationing at his farm in the state of Mato Grosso, Brazil, near the town of Campo Grande, refuses to let his name be made public although it is known to Colonel de Oliveira.

The date: December 15, 1954. The details: The observer was fishing in a river about 400 yards from his home when he saw an unusual craft land a few hundred feet away. His dog became very nervous and began to howl. Having his gun, which was equipped with a telescopic sight, with him the observer employed it and was able to notice two spheres of different sizes, the smaller one rotating around the other. The main object was not on the ground but was hovering about 6 feet above it, and three balls appeared affixed to the underside of it.

Shortly, movement was detected and a few moments later three creatures came down to the ground. They appeared human but quite small, agile, and their movements were very rapid. One had a kind of phosphorescent basket in his hand and another "man" had a metallic tube which was cone-shaped on one end. A large amount of the calcareous material on the edge of the river was collected in the basket and taken inside the craft. Then the two "men" came back to the same spot, and again apparently using the tube, extracted the calcareous material from the ground. The tube was pointed at the ground and the material was "sucked" up into it.

When they were seemingly finished with the latter task, the three little men got into the object, which then took off at high speed.

After the object left, the observer went to the spot where the three little creatures had busied themselves and found square holes had apparently been made in the ground by the cone-shaped instrument. A few days later he learned of the existence of similar holes in the same general area. These holes were so large that they could have accommodated the entire body of a man.

The gathering of the calcareous material aroused the interest of many and some of it was tested at the Institute for Technological Research. The analysis showed that it was made up of 61 per cent silica, 19 per cent aluminum oxide, 11 per cent magnesium, and iron and other components in smaller proportions. Laboratory specialists concluded that this material might be the basis for a very efficient refractory material able to resist high temperatures.

The foregoing report seems to follow the pattern of the 1954 visitations in that it took place in a rural area and involved small entities gathering soil samples. The chemical makeup of the calcareous material is interesting if considered in the context of the theory that these "little men" come here from somewhere in outer space.

One of the first occupant cases to come out of Brazil involved Pedro Serrate and Francisco de Assis Teixeira, residents of the village of Pedras Negras on the Guapore River.

On November 28, 1953, the two men allegedly went duck hunting in an area about two hours' walking distance from the town. Arriving at their destination they separated, as was their custom. Teixeira took up his station near the water of the bay and Serrate climbed a tree to watch for ducks.

Shortly, Francisco sighted an unusual aircraft passing over his head. It passed on and landed on the surface of the water about 150 feet from his location. It made no sound.

Serrate was within 12 feet of the object when it stopped and his view was excellent. We quote his translated report verbatim.

"The craft didn't make a sound. On the rear there was a tube at each side, curved, about 2 inches in diameter. The craft itself was about 4 meters in length (approximately 13 feet), about 2 meters and 50 centimeters wide (about 8 feet) and two meters (6½ feet) in height. The bottom was in the shape of a basin and made of blue metal. The vertical structure, about 1 meter (40 inches) high, was made of glass or similar material. The covering was rounded, supported on the glass, and held by metallic bars existing on the inside with no rivets on the outside. On the rear there was also a kind of rudder, a system like a dolphin tail about 1 meter (40 inches) in length and about 50 centimeters in width (20 inches). The whole craft was dark blue in color.

"On the inside there were six people seated three on each side, four being men and two women, all apparently no more than twenty years old. They appeared to be of medium height and had red hair, white skin, and reddish color on their faces. The women had long hair to the shoulders, parted on the side. All were wearing thick clothes of the same color as the craft.

"As soon as the strangers noticed they were being observed, the craft took off. They made no sign toward me. I was less than 9 feet from them when they discovered that I was watching them. As the object took off it made no sound and I saw no smoke. It disappeared in a second at incredible speed."

A reporter for the newspaper *O Imparcial* edited in Guaruja-Mirim, territory of Guapore, noted that the two hunters spent a very nervous week after the sighting, completely upset by what they had seen.

Another 1954 sighting which took place about a month after the start of the first Brazilian UFO wave of reports was a landing at Santo Amaro, a suburb of Sao Paulo. Dr. Fontes described it as an incredible and disturbing story which he would have hesitated to forward to APRO headquarters had it not been for the fact that it had been released by Colonel de Oliveira (now a brigadier) who was chief of the Brazilian Air Force's UFO project at the time.

Our witness in this case is taxi driver Maurilio Braga Godoi, and the following is a condensed version of his account. On November 2, 1954, at 10:30 A.M. Godoi left the Santo Amaro streetcar terminal and started to walk home. The area was deserted at that hour, and when he arrived at the corner of Andaguara Street, he was startled to see a large object landed in an empty lot between two houses. It was glowing, a circular object about 90 to 120 feet in diameter and surrounded by a strange reddish-blue or violet glow. Curious about it, Godoi decided to investigate and approached it. He soon realized that it was much larger than he had initially thought it to be and hesitated for a moment, a little frightened. The object was like nothing he had ever seen before and he thought he should go to the police or some authority and report it. He felt like running but seemed to be rooted to the ground. Godoi tried to call for help but no sound would come from his mouth. It seemed he was in the grip of some strange feeling that persisted for a time but which finally left him. When the feeling left it was replaced by great curiosity and from his position about 60 feet from the object he approached it.

Godoi noticed an open door (sliding) at one side and entered the ship. He didn't recall afterward if he used a staircase or not but he was in a large, circular room illuminated by a soft light. He saw no lamps. There was no one in sight and the craft seemed to be deserted. At the center was an odd-shaped table and on it were charts and maps. One of these especially attracted Godoi, for it was a map of the South American continent and it had a glowing or phosphorescent quality. He noticed certain symbols and took a closer look. The marks were mushroom-shaped and were seemingly scattered about the map in a random manner.

Godoi had just finished scrutinizing the map when he looked up and froze where he stood. Facing him were three "persons." They seemed quite normal except that they were small—less than five feet in height. They had dark brown skin, black, very short hair, and were dressed in a one-piece garment like an overall which was light gray in color. He saw no buttons, zippers, or the like. Each wore a belt around his waist which appeared to support an object which Godoi thought might be a gun.

The three creatures made no move toward Godoi, but stood in silent appraisal, occasionally conversing among themselves in a completely (to him) strange language. He noticed that the K sound was repeated quite often at the beginning of "words" more often than any other sound.

By now Godoi's fear had returned and he stared back at the trio, paralyzed with fright. He tried to talk to them, to tell them he meant no harm, but they were expressionless and just seemed to look him over intently.

Godoi suddenly became aware that completely against his will, he was backing out of the craft, literally dragging his feet, one after the other, his attention riveted to the "men." They made no attempt to stop him. When he reached the door he jumped to the ground and started to run away. When about 30 feet from the ship he turned his head. The object was by then hovering about 30 feet above the ground, having at the center bottom a "screw without end" (Godoi's exact words).

The craft started to move and climbed up silently at high speed with an eerie bluish-red or violet glow at the periphery.

Shortly after the report was made, Godoi was examined by several psychiatrists in Sao Paulo who concluded that he showed no signs of neurosis or psychosis. The case is still listed as "unknown" in Brazilian Air Force UFO files.

Toward the latter part of November 1961, Cavalheiro Mendes arrived at the beach of Pinhal, about one hundred miles from Porto Alegre, Rio Grande do Sul, Brazil, on business. A retired member of the Porto Alegre police force, Mendes was a dealer in real estate and an agent for people desiring vacation housing.

On the night of his arrival, Mendes was alone in his small beach house. The night was very hot, he couldn't sleep, and he was nudged by an unexplainable urge to go out and walk on the beach. He continued his efforts to sleep but to no avail and he finally gave in to the urge and at 9:30 he left the house and went toward the beach. Almost immediately after going outside he saw a huge light which he estimated to be about 900 feet away. He first thought the light was one used by fishermen, then became aware of a strong desire to approach it and found himself walking in its direction.

As Mendes approached the light he became aware that there was some kind of object resting on the sand, and as he came closer he realized it was a glowing disc-shaped thing. The strange feeling that he had to keep going toward it increased as he drew nearer, and then he saw two figures which came out from behind the craft.

Mendes could not see facial features too clearly because of the brilliance of the light coming from the object behind the forms, but did note that they wore helmets similar to those worn by football players.

At this juncture, Mr. Mendes felt he should retreat. He was not panicked, not even afraid, he said later, but the strangeness of the situation was unnerving. Then he began to get the impression that the creatures were communicating with him: "Don't resist because you can't. It's hopeless—if you doubt us—try to move your body." Mendes tried to move and found that he was like a statue, completely unable to move.

The men came closer, and that was the last that Mendes recalled. His only memory is a fragmentary one—that something was scratching the skin of his forearm with some kind of instrument.

When Mendes recovered his senses he was almost at his beach house again. It seemed that he had walked all the way back from the beach area where the craft had been without being aware of it. He looked back to where the object had been, and it was dark. He then looked at the illuminated dial of his watch. It was 11:30 P.M. Two hours had elapsed since he had walked out on the beach in response to an unconquerable urge.

Cavalheiro Mendes kept his adventure and his doubts to himself for quite some time, but after a few weeks he began to realize that he was ill. Formerly a cool, calm individual, he now showed signs of nervous instability. He felt depressed and anxious for no apparent reason and had an increasing desire to be alone. After several months had gone by he decided to confide in someone, and because of the part the strange object had played in his remembered experience, he contacted Captain F. V. Cardoso, a Brazilian Air Force officer (retired) and Lieutenant Colonel W. C. B. Schneider of the army. Both had had considerable experience investigating UFO reports.

After exhaustive interrogation, the two officers proposed that Mr. Mendes should be interrogated under hypnosis but he refused.

At this point, Fontes closed his files on the case.

In the fall of 1966, after the disclosure of the Hill case in the United States, Fontes decided to reopen the case and rallied his forces. Police Chief Maiolino of Porto Alegre, Rio Grande do Sul, undertook to convince Mendes that he should undergo hypnotic questioning in order to solve the puzzle. Mendes steadfastly refused to cooperate, however.

The man-shaped, silver-suited beings were seen in June 1959 in Boinai, New Guinea, by a Church of England priest, Reverend William Gill. The entities were on the top portion of an object which hovered several hundred feet away from Father Gill and thirty-seven other witnesses. This incident was thoroughly documented and presented in Mrs. Lorenzen's book, *Flying Saucers*. It is one report which bolsters the opinion of many that the UFO occupants are "friendly," because the "men" on the UFO responded to waves from the crowd on the ground. It is an argument but by no means conclusive, for the occupants of that particular craft waved only in response—they did not initiate the exchange of gestures and shortly lost interest and went back to what they had been doing previously.

The cases discussed in our 1967 book *Flying Saucer Occupants* seem to indicate that encounters with, or observations of, UFO occupants are confined to Europe and the Americas but this is not necessarily so. The Gill case at Boinai, New Guinea, is the only recorded observation of occupants in that area. It happened to have been observed by Reverend Gill, an educated white man, and therefore received attention. It seemed likely that other similar observations may have been made by natives in other locations who attached little if any importance to their experiences and therefore did not report them; or if they did report, little attention was paid to them because of their lack of qualification as observers. The same situation could be quite true in Africa and other areas where communications networks are not as advanced as those in Europe and the Americas.

As we have mentioned before, the landings and appearances of UFO occupants seem to concentrate in isolated or rural areas. It is possible then that the landings in some countries could take place and never be observed at all. Australia, for example, which has a good deal of land space which is sparsely populated or populated almost entirely by aborigines, experienced landings in later years. The landing of one disc-shaped object near one already on the ground was supposedly witnessed by aborigines in central Australia in 1951. According to the report, a small being in silvery suit and helmet got out of the second disc and entered the first one, whereupon both craft took off. This case is similar to the one in France in which two of the "pilots" were observed "trading" aircraft. The Australian report was not widely publicized and it is doubtful that the Frenchman who observed the two little men in 1954 could have known about the Australian landing.

Another consideration is the availability and location of investigators and reporters. Landings could take place and receive local publicity but never come to the attention of UFO chroniclers. Although APRO has managed to recruit a substantial international membership there are still many areas which are not adequately covered.

Some of the areas from which few if any reports emanate are those countries under Communist rule. Occasionally a report of a UFO may reach international press wires but it is almost always followed by an official pronouncement that the saucers are merely psychological tools of the imperialistic Americans or some such rot. One gets the definite impression that communist countries are having their problems with the elusive discs, and like their democratic counterparts in the West, try to explain away the unexplainable.

Although APRO has good connections in Japan there has yet to be a good landing or occupant case reported to us. There are several possible explanations for that lack: (1) for whatever purposes the occupants have, Japan is not important to them; (2) it will be reconnoitered at some future time, i.e., they just haven't gotten around to Japan yet; (3) Japan is so heavily populated there is no place where a landing could be effected without detection, therefore the country is avoided; (4) landings may have taken place but have not been reported for the usual reason—fear of ridicule. Unidentificed flying objects have been reported in the sky over Japan both at high and low altitudes, however.

One of APRO's goals has been to gather an adequate international force of investigators so as to effect complete global coverage. The most desirable situation would, of course, be an officially recognized commission for the study of UFOs established within the framework of the United Nations. We went on record concerning the advisability of such a working force in the 1950's, fully aware of the stumbling blocks involved in such an effort.

It seems that politics has no bounds, and would probably deter any sizable effort in this direction, but hopefully could be circumvented in the interest of scientific investigation. The people of this world have managed to put away political disagreements to a large extent where medical and astronomical research are concerned, but whether or not they could do the same in the area of UFO research is a completely different proposition. For one thing, surreptitious beings reconnoitering this planet could be considered by some to lie in the area of a military problem and therefore not a subject for objective scientific scrutiny.

In this respect we are again confronted with the regrettable emotionalism which tinges every facet of the UFO mystery.

We don't need a computer to realize that among the cases listed in this book there are marked correlations.

Features which have been repeatedly described have been large eyes and large craniums and small stature.

Another repetitive feature in certain incidents is the unexplainable "urge" to approach the UFOs and their occupants.

Clothing has probably been the one item which shows a rather large diversity of color and description among witnesses. This could be a result of personal attention to color, ability to perceive color correctly, and attention to detail. There is one other possibility, too, and that is that, just as we have different clothing for different occasions, perhaps the entities do also.

It is natural to assume that if these strangers are from somewhere beyond earth, they are probably members of a military organization of sorts and therefore the observed apparel should be consistently the same within limits. This sort of reasoning is a trap. In any evaluation of these creatures and their ships we should attempt to drop the tendency to compare them with ourselves, for if they are alien, there is little likelihood that there will be much resemblance between them (their thought processes, their motivations, clothing, or anything else for that matter) and us.

The differing descriptions of their hair length and coloring, eye shape and location and coloring, as well as skin color are of little importance either. In the matter of hair length and coloring it could be a question of preference. Where shape and location (widespread or otherwise) of eyes are concerned, there seems to be no great difference between reports within each category, i.e., the small "men," small anthropoid types, or nearly normal (human) types. To illustrate this, we might mention one family of our acquaintance which has a black-haired, brown-eyed father; blond, blue-eyed mother; red-haired daughter with brown eyes; and brown-haired son with blue eyes.

Why do we insist that if these entities are from somewhere other than earth they must all look and dress alike?

There is also a good possibility that several races are involved in this activity which we have dubbed the "UFO mystery." This could mean different races from one planet (we have three distinct ones on earth) or a "planetary alliance" as it were, of several races, all cooperating in exploring various populated planets—earth being one of them. The small anthropoid types might be trained animals used for specific purposes. Or, in a very advanced culture, animals, including the intelligent ones, might be bred for their specific dominating qualities.

Man is currently thinking of the day when the human race could be improved with specialized breeding techniques. Does this necessarily have to be a unique idea?

Another problem which crops up again and again is the prominence of landings and occupant reports in Europe (and specifically France) and South America as opposed to the United States. South America, being a considerably larger land area than the United States would be expected, from a statistical standpoint, to register more, providing the whole earth was subject to landings. Brazil has had a larger number of landings and occupants reports than any other country in South America, but it may be that the presence of competent investigators like Fontes bears on that question. APRO, the only civilian research organization with good world coverage, still does not have a satisfactory number of UFO report chroniclers in South American countries other than Brazil, Venezuela, and Argentina.

But what about France? The fact that France is considerably more densely populated than the United States might be an answer. Isolated or rural areas in France have more people to the square acre than the United States, and it's just that simple. For instance, a landing could take place in a field on a 460-acre farm in Wisconsin after dark and would not be likely to be observed because of the distance from dwellings. People are generally inside after dark. The chances of observation would be even less in areas such as Texas where "farms" often consist of thousands of acres.

Another factor is also involved—that of the tendency of Americans to conceal anything which would, of a surety, bring ridicule. If a respected American businessman, for example, were to come upon a landed unconventional craft somewhere in an isolated area and observe its occupants, he would hesitate to mention it even to his family for fear of the ridicule which would almost certainly follow because of the general attitude toward the subject of UFOs. People have a tendency to ridicule that which they fear. It is our guess that there may have been as many as a hundred or two hundred witnessed landings of UFOs and their occupants within the continental United States which have never been reported to any agency.

We would like, at this point, to ask anyone who has seen an unidentified object on the ground, or a UFO on the ground accompanied by unusual beings, to contact us at the address given in the back of this book. Names will ne needed, of course, for purposes of identification, and investigators will be dispatched, but the witness' desire for anonymity will be respected if requested.

One of the most interesting and at the same time disturbing elements of the whole tapestry of the occupant picture is the Villas-Boas affair. If we discount the possibility that Villas-Boas is a liar or a psychopath (and Fontes' evaluation seems to preclude the latter) we have one remaining answer: the experience was real. But this conclusion only complicates matters for we are immediately led to speculate about the reason for the mating experiment.

A geneticist who recently wrote us about this particular incident offered his opinion that if the Villas Boas affair is true, the occupants of the UFOs must be of human ancestry.

He said: "It is an utter impossibility for living organisms of separate evolutions to sexually unite their genes...it would be impossible...unless they were of common genetic background...."

The possibility that the Villas-Boas affair was in actuality a breeding experiment is logical although not emotionally acceptable to most. The case involving Fernandez in October 1957, preceded the Villas-Boas incident. The two men involved were scouted by a ship, then stopped and scrutinized by the crew. Six of them came and looked at Fernandez and his companion and then a seventh came and looked.

In the Villas-Boas report the farm was visited at lease twice before the experiment actually took place. If it did. Did the female part of the experiment pick her companion? Was she looking for an acceptable mate on October 10 and were Fernandez and his companion rejected? Did the group then scout the Villas-Boas farm and did the woman choose Villas-Boas? Were there other similar incidents in which humans were observed and considered for a part in the experiment?

Going from the Villas-Boas report to the Hill case in 1961, we came upon another strange, though nebulous, tie-in. The Hills were allegedly picked up and examined in September 1961. Only two months later in Brazil, a man was apprehended, and seems to have suffered a loss of memory.

Betty Hill said under *hypnosis* that she and the "leader" had a discussion concerning *old age* which her companion apparently could not understand. Her husband, Barney, revealed, also during hypnotic trance, that samples of skin had been scraped from his arm.

Two months later a sixty-year-old man had an unusual experience and his only conscious recollection was that his forearm had been "scraped."

The Hill case did not become public until 1966. The subconscious minds of Betty and Barney Hill had not even been probed until 1964. We have Doctor Fontes' testimony that the Mendes case was on record within months of the time it is alleged to have happened—in 1962.

When we put all of these minute scraps of evidence together we suspect that not only are we studying the UFOs and their occupants, but that we, ourselves, are the subject of a study.

It is correlations such as these which lead us to dispute the statement that publication of such cases as the Hill incident will "set UFO research back." In our opinion giant strides have been made since John Fuller released the details of the Hill incident. As a result of his presentation of the Hill case, we have *dared* to record publicly the accumulated evidence concerning UFO occupants which is contained in this book.

The whole pattern of UFO activity since the concentration began in the 1940's, following the advent of the A-bomb, indicates that "they" have a plan of activity which has become more concentrated since space travel for man became a reality in 1957. Succeeding space probes launched by men seem to have generated a closer scrutiny of earth by our "visitors," if indeed they are real.

In this book we have specialized and concentrated our efforts on certain aspects: the reported occupants of the UFOs, the psychological portent of the whole situation, an interpretation of the role of authorities. There are many books which provide quite an adequate background for those who are basically unfamiliar with the subject of UFOs in general. They are listed at the conclusion of this book.

In summing up, we are confronted with few choices of theories to explain the reports of landed UFOs and their occupants.

1. The objects and their "operators" are physically real. The remaining speculation concerns their identity and origin and, eventually, motivation.
2. The population of this world is falling victim to a particularly insidious and apparently contagious mental disease which generates hallucinations involving specific types of airships and humanoids. This disease seems to be spreading.

Who will be the next to contract the malady?

You?

CHAPTER XIX

Speculation

In view of the number of occupant reports which have flooded civilian research groups since the heavy UFO activity of the middle 1960's, and the ensuing (although few) correlations, one cannot help but speculate about the meaning of those reports.

Some of the scientists involved in the UFO field look askance at theorizing about the identity and motivations of the alleged UFO occupants, speaking strongly in favor of exotic (and expensive) computer programs while privately espousing the ETH (extraterrestrial hypotheses) as the most reasonable explanation of all those so far considered. As a matter of fact, we have yet to talk to *any* UFO-involved scientist who has not engaged in long speculative conversations concerning the UFO entities, their origin, and their motivations. Yet some of these same individuals publicly take a stance which indicates that they do not put any stock in the ETH or are extremely skeptical of the reality of UFOs, period.

But these same individuals advocate the allocation of millions of dollars of taxpayers' money for "research and investigation" of the UFO problem. This, in our opinion, would be extraneous and prohibitively expensive considering the *fact* that twice the federal government of the United States has sadly failed in its effort to solve the UFO problem. Dr. J. Allen Hynek, for twenty years a scientific consultant to the Air Force's (variously titled Project Sign, Grudge, Blue Book, etc.) UFO project can readily attest to this. Those projects were little more than public relations endeavors and were dismal failures as was the University of Colorado UFO Project (popularly called the "Condon Committee").

Too many researchers have been willing to be influenced by one report or one theory and tend to waver and change attitudes and theories with the weight of only one or a handful of cases. Also there is a tendency to lump all unknown or unidentified phenomena under the heading of UFOs. If we're going to research UFOs, let's stick to unidentified flying objects and forget the leprechauns and ghosts and things of that nature; there's enough mystery to work with in our chosen subject without getting involved in mysticism, spiritualism, and the like.

It may be comforting to some people to have only *one big mystery* rather than face the possibility that this is a universe *full* of mysteries.

We at APRO have been somewhat unpopular in the UFO research community since we began taking seriously the reports of landed UFOs and UFOnauts in the early 1950's. It was apparent that some people were ready to acknowledge the existence of UFO's in the earth's atmosphere, but the idea of them landing or being piloted by intelligent beings seemed to be totally unacceptable, even though these same people espoused the idea that the UFOs were interplanetary in nature. It was our opinion that if they were truly interplanetary, surely whoever was responsible for their presence over the earth would not be likely to send them millions or trillions of miles merely to fly across the sky, and then zip back to wherever they came from in the first place. Perhaps we Lorenzens were egotistical enough to think they might find homo sapiens and our technology of sufficient interest to stay around awhile.

Therefore, when landings were reported, they were not unbelievable, and when UFOs were reported on the ground with occupants nearby or getting in or out of them, that came as no surprise either. We did not believe every report, but conversely, we were not unbelieving. Each report was a part of the whole puzzle and our philosophy was much the same as it had been when we founded APRO collect, study, and store the data.

In the middle 1960's a new facet of the UFO phenomenon was manifested with the revelation of the Betty and Barney Hill case. This news indicated that we should reconsider the Villas-Boas case which had been a stored item and one which we had felt would not be readily acceptable by the UFO field, let alone the general public. In these two cases, we were confronted with the possibility that alien races were actually visiting earth, and moreover that they were carrying out experiments with human beings—with or without their willing participation.

The Villas-Boas incident took place four years prior to the Hill experience. Villas-Boas' conscious cooperation was obviously a prerequisite and possibly his abductors relied on the social mores of the time as well as his natural modesty to keep him from divulging it. Possibly they felt that even if he did make his experience public he wouldn't be believed and the ridicule would prevent him from pursuing the matter.

We don't know for sure what the other entities in the Villas-Boas incident looked like since they were heavily suited and wore helmets which hid everything but their eyes. In contrast with the red pubic hair was the platinum blonde color of the hair on her head. If she and her companions had monitored our television broadcasts to any extent perhaps they learned that gentlemen prefer blondes and thereafter performed a little transformation via the bleach bottle, just for Villas-Boas' benefit. We must also postulate that her very "humaneness" was in actuality a result of cosmetic surgery—she may not really have been as human as she looked and in her natural state might have been thoroughly repulsive to Villas-Boas.

One can learn a lot from television. For instance, visiting aliens would be informed in practically no time at all that humans suffer from bad breath, smelly armpits, bad body odor in general, and constipation is a fact of life. Also, besides our physical afflictions, the aliens would learn in very short order that we habitually commit murder on a large scale with our never-ending border disputes, police actions, and good old-fashioned wars.

Can we wonder, then, about the obvious mind probe of Mrs. P? At about the time that the preliminary report on the Utah case came to our attention, Mrs. Lorenzen, who is deeply interested in the study of psychology, was reading the book titled *I'm Okay—You're Okay* by Thomas A. Harris, M.D. In the first chapter, titled "Freud, Penfield, and Berne", Dr. Harris relates the experiment of brain surgeon Dr. Wilder Penfield, who during surgery on a patient under local anesthetic suffering from focal epilepsy, experimented with stimulating various points of the temporal cortex of the brain with a weak electrical current via a galvanic probe. Harris concluded from examination of Penfield's writings that everything which is a part of our conscious awareness is stored in detail in the brain and is capable of being "played back."

Not only are past events recorded and stored, but the emotion felt at the time—what the patient saw, heard, felt, and understood.

Now let us re-examine what Mrs. P said: they were "taking my thoughts"—this while the needles were in her head. She was sure they had performed such examinations before because of the precision with which they carried out the task. Some of the questions they asked indicated that they were attempting to construct a psychological profile of the human mind. They asked about the birth of her children, for instance. Also they asked whether or not she liked animals. When she replied in the affirmative, she was asked why.

So it would seem that at least the species which abducted the P family already knew quite a lot about humans, but all the same have a curiosity or a need to know about a human's emotional experiences, responses, and needs. The question about animals may have been an attempt to understand man's relationship between non-productive domestic animals such as dogs and cats, or it may have been a standard psychological question.

The idea of humans being abducted and subjected to tests or experiments of which they have no understanding by strange-appearing humanoids is repugnant and frightening, to be sure. However, if we compare the aliens' behavior to that of the human scientist in the laboratory attempting to understand the physiological and psychological make-up and behavior of the lower animals we can begin to understand the behavior of these entities who obviously consider themselves superior to mankind. The dog who is the hapless subject in a laboratory and must submit to brain probes which trigger various physical actions such as salivation, or is forced to exist with a see-into stomach so that scientists can observe the function of that organ, certainly would be elsewhere if he had the intelligence to elude man or could defend himself.

Which brings us to the possibility of contact. If the television and radio networks could be persuaded to begin an "educate the aliens" campaign, contact might be possible. As it is, until now the air waves have been filled with untenable "explanations" such as Venus, balloons, plasma, and swamp gas, following a period of extended and concentrated UFO activity. Can it be any wonder, then, that humans are taken surreptitiously and influenced in some unknown way so that they cannot remember their experiences? If "they" think we are so stupid that we can't recognize the evidence of their presence after twenty eight years, perhaps they find it the better part of valor to keep us in our blissful ignorance. We have speculated before that perhaps the visitors feel that making their presence known would result in problems where our culture is concerned—certainly when there is contact between a greatly advanced culture and a vastly inferior one, the latter suffers. Perhaps, despite Mrs. P's indignation at the treatment, the aliens were acting humanely—by their standards. Their faces were covered with human-appearing masks. Were they covered to prevent the shock which might have ensued were she to look upon their real faces, or did they disguise themselves so that she could not later give a description should she remember the episode?

We come now to consideration of the human aboard the ship in Mrs. P's case. We have few choices where he's concerned—a willing human accomplice, a human completely under their control and performing more or less against his will, or an android (a manufactured item). This particular part of the episode is understandable—a human being or human-appearing, fatherly-looking individual to allay their fears, thus making the task easier for the aliens.

The "human" aboard the ship in the Utah report is only one of the puzzles presented by the whole UFO enigma. If we start with the assumption that UFOs are extraterrestrial and manned by intelligent beings as a working hypothesis, and apply what has been learned from the Hill case, we begin to get some tentative answers. According to Betty Hill, certain routes marked on the three-dimensional star map aboard the ship were designated as trade routes and others were for exploration.

A trade route between stars would indicate trade between the cultures on two planets orbiting different stars. Expeditionary routes would mean that the inhabitants of a planet orbiting a certain star were traveling to various solar systems where they explore any existing planets.

Whether coincidental or not, most interesting is the fact that the National Aeronautics and Space Administration's (NASA) Copernicus Orbiting Astronomical Observatory is scanning three stars for signs that other civilizations may be trying to contact earth with ultraviolet laser beams. Such observations can only be made from an orbiting observatory because the earth's atmosphere prevents ultraviolet radiation from reaching the surface. The stars being scanned are Epsilon Eridani, Tau Ceti, and Epsilon Indi—all approximately eleven light-years from the earth. Tau Ceti is one of the stars in the Marjorie Fish models which is connected to Zeta 1 Reticuli as a trade route. It will be interesting to learn what the results of the intragalactic experiment is. Epsilon Eridani, according to *Astronomy* magazine of August 1975, was the first to be scanned in November 1974, and the data from Copernicus is being analyzed at this writing.

Some scientists claim that the first attempt at communication with earth by other civilizations would be via light or laser beams, the insinuation being that an intelligent race would attempt communication in that manner and if they got no answer would not follow up with manned flights. But what if a race attempted—a few hundred or a few thousand years ago—to contact the human race via laser beam? They would have gotten no answer. But if they were interested also in exploration, might they not send unmanned, remote-controlled space probes calculated to obtain information about the planet's atmosphere, geology, etc.? And what if that probe sent back information indicating the presence of intelligent life? The sponsoring race quite likely would include that planet in its projected manned space expeditions. Therefore, given the technological advances of the human race in the past century, is it not entirely possible that aliens attempted, long ago, to contact earth via laser beams without success? But wanting to learn about the physical features of the earth, possibly with an eye to future mining expeditions, then sent an unmanned probe? If that probe came into the earth's atmosphere, orbited, and began to send back information which included photography of cities and farms, the civilization receiving the information would know they had discovered a civilization which at the time that the laser communication was attempted, lacked the technological knowledge to receive the communication or to respond.

If this hypothetical race had a modicum of scientific curiosity they would want to explore and study the planet in question, and in depth, including the animal life. On the other hand, they might be interested in exploitation, pure and simple, just as were the Europeans who set out for the "new world." Therefore, in a solar system such as ours, the visiting race would explore all the planets, possibly mining some of them for materials which were in low supply on the home planet. It would not be unreasonable to assume that these explorers might set up a base on one planet while exploring others.

In our present predicament of attempting to interpret the machinations and motivations of the UFO occupants we must recall that for many years there has existed a coincidence between heavy UFO activity and the close approach of the planet Mars, approximately every other year. The theory that the UFOs might have been using Mars as a "way station in space" *seems* to have been negated by the information gathered when Mariner made its famous flight, for there appeared to be no evidence of intelligent life on the surface of Mars. But the *surface* of Mars would not be the likely choice of UFOnauts for a base because of the sparse atmosphere. Underground bases would be preferable and not likely to be detected by earth-based astronomers or space probes from earth. There may be another reason why UFO activity happens to coincide with the close approach of Mars, but for the present, at least, the way station hypothesis is still tenable and no alternative theory has surfaced.

One is forced to wonder about the motivations of the scientists who deny the existence of evidence indicating that outer space visitors are here, but at the same time promote the financing of extremely expensive projects designed to attempt contact with other civilizations.

A Swiss student wrote APRO recently to express a rather unique view on specialization versus adaptability.

He recalled an idea expressed by Charles Darwin—that the more specialized an animal becomes, the less adaptable it is, and cited the koala bear of Australia as an extreme example of specialization. The koala subsists on a diet consisting solely of eucalyptus leaves and has become so dependent that his survival depends on the survival of the eucalyptus.

He went on to say that intellectual specialization can lead to a similar lack of adaptability. Those astronomers who depend solely on radio telescopy to contact extraterrestrial intelligence ignore UFO data because it does not have the familiar taste of eucalyptus leaves.

We must eventually face up to the hodge-podge of witness reports of the UFOnauts. There are some general categories, yes—large forms, small forms, tiny forms. Except for a very tiny percentage, almost all of the reports deal with human-shaped occupants. The large disparity in the types of clothing is not an insurmountable problem if we take a look at the availability and variety of colors, fabrics, and styles here on earth. Should space travelers necessarily all dress alike? We tend to think in terms of the military and their uniforms when we consider the dress of alien visitors because our own space efforts involve members of the military and even when civilians do go into space they wear the same kind of garb as the pilots who guide the spacecraft, lunar expeditionary model, etc.

However, as we become more adept (some time from now, of course) at space travel, we are quite likely to be less rigid about the mode of dress. It should not, therefore, be too surprising to learn that other space travelers may be as individualistic in their mode of dress as civilians are on earth.

And then, it is obvious that we are dealing with more than one race of alien visitors. It would seem reasonably certain that they are aware of one another and indeed may be aligned with one another in a sort of cooperative exploration. This would not only explain the large number of *different-looking* entities, but also the vast number of types of clothing.

The entities in the Utah case match up fairly well with those seen on board the craft by Betty Hill as well as the two humanoids seen at Warneton, Belgium. In the Hill case, not much detail was described where clothing was concerned but Mrs. P (the Utah case) described a sort of uniform with an emblem on the collar. The Warneton entities wore much the same general type of "uniform" replete with Sam Brown belt. These uniforms seem to indicate a certain branch of service of some kind, or a certain select group, at least. Those who argue against the reality of the humanoids because they don't seem to wear consistently similar clothing are merely saying that they cannot possibly exist because they don't conform to the dress codes of humankind. In the Warneton report, Mr. X said the faces of the entities were identical (even though they were dissimilar in height), leading to speculation that they, like the humanoids in the Utah case, may have also been wearing masks.

Many skeptics point to the lack of reports which match one another completely and insist that this is a good argument against their reality. But when one takes into consideration the difficulty of getting a detailed description from someone who was excited or frightened or observed an object at night or under very poor lighting conditions, there is nothing surprising about the apparent lack of correlation. However, there have been some instances in which craft which are apparently identical were observed and described.

In December 1970 APRO received a letter from an art instructor in Lexington, Kentucky, telling what she and two companions had seen one night, but could furnish no information about the exact date except that it was sighted during the time that the "Blue Grass Fair" was being held. She thought it might have been five or more years in the past. Subsequent correspondence did not yield the date as the correspondent was rather slow in answering, but we did learn that one of the witnesses had completely turned around her testimony, and her companion said that she was the "kind of person who would wash out all original knowledge rather than be labeled a kook who thought they saw a flying saucer."

The ladies at first thought that what they were viewing was some kind of a clever contrivance to attract attention to the fair. Because it was dark the part of the object which they could best observe was that portion of the craft which was illuminated. The witness who initially contacted us sketched the object, showing a rounded top, a wide rim or platform encircling it, and just above the platform was a lighted, transparent section through which they could see the silhouettes of people who seemed to be "working" at something. The "band of light" or transparent section had upright pieces at regular intervals which the witness took to be structural support members, and these and possibly the rim revolved. They watched the thing hovering in the sky for about five minutes, then went about their business and did not see how it left or if it left. It is interesting to note that all three ladies were responsible, well-educated people. One was an assistant professor of art, the second a landscape artist and design architect, and our correspondent was an art education instructor.

In 1972 Field Investigator Donald Worley of Connorsville, Indiana, interviewed a woman in a small town concerning a strange craft and occupants which had hovered near her home one night in November 1966. Mrs. S is a thirty-six-year-old housewife and mother of three children. On the night in question she was watching television and her husband and children were in bed asleep. She left the living room to go to the kitchen for a drink of water, and happened to glance out the kitchen door. She saw what she first thought must have been a helicopter hovering over the electric lines about a quarter of a mile north of the house. The fastest the object moved was approximately five miles per hour and it seemed to hover for a short period of time over the two other homes on the road where Mrs. S lives. Then it began to approach the S house and stopped at what Mrs. S estimated to be 50 feet away and "two or three stories" high.

Mrs. S described the craft as "big as a house," like a ball with a circular rim around the middle, and windows in the upper part. She, like the ladies in the Lexington sighting, described thin, upright supports in the window section, and the silhouettes of figures inside it which were quite distinct because of the bright light. Looking at the thing, she said, was like looking at a negative, as the figures were dark, the light from within a brilliant white, and the outside of the ship a silvery color. She got the impression of parts of the walls being "full of computers" and that two of the figures inside were smaller and feminine looking compared to the heavier, more muscular figure who was at the side of the object closest to her. The two slender figures she took to be female although she did not see an outline of hips or breasts which would indicate that such was the case. The figure closest to the witness seemed to be staring at her, Mrs. S said, which rather frightened her. She kept calling to her husband to get up and come and see the thing but he did not waken.

What was really striking was the similarity between the sketch made by the trained artist and the crude drawing made by the untrained housewife. The descriptions and drawings indicate that except for the revolving of the transparent part of the craft in the Lexington report and the "feminine" figures (the ladies who observed the ship in Lexington were considerably farther away from the craft than Mrs. S was) in the Indiana case, the figures and ships were identical.

Another correlation is in the number of reports (others are

described elsewhere in this book) where figures are seen close up and in fairly good detail *except that the face area* is *covered.* A very good example of this is a sighting reported by a nurse at the Cowichan Station, British Columbia, Canada, Hospital on New Year's Day, 1970. Ironically, it was the day after the U.S.A.F. announced that they were getting out of the UFO business and that they could find no valid reason to continue their investigation.

At 5:00 A.M. on January 1 Mrs. Doreen Kendall, a practical nurse employed at the Cowichan District Hospital, went into a four-bed extended care ward to begin her early morning chores. As was her habit, she strode to the window and pulled back the drapes. What she saw outside caused talk for several hours in the hospital and for many months throughout Canada. Curiously, although it was a multiple witness case, this sighting did not reach the press wires or American newspapers.

Outside the window, approximately 40 feet from the building, a circular craft with transparent dome was hovering. Inside the dome two figures could be clearly seen. One was at an instrument panel, the other behind him. They had "nice" physiques, Mrs. Kendall said, were more than six feet tall, and their hands were the same color and shape as ours. They wore dark clothing like a pilot's uniform, of soft-looking material, which also *covered their faces.* While she stood watching, one man turned and appeared to look directly at her and then put his hand on the back of the man who was sitting down. The other man then pulled back "a joy stick" similar to those in a large airplane going from first, into second, and then into third gear, and the object tilted sideways giving Mrs. Kendall an even better view of the instrument panel and interior.

At this time she noted that the dome seemed to be lit from below rather than above. Up until this time Mrs. Kendall had been so entranced with what she was watching that she didn't think to call anyone, but when it started to pull away she realized no one would believe her so she ran and called Mrs. Frieda Wilson to come into the room. Mrs. Wilson entered and saw the craft, but no occupants, for it was already some distance away. Several other nurses answered the summons and also saw the craft leave.

The object itself was similar to a sphere with a wide rim at its horizontal midsection. It was situated about 40 feet from the building and was possibly 50 feet in diameter or as Mrs. Kendall put it, "about the width of five hospital windows." She thought that perhaps the men were making repairs on the machine, which was silvery in appearance and with a "necklace" of lights around the outside of the rim.

Mrs. Kendall cooperated with APRO Staff Artist Brian James of Winnipeg, Manitoba, Canada, who did several drawings to her specification. It was noted that the object she described looked exactly like another UFO which had been seen elsewhere at a different time and which had been illustrated in the "Canadian UFO Report," giving us another correlation.

Besides its sensational nature, another reason that APRO "sat on" the Villas-Boas case was because we wanted to keep it in reserve without publicity to ascertain whether similar sightings or reports of similar entities might eventually surface. Note that the helmeted, suited humanoids had the required number of eyes, legs, arms, hands, fingers, etc., and all in the right places. The only thing which set them apart from the entities in other reports was the size of their heads above the eyes—that area was abnormally large.

We had to wait many years—fifteen, to be exact, for such a report to come to our attention. In 1971, the *National Enquirer* launched a contest for proof that UFOs were real and from outer space, giving cash prizes for the most interesting UFO cases. In the process, they received a letter from Mrs. Marilyn Chenarides of Grand Forks, North Dakota, relative to an experience she and her mother shared in August (no exact date recalled) 1962.

Marilyn was eighteen at the time and her mother, Mrs. Anderson, was doing her hair, while her younger brother Roger was in bed asleep. The two occasionally glanced out the window at Lake Movil, only yards away from their summer cabin located in northwest Minnesota.

Marilyn said she was just gazing into space when "this bright red object appeared from nowhere right over our dock." Rather like a flattened ball, it was bright red in color, and had three windows from which shown bright yellow light. Silhouetted in these windows were three figures; no arms could be seen, and they appeared to be very slender with no hipline. The characteristic which made them appear unusual was the size of the head from the eye area to the top—it was elongated.

Mrs. Anderson switched out the cabin lights and went outside toward the object. The light from the object went out and it was just a dark blob hovering over the boat dock. When she was halfway to the dock, the object elevated slowly, then shot off into the sky and out of sight.

The outstanding characteristic of this report which caught our eyes was the elongated "head." Both Mrs. Anderson and her daughter said the entities were wearing "normal" clothing although they were seen only in silhouette, but they emphasized the elongated head. This is a distinct correlation with the entities of the Villas-

Boas case, but unfortunately the only one, because in the Lake Movil case no appendages were viewed—only a general outline of the torso and head.

In this morass of facts, semi-facts, and just pure hokum (the contactee cases) that permeate the UFO subject, one thing seems to stand out clearly:

SOMEONE IS PUTTING US ON!

But who is that somebody? By process of elimination we know it's not a put-on engineered by humans—no one on earth has the technology to build and fly machines with the speed and maneuverability of the UFOs.

Some have been toying with the so-called interdimensional theory. But it's only a theory—something like a pipedream, we might say. We believe in conservation of theory and that is why the ETH is the most rational and practical theory—it's a tried and true possibility. Man has proven that space travel is possible, but no human being has passed from this existence to another dimension and back again to report on it. If and when this is possible and it is a matter of fact, we can consider that IDT (interdimensional travel) is a possible solution to the UFO problem.

Meanwhile, let's look at the evidence compiled by APRO over a twenty-four-year-period. What kinds of crafts have been observed? There are the discs, the egg shapes, the cigar shapes, and the spheres—four *general* categories. When seen in daylight they can be silvery or gray or even black, depending on how the light is striking them. But at night—ah, that is another thing.

Quite often discs are seen with a string of lights around the rim. Sometimes these lights are white and they blink on and off. Sometimes they are red, green, and white and they blink on and off. But sometimes the disc has a red light on top and a white light on the bottom, and practically every color combination possible has been observed—you name it, they've got it.

We find the same condition existing with the cigar-shaped objects, while the eggs and spheres tend to glow all over in different colors. We have postulated that these lighting arrangements might be aircraft recognition signals among the UFO fleets or related to their propulsion, but there may be quite another explanation: a camouflage of sorts. The most common UFO sightings take place at night, and there is a proliferation of them, but the descriptions of the lights, their colors and their arrangement and performance (blinking, pulsating, etc.), are so varied that it is difficult to find any kind of a pattern.

Perhaps that's just the point! Someone doesn't want us to find a pattern.

Those seemingly overt acts on the part of the UFOs should be suspect to anyone engaged in the study of the UFO phenomenon. Just as human intelligence agencies have contingency cover stories ready should sensitive information be inadvertently compromised, we should expect the same of our visitors. One example may be the sighting by William Bosak (see Chapter X).

To our knowledge, this particular description has never shown up in UFO lore prior to 1975. Although some researchers claim a connection between the so-called "Bigfoot," "Sasquatch," "Yeti," or "Abominable Snowman" and UFOs, there is yet to be recorded a case involving a huge, hairy, smelly, man-shaped being getting into or coming out of a UFO. The description given by Bosak does not match that of the "Bigfoot"—it is simply a maverick among UFO occupant reports. Bosak is a man of good reputation and we have no reason to doubt his story. But what did he see?

At the time of the Bosak sighting, Wisconsin was recording several UFO reports each night. If we accept the idea that UFOs are piloted by intelligent beings and if the Bosak report is a legitimate one, then we must tackle the puzzle of WHY?

Why would intelligent beings land one of their ships on a road near a small town in northern Wisconsin? Why would the occupant be so different from all the rest of the UFO reports which involve humanoids? We have three choices.

(1) The UFOs are "manned" by many, many types of beings including what we would consider to be animal-like entities. (2) The Bosak sighting is a hoax. Or (3) the Bosak sighting was an intelligence ploy—i.e., a close scrutiny of a certain area was in the offing and an attempt to discredit future sightings was undertaken. After all, after such an unbelievable incident was publicized, who could take seriously the reports of landed UFOs? It is difficult to think of the Bosak sighting as anything but an intelligence operation.

In the case of the humanoids or occupants or what have you, we find the same situation. Although there are three *general* sizes, about 3 feet tall, about 4 feet tall, and the size which is comparable to an average human being—5 feet, 6 inches to 6 feet, there seems to be a great variety of types. In these categories the entities are generally human in shape with a head, trunk, two arms, and two legs. In some instances claw-shaped hand-like appendages are described (the Pascagoula incident and the Utah case) but generally the differences between them and human beings are negligible.

The fact is that there are precious few humanoid cases in which the witness gets a good look at the facial features. Either they are covered, as we have noted elsewhere, or a helmet obscures them or the lighting conditions are such that little detail can be discerned, and with the Utah case and, we suspect, the Warneton report, masks are worn. We should note that in the reports where humans are *approached by* the UFOnauts the faces are covered, helmets are worn, etc. This suggests that the only cases in which we can rely on the descriptions as being the actual facial features would be those cases where the witness either observes from concealment or accidentally stumbles upon the humanoid.

For if "they" want to sow confusion and really cause a nervous breakdown in our computers, all they have to do is use a variety of different clothing, land on or near highways so that they can be seen, keep their faces either covered or wear masks, and fly their machines from place to place, going about their business, whatever that may be, changing the light arrangement on their ships regularly.

Much has been said about a proposed government-financed agency to study the UFO problem. We are against such a proposal. Civilian research has not done a bad job so far; certainly far better than the Air Force Projects or the Condon Committee, and it is a well-known fact that government money always has strings attached. APRO has never lacked for dedicated, knowledgeable, competent investigators; our only drawback has been a lack of sufficient funds to finance the projects which need to be carried out. But since the Air Force has gotten out of the UFO business, and cases get publicity without benefit of Air Force "explanations," the general public increasingly turns to APRO for information. Thus, membership has increased, providing needed funds.

Considerable has also been said about the computer study of all the data thus far gathered. APRO has its own computer program but not much emphasis is put on facilitating it (mainly because of lack of funds) for we feel that the more important task is that of gathering and investigating reports. We further feel that the UFO enigma will not yield to a computer study because a computer is a subjective tool. This problem will yield only to *human reason,* but only if the humans involved are objective. We have concentrated on keeping our minds open to any new manifestations in the UFO mystery, feeling that if we are able to face each new bit of evidence as it becomes available we are that much closer to the solution. We have long held the opinion that the landings which leave physical traces and the reports involving encounters between human beings and the UFOnauts will ultimately yield most of the an swers, if not the solution.

Of course, we cannot state that we have all the answers now, but among the cases currently pending investigation is some very interesting new material which should cast considerable light on some very perplexing aspects.

Two young men who were engaged in a game of "chase" in the Oklahoma countryside in 1967 took a short cut, ended up on a dead end road and going too fast to turn around ran their car into a ditch, wrecking the fan and the radiator. It was midnight and they set about to find a telephone to call their parents to get transportation home and to let them know they were all right.

There were three houses in the vicinity and after they had walked to one and received no response to their knocks and calls, proceeded to the second one with the same result. Although the dogs barked at them, no one responded to their knocks.

They then set out for house number three and at about that time spotted a bright red light in the sky. It became larger and larger as it approached, and when they realized it was on a course headed straight for them, they changed their fast walk to a dead run, "scared to death" as our informant put it. Then, with no time for transition, they were standing in the road watching the thing leaving with a feeling of sadness that it was going.

In his initial letter witness number one said that the time required to take them from their car to the first two houses, and even house number three, should have taken them no longer than two hours. However, after the disc had left, they headed back to house number two where lights were ablaze and the dogs were again barking furiously. They made their telephone call and eventually got home, but were puzzled about the two hours for which they could not account.

This is another case which is pending. Initial contact has been made and the witness has agreed to regressive hypnosis and, if we wish, a lie detector test. Before we will be ready to comment on this particular case, like the Utah case, considerable more work will have to be done. But it just might be that there will be additional information, however fragmentary, to add to what we already know.

It is our premise that Betty and Barney Hill and Villas-Boas and Mr. X (the Warneton, Belgium case) and Mrs. P in Utah are telling the truth to the best of their ability. Unless illusions about the physical nature of their captors was deliberately planted in their minds, we have our first leads as to the identity and intention and physical nature of the UFOnauts. At this writing it seems logical to theorize that several races of intelligent beings from other star systems are systematically studying the earth and its inhabitants.

It behooves us, at this juncture, to consider the motivations of the aliens and to look into ourselves for some of the answers. The reactions of human beings to their encounters with the occupants has always been most intriguing. Except in rare cases, the human observer has been frightened and/or repulsed. Which brings us to examine some of our own emotional attitudes toward other species.

A small child will approach and embrace any plant or animal with curiosity and sometimes love, simply because it has not been impregnated with adult prejudices. But given a few years of exposure to the bias of "experience," that same child will cringe at the sight of a snake, various types of insects and, if conditioned, at the sight of domesticated animals such as dogs and cats.

Keeping in mind the obvious close resemblance of the visitors to human beings, we must ask ourselves why humans can find a closeness with lower animals such as dogs and cats, but find repugnant the appearance of aliens with an upright stature, head, trunks, arms, and legs much like ours with the main differences being the face and hands? One reason, of course, is that our domestic and wild animals are familiar to us.

This brings us to the current and possible future relationship between humans and the visiting aliens. Man has his prejudices. When we first read the Hill case in John Fuller's *Interrupted Journey,* we were struck by two things; the samples taken of Betty's hair, skin, and nails, as well as the "needle in the navel." In subsequent conversations with Betty, she said that she had considered that the aliens were engaged in sample-taking for the purpose of "cloning." A clone, according to the dictionary, is a group of plants originating as parts of the same individual, from *buds or cuttings.*

Now, consider that every cell of the human body (or plants or animals, for that matter) contains all of the genetic characteristics of the complete entity (color of eyes, hair, build, etc.). "I have visions of little Betty or Barney Hills running around somewhere," Betty told Mrs. Lorenzen.

Were "buds" or "cuttings" taken from Betty for the purpose of producing progeny without the benefit of the usual insemination and gestation process? Semen was taken from Barney, for "test tube babies," perhaps? Which takes us, automatically, back to the Villas-Boas case. Was that breeding experiment unsuccessful? Or, if successful, did "they" look about for semen from other donors for artificial insemination in subsequent breeding experiments? Or are there many races, each with their own methods of experimental breeding?

On the surface, this may seem to be a disgusting proposal, but by all the rules of logic, taking into consideration the mass of testimony we have so far, it does make sense.

Difficult though it may seem, we must consider the possibility of zoos many light years from earth which are waiting for their consignments. Perhaps in the past live earthmen and women have been captured and shipped, only to languish and die, either enroute or after being delivered, from Earth.

Here on our own earth, we have learned that few of the animals taken from the wild survive in zoos—and they are unreasoning animals, at that. In more recent years, having captured wild animals in quantities, we have accustomed them to a certain amount of sequestering and they have begun to breed. Therefore, there is little hunting for zoo stock anymore, because we are breeding "wild" animals in captivity and are able to stock most zoos with the progeny of the captured specimens.

Are some of us potential inhabitants of exotic zoos light-years from earth? Or (and this is more acceptable) have the visitors produced clones for their purposes? Or are we merely the subjects of coldly scientific experiments on "lower animals" by beings so far beyond us intellectually and technologically that we cannot divine their intent? Are cloning experiments taking place in laboratories in space or on remote planets revolving around stars countless miles from earth, utilizing the ovum, semen, skin, hair, and nail samples of the unwilling human donors?

We suggest that the answers to these questions are within our intellectual capability to answer and understand, given more information. It has been suggested that a "lure"—a fake UFO—should be built to attract the UFOs so that we can observe, photograph, and ultimately contact them. Here on earth we have an elaborate means by which we keep track of our aircraft. Why shouldn't visiting aliens have a similar (and probably more efficient) system? Why would they be attracted to a saucer-shaped object on the ground? Certainly they wouldn't mistake it for one of theirs. It is doubtful that they would be curious enough to approach close enough so that they could be photographed; UFOs are notoriously camera-shy. There is a large model of a UFO parked outside a large Dodge dealership in Mexico City, and the Houston astrodome resembles a huge squatting saucer, yet there is no indication that either have attracted UFOs to the areas. We rather view the idea of that sort of lure as being comparable to a fish luring a fisherman.

In reviewing the contents of this chapter, we might point out that there are no *hard facts* about UFOs, only assumptions based on observations of witnesses. However, barring the possibility that we are dealing with a host of liars or incompetents (which, statistically, is not likely), we are dealing with a very clever, intelligent, technologically superior adversary.

And that, precisely, is why they are repugnant to us. Anthropologists and geneticists tell us that ultimately, through the process of evolution, we may lose our little finger. The third or ring finger is little more than an appendage upon which to hang a decorative band called a ring. However, a person can do quite well without each of these fingers, needing the thumb and index finger for grasping and the middle finger for strength. What if a race perhaps a few thousand years in advance of our culture attained space travel? When we say a few thousand years, we are not referring merely to technological advances, but physical evolution. Might they not be lacking a few fingers, also sans lips and protruding proboscis?

We could accept these un-beautiful (by our standards) creatures if they were inferior to man. We can accept our dogs, cats, cows, etc., because, although they resemble us very little, they give us undying allegiance and they are psychologically and mentally inferior and possess no technology with which to defend themselves against us. Conversely, our visitors have a technology which far outstrips our own, their accomplishments make ours appear pitiful. The comparison leaves us only one way in which we can feel superior—our physical characteristics. And that's just a matter of relativity.

Going back to the Hill, Villas-Boas, Warneton, and Utah cases, the writers are concerned that either because of ignorance, incompetence, or deliberate deception by governmental and scientific authorities of the world, unsuspecting people have suffered traumatic experiences because they believed authoritarian pronouncements that UFOs are not real and do not constitute a threat. One is led to wonder if there have been any cases of abduction in which the victim didn't live to tell about it (heart attack due to extreme fright, for instance). Or how about people who have had the experience, do not recall it consciously, but suffer unexplainable and terrifying nightmares and physical discomfort, as well as psychological disturbances as a result?

The time has come for candor.

Now might be the appropriate time to initiate "educate the aliens" radio and television programs and invite them to visit us openly, rather than capturing and terrifying people at random.

Meantime, we invite anyone who feels that he or she has had an unexplainable time lapse connected with a UFO sighting to contact us and we will do our best to accommodate them, allay their fears, and just possibly they might be able to contribute to this most important study.

Appendix A

The following article is reprinted from the APRO *Bulletin*, August 1975 issue.

CIA Documents on UFOs Released
By Brad Sparks

The Central Intelligence Agency (CIA) declassified the long-awaited full report of its 1953 scientific advisory panel on UFOs on 21 January 1975 at APRO request. Chaired by the late physicist-cosmologist, Dr. Howard Percy (Bob) Robertson, the panel was convened on 14-17 January 1953 by the Administration Staff, Office of Scientific Intelligence (OSI or O/SI), directorate of Intelligence (D/I, DDI or DD/I, CIA.)

Most of the information deleted from the "sanitized" version of the 32-page memorandum (released in 1967) has been known to APRO since June 1973 by way of secondhand reports concerning the late Dr. James E. McDonald's notes, painstaking analysis, and other sources.

The formerly SECRET memo was written by Frederick Clark Durant III for Dr. Harris Marshall "Chad" Chadwell, Assistant Director for Scientific Intelligence (ADSI or AD/SI), and is dated 16 February 1953. Durant, a rocket engineer, was a staff assistant to Chadwell, who was a physical chemist and head of OSI. The memo is comprised of six main parts: a title page and index (table of contents); six pages of meeting minutes; eighteen pages of "unofficial" comments of the OSI Panel; the two-page official report of the OSI Scientific Advisory Panel of UFOs dated 17 January 1953 and appended as "Tab A"; a two-page list of documentary evidence presented (Tab B); and a two-page list of Members, Associate Members, and Interviewees of the OSI Panel (Tab C).

OSI Panel Members were: Panel Chairman Robertson, who at that time was on a two-year leave from his post as Professor of Mathematical Physics at California Institute of Technology to be a full-time consultant to OSI; physicist Dr. Luis Walter Alvarez, University of California, Berkeley; the late geophysicist Lloyd Viel Berkner (he did not have a doctorate), President of Associated Universities, Inc., which operated the particle accelerators of the Brookhaven National Laboratories; theoretical physicist Dr. Samuel Abraham Goudsmit, Chairman of the Physics Dept., Brookhaven National Laboratories; astronomer Dr. Thornton Leigh Page, Deputy Director, Office of Operations Research, John Hopkins University.

Associate Members were: Panel recording secretary Durant; and astonomer Dr. Josef Allen Hynek, Ohio State University, who was also a consultant to the U.S. Air Force Air Technical Intelligence Center (ATIC), which included the UFO Project Blue Book.

Interviewees (or witnesses) before the Panel were: intelligence administrator Brig. Gen. William M. Garland (USAF), Commanding General, ATIC; ADSI Chadwell, CIA; the late intelligence administrator Brig. Gen. Philip G. Strong (USMC), Chief Operations Staff, OSI, CIA; atmospheric physicist Dr. Frederic Carl Emil Oder (Lt. Col., USAF), Deputy Chief, Physics and Electronics (P&E) Division, OSI, CIA; philosopher Dr. Stefan Thomas Possony, Senior Civilian, Special Studies Group, USAF Directorate of Intelligence; the late Capt. Edward J. Puppelt (UFAF), Chief, Aerial Phenomena Branch (Project 10073 Blue Book), ATIC; aeronautical engineer Dewey J. Fournet, Jr., The Ethyl Corp. (formerly Project Blue Book officer in USAF Directorate of Intelligence and now NICAP Board member); photo interpreters (PI's) Lt. R. S. Neashan (USN) and Harry Woo, U.S. Photographic Interpretation Laboratory (PIL).

Also present as observers were: weapons intelligence specialist David B. Stevenson, Weapons & Equipment (W&E) Division, OSI, CIA; and intelligence officer Capt. Harry B. Smith (USAF), Estimates Division, USAF Directorate of Intelligence.

Ruppelt died in 1960; Robertson in 1961; Berkner in 1967; and Strong in 1971. APRO has located most of the people listed above who are still living, and is continuing to interview those who will permit it. Former ADSI Chadwell, who was one of the first three CIA officers to be publicly identified in connection with UFOs eight years ago, had told APRO he has been contacted by many amateur investigators and members of the publicity/lunatic fringe since then and consequently refuses to be interviewed.

The existence of a 1953 panel of scientists convened by the CIA to review the UFO subject was first revealed by Donald E. Keyhoe in his 1955 book and confirmed a few months later in a book by Ruppelt, who was present at four of the eight panel meetings. In 1957, then-NICAP-Director Keyhoe secured a one-page, heavily edited summary of the two-page Panel Report (Tab A in the Durant memo) from the Air Force, which disclosed the names of the five panel members. Dr. Donald H. Menzel named the Office of Scientific Intelligence as the CIA unit that sponsored the panel, in his 1963 book. Menzel had been corresponding with the OSI Panel Members and USAF personnel knowledgeable of the panel since 1958.

During the late Dr. McDonald's first visit to Project Blue Book on 6 June 1966, he was allowed to read and make notes from a full copy of the Durant memo, which had been retyped for the Air Force to correct embarrassing typographical errors in the CIA original and which had been "routinely" (but mistakenly) declassified by Maj. Hector Quintanilla on the basis of the twelve-year declassification schedule established by DoD Directive 5200.10 of 1961. McDonald's 20 June request for a Xerox copy of the memo was brought to CIA attention and refused, Quintanilla said on 30 July 1966. The CIA ordered the memo's classification upgraded to SECRET again.

John Lear, Science Editor of *Saturday Review,* received a moderately *edited* twenty-three-page copy of the thirty-two-page Durant memo from the CIA through Quintanilla and the Secretary of the Air Force Office of Information (SAFOI) in August 1966. Editing (as distinguishable from "sanitizing") involves the *rewriting* and *retyping* of a document to omit sensitive material.

McDonald publicly identified Chadwell, Clark, and Strong as being among the CIA officials present at the panel meetings, in his 22 April 1967 address to the American Society of Newspaper Editors. He also revealed the existence of two Associate Members of the panel (Durant and Hynek) and the presence of Gen. Garland at the meetings.

In October 1967, APRO received a thirty-page *sanitized* copy of the Durant memo from SAFOI. (Sanitization is the selective censorship of classified information from a document, usually done by razor blade or white tape on a photocopy of the original, which is then recopied.) This copy was published by the Lorenzens in 1968 (*UFOs Over the Americas*) and is identical to the copy published in the Condon report in 1969. The largest deletion was Tab C, the two-page list of personnel concerned with the OSI Panel. Other deletions mostly dealt with CIA and Air Force intelligence organization, personnel, and personnel titles.

Following inquiries on 21 October 1974, CIA official Robert S. Young offered to declassify the main body of the Durant memo for APRO and did so on 21 January 1975, minus Tab C. The list of evidence presented to the panel (Tab B) was left sanitized as it had been in 1967. (Young is now Records Administration Officer, Of fice of Logistics, Directorate of Administration, CIA, as well as CIA Freedom of Information Coordinator for the new Freedom of Information Act legislation that took effect 19 February 1975.)

Young declassified Tab C for APRO on 28 March 1975, and I then requested the declassification of "Battelle Memorial Institute" in CIA records (this was the only deletion in Tab B). The Air Force agreed on 20 June 1975 and Tab B was declassified five days later. By this time, several other UFO researchers had requested the so-called "Robertson Report" (actually the Durant memo) as well as the complete Tabs B and C.

The results of APRO analysis of the Durant memo and other CIA and USAF documentation of UFOs will be published in the coming months.

Appendix B

Air Force propaganda to the effect that there was really nothing to the UFO mystery became increasingly effective in the years following the convening of the Robertson Panel in 1953. Unfortunately for the intelligence community, this effectiveness so reduced the number of reports being filed through official channels that the intelligence effort was seriously hampered. In an attempt to remedy the situation the following brief was issued to all commands by the office of Inspector General of the Air Force on December 24, 1959.

UFO'S SERIOUS BUSINESS

Unidentified flying objects—sometimes treated lightly by the press and referred to as flying saucers—must be rapidly and accurately identified as serious USAF business in the ZI. As AFR

200-2 points out the Air Force concern with these sightings is threefold: First of all, is the object a threat to the defense of the United States? Secondly, does it contribute to technical and scientific knowledge? And then there's the inherent public information media about what is going on in the skies.

The phenomena or actual objects comprising the UFOs will tend to increase, with the public more aware of goings-on in space, but still inclined to some apprehension. Technical and defense considerations will continue to exist in this area.

Published about three months ago AFR 200-2 outlines necessary orderly qualified reporting as well as public information procedures. This is where the base should stand today, with practices judged at least satisfactory by the commander and inspector.

—Responsibility for handling UFOs should rest with either Intelligence, Operations, or the Provost Marshall or the Information Officer—in that order of preference, dictated by the limits of the base operation.

—A specific officer should be designated as responsible.

—He should have experience in investigation techniques and also, if possible, scientific or technical background.

—He should have the authority to obtain the assistance of specialists on the base.

—He should be equipped with binoculars, camera, geiger counter, magnifying glass, and have a source for containers in which to store samples.

What is required is that every sighting be investigated and reported to the Air Technical Intelligence Center at Wright-Patterson AFB and that explanation to the public be realistic and knowledgeable. Normally that explanation will be made only by the USAF Information Office. It all adds up to part of the job of being experts in our own domain.

Appendix C

Our investigators in late 1966 encountered an increasing number of instances involving mysterious agents who refused to identify themselves or were not who they said they were. Some claimed to be Air Force officers and even carried "proper" identification. Their usual behavior pattern was to confiscate evidence and intimidate witnesses, warning them against talking to any other investigators. What agency or agencies these individuals represented is not known. However, when the matter received press attention, the Air Force made an ostensible attempt to disown them by issuing the following memo.

DEPARTMENT OF THE AIR FORCE
Office of the Chief of Staff
United States Air Force
Washington, D.C. 20330
1 March 1967

Reply to
Attn of; AFCCS

Subject: Impersonations of Air Force Officers

	ADC	AFSC	HQCOMD USAF	SAC
To:	AFCS	ATC	CAC	TAC
	AFLC	AU	MAC	USAFF

Information, not verifiable, has reached Hq USAF that persons claiming to represent the Air Force or other Defense establishments have contacted citizens who have sighted unidentified flying objects. In one reported case an individual in civilian clothes, who represented himself as a member of NORAD, demanded and received photos belonging to a private citizen. In another, a person in an Air Force uniform approached local police and other citizens who had sighted a UFO, assembled them in a school room and told them that they did not see what they thought they saw and that they should not talk to anyone about the sighting. All military and civilian personnel and particularly Information Officers and UFO Investigating Officers who hear of such reports should immediately notify their local OSI offices.

HEWITT T. WHELESS, Lt. General, USAF
Assistant Vice Chief of Staff

Table of Sightings and Occupants

This table attempts to present in abbreviated form the sightings which included occupants set forth in this book. The following abbreviations are used to designate certain characteristics of the occupants, the craft and the date and time of day.

Time of Day	Craft Sighted	Occupant Type
nr (not reported)	nr (not reported)	nr (not reported)
d (daylight) a.m.		
or p.m.	bo (bright object)	m (small monster)
dn (dawn)	c (small cigar)	M (large monster)
n (nighttime) a.m.		
or p.m.	C (large cigar)	0 (small—under 40 inches, humanoid)
tw (twilight)	d (small disc)	O (large—over 40 inches, humanoid)
	D (large disc)	r (small robot)
	e (small egg)	R (large robot)
	E (large egg)	Other
	g (small globe)	
	G (large globe)	
	Other	

Eyes	Hands	Clothing
nr (not reported)	nr (not reported	nr (not reported)
ge (glowing eyes)	claws (animal-like)	un (unusual)
le (large eyes)	nor (normal, humanoid type)	ds (diving suit)
		dh (diving helmet)
nor (normal, humanoid)		br (bright)
	Other	or (ordinary)
Other		

Date (year, month, day)	Location country, state, city	Time	Craft	Occupant	Clothing	Eyes	Hands
1947, 2/3 nr	Peru, Pucusana	d (nr)	D	O	un	one	claws
1947,7,23	Brazil, nr	nr	D	O	ds	le	nr
1947,8,14	Italy, Carnia	d (nr)	d	0	or/dh	lw	claws
1949,8,19	USA, CA, Death Valley	d (nr)	d	o	nr	nr	nr
1950,3,18	Argentina, Lago	tw	D	O	ds	nr	nr
1951,12,nr	USA, NC, Red Springs	d (nr)	d	nr	nr	nr	nr
1952,9,12	USA, WV, Flatwoods	n (p.m.)	G	M	un	ge	nr
1953,1,3	Brazil, Guanabara, nr	nr	d	O	un	nr	nr
1953,5,20	USA, CA, Brush Creek	nr	g	o	un	nr	nr
1953,6,20	USA, CA, Brush Creek	nr	g	o	un	nr	nr
1953,8,nr	Mexico, Cuidad Valley	tw	D	O	ds	nr	nr
1953,11,28	Bolivia, River Guapore	nr	d	O	un	nor	nr
1953,11,28	Brazil, Pedras Negras	d (nr)	d	O	un	nr	nr
1954,3,nr	Brazil, Santa Maria	nr	e	O	un	nr	nr
1954,3,nr	Brail, Santa Maria	tw	e	O	nr	nr	nr
1954,8,23	France, Thonon	nr	e	o	ds	nr	nr
1954,9,nr	USA, KA, Coldwater	n (p.m.)	d	o	br	nr	nr
1954,9,10	France, Mourieras	tw	c	o	dh	nr	nr

Date (year, month, day)	Location country, state, city	Time	Craft	Occupant	Clothing	Eyes	Hands
1954,9,10	France, Valenciennes	n (p.m.)	nr	o	ds	nr	nr
1954,9,17	France, Cenon	n (p.m.)	d	o	nr	nr	nr
1954,9,26	France, Valence	nr	d	o	ds	le	nr
1954,9,30	France, Marcilly-sur-Vienne	nr	d	o	dh	nr	nr
1954,9,30	France, Ligescourt	n (p.m.)	d	o	ds	nr	nr
1954,10,nr	France, Toulouse	nr	d	o	ds	le	nr
1954,10,5	France, Loctudy	nr	d	o	nr	le	nr
1954,10,5	France, Mertrud	nr	d	m	nr	nr	nr
1954,10,9	France, Pournoy-	n (p.m.)	g	o	or	le	nr
1954,10,9	France, Carcassonne	nr	g	o	nr	nr	nr
1954,10,9	Germany, Rinkerode	n (nr)	c	nr	ds	nr	nr
1954,10,9	France, Lavoux	n (nr)	nr	o	ds	le	nr
1954,10,12	France, La Croix Durade	n (a.m.)	nr	nr	nr	nr	nr
1954,10,12	Iran, Teheran	nr	d	o	nr	nr	nr
1954,10,12	Morocco, Pt. Lauttey	d (nr)	nr	o	nr	nr	nr
1954,10,13	France, Bourasote	nr	d	O	ds	le	nr
1954,10,14	France, Meral	nr	D	o	nr	nr	nr
1954,10,16	France, Baillolet	nr	d	o	nr	nr	nr

1954,10,17	Corbierres	nr	d	nr	dh	nr	nr
1954,10,18	France, Doubs	n (p.m.)	nr	O	nr	nr	nr
1954,10,18	France, Fontenay-Forcy	n (p.m.)	c	o	dh	ge	nr
1954,10,18	France, Royan	n (p.m.)	d	o	nr	nr	nr
1954,10,21	England, Shrewsbury	d (p.m.)	nr	nr	or-dh	le	nr
1954,10,27	France, Les Jonquets-de-Livet	n (nr)	c	O	ds	nr	nr
1954,11,2	Brazil, Santo Maro	n (a.m.)	D	O	or	nor	nr
1954,11,8	Italy, Monza	n (nr)	d	nr	ds	nr	nr
1954,11,14	Italy, Isola	nr	c	o	ds	nr	nr
1954,11,14	Brazil, nr	n (a.m.)	e	o	nr	ge	claws
1954,11,28	Venezuela, Caracas	n (p.m.)	d	o	nr	nr	nr
1954,12,4	Brazil, Pontal	d (nr)	d	o	or	nr	nr
1954,12,9	Brazil, Linha Bela Vista	n (p.m.)	d	O	ds	nr	nr
1954,12,10	Venezuela, Caracas	n (p.m.)	d	o	nr	nr	nr
1954,12,10	Venezuela, Chico	n (p.m.)	d	o	nr	nr	nr
1954,12,11	Brazil, Linha Bela Vista	d (p.m.)	d	nr	un	nr	nr
1954,12,15	Brazil, Campo Grande	d (nr)	S	o	nr	nr	nr
1954,12,16	Venezuela, San Carlos	n (p.m.)	d	o	nr	nr	nr
1954,12,19	Venezuela, Valencia	n (p.m.)	d	o	nr	nr	nr
1955,3,nr	US, O, Loveland	n (a.m.)	nr	o	un	nor	nr
1955,7,3	US, GA, Stockton	n (nr)	nr	o	un	le	claws

Date (year, month, day)	Location country, state, city	Time	Craft	Occupant	Clothing	Eyes	Hands
1955,8,nr	US, O, Cincinnati	n (p.m.)	nr	o	nr	nr	nr
1955,8,22	US, KY, Hopkinsville	n (p.m.)	nr	m	nr	le,ge	claws
1957,4,nr	Argentina, Pajas Blancas	nr	D	nr	ds	nr	nr
1957,5,nr	US, PA, Melford	dn	d	o	un	nor	nr
1957,5,10	France, Miramont-Beaucourt	n (p.m.)	nr	O	nr	le	nr
1957,10,10	Brazil, nr	nr	D	O	ds	nr	nr
1957,10,10	Brazil, Quebra-Coco	n (p.m.)	C	O	un	nr	nr
1957,10,15	Brazil, Sao Francisco de Salles	n (a.m.)	C	O	ds	le	nor
1957,11,5	US, NB, Kearney	d (p.m.)	E	O	or	nor	nr
1957,11,6	US, TN, Dante	d (a.m.)	E	O	or	nor	nr
1957,11,6	US, NJ, Everittstown	tw	e	o	un	le	nor
1957,11,6	US, CA, Playa del Rey	dn	e	O	un	nor	nr
1957,11,7	US, MS, Meridian	nr	E	O	un	nor	nr
1957,11,18	Brazil, Maracaja	d (a.m.)	d	O	ds	nr	nr
1957,12,16	US, CT, Old Saybrook	n (a.m.)	e	r	nr	ge	nr
1958,6,nr	Argentina, Boca del Tigre	n (a.m.)	n	O	un	nr	nr
1958,11,nr	England, Deeside	n (a.m.)	D	M	nr	nr	nr
1958,11,23	El Salvador, Cojutepeque	n (p.m.)	D	O	un	nr	nr

1959,6,26	New Guinea, Boinai	n (p.m.)	D	C	nr	nr	nr
1959,6,27	New Guinea, Boinai	n (p.m.)	D	O	nr	nr	nr
1959,9,29	Sweden, Mariannelund	n (p.m.)	nr	o	nr	le	nr
1960,5,14	Brazil, Paracuru	n (a.m.)	d	o	nr	nr	nr
1960,6,9	US, AZ, Globe	n (a.m.)	nr	m	nr	ge	nr
1961,4,18	US, WI, Eagle River	d (a.m.)	d	O	nr	nor	nor
1961,9,19	US, NH, (Hill case)	n (a.m.)	D	O	or	le	nr
1961,11,nr	Brazil, Pinhal Beach	n (p.m.)	D	O	nr	nr	nr
1962,5,24	Argentina, La Pampa	nr	D	r	nr	nr	nr
1962,7,28	Argentina, Bajada Grande	nr	nr	nr	nr	other	nr
1962,8,nr	US, MN, Lake Movil	n (p.m.)	d	O	nr	nr	nr
1963,nr,nr	Argentina, Chaco Pr.	nr	nr	O	nr	nr	nr
1963,10,12	Brazil, Monte Maiz	n (nr)	E	R	un	nr	nr
1963,10,21	Argentina, Trancas	n (p.m.)	D	nr	nr	nr	nr
1963,11,nr	England, Kent	nr	nr	M	nr	nr	nr
1963,12,nr	Argentina, Sauce Viejo	n (nr)	nr	O	nr	nr	nr
1964,1,23	US, VA, Lynchburg	tw	nr	o	nr	le	nr
1964,4,24	US, NY, Tioga City	d (a.m.)	E	O	un	nr	nr
1964,4,24	US, NM, Socorro	tw	e	o	or	nr	nr
1964,6,5	Argentina, Poajas Blancas	n (nr)	bo	O	nr	nr	nr
1964,7,16	US, NY, Conklin	d (p.m.)	nr	o	un	nr	nr

Date (year, month, day)	Location country, state, city	Time	Craft	Occupant	Clothing	Eyes	Hands
1964,9,24	US, CA, Cisco Grove	n (a.m./p.m.)	D	O-R	ds	nor, ge	nr
1964,11,25	US, NY, New Berlin	n (a.m.)	D	O	un	nr	nr
1965,3,3	US, FL, Brooksville	d (p.m.)	D	O	ds	le	nor
1965,7,nr	Argentina, Buenos Aires	d (nr)	E	O	ds	nr	nr
1965,7,1	France, Valensole	dn	e	o	or	nr	nr
1965,7,26	Brazil, Carazinho	n (p.m.)	D	O	ds	nr	nr
1965,8,nr	Canada, Ont., Ottawa	n (p.m.)	nr	o	nr	nr	nr
1965,8,nr	US, IA.	d (p.m.)	D	o	nr	nr	nr
1965,8,nr	US, WN, Renton	n (p.m.)	nr	m	or	le	nr
1965,8,15	Uruguay, Saleo	n (p.m.)	bo	O	nr	nr	nr
1965,8,20	Peru, Cuzco	d (a.m.)	d	o	nr	nr	nr
1965,8,20	Argentina, Mar del Plata	n (p.m.)	bo	O	nr	nr	nr
1965,8,23	Argentina, Apostoles	n (a.m.)	c	O	un	nr	nr
1965,9,1	Peru, Huanuco	nr	e	o	nr	le	nr
1965,9,10	Brazil, Sao Jao	d (a.m.)	d	o	un	nr	nr
1965,9,12	Peru, Andes	n (nr)	nr	o	nr	nr	nr
1965,9,20	Peru, Picacha	d (p.m.)	bo	o	un	nr	nr

1965,10,23	US, MN, Long Prairie	n (p.m.)	C	r	nr	nr	nr
1965,11,11	Brazil, Mogi-Guacu	nr	nr	o	nr	nr	nr
1965,11,13	Brazil, Mogi-Guacu	n (nr)	nr	o	or	nr	nr
1066,3,23	US, OK, Temple	n (a.m.)	E	O	nr	nor	nr
1967,2,14	US, MO	d (a.m.)	D	o	nr	le	nr
1967,3,28	US, O. Munroe Falls	d (a.m.)	other	o	un	nr	nr
1967,6,13	Canada, Ont, Caledonia	n (a.m.)	c-d	o	nr	nr	nr
1967,8,7	Venezuela, Caracas	n (a.m.)	other	o	nr	nr	nr
1967,8,13	Brazil, Goias St.	d (p.m.)	D	o	un	nr	nr
1967,8,23	Venezuela, Caracas	n (nr)	nr	o	nr	nr	nr
1967,8,24	Australia, Vic., Kilda	d (p.m.)	D	O	ds	nr	nor
1967,8,26	Venezuela, Puente del Rio Tigre	nr	nr	o	nr	le	nr
1967,8,26	Venezuela, Maiquetia	n (a.m.)	nr	o	un	le	nr
1967,8,29	France, Cussac	d (a.m.)	S	o	nr	nr	nr
1967,9,23	Venezuela, Caracas	n (nr)	nr	o	nr	le	nr
1967,9,8	Venezuela, Caracas	n (a.m.)	nr	o	un	nr	nr
1967,9,9	Venezuela, Caracas	n (a.m.)	d	o	un	le	nr
1967,9,15	US, CT, Winsted	n (p.m.)	e	o	nr	nr	nr
1967,9,22	Venezuela, Caracas	n (nr)	nr	o	nr	nr	nr
1967,9,26	Brazil, Hospital da Baleia	n (nr)	D	O	ds	le	nr
1967,10,21	US, OK, Duncan	n (p.m.)	nr	o	un	nr	nr

Date (year, month, day)	Location country, state, city	Time	Craft	Occupant	Clothing	Eyes	Hands
1967,10,28	US, CO	n (p.m.)	nr	o	nr	nr	nr
1967,11,25	Brazil, Rio de Janeiro	d (p.m.)	D	O	nor	nr	nr
1968,7,31	Reunion, La Plaine des Cafres	d (a.m.)	d	o	ds	nr	nr
1968, 10, nr	Brazil, Sao Paulo	n (a.m.)	d	O	or	nr	nr
1968,11,1	Philippines, Baras	n (a.m.)	other	O	or	nr	nr
1968,11,1	Philippines, Baras	d (a.m.)	other	o	nr	nr	nr
1968,11,1	Philippines, Baras	d (a.m.)	other	O	or	nr	nr
1969,1,nr	US, MO, Edina	n (p.m.)	other	o	un	other	nr
1969,2,7	Brazil, Parassununga	d (a.m.)	d	o	un	nr	nr
1969,7,4	Columbia, Anolaima	n (p.m.)	g	nr	nr	nr	nr
1970,1,7	Finland, Imjarvi	d (p.m.)	d	o	other	nr	claws
1970,6,21	Brazil, Rio de Janeiro	d (a.m.)	d	o	dh	nr	nr
1971,6,9	Canada, Ont., Rosedale	n (p.m.)	other	O	nr	nr	cl
1971,9,22	Brazil, Tombos	n (p.m.)	nr	o	un	nr	nr
1972,6,6	US, IA	d (p.m.)	e	o	nr	nr	nr
1973,10,7	Yugoslavia, Ljubljana	d (a.m.)	nr	o	un	nr	nr
1973,10,11	US, MS, Pascagoula	n (p.m.)	E	O	un	nr	claws
1973,10,17	US, confidential	n (p.m.)	D	O	un	le	claws

1973,10,22	US, IN, Hartford	n (p.m.)	nr	o	un	nr	nr
1973,11,2	US, NH, Goffstown	n (a.m.)	G	o	un	le	nr
1973,12,nr	Belgium, Vilvorde	n (p.m.)	d	o	ds	le	nor
1974,1,7	Belgium, Warneton	n (p.m.)	D	O	un	nor	nr
1974,2,28	France, Origney-en-Thierache	d (a.m.)	D	O	ds	nr	nor
1974,3,21	Spain, Pineda	n (p.m.)	D	O	un	nr	nr
1974,7,22	Canada, Que, St. Cyrille	n (a.m.)	D	O	un	nr	nr
1974,10,7	Canada, Que, St. Mathias	d (a.m.)	D	o	un	nr	nr
1974,10,24	US, WY, Medicine Bow Nat. Forest	n (p.m.)	other	O	un	nor	other
1974,12,2	US, WI, Frederic	n (p.m.)	D	O	nr	nr	nr
1975,1,4	Argentina, Bahia Blanca	n (a.m.)	other	O	un	other	other
1975,8,13	US, confidential	n (a.m.)	D	O	nr	nr	nr

About APRO

The Aerial Phenomena Research Organization (APRO) was founded in 1952 by Mrs. Lorenzen. Its purpose is to resolve the many questions posed by the existence of UFO reports.

Its journal, the ***APRO Bulletin,*** has been published continuously since 1952, informing the members and subscribers of developments in the UFO field worldwide. It is issued on a monthly basis.

Throughout its history, APRO has led the UFO research effort, pioneering those concepts which are now mainstays of the field. It sought interest and support from the academic community and established an ever-growing panel of scientific consultants. It initiated the concept of UFO symposia as a means of providing these consultants an opportunity to exchange and publish their ideas on the subject.

The idea of recruiting a special contingent of Field Investigators to conduct on-site research was also initiated by APRO.

Incorporated as a not-for-profit educational organization, APRO fulfills its public information function by producing an ongoing radio program of five-minute shows, five days per week. The shows are written and produced and voiced by Hal Starr, an award-winning 37-year veteran of radio announcing, writing and production. They are syndicated nationally by:

Creative Radio Shows
9121 Sunset Blvd.
Los Angeles, California

Subject material consists of cases from the APRO files, interviews with principals, witnesses, experts, etc.

Also, audio-visual material is under preparation for use in schools. This material will avoid dogmatic treatment of the subject and will strive mainly to use the UFO subject as a learning stimulus.

Inquiries concerning membership or any of the above should be addressed to:

APRO
3910 E. Kleindale Road
Tucson, Arizona 85712

APRO STAFF

International Director	L.J. Lorenzen
Director of Research	James A. Harder, Ph.D.
Public Relations	Hal Starr
Secretary-Treasurer	Coral E. Lorenzen
Membership Secretary	Madeleine H. Cooper
Staff Librarian	Allen Benz
Office Manager	Sheila Kudrle

CONSULTING PANELS

BIOLOGICAL SCIENCES

Anatomy	Kenneth V. Anderson, Ph.D.
Biochemistry	Vladimir Stefanovich, Ph.D.
Biophysics	John C. Munday, Ph.D.
Botany	Robert J. Hudek, Ph.D.
Botany	Robert Mellor, Ph.D.
Exobiology	Frank B. Salisbury, Ph.D.
Microbiology	Mohammed A. Athar, Ph.D.
Physiology	Harold A. Cahn, Ph.D.
Zoology	Richard Etheridge, Ph.D.
Zoology	Burt L. Monroe, Jr., Ph.D.

MEDICAL SCIENCE

Medicine	Louis E. Daugherty, M.D.
Medicine	Benjamin Sawyer, M.D.
Medicine	B.A. Te Poorten, D.O.
Medicine	R. Donald Woodson, M.D.
Psychiatry	Jule Eisenbud, M.D.
Psychiatry	L. Gerald Laufer, M.D.
Psychiatry	Berthold E. Schwarz, M.D.

PHYSICAL SCIENCES

Aeronautics	Rayford R. Sanders, M.S.M.E.
Astronomy	Daniel H. Harris, B.S.
Astronomy	Leo V. Standeford, Ph.D.
Astronomy	Walter N. Webb, B.S.
Astrophysics	Richard C. Henry, Ph.D.
Civil Engineering	James A. Harder, Ph.D.
Civil Engineering	Charles E. Martin, B.S.
Computer Technology	Vlastimil Vysin, Ph.D.
Electrical Engineering	Kenneth Hessel, Ph.D.
Electrical Engineering	Brian W. Johnson, Ph.D.
Geochemistry	Harold A. Williams, Ph.D.
Geology	Philip Seff, Ph.D.

Mechanical Engineering	Arlan K. Andrews, Sc.D.
Metallurgy	Robert W. Johnson, Ph.D.
Metallurgy	Walter W. Walker, Ph.D.
Oceanography	Dale E. Brandon, Ph.D.
Optics	B. Roy Frieden, Ph.D.
Physics	Michael J. Duggin, Ph.D.
Physics	Richard F. Haines, Ph.D.
Physics	Gerhard H. Wolter, Ph.D.
Physics	Robert M. Wood, Ph.D.
Radiation Physics	Horace C. Dudley, Ph.D.
Seismology	John S. Derr, Ph.D.

SOCIAL SCIENCES

History	David M. Jacobs, Ph.D.
Linguistics	P.M.H. Edwards, Ph.D.
Philosophy	Norman J. Cockburn, Ph.D.
Philosophy	Robert F. Creegan, Ph.D.
Philosophy	Emerson W. Shideler, Ph.D.
Philosophy	Kathleen M. Squadrito, Ph.D.
Psychology	Terry L. Maple, Ph.D.
Psychology	Michael A. Persinger, Ph.D.
Psychology	R. Leo Sprinkle, Ph.D.

REPRESENTATIVES

Argentina	Guillermo Gainza Paz
Australia	Peter E. Norris
Belgium	Edgar Simons
Bolivia	Fernando Hinojosa V.
Brazil	Prof. Flavio Periera
Britain	Anthony R. Pace
Ceylon	K.P.K. DeAbrew
Chile	Pablo Petrowitsh S.
Columbia	John Simhon
Costa Rica	Rodolfo Acosta S.
Cuba	Oscar Reyes
Czechoslovakia	Jan Bartos
Denmark	Erling Jensen
Dominican Republic	Guarionix Flores L.
Ecuador	Gen. Raul Gonzales A.
Finland	Kalevi Hietanen
France	Richard Niemtzow
Germany	Capt. William B. Nash
Greece	George N. Balanos
Guatemala	Eduardo Mendoza P.
Holland	W.B. van den Berg
Honduras	Julian Lanza N.

Ireland . . . . Martin Feeney
Italy . . . . Roberto Pinotti
Japan . . . . Jun' Ichi' Takanashi
Lebanon . . . . Menthis El Khatib
Malta . . . . Michael A. Saliba
Mexico . . . . Roberto Martin
New Guinea . . . . Rev. N.C.G. Cruttwell
New Zealand . . . . Norman W. Alford
Norway . . . . Richard Farrow
Peru . . . . Joaquin Vargas F.
Philippine Republic . . . . Col. Aderito A. deLeon
Puerto Rico . . . . Frank Cordero
Rumania . . . . Tiberius A. Topot
Sierra Leone . . . . Bernard J. Dodge
Singapore . . . . Yip Mien Chun
South Africa . . . . Frank D. Morton
Spain . . . . Pedro Redon
Sweden . . . . K. Gosta Rehn
Switzerland . . . . Dr. Peter Creola
Taiwan . . . . Joseph March
Tasmania . . . . William K. Roberts
Trinidad . . . . Enrico Jardim
Turkey . . . . Adnan Gur, Ph.D.
Venezuela . . . . Jose M. Pascual
Yugoslavia . . . . Milos Krmelj

APRO Membership including Bulletin:
U.S., Canada and Mexico . . . . $8.00/yr.
All other Countries . . . . $9.00/yr.
Subscription to **Bulletin** Only:
U.S., Canada and Mexico . . . . $8.00/yr.
All other countries . . . . $9.00/yr.